THUNDER OVER THE HORIZON

From V-2 Rockets to Ballistic Missiles

Clayton K. S. Chun

War, Technology, and History
Robert Citino, Series Editor

3 1336 08062 3359

PRAEGER SECURITY INTERNATIONAL
Westport, Connecticut • London

Library of Congress Cataloging-in-Publication Data

Chun, Clayton K. S.
    Thunder over the horizon : from V-2 rockets to ballistic missiles / Clayton
K. S. Chun.
        p.   cm.—(War, technology, and history, ISSN 1556–4924)
    Includes bibliographical references and index.
    ISBN 0–275–98577–6 (alk. paper)
1. Rocketry—History.   2. Rockets (Aeronautics)—History.   3. Rockets
(Ordnance)—History.   4. Guided missiles—History.   I. Title.   II. Series.
    TL781.C488   2006
    621.43'56—dc22   2005032678

British Library Cataloguing in Publication Data is available.

Library of Congress Catalog Card Number: 2005032678
ISBN: 0–275–98577–6
ISSN: 1556–4924

First published in 2006

Praeger Security International, 88 Post Road West, Westport, CT 06881
An imprint of Greenwood Publishing Group, Inc.
www.praeger.com

Printed in the United States of America

The paper used in this book complies with the
Permanent Paper Standard issued by the National
Information Standards Organization (Z39.48–1984).

10 9 8 7 6 5 4 3 2 1

Contents

Introduction   vii

1. Ballistic Missile Fundamentals: How Ballistic Missiles Work   1

2. V-2: The Dawn of a New Age   39

3. Cold War: Push-Button Warfare   57

4. The Cuban Missile Crisis   87

5. Ballistic Missiles at War: The Case of Iraq   109

6. Ballistic Missile Proliferation   141

7. Ballistic Missiles Reinvent National Strategy and Policy   169

8. Ballistic Missiles and the Impact of Technology   183

Appendix: Tables   199

Selected Bibliography   209

Index   213

Introduction

HISTORY IS FILLED WITH examples of new weapons and technologies that have revolutionized warfare. Man's introduction of gunpowder, the airplane, and other discoveries have changed the nature of warfare forever. Ballistic missiles have done the same since World War II. These new weapons have provided a nation the capability to bypass the battlefield and hit a capital city or strategic target with relative impunity. Ballistic missiles, coupled with nuclear weapons, have made profound changes to international relations, regional balances of power, and how countries think about conflict. Whole national strategies have been devised to incorporate their effects and how a state should treat an enemy who possesses them.

The United States and the former Soviet Union developed and controlled vast missile inventories that threatened mutual annihilation all within thirty minutes. Fortunately, these weapons were never used, but their legacy continues to haunt the world. The cold war ended with the United States and countries from the former Soviet Union trying to disarm their strategic nuclear force. However, these delivery systems have found new lives among nations wishing to influence regional and global rivals. Today, one can see these weapon systems and others in North Korean and Iranian arsenals. Some countries have acquired ballistic missiles to expand their ability to hit only battlefield targets and treat them as mere extensions of field artillery. Others have sought them as a way to counter an existing threat that they could not counter with conventional weapons. These weapons also offer a path to expand technologies to allow for space launches or a means to demonstrate national pride. Ballistic missile development and deployment offer a wide range of ways to enhance a country's military, political, and economic capabilities.

For many nations, the introduction of ballistic missiles by a regional rival or foe has sparked an almost instant panic and movement to counter this threat. As in the cold war, nations have rushed to build rival systems, create a capability or policy to counter the threat, or press for negotiations to stop or remove the threat. Some of these fears are legitimate, while others are mere rhetoric. This book explains many questions and issues concerning these delivery vehicles. It explores how they work, their use, and their impact in war and peace. Specially, the book examines how the systems and components operate. Understanding how these weapons work provides the reader an awareness of the technical challenges that scientists and engineers had to overcome. Next, several case studies are presented to illustrate how nations have used and developed these systems. The case studies include the Germans' use of the V-2 in World War II, the United States' development of ballistic missiles, the Cuban Missile Crisis, and Iraq's conflicts with Iran and the 1991 Persian Gulf War. Additionally, this study examines how the United States' nuclear strategy developed with the introduction of these systems. The book also investigates today's proliferation of ballistic missiles. This study presents the reader a summary review of nations that pose the biggest threats to the United States or its interests. Finally, the book ties the effects that technology had on several key national and military security topics. New technology changed warfare concepts, national strategy, and organizations and helped introduce a new military field, space, during this period.

Today the spread of technology through instant information, globalization, shifting international and political interests, the rise of regional rivalries, and other factors have contributed greatly to ballistic missile proliferation. In many cases, this proliferation has complicated the national strategies and security of countries from the United States to China. Nations that have little to lose from an attack that includes conventional weapons or weapons of mass destruction may find ballistic missiles a way to stay in power. Nuclear weapons also provide a relatively inexpensive way to maintain a military advantage over foes. Demystifying the process of building nuclear weapons and their delivery systems has increased the fear that nuclear weapons will be used. Instead of relying on conventional forces to win wars, states today can use ballistic missiles to immediately attack cities, economic targets, or targets deep in an enemy's territory and create tremendous devastation. These new delivery systems have complicated national security policy and defense planning.

The leaders of nations that have a nuclear capability might contemplate actions they never considered before. If both sides in a confrontation have the ability to release nuclear weapons, then one side might want to use those systems to disarm its opponent first. Because defenses against these types of weapons are not widely available, a nation's military capabilities, cities, capital, and infrastructure are inviting targets in an enemy's gun sight, and if attacked, their destruction would be certain. Relatively fragile or unstable countries that possess these weapons are vulnerable to terrorist or revolutionary attacks and may become susceptible to control by radical groups. Such groups might not be influenced by international diplomacy or internal government mechanisms to control the release of chemical or nuclear warheads. This situation could provide a radical group the instant capability to create massive destruction against its neighbors or other nations.

Ballistic missiles today offer countries a way to equalize disparate military capabilities that may have taken great time and expense to create comparable conventional capabilities. Now, any country that possesses the willingness, resources, and access to obtain these weapon systems can join a growing club of nations that have deployed them. Some states might desire a single missile armed with one nuclear device as an insurance policy against a foe. This weapon might ensure that the country is not invaded or attacked. The rival's expensive conventional forces might become obsolete and its national leadership might become hostage to a potential nuclear attack. The United States faces problems with nations such as North Korea and Iran that may have such capability. The United States and its regional allies could be blackmailed by countries that have a limited number of nuclear weapons. In the case of Iran, for example, Washington or London might now be in danger along with Jerusalem.

Ballistic missiles caused a profound change in the world during the post–World War II era. In the cold war these delivery vehicles affected economic, political, military, and social policies that have shaped today's world and the world we will inhabit in the future. Balances of power, defense spending, intergovernmental relations, and a host of issues surrounded the advent of the nuclear age. The nuclear arms race between the United States and the Soviet Union dominated relations between them and with other countries around the world. Some of the systems involved in the arms race resulted from a dedicated effort to build advanced weapons, others by unintended discoveries. In many cases, these changes were caused by the growth of technology or ways to counter new systems. Ballistic missiles were merely the result of scientific and engineering efforts to understand and improve a way to deliver a weapon. Small, incremental steps aided this development. These technological changes created improved capabilities, some unforeseen, which spurred nuclear weapons to prominence over other devices. Unexpected changes to a rival's military technology forced rapid changes in force structure and national policy.

Technological progress was also instrumental in changing the organizational structure of the military. The U.S. Air Force and the U.S. Navy experienced modifications to their roles and missions after the introduction of ballistic missiles. For the air force, these weapons reinforced its assumed role of providing the premiere strategic nuclear retaliatory force to guard the nation against a surprise Soviet attack. These capabilities cemented the air force's belief in strategic bombardment that seemed like a natural extension of its World War II role. Despite the use of tactical aircraft to support close air support missions to aid ground forces and attacking an enemy's ability to support ground operations, strategic bombardment and nuclear weapons created a new set of ideas for military leaders to consider. Nuclear weapons became a cheap source of security because they could destroy an enemy's society and ability to conduct war.

The navy extended its missions beyond the control of the seas by creating a mobile ballistic missile force. Submarines armed with these systems allowed the navy to expand its power projection from the seas into the enemy's heartland. The navy now had the capability to strike targets at sea, in the air, and further inland to fight the nation's wars. Ballistic missiles also allowed the navy to justify nuclear propulsion that would extend their reach and capability to maintain a fleet at sea. Like the air force, the navy found ways to extend its organization's roles and missions through these new capabilities and technology.

Ballistic missiles also gave the nation a push into a new realm, space. Advanced delivery vehicles gave the nation an ability to launch satellites and later expand the manned space programs. Nuclear weapons also forced the military to find better and faster means to detect enemy activities. This created an urgent need for early warning, intelligence, and command and control capabilities that would come from space. Today, space has dominated many aspects of military operations that range from nuclear warfare to peacekeeping operations.

There is an extensive literature about ballistic missiles. This work attempts to only introduce the general reader to many of the main concerns and subjects concerning them. For example, the question about nuclear arms control can take volumes. This introduction to the essential components of arms control should give the reader an appreciation of the instruments available to national leaders and diplomats for limiting potential weapons proliferation. Issues such as missile defense have become key elements of our national security. Understanding types of missile defense on the national and theater levels can shape opinion and public policy.

My hope is that readers will come away from this book with an appreciation of why ballistic missiles had such an important role in history and why these weapons will continue to affect international events and relations for the foreseeable future. As technology spreads, nations that could at one time only dream of creating a nuclear force will be able to do so, albeit with some effort, and use them to enhance their security or threaten regional or international powers. The development of nuclear weapons and one of their main delivery systems, the ballistic missile, was once the province of major powers that could afford vast sums to produce such weapons. Today, powerful chemical, biological, chemical, radiological, and high explosive devices can also give a country the ability to cause mass casualties and destruction on an enemy. Nations that might seem unstable may claim to have a wholly rational reason to bring these weapons into their inventories. These systems have become widely available in black markets and through internal promotion. Given the deadly nature of ballistic missile systems and increased tensions among nations willing to use these devices, the United States and the world may one day face conflicts of potentially horrendous destruction that will not be limited to a particular region.

1

Ballistic Missile Fundamentals: How Ballistic Missiles Work

MISSILES ARE USED TODAY to deliver a variety of weapons to a target. Not all missiles are ballistic ones. Depending on the factors that affect the flight of a projectile, it can have ballistic characteristics. For example, bullets may have ballistic characteristics. After leaving a rifle barrel, a bullet relies initially on the force created by expanding gases from its gunpowder charge to propel it from the weapon. Once that force dissipates, gravity pulls the bullet toward the ground and atmospheric friction will slow its initial speed. A ballistic missile is guided during a powered flight and increases velocity during its flight, unlike a bullet, and becomes subject to an unguided flight or trajectory influenced only through gravity and atmospheric drag. This vehicle then relies on gravitational force to influence its path and impact on a target. A ballistic missile uses its internal rocket engine or motor to create initial velocity and direction of a body in motion to attain sufficient altitude, distance, and direction to a target. Once this is achieved and the rocket stops operating, either for lack of fuel or by design, then it relies on the earth's gravity to influence its flight path. Conversely, some missiles or projectiles might continuously use their own power to guide them to their destinations. Air-to-air missiles that require constant corrections and high speed may need to use their internal power source up to the interception point of their intended targets. The air-to-air missile uses powered flight throughout its use. This type of flight is not ballistic.

Ballistic missile launches can occur over several mediums. Most countries that operate these systems normally do so from land-based facilities that include fixed locations or on mobile transporters. Fixed sites can be in underground silos or surface launch support facilities. Mobile transporters can range from sophisticated tracked vehicles to a truck with sufficient launch railings. Nations also deploy these weapons as submarine launched ballistic missiles (SLBMs) or can place them on surface ships. The United States experimented with launching these devices from aircraft.

One can distinguish classes of ballistic missiles through their ranges. The first is the short-range ballistic missile (SRBM) that strikes targets at less than 1,000 kilometers (620 miles). Next is the medium-range ballistic missile (MRBM) that has a range between 1,000 and 3,000 kilometers (620 to 1,860 miles). The intermediate-range ballistic missile (IRBM) is defined as having a range from 3,000 to 5,500 kilometers (1,860 to 3,410 miles). The longest-range ballistic missile is the intercontinental ballistic missile (ICBM) that can attack targets at greater than 5,500 kilometers away from its launch site, normally from a land-based site.

BALLISTIC MISSILE PHASES

A ballistic missile follows three distinct flight phases as it moves from its launch point toward its intended target. These phases require particular capabilities and systems for the missile to successfully pass from one phase to the next. Each phase's duration depends on the intended range to the target. These phases also help define when systems are vulnerable to particular defensive action. Countries can launch them with variations in their flight path such as a depressed or lower than normal trajectory that may reduce its range but also not allow it to enter space where it would be subject to detection and interception. The following description illustrates the typical ICBM flight path.

The first activity is the boost phase. This phase begins when the rocket engines or motors of the missile ignite and ends at the conclusion of powered flight. The ballistic missile's rocket engine or motors must provide sufficient propulsion to lift off from a launch site. The missile's propulsion system needs to push the entire vehicle from the earth's surface or from its sea base, if launched from a submarine, to a point where it can escape gravity. A missile's flight path, once the missile is launched, will not always appear to be perfectly vertical from the missile's launch site. Onboard computers will direct the missile to make certain movements to align itself to reach a particular trajectory or flight path. These preprogrammed movements help ensure that the vehicle's flight path to a target bearing has the correct azimuth, or angular direction to a target. The missile continues to use powered flight at very high altitudes including an entry into space.

If the ballistic missile has several stages, or missile segments, in its propulsion system, it starts to separate these stages once their propellants are used up or when the missile reaches a particular altitude. The vehicle's sensor will

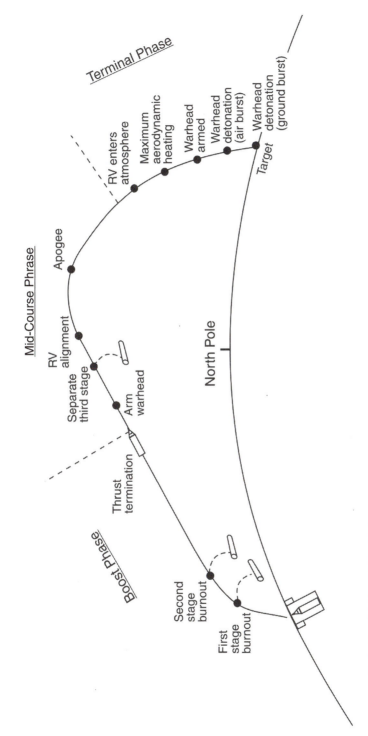

Notional Ballistic Missile Flight Path

send a signal to a computer when the rocket engines or motors near completion of propellants in a stage. The computer generates the command to end that stage's rocket operation and separates the used stage. Using multiple stages helps accelerate the missile toward its target at a more efficient rate than using a single rocket stage. The missile normally starts its journey with the ignition of its first stage, which carries the entire system's weight. Once it reaches a preprogrammed height, the rocket shuts down and the stage is discarded. This action reduces the weight carried by the missile since the first-stage rocket engine or motor and support equipment to that propulsion unit are jettisoned. The ballistic missile is at a higher altitude, under less gravitational force and total weight, when the next stage's rocket ignites and pushes the vehicle to a higher altitude. Velocity increases, then decreases with each stage separation, and then the missile accelerates again. This method moves the vehicle along with less fuel and reduced need for larger rockets. This staging occurs until the ballistic missile is placed into the proper trajectory. If one could view the trajectory from a point in space, the flight path would look elliptical.

These activities last from 180 to 320 seconds, or about three to six minutes. This phase's duration depends on the type of fuel used by the rocket engine or motor, range to the target, and acceleration of the missile in flight.

The mid-course phase begins after the last rocket stage burnout but before the delivery vehicle deploys its payload or warhead. The warhead or weapons payload travels in space for thousands of miles at speeds of up to four to five nautical miles per second. The payload can include a single warhead or several. The system can also carry a small unit that has defensive countermeasures and a small propulsion system to aid placement of warheads into proper attitude for reentry. During the mid-course phase, the missile can reach its apogee, highest point in its flight, in less than 1,000 seconds and an altitude of about 1,100 to 1,400 kilometers (682 to 868 miles). This phase is the longest and can last about thirty minutes.

The terminal phase is the last action taken by the ballistic missile. The warhead reenters the earth's atmosphere and deploys against the target. The reentry vehicles containing the vehicle's warheads start to heat up at an altitude of about 100 kilometers (sixty-two miles). However, this part of the missile still travels at a fairly defined trajectory until it faces heavier layers of the atmosphere, about forty kilometers (twenty-five miles), where aerodynamic drag and gravity can affect its landing. This phase lasts about 2,000 seconds or more.

Each of the phases poses challenges to a rocket engineer or missile designer to ensure the ballistic missile can accomplish its mission. Several factors can affect the missile's ability to move it into a proper flight path. Although not

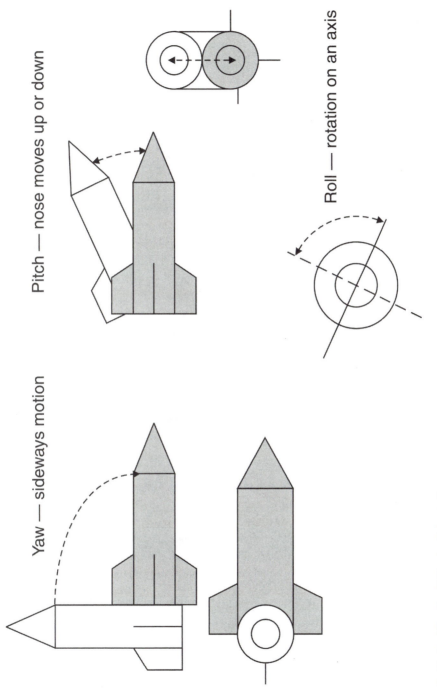

Yaw — sideways motion

Pitch — nose moves up or down

Roll — rotation on an axis

Ballistic Missile Attitude Orientations

the singular concern of engineers and designers, it was one of the largest challenges to early missile efforts to reach a proper flight path. These particular phases also determine how a missile defense might attempt to destroy or disable incoming ballistic missiles in an attack.

MISSILE COMPONENTS AND SUBSYSTEMS

A missile requires the integration of complex systems to work in concert to achieve maximum results. Any one component that fails or does not perform to specification can degrade its performance.

Missiles rely on several components or subsystems that allow them to operate. Missiles have several common components that include an airframe, propulsion system, guidance systems, control surfaces, and most important, a payload or warhead. Additionally, an integral part of the missile system includes a support infrastructure to operate and maintain the weapon. This includes launch sites, maintenance, and operating crews. However, the main focus is the missile itself. The size and type of missile used for a particular mission may depend on the intended target; what range is required to deliver the weapon; selected delivery method; and how crews will launch the weapon.

A ballistic missile's airframe provides a chassis to assemble flight components in a single system. Additionally, the airframe helps to support and protect many critical and delicate components while the missile is in flight. The shape of the airframe also influences the flight path and performance of the missile during flight. One of the most critical factors that influence the size and shape of the airframe is the propulsion system that includes the number of rocket engines or motors, the type and quantity of propellant, equipment components carried on board the missile, and number of stages used to boost the missile in flight.

Missiles generally have two types of propulsion systems based on the type of fuel: liquid or solid. Rockets that use solid fuel propellants are normally called motors, while liquid fueled systems are engines. Each system has benefits and drawbacks that affect their use, storage, and performance and the cost to operate and maintain them. Each system has some commonality such as the requirement to supply fuel or propellant and a means to provide oxygen to enable the fuel to burn while at high altitude or in space. Propulsion systems allow the missile to produce sufficient thrust to increase the vehicle's velocity to escape earth's gravity. Thrust is measured in pounds. If the rocket can deliver more thrust than the given weight of the vehicle, it will push it into the atmosphere and escape gravity. This thrust-to-weight ratio affects the velocity of the ballistic missile, its range, and its flight path. Thrust-to-weight ratio for the Space Shuttle is about 1.6, and early ICBMs had ratios of about 1.2. Depending on the missile's propulsion system, the range or amount of payload can vary. Increasing the missile's thrust can improve the amount of payload or range for the vehicle. If the missile propulsion system can deliver sufficient thrust to the overall missile's body weight, then it can lift more. This efficiency can provide the benefit of less expense and more weapons payload carried by the missile. The propulsion system is by far the heaviest system in the missile. Normally, the fuel (and oxidizer in the case of a liquid system) makes up 93 percent of the missile's weight; the missile's airframe and other systems make up only 7 percent, of which only 3 percent is made up of the payload.

Liquid fueled propulsion systems are the most complex and expensive ballistic missiles in service. This missile type may include a series of systems such as the fuel and oxidizer storage, a pump system to draw the fuel and oxidizer from storage at a high rate, a combustion chamber that mixes the fuel and oxidizer, a nozzle to direct exhaust that produces thrust, electrical systems, an ignition system, and a plumbing system.

Normally, a liquid fueled missile will use separate fuel and oxidizers that mix and then burn. Oxidizers supply oxygen to burn fuel at high altitudes or in space where oxygen is rare. Many of the current classes of fuels and oxidizers are hypergolic: once combined, they will chemically burn and not require an ignition system. For example, the United States used unsymmetrical diethyl hydrazine and monomethyl hydrazine as a fuel and nitrogen tetroxide as the oxidizer for its Titan II ICBMs. Other liquid fuels have included kerosene, liquid hydrogen, and alcohol. Missile propulsion systems also used liquid oxygen as an oxidizer. In a single-staged missile, the oxidizer tank is on the bottom and the fuel tank rests above it to lower the missile's center of gravity. A missile propulsion system normally uses more oxidizer and is heavier than the fuel. The order of fuel and oxidizer is reversed in multistaged missiles to move the center of gravity higher. Some tanks are manufactured from steel sheet, while smaller tanks may use aluminum sheet milled in a waffle pattern as thin as .015 inch. Normally, there is a transition section between stages in multistaged liquid fueled ballistic missiles. These transition stages allow space between fuel or oxidizer tanks to give them insulation or to store electrical or mechanical systems to support the propulsion system.

Many types of fuels and oxidizers tend to be highly volatile and corrosive. The fuel and oxidizer are physically combined in the combustion chamber. Once the fuel and oxidizer burn, exhaust gas is produced within a combustion chamber. Pressure and temperature within the combustion chamber increase from the production of exhaust gas. This gas is converted into kinetic energy as it is expelled from an exhaust nozzle. The escaping gas creates force called thrust that powers the missile along its flight path. Thrust is composed of the velocity and mass of the escaping gas.

The combustion chamber in a liquid fueled system is cylindrical. Usually, this combustion chamber requires a large volume to allow sufficient fuel and oxidizer to mix and burn and to allow a continual amount of combustion to take place. Once mixed and burned, the gases escape through a thrust chamber or exhaust nozzle that concentrates the exhaust gases to increase the missile's velocity. One can imagine the high pressure and temperatures that the walls of the combustion chamber and the exhaust nozzle must withstand. If the system is not cooled, metal components may melt and weaken the entire combustion chamber or other critical sections of the propulsion system. An innovative method used by missile designers is regenerative cooling. This process directs relatively cold liquid fuel from the front wall of the exhaust nozzle to a point above the combustion chamber. This system can run cooling fuel through coils inside and outside the combustion chamber, exhaust chamber, and other critical areas. This process cools the system from its 5,000°F (2,760°C) internal temperature and warms the fuel that increases its potential energy for combustion.

The amount of thrust depends on several conditions. First, the size of the burn area for the fuel determines the amount of gas and mass created. Second, the length of time that the fuel is burned affects how long thrust is maintained. Third, the rate of fuel and oxidizer burned directly influences the amount and temperature of the exhaust gas that affects pressure. Fourth, the shape of the exhaust nozzle can influence the direction and concentration of the exhaust gas.

Once a crew initiates its sequence to launch, a liquid fueled missile's propulsion must generate a high flow of fuel and oxidizer through its pump system to the combustion chamber. The pump system uses an independent power source, normally using two pumps, to move fuel and oxidizer separately through a plumbing system. The pump assembly uses an impeller, turbine wheel, and a gear train that connects the impeller and the turbine wheel. Power for the pump system comes from a gas generator that uses fuel and oxidizer to generate high-pressure gas that drives the impellers that draw the fluid toward a mixing area in the combustion chamber. Some fuel and oxidizer may be returned to their respective storage tanks to maintain pressurization throughout the process. This action helps improve the flow of propellant throughout the pumping system. An initial charge or device used to power the pump assembly can help initiate pumping action that generates fuel and oxidizer flow to the combustion chamber and powers the pump system. The gas generator operates if fuel and oxidizer are present.

Pershing I second stage. Combustion chambers must withstand intense temperatures and pressures when the rocket motor or engine operates. This Pershing I solid fueled rocket motor illustrates a typical combination chamber that concentrates the rocket exhaust to increase thrust. (Courtesy, Department of Defense)

When the missile is on its flight path, it might make directional changes from aerodynamic control surfaces like fins. However, these control systems can slowly lose their effectiveness as the missile gains altitude. Some missiles use exhaust vanes to deflect exhaust gas, while other missile propulsion designs use gimbaled rockets that direct the exhaust gases in a particular direction.

Another propulsion option is to combine fuel and oxidizer into a solid mixture that burns as one. This system offers a lower-cost alternative and avoids the storage problems, pumping, internal structure, and use of corrosive substances. The fuel and oxidizer mix is ignited and continues to burn at a relatively constant rate, unless designs are used to modify the burn. Unlike the liquid fueled system where the rate of burn is controlled by the pumping rate of the fuel and oxidizer, in the solid fueled system the burn rate is adjusted by the exposed propellant surface that is ignited. The burn rate also depends on the size and shape of the material, composition of the fuel, combustion chamber temperature, velocity of exhaust gases next to the burning surface, quantity of fuel, and pressure. The solid fueled missile normally requires a heavier construction to withstand the higher pressures over a shorter period of rocket motor burn than a liquid fueled system requires.

The solid fueled propulsion system includes the propellant, combustion chamber, an ignition system, and the exhaust nozzle. The propellant is enclosed within the combustion chamber. The solid fuel propellant's combustion chamber can be rather large relative to a liquid fueled system's combustion chamber. There are also devices to trap and prevent any residue or discarded burning material from clogging the exhaust nozzle and reducing thrust. The solid fueled system uses a chemical mix that includes fuel and oxidizer. For example, the United States' Minuteman III uses a solid fuel based on acrylic acid and oxidizer based on ammonia percolate and aluminum.

The solid propellant is cast as a single block. However, the cast is usually made with a hole or indentation at the bottom called a perforation. This perforation serves as a way to control the shape of the burning surface, rate of burn, and thrust. The perforation can take the shape of a star, rod and tube, or other shape. These perforation shapes affect the rate and surface of the burn area. A single perforation or star shape has a constant burn area that will keep the thrust stable. Conversely, a multiperforated rocket motor has an increasing rate of fuel consumption that will reduce quickly its burning surface area. The reduction in burning surface and thrust cause a decrease in exhaust gas pressure that will slow the missile down. The cast may have a hole throughout the entire fuel system that can increase the burning surface and several holes driven through the cast to relieve internal pressure.

Minuteman first stage. The United States converted its land-based ICBMs from liquid to a majority solid fuel-based force. The Minuteman's first stage used four combustion chambers to power it into flight. (Courtesy, Department of Defense)

A solid fueled ballistic missile has several ways to control the burning of fuel and the thrust delivered in flight. Designers can control the rate of burn by inhibiting the amount of area subject to ignition. Placement of a plastic resistor or other device could slow the rate of burn, which would increase the period of powered flight. Also, engineers could avoid casting the fuel as a solid block and instead introduce gaps in the fuel. This action could increase or decrease thrust during a preprogrammed flight. Another method to decrease thrust is to employ a thrust termination system. A missile design could include forward-facing thrust units that when fired would slow the ballistic missile. The rate of thrust reverse could stop forward momentum. Engineers have many options to ensure a solid fueled propulsion system can deliver its warhead.

An ignition system is used to start the fuel and oxidizer burning. An electrical system or some type of pyrotechnic device can deliver sufficient spark to start the burning of the fuel. The igniter may have a small amount of gunpowder or other substance that initiates a spark or heating element to start the solid propellant to burn. Once started, the solid propellant continues to burn until all of the fuel is consumed.

The solid and liquid fueled systems operate in environments within the atmosphere or space. There are specific advantages and disadvantages to each system. Liquid fueled ballistic missiles are complex systems that require extensive internal components to operate. They may need a long checkout sequence before launch, and fuels and oxidizers cannot be stored within the missile for long time periods without adequate maintenance. For some systems, fuel and oxidizer must be recycled in the missile to allow for inspection of the tanks. There are also some stringent and extensive technical and logistical requirements for the liquid fueled system. For example, if the missile is designed to use liquid hydrogen or oxygen, that requirement forces launch crews to keep the temperatures at −297.4°F for the oxygen and −423.04°F for the hydrogen. Such constraints and fueling activities would make field operations difficult before liftoff and would slow the reaction time to launch a missile. However, a control system can precisely regulate rates of fuel and oxidizer consumption to affect the flight path in liquid versus solid fueled propulsion systems. Once a certain velocity or distance along a flight path is achieved, a control system can turn off the pumping system and terminate all thrust in the propulsion system.

Solid fueled systems do have some problems. The fuel casting must be exact, because cracks or gaps may create uneven burns or structural concerns. The system is also sensitive to environmental conditions and is fragile. Solid fueled systems are normally less complex (they have no moving parts), are ready to launch at an instant, and have fewer storage problems than liquid

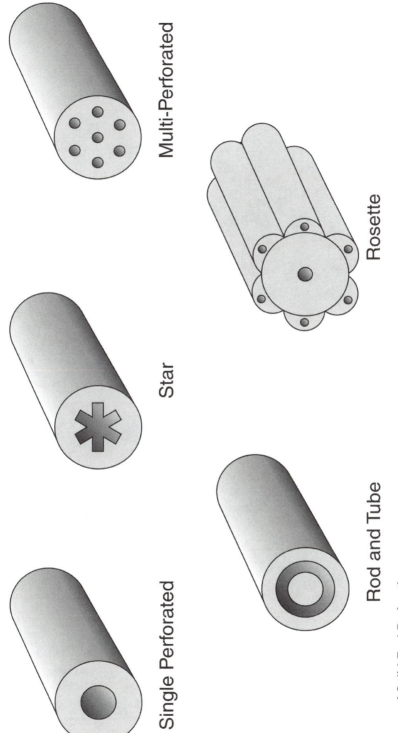

Single Perforated

Star

Multi-Perforated

Rod and Tube

Rosette

Types of Solid Fuel Perforations

Minuteman in silo. Ballistic missile operations moved from above ground sites to underground silos. This Minuteman ICBM silo provides not only environment protection, but secures the missile against a near nuclear explosion. (Courtesy, U.S. Air Force)

fueled systems. A solid fueled system generally has a greater acceleration rate than liquid fueled ones. For example, the United States' solid fueled Minuteman III ICBM has a speed of 16,000 miles (25,770 kilometers) per hour compared with the liquid fueled Titan II (now retired), the United States' largest liquid fueled ICBM, which has a speed of 15,000 miles (24,150 kilometers) per hour. The solid fueled rocket motor system can deliver a high amount of thrust for a short period of time, unless it has inhibitors or resistors embedded in the fuel. Rapid acceleration and high speed have advantages: they reduce the time in the boost phase and could make shooting down the solid fueled ballistic missile more difficult than a liquid fueled one in its boost phase.

An engineer can design a missile to travel a certain distance. Construction of a missile launch site can include positioning the missile to launch at a certain angle. Maintenance crews can also maintain the proper level of liquid fuel for flight. Still, states of nature such as the weather or human error such as an improper initial calculation of longitude and latitude can force small perturbations from the missile's intended flight path. These small factors can mean the difference between mission success and failure.

One of the most important ballistic missile elements is the guidance system that directs the ballistic missile to its target. Guidance systems allow a missile to generate commands that correct for navigational errors and help maneuver the missile into a corrected path to its intended target. A ballistic missile guidance system can include some type of homing, celestial navigation, programmed maneuvers, or other method. The most common guidance system is the all-inertial or radio-inertial guidance systems. A vehicle using an inertial guidance system contains appropriate devices for the control and direction of the missile internally. A radio-inertial guidance system must rely on external information to correct flight path deviations and has internal components. Some guidance systems now use satellite navigation or other external data, such as digital imagery.

A missile must overcome several problems that require an accurate and reliable guidance system. If the ballistic missile were launched from one point on earth to another, the problem would be relatively easy. However, the earth rotates and the missile must hit, in some respects, a moving target. The Coriolis Effect involves the earth's movement that seriously affects a missile's guidance. The missile's guidance system must compensate for a move that is proportional to the total flight time and also depends on the movement of the earth at the latitude of the target. If one aims at the equator, the target might move about 966 kilometers (600 miles) because of the earth's rotation. Additionally, the earth is not a perfect sphere, but is an oblate spheroid, like a grapefruit, which affects the accuracy of the vehicle's flight path to its tar-

Minuteman dual launch. Solid fuel-powered ICBMs like these Minuteman III missiles begin launch operations with the ignition of its first stage within its silo. A Minuteman III launch crew controls up to ten missiles. (Courtesy, Department of Defense)

get. The earth bulges at its equator as it spins on its axis. The equator is about twenty-two kilometers wider at its axis than if we measured the radius of the earth through the poles. Another impact is centripetal force, which tends to pull an object that moves in a circular path toward the axis of rotation. The earth's rotation pulls an object such as a missile toward the center of the planet. Another factor that affects guidance is the combination of speed and altitude that a missile must reach to attain its proper range. An engineer can extend the vehicle's range by increasing its altitude or speed. Combinations and adjustments to one or both of these factors can adjust the ballistic missile's performance.

A guidance system needs to adjust speed, altitude, direction, and other flight characteristics. These changes require close integration of the guidance system and any flight control systems. The guidance system must first sense that there is a deviation between its intended and actual flight paths. The information for the missile must come from internal sensors or calculations or from an external source, like a radio message or satellite data. Although most missiles today use an internal guidance system, early systems sometimes relied on radio guidance. The second guidance system requirement is to transform the guidance information to an appropriate signal to activate a control system to make the correction by using a flight control system.

The guidance system can use several devices to measure deviations from its intended flight path. The two most common devices are gyroscopes and accelerometers. A gyroscope is used to ensure the missile has the proper attitude. Attitude in this case is the orientation of the missile relative to its direction of motion. The motions involved in attitude are roll, pitch, and yaw. If one can view a static missile body, then one can imagine roll as the motion of a missile as it spins or revolves. Pitch is the movement of the missile's nose as it moves up or down. Yaw involves change of sideways direction or turn left or right. The roll, pitch, and yaw movements help stabilize the ballistic missile. The guidance system must ensure that the speed, staging, and other actions take into account these movements that affect guidance system measures. Gyroscopes help determine the effect of these actions. Normally, a gyroscope uses the earth's gravity as reference. Information may include angular reference directions based on the earth's spinning mass.

The gyroscope helps the missile guidance systems in flight to assume the proper attitude and direction by keeping guidance instruments in proper alignment on a stable platform. The gyroscope contains an accurate, balanced rotor system that allows it to move in any direction about its center of gravity at a very high speed. The device maintains gyroscopic inertia or rigidity. The gyroscope resists or compensates for forces that displace rotors and other devices in motion, like gravitational influence. Added weight or speed of the rotor improves gyroscopic inertia. If a gyroscope, a spinning mass, is pointed at a relative position and is in motion, it will continue to do so unless acted upon by an outside force. If one mounts the gyroscope on gimbals, it will appear that the gyroscope is moving, but it is really fixed. If the gyroscope continues to point at the initial reference point, this can help create conditions where a system can measure deviations from a planned position for a missile from its actual one. This characteristic can help stabilize a platform to keep its position so that devices that measure position or velocity, like an accelerometer, stay in alignment and add to the precision of the missile's alignment.

Second, a gyroscope is affected by precession. Movement may affect the rate or direction of the gyroscope's spin. Suppose one were to place a gyroscope on the body of a missile. As the ballistic missile rotates or spins through its flight path, the force can affect the spinning gyroscope. The gyroscope will react by spinning about its axis at 90° away from the direction of the force that is acting upon it. Measuring the amount of precession, one can determine the amount and direction of the missile's rotation. This information can help calculate the missile's attitude.

The second common device for the guidance system is an accelerometer that calculates the missile's acceleration (the rate of change in velocity over time) and combines a clock to determine the distance that the missile has traveled. These activities allow a computer to find the differences between what its programmed values for the flight should be and its actual values. The accelerometer's measurements can also help determine whether the missile is on or off course. The accelerometer, with help from the gyroscope, creates sufficient data to uncover the missile's true direction and nongravitational acceleration.

Different forces that act upon the ballistic missile can affect its acceleration. This can include the rocket operations, control systems, or the effect of gravity. The accelerometer takes time signals and can calculate velocity and ultimately the distance traveled by the missile. A missile can use three different direction values: vertical, lateral, and target. This may require three accelerometers and an integrating computer to calculate the appropriate speed, direction, and position of the ballistic missile in flight.

The gyroscope, accelerometers, a stable platform for the instruments, and other support instrumentation make up the guidance system that allows the ballistic missile to navigate through its flight path. This system directs the path of the missile based on sensed acceleration and other data given a coordinate system or reference measured solely within the vehicle. The accelerometers and gyroscopes work entirely on the laws of classical motion and gravitation from Newtonian physics. An inertial measurement unit, a part of this guidance system, is a specific platform that gyroscopes stabilize, which allows mounted accelerometers to make their measurements and calculations.

A guidance system creates conditions within the missile to accurately determine where it is relative to a referenced coordinate. This referenced position, if seen from afar, would appear to be fixed in terms of a reference point such as a star. Although stars are in motion, their relative distance from the ballistic missile makes them seem fixed and thus good reference points for coordinates. The guidance system is one of the most critical missile systems. If a nation wants to deliver a weapon against a target, it can use a very large weapon to ensure its destruction, given an inaccurate delivery, or it can use a relatively smaller weapon that employs a precisely aimed missile. Nations using a less accurate missile, through its guidance system, may have to use more expensive, large propulsion systems to move the larger weapon to its target.

Radio-inertial guidance systems still serve as an option. These systems rely on commands provided outside the missile's internal systems. This control arrangement includes a two-way communications scheme and a ground station. This radio-inertial guidance system includes a control point (ground, sea, air, or in the future, space) that tracks the missile's powered flight and determines if it is on the correct path. The control point then sends out commands via a radio link or other signal to the missile to correct any problems. The missile can then signal back to the control point that it made the corrections. This control system uses a combination of external signals and internal control systems. Radio-inertial guidance systems have some deficiencies such as range. A radio signal may not have sufficient strength to communicate with the missile, or a country's ability to determine flight path deviations may have constraints. The guidance system may require many ground stations depending on the distance the missile must travel. Additionally, the signal may be jammed, or other interference problems may affect the command links between the missile and the control point. Depending on where targets are located and the extent of territory controlled, the use of ground-based control or signal systems may have severe limits.

Unlike the all-inertial guidance system, a missile using radio-inertial guidance has other problems as well. Radio-inertial guidance relies on a complex interrelationship between radio and radar signals. Surface or airborne assets must continually monitor the missile and provide data to computers to interpret signals. These support programs are costly and subject to attack. Problems such as weather or readiness concerns, other than enemy jamming or attacks, could degrade the ability of the nation to launch a ballistic missile strike. An enemy could also send the wrong signals to incoming missiles that could explode the ballistic missile prematurely or send it to a different target.

Inertial guidance programmed ballistic missiles do not rely on such an extensive system.

If a targeted nation does not have a space-based radar system or other means to detect a ballistic missile launch, it might use a radio-inertial guided missile force against an opponent. Because the radio-inertial guided ballistic missiles must use radar, radio, and other signals, those signals may provide a warning to a potential foe. Unless a country routinely sends false messages to confuse a potential enemy, those signals use certain frequencies, and the level of activity may signal a change in an enemy's posture to launch an attack. Countries that only use this method for early warning may launch their ballistic missiles or aircraft in response, even if the other nation is merely undergoing an exercise or test of its ballistic missile force.

The destruction of ground stations by commandos or an air attack can instantly disable a ballistic missile program. An expensive ballistic missile program that relies on a single ground or radar control station program is subject to a critical weakness. An opponent might not require a ballistic missile as a counterweight, just an effective means to attack the missile's ground control element. All-inertial-guided ballistic missiles can operate regardless of whether ground stations or any other facilities exist after their launch.

An alternative guidance system may involve taking navigational references from relatively fixed sites. Celestial navigation by the stars or signals from a satellite, like the Global Positioning System (GPS) satellites, or other space navigational systems like the European Space Agency's Galileo or Russia's GLOSNASS program, is possible. Navigation by stars, however, may be limited by the weather until the missile reaches into space. GPS navigation is possible, but depending on the level of warfare, who is at war, and the desired accuracy, this type of navigation may be denied. For example, a country might want to jam GPS signals for a variety of reasons during a conflict that would render a host of systems inoperable, including this type of missile guidance system. Another technique involves a guidance system using radar or digital images and comparing them to a preprogrammed path. This method can result in a very accurate guidance system.

The ballistic missile's main purpose is to deliver a weapon to its target. That weapon must survive the stress and shock of high speed acceleration into a flight path, transition to conditions in an atmosphere to low gravity, and then survive a fiery reentry back to the earth's surface. The ballistic missile's payload can contain one warhead or reentry vehicle (RV) or several devices. To protect the RV during the initial powered flight operations, the ballistic missile has a shroud that houses the warhead section.

An RV includes the structure that contains the warhead, arming and fusing components, and support systems. A ballistic missile carries a single or several RVs in a bus or post-boost vehicle. The bus may contain defensive countermeasures (penetration aids, or penaids) or other devices such as a small propulsion system to align the release of the weapons to different targets. Advanced buses can support improved accuracy for a ballistic missile armed with a single RV since it can make attitude corrections with its own propulsion system. Similarly, a bus system with sufficient propulsion units can deliver its load of many RVs, a multiple independently targetable reentry vehicles (MIRV) system, and can move to several locations, separated by hundreds of miles, to detach an RV and let it fall to earth. Some MIRV systems may have up to ten RVs. A control device can separate these RVs on a preprogrammed time or distance to strike their targets. Normally, the RVs separate from the post-boost vehicle before the system reaches its apogee. These RVs can contain several types of weapons such as nuclear, chemical, high explosive, radiological, or biological devices. The speed, range, and limited defenses against ballistic missiles make them a highly effective weapon against another state. These weapons can strike foes ranging from countries that have huge military resources to countries that have more meager resources.

A missile's flight path will put its RV into position where it can deliver the weapon on target. Depending on the size and ability of the ballistic missile, the delivery vehicle's payload could carry a sizeable RV. Similarly, the accuracy of the missile's guidance system can certainly determine the RV placement into its ballistic path to the surface. The RV must accomplish several operations to successfully deliver its intended cargo. First, it must survive a relatively hostile environment. Second, the RV needs to position itself precisely at its intended location. Third, the RV may need to use countermeasures to avoid a ballistic missile defense system. Fourth, the system needs to deploy successfully its weapon and initiate the weapon's burst over the target. Designers must meet exacting requirements for precision in their extensive criteria for RV design. Along with RV protection, the ballistic missile's engineering must ensure that the missile also maintains minimum vehicle weight. Extra weight requires the use of more powerful propulsion systems and larger ballistic missiles.

The largest problem faced by RV designers is protection of the missile's cargo from the atmospheric reentry heat. An RV faces tremendous heating as it returns to the atmosphere from its flight path, starting several kilometers above the earth's surface, which may last for several minutes. The most intense heating can last over a minute. The RV's external temperatures can reach about 15,000°F, which will melt most materials. The RV must protect sensitive internal components for the weapon to operate upon delivery by keeping those items cool during its return. Along with RV design and shape, the internal components must have thermal insulation to protect them during reentry and allow them to operate in the cold of space. However, the heat from reentry is one of the most immediate concerns. Heating from friction, convection, and space radiation can transfer energy onto the RV and damage components.

If the heating problem is not solved, then the warhead might vaporize in the upper atmosphere. An RV design can take two approaches to combat atmospheric heating. The first involves treating the RV as a heat sink. This approach is one of the simplest and earliest used designs. As the RV reenters the atmosphere, friction creates large amounts of heat. An approach to dissipate the heat is to create a large volume of a heavy metal to reduce the RV's temperature.

The RV's designers would shape the device as blunt bodies that have high-drag characteristics that help protect it. The RV's return to earth is made at great hypersonic speeds, up to Mach 20, which create shock waves. The heat sink's design can help dissipate up to 90 percent of the heat energy by manipulating the impact of the shock waves. As the vehicle enters the atmosphere, shock waves can shield it from damaging thermal conditions. Unfortunately, all heat sinks were manufactured using metals such as beryllium, steel, cast iron, or copper. These metals are heavy and add significantly to the ballistic missile's weight. The United States used copper heat sinks in its early missile programs, and weight and design size thus became significant issues. Demands for larger weapon yields also created pressure to increase the RV size. Heat sink designs could not accommodate these requirements. This mode of reentry had another troubling characteristic: it did not have sufficient performance to deliver its weapons with the precision required. Guidance systems did not significantly improve delivery accuracy until much later.

The second design calls for ablative materials. This approach reduces the demands for weight and powerful rocket motors or engines to carry larger RVs. In this approach, successive layers of material heat up and melt or burn off. The heated, ablative material is cast off or vaporized, leaving the RV to cool by heat transfer. Although other methods were tried, such as internal cooling, the ablative RV system seemed the simplest and most effective. Missile engineers can use several types of materials such as pure plastics, a combination of plastics and organic or inorganic fibers, silica, carbon or graphite, and Teflon. Teflon, used in everyday kitchenware, was a technological spin-off from the United States' ballistic missile program. The material dissipates heat well, a characteristic that greatly benefits the RV. The ablative approach is one of the most commonly used today.

The RV must also create conditions that shield its weapons from these forces and its deceleration of up to fifty times the gravitational force of being on the surface. One of the final effects is severe vibration caused by the RV meeting the atmosphere. Components must have some type of cushioning that can counter this and the aforementioned effects. The RV's deceleration also places a high gravitational load on the components. Delicate arming, fusing, and sensing equipment needs to have uninterrupted operating conditions throughout this critical flight phase.

Another problem faced with atmospheric reentry is the return of aerodynamic lift effects. As the RV reenters the atmosphere, friction may cause deflections in its flight path. The RV must have some designs or approaches to maintain its stability in flight by compensating for this deflection impact. If not corrected, the RV's arming and fusing for the warhead might not operate correctly. This condition could lead to a premature detonation or prevent the RV from functioning. To compensate for this effect, the RV might carry a sensing device to determine the proper distance and timing to arm the warhead. One measure of a ballistic missile's accuracy is its circular error probable (CEP). CEP is a hypothetical calculation that uses the target as a center and measures the radius where half of all missiles fired would fall closest to that target. For example, early U.S. ballistic missiles, like Atlas, had a CEP of about 3.24 kilometers (about 2 miles). Accuracy has been improved so that a modern missile's CEP is a mere fraction of the CEP of an Atlas. Today, technology has reduced CEP to measurement in feet. These devices and approaches which help place the RV very close to its target, require additional space and weight that can reduce the size of warhead used in the ballistic missile.

RV designers also need to consider defensive countermeasures. The advancement of ballistic missile defenses has increased the vulnerability of these delivery systems. Nations, if they have adequate warning, can reduce the effect of a ballistic missile attack, launch a counterattack, or shoot down enemy missiles. The technology to determine where a missile launch took place and the probable impact point already exists and has existed for years. Surface, airborne, ship-based, and space-based systems can detect a ballistic missile launch. Space-based infrared satellites can detect launches through the intense heat plume created by exhaust gases from the rocket. Ground stations can use radar. Similarly, a missile traversing the sky is also viewable. Nations could warn their military forces to take precautions such as donning chemical protection suits or seeking shelter.

Nations that use ballistic missiles might do so in a preemptive or surprise attack. These states could gamble with a decisive action to incapacitate an opposition's leadership or military and economic strength or to destroy the population. If the attacking party can swiftly dispatch a foe, then it can use a conventional military force to follow up the action. Adequate warning about an imminent nuclear attack could allow sufficient time to prepare and launch a counterattack that would be strong enough to defeat the attacker.

Countries could avoid an attack by using an active missile defense system to shoot down the delivery vehicles before they detonate their weapons. Specifically designed active defensive systems can counter an attack at many points throughout a missile's flight paths. These defensive systems must quickly react to a strike by determining where it was launched and how many missiles are being used and launching a sufficient amount of antimissile interceptors. Missile defense systems during the cold war used nuclear devices to destroy incoming warheads. Today, conventionally armed, high explosive and kinetic vehicles can attempt to strike down RVs or ballistic missiles during their flight path. Directed energy weapons can also be used for defensive purposes to destroy missile components in flight.

If a nation wants to ensure that its ballistic missile's RVs can penetrate these defenses, it can design defensive countermeasures for these systems. There are several approaches that a country can take. These countermeasures can range from a change in attack tactics to deliberate means to obscure an RV's location or identity. These countermeasures are relatively easy to modify, much more than a fixed active defense system that may not have the flexibility to adapt to changing technologies. The countermeasures include using a simple penaid device to confuse radar, trying to jam an enemy's surveillance system, creating dummy warheads, or creating more warheads that will overload the active missile defense system. The missiles could deliver an RV at a very steep angle or high speed to avoid defenses. Engineers can also design a maneuverable RV to avoid defenses and improve accuracy.

Once the RV gets through the missile defense system, the accuracy of the warhead in hitting its intended target becomes paramount. Depending on the target size and type, accuracy requirements can vary. Suppose that the target is a command and control bunker embedded in a mountainside. If the target is not hit with precision, the warhead is wasted. Conversely, what if the target were a city or large industrial area? A missile launched into the middle of a population center can serve the purpose of creating panic or confusion in the area; destruction of a particular object or area may not be necessary. Still, the drive to improve a missile's accuracy by lowering its CEP has been a challenge for most engineers, scientists, and technicians for years.

The improvement for missile and RV delivery can take several approaches. Designers can try to plan and manufacture better RVs that will improve flight characteristics and compensate for aerodynamic lift concerns during reentry. Additionally, missile engineers can use better control systems to enhance the RV once it travels above the atmosphere. Thrusters or devices on the bus could help the RV to move to a better trajectory for its return to earth. The RV could also use a terminal homing device that has a terrain recognition capability or uses a sensor that could guide the RV to the target. A more accu-

Minuteman launch sequence. After the first-stage ignition, the Minuteman III completes its boost phase with its second-stage rocket motor "burn" that increases the missile's velocity. (Courtesy, U.S. Air Force)

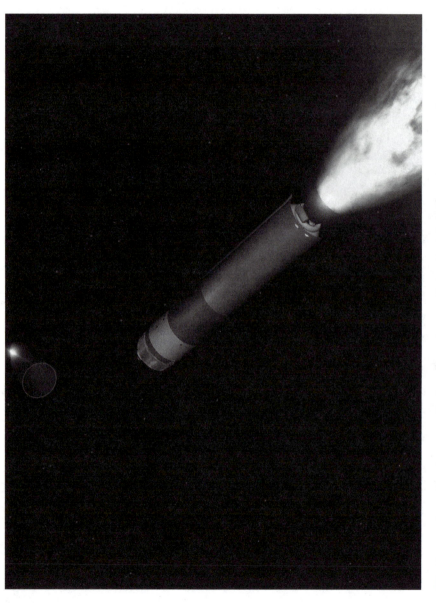

Minuteman launch sequence. During second-stage flight, the Minuteman III prepares for its mid-course phase by shedding its warhead's nosecone. The second stage's solid fuel is almost spent and it will soon separate from the remaining components. The Minuteman can travel upward to 6,000 miles. (Courtesy, U.S. Air Force)

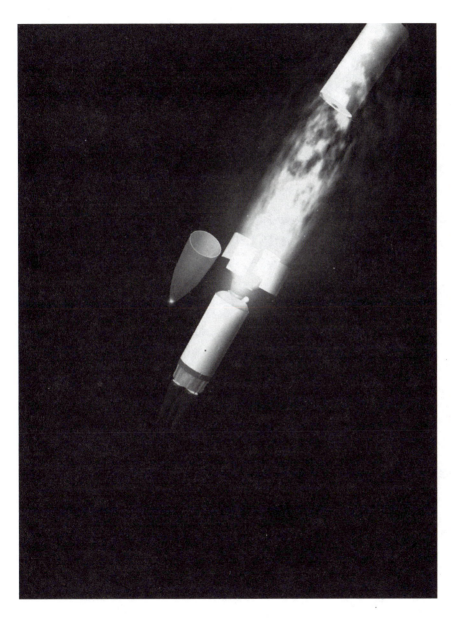

Minuteman launch sequence. The Minuteman III third stage produces sufficient thrust for the RV bus to put it into a proper ballistic flight path. The warhead's protective cover is jettisoned to reveal three RVs. (Courtesy, U.S. Air Force)

Minuteman launch sequence. Third-stage separation puts the RV bus into the mid-course phase of the bal-listic missile's trajectory. (Courtesy, U.S. Air Force)

Minuteman launch sequence. Minuteman III's RV bus will carry its nuclear cargo through space. The mid-course phase is the longest portion of the flight path. (Courtesy, U.S. Air Force)

Minuteman launch sequence. The terminal phase begins with the ballistic missile's release of its RV and penetration aids, like decoys. RVs reenter the atmosphere with great speed and under intense pressure and temperatures. Detonation can occur at a certain altitude, on the surface, or below the earth's surface. (Courtesy, U.S. Air Force)

Titan II RV. The Titan II RV system contained a nine-megaton yield nuclear weapon. The missile was deactivated due to arms control treaties and was later used as a space launch booster. (Courtesy, U.S. Air Force)

rate RV delivery can allow attacks on another nation that would reduce collateral damage to civilians, cultural or religious sites, infrastructure, and other concerns. If an attacker's goal is a swift destruction of a military force or the elimination of enemy leadership, the attacker could risk expanding the conflict beyond its intentions if the attack's path of destruction is too wide. An inaccurate weapon may require a larger weapons yield and consequently more weight to compensate for its lack of precision. A more precise weapon can reduce the need to carry a weapon larger than necessary and thus allow the ballistic missile to carry more warheads intended for other targets. Carrying more warheads would multiply the lethality of the missile by extending its range.

Engineers and scientists developed technology to make ballistic missiles so powerful that a launch crew operating a tactical weapon could destroy a major city. One system, Pershing II, provided both a tactical and a significant strategic advantage to the United States in Europe in the 1980s. This mobile Pershing II also presented the army with new options. The warhead could penetrate the earth up to thirty meters (ninety-eight feet) before detonation. This capability allowed the Pershing II to destroy command and control centers, bunkers, and other buried targets. One of the most significant improvements was the RV guidance system. The Pershing II used an inertial guidance system that directed activities up to second-stage separation. After RV separation, a radar area guidance (RAG) system would start to take images below the warhead. The RAG rotated at 120 revolutions per minute as it gathered digital images and updated the guidance system until impact. Pershing II used radar area terminal guidance to help correct the warhead's flight path by using steerable control vanes. This system took radar images of the area and compared them with stored target area digitized images. The preprogrammed images were placed on magnetic disks that included information on terrain types, physical features, and other distinguishing characteristics. A computer analyzed the images and sent corrections to the inertial guidance system. This computer system simply charted the differences from the actual to predicted images that it received.

This maneuverable reentry vehicle (MARV) system allowed the U.S. Army to improve greatly its missiles' accuracy. The MARV capability allowed greater flexibility to mobile operations. Although Pershing I had a system to quickly determine launch position, the MARV could correct for a number of variations in the Pershing II's flight path. The greater accuracy and smaller yield reduced fears of collateral damage. Some critics believed that these characteristics would also encourage the missile's use. This technology was developed in the 1980s, but the system was deactivated due to arms control limitations with the Soviet Union. Today, this same technology is available, and other countries could adopt it against their neighbors or the United States.

FACTORS AFFECTING BALLISTIC TRAJECTORY

The ballistic trajectory, the path of a body in motion, of a ballistic missile is measured after its initial powered flight. Several factors can affect the path's duration, range, and shape. Engineers and designers can influence a missile's performance by manipulating certain characteristics that change ballistic trajectory. Instead of using powered flight from launch to intended target, an engineer can build a missile that carries a large payload containing a high explosive or nuclear device by exploiting ballistic principles in lieu of using that same weight for fuel to power the missile's rocket engine or motor. A missile designer could also use weight savings to make the ballistic missile transportable on a wheeled or tracked vehicle, which allows a force to escape detection or advance forward in battle to ensure the ballistic missile is in range of its target.

An innovative design can affect the missile's flight and subsequently affect its ability to destroy a target. Guidance systems that are used to make flight corrections may under- or overcompensate for the missile's path and change the ballistic trajectory. External factors such as atmospheric and other physical forces change the flight characteristics and how the missile operates. The velocity and time when powered flight terminates shape the ballistic path. The location, in terms of longitude and latitude, of launch acts on a missile's ultimate trajectory. The shape and length of the ballistic missile's "free-flight" through its ballistic trajectory is also affected by a number of human decisions. These decisions to send the missile into its flight path can be made for operational reasons. An engineer can use a combination of these factors to overcome a lack of powered flight capability or compensate for a location that is disadvantageous for launch.

A ballistic missile's speed and range are influenced, like other bodies in motion, by its shape. The missile operates in the dense atmosphere when it is launched and may, depending on how it travels to a target, need to compensate for air friction. Friction, resistance between two bodies that restricts the relative motion of one of the bodies to the other, can limit the ability of a missile to travel. Friction restrains the missiles from traveling the desired distance within an atmosphere because of its effects on aerodynamics. Aerodynamic shaping can reduce this resistance. Many missile designs are long, thin, and cylindrical, while others may appear as an elongated bullet. These designs are an attempt to reduce friction.

Missile designs can also improve performance in early launch stages and during flight. Some missiles may have aerodynamic fins that help stabilize the missile's flight path. The design of the missile also involves the changing center of gravity while fuel or propellant is used throughout the flight. This change in the missile's distribution of weight can affect its position in flight. The missile's rocket strength can also affect the speed of the system as it travels through the atmosphere and thus influence several flight characteristics such as the altitude and amount of payload carried by the missile.

Small perturbations such as earth movements and weather can affect the final landing impact of the missile. Technical measurements that include exact launch location, landing impact site, vehicle weight, and other parameters help engineers and technicians calculate the angle of launch, amount of fuel, rocket engine or motor shutoff, and other factors that determine where the missile's payload will land. The environment or other conditions can force small changes in the flight path. An effective guidance system on the ballistic missile can correct the missile's flight to a proper trajectory.

Missile operations personnel can significantly shape the ballistic missile's trajectory. The missile's position in its launch site is not always perfectly vertical. A launch crew can launch the missile at a slight depression or have a preprogrammed maneuver in the missile to move toward a particular angle in flight. These actions affect how steep the ballistic missile's trajectory appears, complicating efforts to detect or defend against an attack. Combined with the speed of the missile, the steepness of a missile's flight path can leave it with a flat, medium, or high trajectory.

Missile designers can program the speed of the ballistic missile by increasing or decreasing the engine or motor size. Engineers and scientists can build ways to control the amount of fuel used by the missile's rockets that control speed and range. Depending on the type of missile propulsion system, the shutoff to the rocket is possible by controlling the amount of fuel. A control system that reduces the flow of fuel or the quantity of fuel available to burn could affect the flight path. Reduced flight speeds tend to flatten the trajectories. A flight trajectory and angle of missile flight that are too steep can create problems with the reentry of the missile's warhead: its speed may be too great, causing heating problems on the payload. A very flat trajectory could create a flight path that is too long within the upper atmosphere. A flight path that is too long creates aerodynamic drag on the vehicle that can slow down the missile or decrease its range. Such a flight path is not efficient for using the rocket fuel available to extend the missile's range to hit other targets.

PROBLEMS BUILDING BALLISTIC MISSILES

The United States and the Soviet Union had great motivation to build many types of ballistic missiles. Other nations have also sought these delivery vehicles for self defense or other purposes. However, unlike some nations, the United States and Soviet Union had sufficient scientific capability, production facilities, test centers, and wealth to develop and refine these complex systems. Many nations have sought to purchase complete systems, but many of the available ballistic missiles are still unaffordable to poorer nations. Additionally, some nations that only desire to use these weapons against an aggressive neighbor may not want to build a much more capable weapon than what is available in the market. A nation wanting to purchase a missile system also must get the approval of a selling country. International pressure or other conditions to the sale may discourage the selling nation. One means to avoid these concerns is to build an indigenous missile design and production program.

Although many of the technical facets for building missiles or component systems are available or are relatively inexpensive, countries wishing to build these devices face many challenges. A nation that wants to build a ballistic missile will face many of the problems encountered by the United States and the Soviet Union. Devoting many resources to the problem can create a shortage in other defense programs and limit social or economic programs within the nation. If the nation wants to build its initial missile program in secrecy, it might not take advantage of buying existing technology or components. Still, several countries have successfully built vehicles independently or with foreign technical or assistance and component sales.

One of the most complex components to build is the guidance system. An inaccurate ballistic missile would negate the impact of the warhead's payload. A nation could use available computers and satellite navigation systems, but precision production of gyroscopes or accelerometers require technical skill and production facilities. If the guidance system cannot accurately send the RV to its target, then the country has created a very long-range artillery piece that is more expensive even though other means to attack a nation may be more readily available.

The nation must also build an adequate warhead. Small payloads with high explosive yields are available, but they are nothing more than a substitute for long-range aircraft bomb loads that are single-use weapons. Depending on the size of the warhead, aircraft might carry a larger payload than the missile. Most nations that field a ballistic missile force also want to build a chemical, biological, radiological, nuclear, or other weapon that can cause massive damage or casualties. These programs, like ballistic missile development, are expensive and have a high political cost in terms of international criticism and potential sanctions. A nation must build an RV capable of supporting and deploying these weapons given size and launch constraints. The RV must survive heat, shock, and high speed that requires extensive efforts to achieve.

The last major problem is to develop a reliable rocket propulsion system. Solid fuels are very dependable, but they demand specialized chemical research and production methods. An easier path is the use of liquid fuels. Liquid fuels can be highly available liquid oxygen and alcohol. Manufacturing sufficient liquid oxygen and fuel may not be a problem, even in a less developed nation. However, liquid fuels are difficult for crews to handle in the field and take time to load. Building the internal liquid fueled propulsion system requires some sophistication to store, mix, and ignite the fuels and ensure the missile does not blow up in flight.

BALLISTIC MISSILES AS A WEAPON IN THE FUTURE

Ballistic missiles provide a long-range and very versatile strike weapon that countries can use against regional rivals or states that could be continents away. Armed with a nuclear, radiological, chemical, biological, or high explosive warhead, ballistic missiles provide a means to directly affect the outcome of a conflict. Globalization has allowed the transfer of technology and systems at a much more rapid pace than in the past. Rapid wealth accumulation, the reappearance of ethnic and historic conflicts, and other problems have produced an arms race that includes ballistic missiles. China, India, Pakistan, Iran, North Korea, and other nations have sought many types of ballistic missiles from SLBMs to SRBMs for battlefield use. Despite its potential peaceful use, space satellite launch capability has become a way to develop many of the elements into an effective delivery vehicle.

Ballistic missile proliferation among nations has led to the specter of a conflict's spreading from regional to international consequences. Nations that have an IRBM or ICBM capability could use ballistic missile systems to threaten another country, for example, from intervening on the side of that nation's enemy. Similarly, if its weapons are armed with a nuclear explosive or other device, a small nation could blackmail a much larger nation that does not have similar weapons. This can precipitate an arms race or a sudden pre-emptive attack.

Although ballistic missiles were sought mainly by superpowers in the cold war, the acquisition of these delivery vehicles has continued to spread to nations that can hardly afford a large military budget, let alone ballistic missiles. Unfortunately, the world has seen the combat use of them in a number of situations. Middle Eastern countries have seen the most recent use of ballistic missiles in combat. Nations such as India, Pakistan, or North Korea have openly courted the development and deployment of these systems and nuclear capability. This proliferation has increased research on extending the range of these vehicles. North Korea has tested its versions of these weapon systems that might one day reach the continental United States.

2

V-2: The Dawn of a New Age

MAN HAS USED ROCKETS for centuries. Chinese inventors introduced rockets, in the form of fireworks, to the world in 1150. The first military use of rockets was by Chin Tarters, who used rockets against Mongols attacking Kai-feng-fu in China around 1232 A.D. These rockets were not ballistic. Throughout their history in warfare, rockets were used as long-range projectiles and signaling devices, but were more of a curiosity than a primary means to wage war. As technology advanced, the dream of using rockets and missiles as a military weapon became a reality. In several instances, ballistic missiles played a vital role in a campaign or even settled a war. The next four chapters will explore cases that illustrate the impact of ballistic missiles on war.

One can trace the history of ballistic missiles in the first case to World War II. German efforts to create weapons that did not violate post–World War I peace treaties found these vehicles to be potential substitutes for banned long-range artillery. From the 1930s, the German military developed a rudimentary missile. The Germans used this weapon primarily against England, France, and the Netherlands. This campaign was the largest use of ballistic missiles to date.

The second case traces the ballistic missiles' evolution through the cold war to the Cuban Missile Crisis. The systems in this case provided several advantages for a nation to exploit. Although the world never saw these weapons used by the Soviet Union and the United States and its allies, their presence influenced international events. U.S. efforts to develop ballistic missiles involved technological, political, strategic, and organizational challenges to overcome. Power struggles developed between opposing camps that centered on the number and capabilities of both land-based ICBMs and SLBMs.

The third case involves events in Cuba that affected the United States and the Soviet Union. The two nations almost came to nuclear blows over the placement of ballistic missiles near each other's borders that was capped off by events in Cuba during October 1962. Nuclear delivery vehicles became the currency of cold war conflict after Cuba but also raised questions about their dangers and created a new political dynamic for arms control that would challenge the world even today.

The last case involves Iraq. Surprisingly, the next instance of nations actually launching ballistic missiles against one another after World War II was not made by the world's superpowers, but by two developing nations, Iran and Iraq. During their long conflict in the 1980s, Iran and Iraq used Soviet-designed missiles to strike cities and other targets. These long-range attacks attempted to weaken civilian morale and damage key military installations. One might argue that Iraq's use of these ballistic missiles forced the Iranians to negotiate a peace.

Iraq was not finished with using ballistic missiles after its war with Iran. In this case, Iraq's opponent was the United States. However, unlike other cases of actual missile attacks, the United States had an effective means of early warning and a limited missile defense system. Although there were casualties in these attacks, Iraqi efforts to use their weapons did not create significant damage. The attack's physiological and political impacts did cause the United States and its allies to devote resources and effort to counter these threats.

VENGEANCE FROM AFAR: THE V-2 AT WAR

Germany's defeat after World War I created the conditions for a revolution in the use of technology to military applications. The 1919 Treaty of Versailles limited the vanquished German military effort to a very small force. Combat aircraft and long-range artillery were strictly prohibited so that if a hostile German government and military came to power, they would not repeat their World War I actions. During the 1920s, scientists, engineers, and rocket enthusiasts spawned a dream of future space travel. These individuals envisioned travel to the moon and beyond with powerful rockets. Books, articles, and movies glorified future space exploration. This interest not only fired the public's imagination, but also inspired the German military. The combination of the emerging field of rocketry and a military need to replace aircraft and long-range artillery created an opportunity for the German military after World War I. The Germans had bombed London with primitive bombers, albeit with small payloads, and had used its Paris Gun to lob shells over 130 kilometers (eighty miles). However, technology would allow for a different war.

The marriage of convenience between technologies, need, and vision created a situation where German army scientists created the world's first operational ballistic missile. This effort culminated in the launch of 3,255 V-2 ballistic missiles in anger against Allied cities and other targets. The German launch program represents the single largest demonstration of ballistic missile operations in war. Although the German endeavor failed to substantially change the strategic picture for Germany, it created much concern in Allied senior leadership circles. These concerns were muted as the German military position crumbled in late 1944. Out of the ashes of defeat, as in World War I, new ideas and technologies evolved to improve the ballistic missile's future. These delivery vehicles and the atomic bomb provided the opportunity for visionaries to seek a new type of warfare that was almost instantaneous and unstoppable: nuclear armed conflict.

How the German military developed and used their *Vergeltungswaffe* (vengeance weapons)-2, or V-2 (most German army sources called the missile the A-4), illustrates many of the issues involved in applying new technology to problems, developing a weapon system, and then trying to operate that weapon effectively. The V-2 was also subject to much political debate about its control. These types of concerns and issues are still relevant today, whether they involve ballistic missiles or some other kind of technology and weapon. How one country used this weapon and its opponent's reaction to it at the time and its future uneasiness about the development of these systems illustrates problems that this nation and others face today.

A German army officer, Colonel Karl Becker, with an interest in field artillery and ballistics, initially conceived the idea of bringing rockets into a more active role in the military. Becker was an engineer who was heavily involved in the army's ordnance testing and development of new weapons. He was fascinated with the prospects of using rockets as a substitute for long-range artillery as a means to deliver poison gas against an enemy. As chief of the army weapons bureau (*Heereswaffenamt,* or HWA), Becker started to explore rocket technology. Armies had used small solid fueled rockets for signal purposes in the war, and developments around this technology continued into the 1920s. However, other scientists and engineers believed that liquid fueled systems using gasoline or kerosene as fuel and liquid oxygen might deliver better results. Undaunted, with a relatively small budget, Becker attempted to advance the use of solid fueled rockets as short-range weapons.

Becker pushed through a modest rocket program in the Reich's defense ministry. Skeptics believed the program to be a waste of limited military funding. However, Becker, strengthened by his convictions in new technology, was able to acquire funds and personnel for the effort. One army officer, Captain Walter Dornberger, an engineer and veteran artillery officer assigned to

Becker, would eventually become a key player in the V-2 development. In 1930, Dornberger started to explore ways to use solid fueled rockets to deliver weapons to a range of about seven to eight kilometers (less than five miles).

Civilian rocketry advances in liquid fueled systems soon eclipsed those in solid fuel research. German amateur rocket groups, such as the Society for Space Travel (*Verein für Raumschiffart,* or VfR), were actively experimenting with combinations of gasoline and liquid oxygen rockets that promised greater range and payloads than solid fueled systems. Becker's desire for long-range artillery capability soon translated into a higher priority than the shorter-ranged solid fueled rocket developments. Dornberger was soon working on liquid fueled, longer-range missiles. He became involved in VfR activities that included information exchanges and allowed VfR members to use the HWA's rocket test ranges for their experiments. This test range, Kummersdorf, was near Berlin. Dornberger also recruited VfR members to work for the HWA. One of his biggest catches was a young engineer, Wernher von Braun, who came to work for the HWA in 1932.

Rocket development accelerated. Dornberger became more heavily involved in development of longer-range missiles. He tested an initial trial missile, the *Aggregat 1* (Aggregate or Assembly 1) or A-1. Von Braun was instrumental in the design of the weapon, which was an attempt to test the feasibility of using lighter materials for rocket construction, such as aluminum; to use ignition and pressurization of fuel and oxidizer tanks; and to construct a rocket with features such as a gyroscopic stabilization program. The A-1 allowed the scientists and engineers to experiment with structural designs. Although the A-1 was not a launch success, it was the beginning of the HWA's efforts to begin a ballistic missile program.

Launch operations at Kummersdorf were limited due to range and local complaints. Dornberger was able to move some launch activities to the Baltic coast on the island of Borkum, but this was only a temporary solution. Von Braun and a growing number of rocket designers advanced the work of the A-1, especially with the placement of fuel and oxidizer tanks, improved stabilization, and other refinements. A new test missile, the A-2, was in its planning stage. The A-2 used an alcohol and liquid oxygen combination that produced a 300-kilogram thrust. On December 19, 1934, a test A-2 rocket was launched that reached an altitude of nearly 1,700 meters (5,600 feet). The next day, missile crews duplicated the successful launch of another A-2. The German army's ballistic missile program was on its way up.

Like most military developments, advancement of weapons technology required resources. The German government was now in the hands of Adolf Hitler and his National Socialist Party. They pledged a strong nation while conducting secret efforts to build up Germany's military. Despite these goals,

Dornberger had to convince a skeptical German army to not only continue but also expand his A-series rocket program to include more funds and a larger research center. The army was not the only service interested in rocket development. The German air force, or *Luftwaffe,* had shown a keen interest in this technology. Instead of competition, Dornberger sought cooperation with the *Luftwaffe* to develop solid fueled rockets for the service. The *Luftwaffe* was interested in developing rocket-assisted takeoff systems for heavy bombers, building rocket planes, and other pursuits. Dornberger received agreement from *Luftwaffe* leadership to help build a joint research and test center on the Baltic at Peenemünde.

The only stumbling block for Dornberger was approval to proceed on testing. He needed to convince top army leadership about the feasibility of long-range ballistic missiles. In March 1936 he invited the commander-in-chief of the army, General Werner von Fritsch, to Kummersdorf. HWA engineers and scientists put on a test demonstration of three rocket engines and made presentations about the use of these new weapons. Von Fritsch was convinced, and funds started to roll into the HWA coffers for further research.

Development of the next series of test vehicles proceeded, as did the construction of Peenemünde, but this next series of missile developments was unsuccessful. The A-3, successor to the A-2, failed. The A-3 was supposed to test larger liquid fueled motors. After several launch problems, Dornberger and his team moved on. The goal of his research team was to build an operational ballistic missile as soon as possible, but technical delays impeded progress. German army officials envisioned a missile with a range of about 250 kilometers (155 miles) and a warhead weighing about 1,000 kilograms (2,200 pounds). This operational missile would become the A-4. The abandoned work on the A-2 took its toll on the A-4 as its development had slowed.

A new test program, the A-5, experimented with vital components needed to make the A-4 operational. Gyroscopic control, ignition, propulsion, and other issues were examined and solutions found. During 1938, test teams launched four successful A-5 test missiles. Scientists and engineers incorporated these lessons into the A-4, and the system seemed ready to pass the milestone of becoming operational.

By 1939, war was on the horizon for Germany and Europe. Rapid success on the battlefield ensured German domination of the continent as nations fell under the heel of the German military. By 1940, the only power that remained unbeaten was Great Britain. The Soviet Union had signed a nonaggression pact with Germany in 1939. Although the British seemed safe on their island fortress, the *Luftwaffe* was unleashing a massive assault on England. The Royal Air Force (RAF) and the rest of the British nation seemed ready to crack, which would either force a peaceful settlement or allow the degraded British military to succumb to a German invasion. These events put into question the need for Dornberger's experimental ballistic missile program. If the *Luftwaffe* or the German army could perform without these missiles, then why should the government continue to fund and devote productive capacity to a program that would deliver little that was new?

The *Luftwaffe* failed in its efforts to conquer the RAF, however. More important, long-range bombardment became a secondary interest as the German army moved against the Soviet Union. Instead of ballistic missiles, the need for existing weapons was paramount as the campaign slowed into an attrition campaign, in contrast to the lightning campaigns of 1939 and 1940. The development of the A-4 slowed but was not stopped. Research continued to make rocket advancements throughout 1940 to 1942 despite the limited resources and official indifference.

By 1942 the fortunes of war started to turn in favor of Dornberger. German military operations had started to turn into disaster. The advantage of additional men, materiel, and time was slowly moving to the Allies. The United States, as the key producer of military goods, was now supplying the Allies with everything from munitions to food. The infusion of resources started to tip the balance of power. This showed on the battlefield. Soviet forces turned the initial German advance into a stalemate. The combined American and British efforts in North Africa started to push the Germans out of that region. Germany was having problems sustaining its war efforts. Allied operations began to pressure the Axis powers along the peripheral edges of their conquests. Increasingly, the Allies struck at targets in Germany's heartland. By the summer of 1942, a bombing campaign against Germany started that would increase in size and scope to the end of the war. The Combined Bomber Offensive (CBO), conducted by American daylight and RAF night strikes, began to target the economy and parts of German national power. German industrial strength and military activities, once thought immune, were routinely bombed by Allied air forces.

Military need and national leadership collided in Berlin. Increasingly, the *Luftwaffe* devoted additional fighter and antiaircraft artillery units to defend the Reich from the CBO. Frontline units were stripped of badly needed aircraft. The need to protect the country and maintain operations took a serious toll on German military and economic resources. As early as February 1942, Albert Speer, overseeing German armaments production, saw technology as a way to offset Allied materiel advantage. Experimentation expanded on surface-to-air missiles and increased fighter production. By 1944, Germany was feeling the brunt of the CBO and faced increased pressure on the eastern front. New ways and means could also help slow the Allied advance in the west and perhaps make direct attacks upon England. However, the most important impact on the CBO bombing campaign was Hitler's desire for revenge. There was no hiding the evidence that German cities and factories had suffered attacks.

Adolf Hitler's desire to respond to Allied attacks on the country began to take shape. He had his eyes on a series of future *Vergeltungswaffe* systems. The *Luftwaffe* created an unpiloted, jet-powered flying bomb called the V-1. *Luftwaffe* V-1 engineers were ahead of A-4 developers and would field their weapons first. The army had its burgeoning A-4. The A-4 test program still required more work to demonstrate its practicality as a long-range ballistic missile.

Hitler was much intrigued by the A-4. Dornberger and von Braun, supported by top army leadership, had briefed Hitler at his Wolf's Lair command headquarters in East Prussia on August 20, 1941. Using film, persuasion, and supposition, Dornberger had made a good impression on Hitler. Images of thousands of ballistic missiles falling onto England and against Allied military forces seemed to convince Hitler that the A-4 could stem the tide. Hitler foresaw the A-4 as a revolutionary weapon, but Germany would need hundreds of thousands of the missiles. Still, Hitler did not order the mass production of the A-4, because it had not flown and there were technical problems. The Peenemünde research and test staff was in a terrible position. They had successfully convinced Hitler of the A-4's merits, but they had not received any significant resources to start large-scale production at their relatively small facilities.

Hitler sought weapons that could deliver a series of long-range attacks upon the Allies. The *Luftwaffe* demonstrated it was incapable of a sustained aerial strategic bombing campaign because of its force structure, doctrine, training, and leadership. One promising technology that started to take on new luster was Dornberger and von Braun's ballistic missile research. The Peenemünde group still had to improve rocket engine performance to push the larger A-4 to its target hundreds of kilometers away. Additionally, the vehicle had to withstand supersonic flight that put aerodynamic pressure on the missile. Finally, the guidance system would require new technology and systems to allow some modicum of accuracy. Designs changed constantly. Over the A-4's development, engineers allegedly had to make over 65,000 design changes to the system. Still, by October 3, 1942, the technical persistence from Dornberger's crew allowed a successful launch of an A-4 about 201 kilometers (125 miles) across the Baltic. The test A-4 landed 4 kilometers (2.5 miles) from its intended impact point.

Although the missile demonstrated its technical feasibility, the army still had to produce significant A-4 quantities. Competing needs to defend the Fatherland by fighters, military vehicles, ordnance, and other military equipment constrained the shrinking industrial base. The *Luftwaffe*'s own V-1 was a rival for the same resources. Manpower was an issue as more women and foreign laborers, many from occupied countries or prisons, were pressed into service. The grueling campaign in the east started to draw more of Germany's dwindling male population into military service. The drain on oil and other resources forced cuts in production activities as Allied military operations started to curtail Germany's access to raw materials, which affected all German economic activities.

Another rivalry threatened the A-4 program. Political jockeying to control the A-4 started to arise. *Reichsführer* Heinrich Himmler, in charge of the *Schutzstaffel* (SS), had taken an interest in the ballistic missile development ever since Hitler's attention had peaked with the proposed weapon. Himmler believed that the military arm of the SS, the *Waffen*-SS, could operate the missile that would not only please Hitler but also increase Himmler's influence among top Nazi leadership. The German army and SS were rivals on the battlefield and for military resources and influence. This rivalry would spill over for control of the A-4.

After much internal discussion, Speer was able to get a decision about full production for the A-4 or V-2. Growing Allied strength on the British Isles and the decided turn of strategic advantage against Germany convinced many in the German national leadership to support these revolutionary weapons. Speer believed that the V-1 and V-2 could provide complementary service and avoid the growing competition between the army and the *Luftwaffe* if they were both approved for production. By June 2, 1943, the V-2 was given a big push toward operational reality when it was made the top priority of all German armaments production programs.

Although the army developed the program, the SS had not given up efforts toward controlling the V-2 launching. The army had already planned some base construction that would affect the V-2's operational use. Dornberger and von Braun had already started to survey potential launch bases in 1942. The first was Watten near Calais. The V-2's planners believed that Watten would become the primary hub for missile operations. This launch site would allow German launch crews to send V-2s from locations closest to southeastern England. London, industrial sites, and potential basing and logistical sites for an Allied invasion were within the V-2's range. The other site was nearby at Wizernes. This site would act as a secondary operating location. Launch bunkers were constructed to include storage and other facilities. Although these sites were subject to Allied aircraft attacks, German army leadership believed that the multiple launch sites would allow V-2 launch units to maintain a constant stream of missile bombardment.

Launch site vulnerability was not lost on the German military. Another insightful development was the way the V-2 was launched. Missile launch crews could send the V-2 off to its target by igniting it from a fixed site. However, army designers recognized that Allied air power was increasing the Allies' ability to destroy targets from factories to moving trains. American and British air forces were making such targets' longevity problematic. Dornberger built support systems to ensure the V-2 was a mobile weapon system. A V-2 launch unit could move to fixed launch positions and set up for launch. German crews did have to operate many support vehicles and had to operate near railways to have access to large quantities of fuel and oxidizer. Despite these designs, the V-2 fixed sites were still subject to attack. The Watten launch facilities were hit by two American air raids on August 27 and September 7, 1943. These raids highlighted the problem facing the German military. Later in the war, Allied ground forces would overrun these V-2 sites and stop operations. Until the invasion of western Europe, however, the only practical method to interfere with missile operations was an air campaign. Photographic and human intelligence sources could identify these types of fixed launch systems, and a bombing campaign could then be waged against them.

American and British intelligence had received reports of rocket launches from the Baltic. Peenemünde also became a target of raids throughout August 1943. These raids did not hit any research or production facilities, but they did destroy worker housing. The attack on these V-2 activities highlighted the Germans' problems from concentrating many V-2 operations at one location. Components and supplies were produced by companies throughout the Reich, but the missiles were assembled at Peenemünde. The air attacks forced production and assembly activities from the Baltic coast to more secure locations. Eventually, missile production and assembly would move underground. Production also suffered from a lack of capacity to build the maximum number of missiles. Hitler had envisioned that Speer could maintain a monthly production rate of 1,800 V-2 units. This rate assumed that sufficient liquid oxygen and fuel, fabricated components, and skilled labor were available.

The V-2 connection with the SS was not limited to potential future missile operations. Scarce workers forced the V-2 production managers to use concentration camp labor. As the war progressed, Allied military operations would pressure the German economy to use more concentration camp labor and conscripted manpower from occupied nations, including V-2 production and assembly centers. Increasing bombing also forced Dornberger to use an SS test site in Bliszna in the heart of Poland. V-2 testing was delayed, but more important, the SS was slowly gaining influence in the V-2 program. Himmler's interest in the V-2 increased as the system became operational.

Hitler had put Dornberger in charge of all V-2 military operations on October 4, 1943. Himmler increased his influence on V-2 production, however, by helping convince Hitler to move the missile construction underground using concentration camp labor. The move would protect the production from future bomber raids and ensure a flow of V-2 weapons to hurl against England and other targets. Additionally, Himmler claimed he could comb the concentration camps for skilled engineers, managers, and laborers. The underground camps provided a secure facility from which intelligence sources would find it difficult to get information. Himmler had selected an individual to construct the underground facility, *Brigadeführer* Hans Kammler. Kammler was a civil engineer who helped build three concentration camps. Himmler believed that Kammler was adept at building facilities quickly and efficiently, perfect for constructing the V-2 facilities.

Kammler helped in the construction of the underground V-2 assembly plants. A facility was built in Germany near Nordhausen that became the primary production center. It was later called *Mittlewerke,* or Central Works. The Peenemünde activities had also been renamed as the *Electromechanische Werke* (EMW), a quasi-commercial firm that built components such as the rocket engine.

The V-2 bombardment against England was planned to start in late 1943. Production was delayed, however, because of the bombing raids, moves to secure production facilities, continuing technical problems, and lack of skilled labor. Despite the SS efforts to get skilled labor, the poor treatment of workers and conditions contributed to questionable workmanship, such as faulty welding efforts. These delays added to increasing concerns among Hitler and others about the viability of the V-2 and the army's ability to run the program. By September 1943, Dornberger had completed thirty-one test flights. Scientists and engineers concentrated on solving many problems that appeared. However, V-2 technical problems were not the only concern for Speer. Competing needs for other weapons created further pressure to delay V-2 production. Existing weapons production programs needed to replace increasing losses among all three branches of the armed forces against the Americans, British, and Soviets.

The *Luftwaffe* was able to start its V-1 bombing campaign against Britain in June 1944 and soon increased the raids by hundreds of missiles. The V-1 missiles were cheaper and simpler to build than the V-2, and the number of attacks impressed Hitler. However, the V-1 campaign did not have the effect that the German military had hoped for. Although production of the V-2 hit a high of 437 missiles in May 1944, Dornberger's missile program produced only eighty-six in July. These efforts fell far short of Hitler's desire for 1,800 units per month.

Germany's strategic outlook had taken a decided turn for the worse after June 6, 1944. American and British forces had landed in Normandy in France.

The German efforts to stem the Allied offensives in the western and eastern fronts called for new ways to pressure the Allies. Hitler, despite the V-2's problems, regained his confidence in the weapon.

For Himmler, the attempt to grab the V-2 was at hand. The SS would not give up in their quest for control of the V-2 program. Through political pressure and intimidation (von Braun was arrested for a period) and other tactics, Himmler and Kammler started to take greater control over the program. The German army's lack of performance in the field had caused Hitler to pause and question its effectiveness. Throughout the eastern front, Germany's army operations could not defeat or stop Soviet forces. Army leaders, in Hitler's opinion, had failed him in Moscow, Stalingrad, and other areas. The German army also was unable to stem the American and British invasion at Normandy. Although the SS took part in these campaigns, Hitler's impression of the SS was colored by their zeal and loyalty, even though they were savaged by Allied ground forces just like the army. The V-2 was one of the few options available to Hitler to stem the tide of Allied advance. If the Allies established a foothold in Europe from France, Germany could expect another slow war of attrition like that on the eastern front. A major two-front war would drain German military and economic resources. V-2 operations offered a chance, albeit a slight one, to change the direction of the war. The German government had already committed resources to these weapons, but the army might not be able to handle the V-2 operations. The SS might give a boost to the V-2.

Dornberger and the army's days of V-2 control were nearly over. Kammler's growing influence over *Mittlewerke,* labor, and other production activities could not be stopped. By the first week in September, V-2 operational control fell to Kammler. The SS would control all operational launches against England and other targets.

The V-2 was about to make its operational debut. The missile was a single-staged vehicle that did not have a reentry system. Instead, the entire missile would hit the target. The mass and kinetic energy in the missile's impact would magnify the damage to the target. Additionally, any unused fuel and oxidizer would add to the effect of the attack. Dornberger and von Braun's final design for the V-2 included five major subsections for the missile. These subsections included the warhead, a control compartment, a midsection that included the liquid fuel and oxidizer tanks, a propulsion unit, and a tail assembly.

The fourteen-meter (forty-six-foot, one-inch) ballistic missile was capped by a single warhead. Engineers built the missile with a maximum diameter of 1.68 meters (roughly five feet and one inch). The V-2 weighed about 12,870 kilograms, approximately 28,300 pounds. The missile was built primarily

V-2. German V-2 crews attempted to knock out Antwerp, a major port, to stop the flow of supplies to Allied forces. Although there were relatively few casualties, these attacks did kill several thousand people. Supply operations were affected with a slowdown. (Courtesy, U.S. National Archives)

from steel. This missile had a maximum speed of about 5,760 kilometers per hour, or roughly 3,110 nautical miles per hour. The rocket engine would operate for about fifty-one seconds, which provided sufficient thrust to push the V-2 to a maximum altitude of about 96,000 meters (a little less than 315,000 feet). Flight time, from launch to impact, was about 310 seconds. The ballistic missile had the capability to hit a target from approximately 330 kilometers, or less than 180 miles. Although in present terms this missile seemed short ranged, it was the start for a new weapon that would have far-reaching effects in the future.

The warhead was simple. Conical in shape, it contained a highly explosive material in a welded steel shell. German ordnance specialists used about 735 kilograms (1,620 pounds) of cast amatol for the explosive. Amatol is a compound composed of 60 percent ammonium nitrate and the remainder TNT. The V-2's manufacturers had a choice of warhead explosives. One concern revolved around internal temperatures that could have ignited the explosives and destroyed the missile. Amatol provided a relatively stable composition that could withstand reentry temperatures.

LAUNCH OPERATIONS

German forces launched 3,255 V-2 weapons against a host of targets in western Europe. Although Hitler wanted to strike England, London in particular, most of the targets that launch crews prepared missiles against were in Antwerp. When the V-2 was in development, the Germans had controlled the continent. Britain was on the edge of defeat, the United States had not entered the war, and the Soviet Union was abiding by the nonaggression treaty. The military and political environment had changed dramatically with Allied forces converging on the Reich from the west, south, and east. The V-weapons could offer a way to stem the flow of the western Allied advances.

Despite pressure on production from bombing and advancing Allied ground forces on all fronts, V-2 production continued. These pressures, however, ultimately affected the general supply distribution of resources, which would ultimately affect V-2 production and other war materials. Still, the German economy was able to produce upward of 7,500 V-2s in 1944 and an additional 2,500 by March 1945. Although these production figures appear significant, many of the missiles had flaws. Poor production methods, labor quality, and supply disruptions created conditions for inferior workmanship. For example, inadequate welding or problems with corrosion forced crews to scrap the missile or caused its flight performance to falter. Despite these problems, by September 1944, the SS had an inventory of missiles to attack the West. Other challenges also hit the program. Many of the prepared launch sites that the Germans had built, Watten, Wizernes, and locations in Cherbourg, were now under Allied control. American and British ground forces had simply overrun the sites. Fortunately for the SS, the V-2 did have a mobile launch capability. Allied intelligence sources were not aware that the V-2 could be launched without the use of the fixed sites. American and RAF bombers and fighters pummeled seven V-2 fixed launch locations with the belief that this would end the V-2 threat. Subsequent examination of the sites by intelligence sources indicated that these sites were primarily liquid oxygen–producing facilities, storage dumps, repair facilities, or activities other than launch sites.

Allied ground advances forced the German military to retreat throughout the western front. The German reliance on large quantities of consumables, like liquid oxygen, required V-2 operations to have access to working railroads and facilities that could swiftly produce the materials. V-2 operations had shifted to the area around The Hague in the southwest Netherlands. From this location, German V-2 launches could strike a number of targets in England, France, and Belgium. Two mobile launch groups conducted the V-2 actions. The northern group focused on England, and the southern group concentrated on France and Belgium. Under SS control, attacks on London were planned to sap the morale of the British people in hopes that they would sue for peace.

The first V-2 attacks occurred on September 8, 1944. Paris was the initial recipient of a V-2 launch that morning. Crews aimed the missile at Paris, but it never reached the city. The London area would receive two V-2s later in the day. One V-2 hit a London suburb, Chiswick, at 6:30 p.m., destroying some homes and killing three people. Unlike the V-1, the V-2 attacks came without warning, since the V-2 arrived on the target area at a supersonic speed. Radar, aircraft, and observers had been able to detect the V-1s flying to England. This use of the V-2 was the start of a campaign that would last until March 1945.

The launch of V-2s against London and Paris came as a shock to American and British military staffs. Unlike the subsonic V-1 that fighters and antiaircraft artillery could at least shoot down, the V-2 sped down on its target at supersonic speeds. There was no effective warning or defense against a V-2 attack. Some British military analysts reasoned that although the V-2 was a new terror threat, it did not have a larger payload than the V-1 and there were fewer V-2 attacks than V-1 strikes. Additionally, V-1 and V-2 attacks on locations other than London had moved the focus away from England to a wider application against the Allies. Still, the Allies had to devote time and resources to stem the V-2 launches. Since there was no effective way to shoot down a V-2, the Allies had to concentrate on passive defenses such as building shelters. The Allies had to take a more active stance, however, by searching out

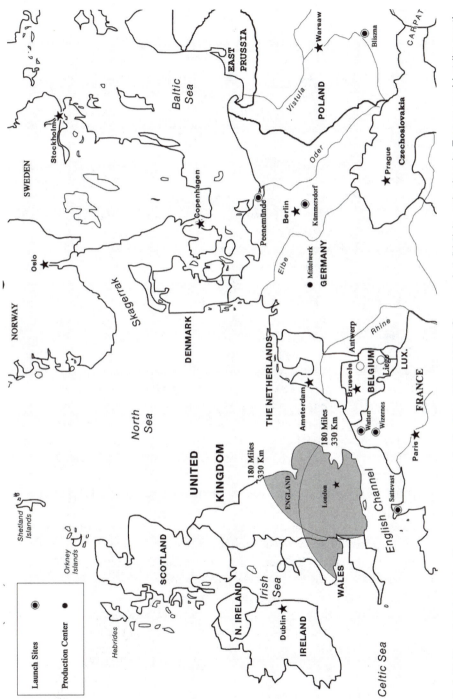

A-4 (V-2) rocket launch sites and ranges of missiles, 1943–1944. German A-4 (V-2) launch sites in France could strike southern England. Later, the missiles hit Antwerp and Liege. (Courtesy, Mapcraft)

and destroying the capabilities of launching the V-2. There was little success in finding mobile launchers; instead, the Allies had to disable the resources and support activities used to launch the missiles.

American and British air forces had to move from CBO missions and tactical air support for ground operations to bombing suspected launch facilities, manufacturing locations, rail lines, and other activities for the V-2. The V-2's psychological impact on Allied political and military leadership forced changes in military strategy to divert limited resources to combat these weapons. Ultimately, these actions did not have the intended result desired by Allied airmen. Once a V-2 crew launched its missile, it could simply move on to another location to set up and prepare for the next round. Instead, ground advances paved the way to ultimate success. The drive through northern France started to push the Germans away from locations that could strike London. The V-2 attacks would continue against England, but German focus soon concentrated on Antwerp.

Allied ground operations required massive logistics. Supplies had to move from the United States to England and then be transported to the Continent. American and British ground forces had captured Antwerp, a major harbor in Belgium, in early September. This key logistical center would save the Allied war supply effort countless days and miles of travel to support their offensive. On October 12, Hitler had selected Antwerp as a target to destroy its port facilities in the hope of slowing down the Allied move east. Later, during his ill-fated Ardennes offensive in December 1944, Hitler selected Antwerp as the major objective to stop the Allies. German officers also directed more attention to Liege, a vital communications and rail center for the Allies. The U.S. Army's main supply route for operations in northwest Europe fed through Liege. The V-2 had now changed from a mostly terrorizing weapon to one aimed at specific military threats. These efforts highlighted the desperate actions that the Germans had taken not only in their V-2 program, but also in other activities such as lowering the minimum and raising the maximum age for enlistment into the army to get more personnel into uniform.

Although the Allies advanced throughout northwest Europe and the eastern front, the Germans managed to launch over 3,000 V-2s in World War II. Throughout the war, the Germans claimed to have launched 1,359 missiles at England, but they took an active interest in knocking out Antwerp with an additional 1,610 V-2s. The remaining attacks hit locations throughout France and Belgium. Hitler had envisioned a massive, single 5,000 V-2 missile attack on London and Antwerp. The V-2's results as a weapon for vengeance were a far cry from this vision. Only 517 V-2s hit London, and another twenty-seven missiles struck the Norwich area. Unfortunately, 2,754 people perished in these attacks and 6,523 were injured. The V-1 and V-2 attacks did disrupt activities in London. The British government saw over 1,450,000 people evacuate London because of to these attacks. People panicked, but the British people survived this threat as they had during the Blitz by *Luftwaffe* bombers, their will intact.

The V-2 attacks on Antwerp did affect the U.S. Army's port discharge operations. For example, during the first week in December 1944, port handlers processed 19,000 tons per day. V-2 attacks reduced the process to 13,700 tons per day two weeks later, a 27 percent reduction. Morale flagged among port workers and railroad workers as they became V-2 targets and productivity started to fall. In the V-2 attacks on Antwerp and Liege, the German ballistic missiles killed 5,400 persons, about wounded 22,000, and destroyed more than 90,000 homes. A V-2's impact created a larger destructive path than the impact created by the V-1. The kinetic energy produced by the mass and speed of the V-2 caused a greater destructive power than that of the V-1. V-2s pulverized buildings and created blast effects that killed more people and created significant damage. The destruction caused by the V-2 was not enough to slow the Allied advance in the west, but these attacks did force the Allies to respond and concentrate on the V-2.

Allied air forces were forced to address efforts to stop the V-2. This weapon did not create catastrophic impact on the war, but the ballistic missile campaign had a great psychological impact on civilians and politicians. This psychological impact forced changes in the U.S. Army Air Forces (AAF). Heavy bombers from the AAF Eighth Air Force and the RAF used 1,000 aircraft sorties that dropped 48,000 tons of bombs on suspected missile production facilities. Smaller tactical fighter-bombers from both the United States and England strafed or bombed suspected mobile launch sites and targets. Pilots flew about 10,000 sorties and used 2 million kilogram (about 2,000 tons) of weapons in this effort.

Faulty missile construction and launch crew errors caused many of the missiles to fail to lift off or explode on the launch pad. The U.S. Army evaluated V-2 performance against targets in England through December 1944. Analysts classified approximately 24.5 percent of all V-2 launches as failures. This category included canceled launches, missiles that failed to ignite, or V-2s that left the launch pad and exploded. Another 10.5 percent of V-2 missiles launched, but intelligence officers viewed them as wild rounds. These vehicles landed outside an eighteen-mile radius of the intended target. U.S. Army officials considered the V-2 rounds that landed within an eighteen-mile radius, which was 65 percent, to be within acceptable accuracy. They believed that any missile that hit within a six-mile radius of London was a great success in terms of accuracy. From December 1944 to March 1945, practice and improved missile production quality reduced the failure rate from 24.5 percent to 17 percent. Still, the V-2 did not achieve its intended objective of crumbling London's will or stopping the Allied advance.

3

Cold War: Push-Button Warfare

THE END OF WORLD War II forced dramatic changes to world politics. While the Western powers wanted to rebuild the devastated nations after the war, the Soviet Union wanted to extend their communist empire. The Western powers started to demobilize their military forces. In 1945, the United States had over twelve million uniformed personnel; by 1947, there were only 1.5 million military members. Soviet leaders responded by consolidating their control over their new territories. Soviet leader Josef Stalin viewed capitalism and the West on an inevitable path to conflict with communism in February 1946.

On both the free and communist sides, military leaders had marveled at the German technologies. V-2 operations demonstrated that long-range bombardment was possible without a manned airplane. Countries did not have any effective missile defenses to protect the population. Even before the formal end of the war, a mad scramble occurred between powers to capture German personnel and equipment. The race led to a major impact on future ballistic missile development. Although these weapons were not used actively in combat, the fielding of nuclear armed missiles had a major political, military, and economic impact on the world for decades.

U.S. BALLISTIC MISSILES IN THE COLD WAR

These weapons offered a major boost to a nation for several reasons. The means of delivery for a weapon was increased greatly with these new systems. Speed and a way to avoid enemy defenses seemed to give a country a way to strike immediately at a rival's capital. Although strategic aerial bombardment campaigns did target Berlin and Tokyo, they came at a huge cost in terms of lost aircraft and crews due to enemy actions. World War II AAF losses over Europe alone included over 18,000 aircraft and 79,265 crew members. A longer-range V-2 could serve as a natural extension of artillery that would allow bombardment to occur without such losses. Visionaries, scientists, military officers, and others saw the value of the ballistic missile. Still, many technical, financial, political, and other concerns would plague the development of these systems throughout the early cold war.

The early V-2 relied on a conventional warhead that did create damage, but the damage was limited to a few square city blocks. By August 6, 1945, the United States had introduced a more powerful weapon, the atomic bomb. An unstoppable delivery system and the tremendous devastation of nuclear weapons offered an opportunity to destroy whole societies without deploying a single soldier on foreign soil. Such a weapon might counter a foe with a large standing force and provide a significant advantage to an actor with a ballistic missile force. Although the atomic bomb unleashed a new era of weapons, scientists doubted that a missile that could carry a weapon thousands of miles away, with accuracy, was possible, at least not for a few years. The V-2 could hardly reach its range of 200 miles with a relatively small payload. The V-2 carried a 1,620-pound warhead; the United States dropped an atomic bomb on Hiroshima that was almost five and a half times larger. Assuming nuclear yields would increase, how could a missile carry a much heavier atomic bomb in the future?

The United States, traditionally, did not support large standing armies. After a major conflict, the nation demobilized its military forces partly for political and economic reasons. World War II was no different; the United States quickly returned soldiers, sailors, airmen, and marines to civilian life. The military was a skeleton of its former self. The United States was also getting back on its feet economically from pent-up consumer demand for household goods and services that were shortcut during the Great Depression and war years. The U.S. government had to cut expenditures to ensure a growing economy and return to normalcy. One target was military spending.

Atomic weapons, delivered by jet aircraft or ballistic missiles, offered a less expensive alternative. Although critics argued about the credibility of using nuclear weapons in all cases, the pressure to move to an instant nuclear response offered an option to cut defense spending. Others argued that a single-use and single-mission weapon, like a ballistic missile, was not as flexible as the proven manned, long-range bomber. Once the missile was launched, it was programmed to hit a specific target only. A piloted aircraft allowed for changes in course or mission that would allow more flexibility in planning and for the vagaries of war. Replacing the manned bomber with unmanned missiles was anathema to many pilots. The unproven long-range technology threatened future aircraft systems and a way of life for many of these officers.

The rise of atomic weapons also served another purpose. Service independence for the fledgling U.S. Air Force from the U.S. Army was helped by a focus on the future of strategic bombardment. The air force touted the nuclear weapon as a means to check the perceived threat of a growing Soviet military force. Adding a nearly instant means to counter this threat equaled a broader role and expanded service missions. In a competition for limited defense funds, this translated into a means to acquire new weapons and influence. The cold war witnessed the rise of a range of nuclear weapons from mines to weapons ranging in the megaton yield. The ballistic missile was front and center in the race for development funds. Important questions soon appeared. What service should develop these weapons? Interservice rivalry, fueled with limited budgets, intensified with the issue of missiles in the 1950s. Integration of missiles and aircraft would be slow.

Ballistic missiles also acted as a visible sign of a nation's military capability. These delivery systems allowed the United States to showcase its commitment to defend the nation and counter similar systems by the Soviet Union. This commitment was aimed at both the domestic and international communities. The 1960 presidential election between John F. Kennedy and Richard M. Nixon showcased allegations that a "missile gap" had grown between the United States and the Soviet Union. Kennedy alleged that the Republican administration of President Dwight D. Eisenhower had allowed the Soviets to develop a massive ballistic missile force that overshadowed the nation's arsenal. As president, Kennedy would erase such a gap to ensure security for America. Still, questions arose about the true numbers and development of these vehicles by the Soviet Union. Did the Soviets have and intend to develop an overwhelming force of weapons? Or was the threat of a missile gap only a political ploy or a product of faulty intelligence?

DEVELOPING THE BALLISTIC MISSILE

American forces had captured German scientists like von Braun and Dornberger, documents, some equipment, and operational V-2s. Debate about the ability to replicate the same German capabilities and extend them for the United States dominated discussions within Washington. Technological advances in rocketry, electronics, and nuclear energy and a different geopolitical environment in the post–World War II era translated to new opportunities for the U.S. military to explore. AAF Chief General Henry "Hap" Arnold was concerned about the future of the nation and service after the war. Although victorious, the country had to struggle to develop weapons that would match those of Nazi Germany. In the war, the United States was protected by two oceans from the threat of invasion or strategic bombardment. This physical barrier allowed the nation time to mobilize its industry and population to produce weapons and fighting forces.

Scientific advancement provided an avenue to pursue victory. The V-2, advanced bombers, and other weapons created conditions in which a future enemy might use those tools of war to strike at the heart of the country. The next war might not allow the United States the luxury of time and security to rebuild a military. Arnold, impressed with these scientific advancements, explored the AAF's future and the nation's security.

Given the general disarmament fever and calls for massive defense spending cuts, Arnold was limited in his options. Ballistic missile progress would have to be delayed while other pressing needs, such as AAF postwar reorganization into a separate service, took place. Arnold believed that one day these long-range missiles would become a reality. He successfully allocated funds from a limited AAF 1946 budget to begin detailed studies to determine the feasibility of advanced missilery that included air-to-air, air-to-surface, and short- and long-range surface-to-surface missiles. Arnold also was instrumental in forming the RAND Corporation, an independent think-tank, which would apply scientific analysis to defense problems such as ballistic missiles. RAND would become very influential in future weapons development, strategy, and policy. Allowing these research studies to flourish provided Arnold with the ability to select the most promising technologies for further development. Instead of relying solely on government laboratories or arsenals to explore these options, as in the past, Arnold widened these activities to industry and the scientific community.

Fiscal reality forced priorities. With few funds to field new weapons, missile development was centered on air-to-air missiles. Atomic bomb delivery became paramount, not by ballistic missile, but by existing manned bombers. These manned bombers would need to defend themselves against interceptors and so required better defensive capabilities. Crews would also need an air-to-surface missile armed with a nuclear device. A more pressing constraint was the number of scientists and engineers available to conduct the research. Finally, the AAF had to compete against other missile developments by the navy and the army ground forces. The army wanted to develop surface-to-air defense missiles and short-range missiles to support ground operations. Despite these limitations, in April 1946 the AAF awarded a $1.4 million contract to the Consolidated Vultee Aircraft Corporation (Convair) to study designs called for a missile to transport a 5,000-pound (about 2,270 kilograms) warhead up to 5,000 miles (more than 8,000 kilometers). Convair's Project MX-

774 would examine a subsonic, winged missile and a supersonic ballistic missile, Hiroc.

Convair engineers used the V-2 as a natural point of departure to study the possibility of expanding missile range and payload. MX-774 project results included redesign of the V-2 by using rocket sections to hold the fuel and oxidizer instead of using separate tanks; increased use of nitrogen pressurization within the missile that would reduce structural bracing support; focus on a warhead reentry instead of using the entire missile; and the exploration of swiveling rocket engines for better directional control that would eliminate fins and aerodynamic drag.

Unfortunately, budget cuts took their toll on the project. Cruise missiles, using aerodynamic lift, seemed to provide the fastest way to introduce an intercontinental strike system. These missiles would be longer-range versions of the V-1. Effective missile operations still seemed at least a decade away from serious technical consideration. Fuel, guidance, propulsion, reduced weight, and other issues forced the MX-774 project to be canceled. Convair's contract had stipulated that the weapon study examine guidance systems that put the warhead within 5,000 feet (about 1.5 kilometers). Given the current size of atomic weapons and yield and the lack of accuracy seen in the V-2, the missile might not destroy military targets with any precision. Technical advances in nuclear weapons had to either increase a ballistic missile's yield or reduce its weight to make the missile operational. Convair was not dissuaded about the future of its creation. The company continued independent research on many of these problems.

Scientific personnel were at a premium. The United States continued to rely on captured German scientists and engineers. The U.S. Air Force and its predecessor, the AAF, allowed Dornberger to help draft much of the service's missile research and development plans. Under Project Paperclip, these German scientists and engineers came to the United States to support missile development. Von Braun went to work for the U.S. Army. He and 120 German personnel supported postwar V-2 research into high-altitude flight. Similarly, the U.S. Navy supported its own research. These actions were not enough. The only alternative, early on, in all missile programs was to rely on private industry and give many study contracts. These activities bolstered competition of ideas, but they also fostered expensive duplication.

Service infighting was still a problem. Whoever built ballistic missiles would have a decided advantage for roles and missions in future warfare. The AAF had the edge over army ground forces to develop guided missiles when both were under the War Department. AAF personnel were responsible for all guided missiles developed for the army. However, this all changed when the air force became independent through the National Security Act of 1947.

Now, the U.S. Air Force was responsible for only its own missile development and not those that affected the army's roles and missions. Many critics argued that one role for these systems fell into the purview of the army. Army leadership viewed any guided missile launched from the ground its responsibility. They believed that the weapons were nothing more than an extension of long-range field artillery. The U.S. Air Force leadership believed that its role of conducting strategic bombardment would be erased by allowing the U.S. Army to have the sole responsibility for missiles. Instead, they advocated that it and the U.S. Navy develop "robot aircraft" and that all three services produce guided missiles that included ballistic ones as well as air-to-surface and surface-to-air weapons that allowed them to conduct their missions.

Determining which service would build missiles became a point of serious contention and was unresolved for years. At the start of the Eisenhower administration in January 1953, circumstances had changed dramatically. The Soviet Union had exploded an atomic bomb in August 1949; the nation had fought a bloody three-year conflict in Korea that turned the heat on in the cold war; the Atomic Energy Commission had successfully reduced the size of nuclear weapons and boosted yields; and several technological breakthroughs made an ICBM possible. The Korean War had shown that the communist powers were willing to shed blood in direct confrontation with the United States. Earlier, Soviet forces had blockaded Berlin and threatened military action that ended in a communist retreat on May 12, 1949. Threats and strategic objectives changed during the early years in the 1950s, and the United States recognized that its need to strengthen its military forces.

Technical concerns still plagued advocates of an ICBM-range vehicle. However, the reduction in the size of thermonuclear weapons was significant. A thermonuclear weapon was developed that reduced weapon weight. A thermonuclear weapon was developed that increased nuclear yield and was small enough to fit on the Atlas. This weapon, compared to the earlier fission atomic bombs used in Hiroshima and Nagasaki, was more powerful and produced effects in the megaton TNT range, compared with the relatively smaller kiloton range of the atomic bomb. Nuclear testing of the hydrogen bomb had successfully concluded on November 1, 1952. These weapons could weigh from 1,500 to 3,000 pounds (680 to 1,760 kilograms).

This single technical achievement solved a tricky problem; an MX-774 vehicle could now carry a one-megaton warhead with sufficient range. Accuracy was relaxed. Increased accuracy was expensive and difficult to achieve. The Atomic Energy Commission could now build larger thermonuclear weapons that could deliver a two- to three-megaton yield, yet the weight was reduced enough to be carried on a smaller version of Hiroc, called Atlas. Air force officials thought Convair had studied the concept far enough to allow it into initial development by January 1951. Instead of having to land Atlas

V-2 on launch pad. The German V-2 was a key element of early U.S. and Soviet ballistic missile development. This V-2, at White Sands in New Mexico, served as a test bed for the U.S. Army and allowed engineers to experiment with several new technologies. (Courtesy, U.S. Army)

on a target within 1,500 feet with a one-megaton yield, the missile's guidance system only had to get the missile to within five miles with a thermonuclear device.

President Eisenhower ordered a thorough review of all weapons including the ballistic missile. Committees investigated service missions and the growing Soviet threat. Russian scientists and engineers had started a guided missile program after the World War II and intelligence sources indicated that they were ahead of the United States. More important, by August 1953 Moscow had successfully exploded its hydrogen bomb. The move from defensive missiles, such as air-to-air or surface-to-air weapons, had not stopped work on ballistic ones. The U.S. Army had allowed von Braun and other German scientists to improve their work on the V-2. The Redstone became a weapon that could hit a target about 322 kilometers away (about 200 miles) with a nuclear payload. Army advocates pushed for a new missile with greater range of over 2,400 kilometers (1,500 miles).

The United States was poised to open the budget floodgates to develop nuclear weapon delivery vehicles. Still, the early Eisenhower administration believed that the United States had the strategic capability to outmuscle the Soviet Union with existing systems. Service competition remained keen. However, the U.S. Air Force could not rely solely on the proposed Atlas. Instead, air force leadership ordered parallel development of another ICBM. Atlas would become the first generation of long-range ballistic missiles. A follow-on system, Titan, would start development to replace the Atlas and ensure advancement in ballistic missile technology. Similarly, as the army expanded its role in developing an IRBM that became the Jupiter, the air force was not as eager for this type of short-range weapon. Developing a limited-range missile might drain resources from the Atlas and Titan. Additionally, if the air force could build an ICBM, it could certainly build a smaller IRBM. Critics of the IRBM also argued that supporting such a force would become a difficult chore because their range dictated that the IRBMs be stationed in foreign countries. Although the air force and army could emplace IRBMs in Alaska that could hit parts of the Soviet Union, most plans called for European bases. Basing missiles in Europe brought other problems such as reduced warning time of attack and subsequent questions about reaction time to launch. IRBMs seemed only a temporary fix to a longer-term problem.

Since 1953, the president, secretary of defense, and the air force had formed several committees to examine the question of ballistic missile development. These committees spilled much ink on missile priorities, but they failed to resolve the basic issue of when to build IRBM or ICBM systems. On February 14, 1955, the president's Science Advisory Committee's Technological Capabilities Panel, formed by James R. Killian, published its findings and briefed Eisenhower that it found the United States' security was at risk by Soviet advances in nuclear weaponry. Killian recommended that Eisenhower make ballistic missile development a national priority.

The air force's initial reliance on the manned bomber was challenged. Intelligence sources indicated that the Soviets had started to build sophisticated air defense systems that included antiaircraft artillery, interceptors, and other systems that might threaten the bomber flight. On the May Day 1955 parade in Moscow, the Soviets unveiled a production strategic bomber, the MYA-4 Bison, which had been seen a year earlier as a prototype. The May Day parade fly-over of several Bison aircraft shocked top national and air force leaders. If the Soviets had stepped up production of strategic bombers, what other surprises were in store?

Eisenhower finally resolved the issue by accepting the recommendations of the Killian Committee and his National Security Council to make the Atlas, Titan, Jupiter, and the new air force IRBM, Thor, national priorities. Eisenhower ordered the ballistic missile program to be the Defense Department's primary priority on September 13, 1955. The army and navy had responsibility to develop Jupiter. The navy wanted a missile fired from the sea. By default, the air force would build the ICBM force because they had programs in place to start rapid development and production. Additionally, army leadership had been more interested in fielding a missile for tactical support, at most an IRBM, than in an ICBM. Later, on November 26, 1956, interservice squabbling forced the secretary of defense, Charles E. Wilson, to delegate new missile responsibilities. The army was limited to operating missiles with ranges of less than 200 miles. The air force would take over IRBMs; they now had Jupiter and Thor. The navy could develop IRBMs for shipboard operations.

BALLISTIC MISSILES BECOME A NATIONAL PRIORITY

Despite the rising interest in Soviet military activities, the Eisenhower administration was still committed to reducing defense expenditures. Eisenhower had come to office wanting to end the war in Korea, reduce defense expenditures, and revive the economy. Some critics argued that we should not fight large-scale land conflicts. Instead, the policy of massive retaliation grew. First championed by Admiral Arthur W. Radford, chairman of the Joint Chiefs of Staff, in January 1954 and later Secretary of State John Foster Dulles in 1955, the policy of massive retaliation relied on the threat of nuclear attack against a Soviet or Chinese act of aggression at a time or place of our choosing. Air power and missiles would make excellent platforms for this new policy. Eisenhower also believed that true national security depended on a strong economy. Unnecessary government expenditures were opposed to this goal. Eisenhower thought he could use nuclear weapons to replace land power.

General Curtis E. LeMay, the commander of Strategic Air Command (SAC), was slated to eventually control the ICBM and Thor. LeMay, who had doubted the worth of ballistic missiles, was now charged with integrating them with the bomber. LeMay believed that the ICBM might give him a very rapid, accurate, and powerful weapon, if properly designed. There were no known missile defenses, and these new weapons could provide an initial penetration against an enemy and allow bombers a follow-up attack. Still, SAC bomber pilots were skeptical of this new weapon.

By December 1955, air force headquarters planned on having an operational ICBM force by 1959. The Air Research and Development Command (ARDC) would construct an initial force of only ten missiles by April 1, 1959. The weapons would, like the V-2, be launched in the open, but from fixed sites only. Air force crews would operate eighty Atlas and forty Titan missiles at sixty launch sites by January 1960. Due to the importance of these systems, the air force planned to locate these bases in three areas in the eastern, central, and western United States. Crews at each base would launch ten missiles within fifteen minutes and another ten missiles within two hours. These missiles had to have a relatively fast reaction time because they could not survive an attack in their unprotected launch sites. The base deployment scheme was, in part, a way to avoid presenting all of the missiles as a single, vulnerable target.

The Eisenhower administration only planned for an original total force of 120 ICBMs. Beliefs that the United States would continue to lead the Soviets in the missile race and demands to reduce defense spending forced changes in that plan. The number of total operational ICBMs dropped to eighty missiles by March 5, 1957. SAC would have an equal number of Atlas and Titan missiles. A single ICBM wing was composed of separate Atlas and Titan groups. A group was supposed to have four squadrons that operated ten launchers each. The first Atlas was supposed to be operational by March 1959.

The Atlas would represent America's commitment toward keeping a nuclear edge over the Soviet Union. Air force and Convair design efforts would center on a progressive test program. Engineers would develop Atlas prototypes to evaluate design features proposed for the missile. From 1955 to 1957, engineers surged toward creating a flight test program. By June 11, 1957, the first Atlas lifted off the pad, but it exploded soon afterward. Undeterred, the engineers continued testing, determined to do so because the planned initial operational deployment was less than two years away.

Budget concerns again forced the Eisenhower administration to curtail system development. The secretary of defense, Charles E. Wilson, proposed changes to the ballistic missile program. Now, only the Atlas was planned for production. Despite reports that the Soviet Union had tested an ICBM, called the R-7, on August 26, Eisenhower approved the change. Titan languished as a development-only program. The Soviet assertion of an operational R-7 was dismissed since the nation could not verify any of the Soviet claims. This situation changed when the Kremlin boasted that they had successfully launched the world's first man-made orbiting satellite, Sputnik I, using the same R-7 vehicle.

By launching Sputnik I, on October 4, 1957, the Soviets proved they had a weapon capable of placing a payload into space that might also serve as an ICBM. Panic ensued throughout the United States. The apparent lead in ballistic missiles that the United States thought it had over the Soviet Union had evaporated. Eisenhower administration officials scrambled to explain the implications to a worried nation. Then, on November 3, another Soviet blow hit the United States: Sputnik II's launch and orbit. These events fueled a new missile race. The entire proposed U.S. ballistic missile force that had been threatened with extinction by budget cuts only a few months before was now rescued. Congress demanded action; the missile programs again surged to put operational systems on launch pads.

Although Soviet Premier Nikita Khrushchev's claims of using a production ICBM as a Sputnik booster garnered political points around the world, many in the Eisenhower administration were skeptical. SAC still had the ability to launch a nuclear attack on the Soviet Union. The Central Intelligence Agency (CIA) did not have a reliable means to detect or gather vital information about Moscow's ballistic missile programs. CIA activities would soon involve building a series of radar stations in Turkey to monitor test missile launches in the Soviet Union. The psychological impact of exposing American scientific and military weaknesses, however, had occurred.

THOR AND JUPITER COME TO THE RESCUE

Khrushchev had gained a political coup, but it had some unintended consequences. The apparent lack of American scientific and technical education forced national action. Congress soon passed the National Defense Education Act, which promoted graduate study in the hard sciences and engineering. Science and math education from primary to graduate schools took on the added emphasis that it would pay future military and economic dividends. Likewise, the fear of growing Soviet influence in Europe was not confined solely to the United States. Britain and France did not want to be caught unprepared as they were in World War II. They too sought a means to procure a missile. They did not think they needed an ICBM, but thought they could use an IRBM-range weapon.

The U.S. Air Force had at least the Thor and Jupiter to offer. Development of the Thor IRBM was an afterthought by the air force. Focus on an ICBM was its primary concern. Great Britain and France had shown much interest in getting their own nuclear force to counter that of the Soviet Union. British government officials had expressed great interest in a ballistic missile in February 1955. They would eventually acquire Thor missiles. France would later reject American moves to place IRBMs on their soil and opt to build their own weapon systems.

The U.S. Army's work on Jupiter had started as a joint collaboration effort with the U.S. Navy. Engineers designed the system to use gimbaled rocket engines. Navy officials wanted a solid fueled rocket motor, not a ponderous liquid fueled one that required much support on limited ship space and used volatile liquid fuels. Now that Jupiter was becoming a reality, its development and production proved a problem for the air force. Two competing IRBMs consumed funds, personnel, and time. Besides, the Jupiter was an army missile. Army officials had designed Jupiter as a field-mobile weapon. Air force planners believed the Thor was better suited to launch from a fixed site. The air force had to meld a force of Thor and Jupiter vehicles. Thor and Jupiter did offer some benefits. They could supplement the ICBM force and complicate Soviet targeting. However, nuclear war would then spread to other European and potentially Asian countries depending on the missiles' deployment. Unfortunately, those nations agreeing to deployment by the U.S. Air Force would now become targets.

ARDC officials believed that Thor and Jupiter were merely limited sideshows. In the early 1950s, U.S. Air Force officials believed that they could build Thor as a derivative of Atlas. The 1955 Killian Committee had sold the idea of IRBM development to Eisenhower. The air force leaders were forced to build an IRBM that they could field quickly and operate. To reduce development time, air force engineers decided to use existing Atlas technology. For example, the inertial guidance system and RV designed for the ICBM were selected for Thor. Similarly, the Jupiter rocket engine was chosen.

Air force and contractor development engineers had an ambitious schedule to meet. Full production was authorized for the Thor even though the missile had never flown. The first test, conducted on December 26, 1956, ended in a failure, and a continual stream of problem test shots occurred until September 20, 1957. A Thor was able to reach a range of about 1,500 miles, days before Sputnik I. The first successful test missile was launched on December 19, 1957. This was a small success in a period dominated by concerns about ballistic missiles and cold war threats. These vehicles were the only long-range missiles that the nation could offer to counter the supposed Soviet ICBM.

Great Britain made a formal agreement, by June 1958, with the United States to base Thor in Britain. British officials would eventually allow stationing four Thor squadrons armed with nuclear weapons. Each missile carried a 1.44-megaton nuclear yield. Unfortunately, the U.S. government was very sensitive about nuclear technology and control of these systems. A sale or transfer of nuclear weapons, albeit to an allied nation, was impossible. Instead, a dual arrangement was created between SAC and RAF personnel. RAF missile crews would maintain and operate the Thor. SAC officers would authorize release of the nuclear warhead.

European opposition to allow Thor emplacement in Europe limited deployment to only Britain. U.S. Air Force personnel started to deploy the Thor to Britain by August 1958. Construction problems and inadequate training delayed RAF officials' ability to declare the weapons operational. Some success was made when seven out of a fifteen missiles of a RAF Thor squadron had been deployed by December. Trained SAC crews could provide an emergency launch capability, after hours of preparation, but this capacity was largely symbolic. The first of four squadrons, the 77th RAF Strategic Missile Squadron (SMS), became operational on June 30, 1960.

A launch crew was supposed to load the liquid fueled missile and send it toward the Soviet Union within fifteen minutes. Each RAF SMS had three launch complexes with five launchers each. Once ordered to launch, the Thor was erected from a horizontal to vertical position from its shelter. These shelters could not withstand a nuclear attack since they were above ground. Construction crews had built the complexes twelve missiles apart to reduce their vulnerability as targets from a Soviet nuclear attack. The single-stage, one-rocket-engine Thor required 100,000 gallons of liquid oxygen and kerosene fuel. Fuel handlers could load these propellants into the missile within eight minutes. The CEP (circular error probable) was about two miles (3.2 kilometers); given the size of the warhead, this accuracy was sufficient. Despite its elaborate launch procedures and delicate support equipment, the Thor enjoyed a 98 percent alert rate of its assigned vehicles.

The United States had concerns about Thor. Fueling the missile was slow and limited reaction time. Although housed in a shelter, Thor was still vulnerable to attack. By 1962, Secretary of Defense Robert S. McNamara informed the British Minister of Defence Peter Thorneycroft that SAC would no longer support any Thor operations in Britain. The first Thor was removed from alert on November 29, 1962, and the last weapon became nonoperational on August 15, 1963.

Jupiter was another system that the U.S. Air Force would field. The army would work with the missile in conjunction with the navy. The primary focus was to build a shipboard IRBM for the navy and act as a backup to the Thor. Naval requirements differed markedly from the army designs. Corrosive fuels, limited ship space, and slow reaction time due to fueling brought demands for change. The army had already started engine tests by November 1955, and the army's missile design and engineering center at Redstone Arsenal near

Huntsville, Alabama, were reluctant to change. The navy decided to build a modified ballistic missile, the Jupiter-S (solid). Although the navy would design a much different solid fuel program, it continued to work with the army on the liquid fuel version.

Army engineers had used some components of their successful Redstone in Jupiter's development. Jupiter's development by the army and the Chrysler Corporation culminated in a test launch of Jupiter on September 20, 1956, at Cape Canaveral, Florida. This test flight was a great success. The test missile flew 3,400 miles (5,500 kilometers) and reached an altitude of 650 miles (1,050 kilometers). Jupiter had potential as a weapon. Secretary of Defense Wilson had decided that the air force would become the lead service to operate IRBMs, but the Redstone Arsenal would continue to build Jupiter. Jupiter's success seemed to far surpass Thor's continued test problems. Thor did have some advantages, however. The Thor missiles used in tests were production versions, and Douglas contractors had already begun work on support equipment. Efforts on Jupiter were confined largely to test elements.

Jupiter offered several valuable characteristics to the nation's nuclear delivery force. Since the Jupiter was a field-mobile system, its crews could launch it from several possible sites. Like the V-2, this capability would compound an enemy's required effort to destroy the missile. The Soviets might use more of their limited resources trying to eliminate this threat than would be necessary. Jupiter also involved a different warhead design than Thor. Thor used a heat sink RV, while Jupiter's designs called for one using ablative material. This change made the Jupiter more accurate than Thor. Jupiter's approximate CEP was about 0.9 miles (1.4 kilometers).

Air force planners believed that the reduced range required basing closer to the Soviet Union. France had already rejected IRBM basing, Germany was too vulnerable to attack, and other nations were too far away for Jupiter basing, so bases in Italy were sought as the prime launch sites for Jupiter. The United States and Italy agreed, on March 16, 1959, to base two fifteen-missile squadrons at Gioia del Colle in southern Italy. Missile crews were organized to launch groups of three Jupiter missiles. The crews had to prepare the site for launch and fuel their weapons. The Italian squadrons were collectively called NATO (North Atlantic Treaty Organization) I. As in the agreement between the United States and Britain, the Jupiters in Italy became a dual-nation responsibility. Italian air force crews would launch the vehicle when SAC crews released the nuclear weapon.

Two Jupiter squadrons were not sufficient. General Frederic H. Smith, Jr., commander of the U.S. Air Forces in Europe, requested that another fifteen-missile squadron, NATO II, become operational in Turkey. Turkey agreed to emplace a single squadron at Cigli with the understanding that Turkish crews

Thor. Thor was the first operational IRBM stationed overseas by the United States. The RAF operated four squadrons, but U.S. officers controlled the nuclear warheads. U.S.A.F. crews would later use Thor as a space booster and anti-satellite device. (Courtesy, U.S. Air Force)

would launch the missile with American officers controlling the nuclear weapon. NATO I became operational on April 14, 1961. The Turkish-manned NATO II's Jupiter missiles became launch capable on March 5, 1962, and the squadron became fully operational in May 1962. SAC crews operated the missiles until the Turkish crews could demonstrate launch proficiency.

Jupiter would have the shortest operational life of all early American ballistic missiles. Concerns about the limited production of missiles—few operational test launches, logistical support, and other technical issues—forced U.S. Air Force officials to question the weapon's effectiveness. Additionally, as more advanced weapon systems became operational, the need for Jupiter declined. Jupiter's days were numbered. The air force wanted to press ahead for ICBMs, not continue reliance on IRBMs.

SOVIET BALLISTIC MISSILE THREATS DEMAND INTELLIGENCE

Early in the Eisenhower administration, the growth of Soviet military power concerned many in government. The successful explosion of an atomic bomb, bomber development, and the Korean War offered evidence that Moscow wanted military parity with or even superiority over the West. When the Soviets exploded a hydrogen bomb in 1953, concern about a potential nuclear Pearl Harbor clouded Eisenhower's mind. The Soviets could strike at the nation, but they would need appropriate delivery vehicles. By 1954, the U.S. Air Force and the CIA had agreed on a joint photoreconnaissance project that would allow aerial intelligence missions over the Soviet Union by the U-2. The U-2 made its first debut over the Soviet Union on July 4, 1956. U-2 pilots flew missions over the Soviet Union from West Germany, Alaska, Turkey, Pakistan, and other locations. Future flights provided valuable information about the Soviet military developments. For example, after a few U-2 missions, the Soviet bomber threat was debunked. Bomber production and operational bases indicated that the Soviets were not building a large number of long-range bombers. The Soviet ballistic missile programs became the focus of American intelligence efforts.

The Soviets' R-7 ICBM test flight proclamation forced defense and CIA officials to take more interest in the Tyuratam Missile Test Range in Baykonyr. On August 28, 1957, two days later after the proclamation, a U-2 flight determined that there was only a single launch pad. U-2 pilots followed a telltale sign of launch pad support, rail lines. U-2 missions provided valuable information about the Soviet missile and nuclear activities. Intelligence data flooded in about nuclear test and production facilities, and another missile test center at Saryshagan was found. U-2 flights were detected by Soviet air defenses, however. Official protests by the Soviet government to Washington charged violation of sovereign airspace. Additionally, fears of Soviet advancements in fighter interceptor capability, air-to-air missiles, and surface-to-air missiles caused some concern about the U-2, though no aircraft had been shot down. Eisenhower sought international agreements to allow for aerial surveillance and reconnaissance that allowed a more secure system of intelligence, photoreconnaissance satellites, Project CORONA.

Disturbing news about Soviet missile production claims started a slow drumbeat for more accurate information. Fears that the Soviets would overtake the United States in ballistic missile capability created claims of a new "missile gap" in early 1959. Throughout late 1958, Soviet officials, at a series of Geneva conferences on reducing the possibility of nuclear surprise attacks, hinted at Moscow's mass production of ICBMs. By December 9, 1958, Khrushchev had heightened the United States' angst by declaring that his country had a ballistic missile that could strike 8,000 miles with a five-megaton warhead. Other Soviet claims in early 1959 predicted that Soviet missiles had perfected an accurate nuclear delivery for their systems. Fears of American military inferiority fueled a public debate about the adequacy of missile capability and overall military capability. The American public and Congress wanted answers. Although earlier U-2 flights had indicated only a single launch pad in operation at Tyuratam and no large-scale ballistic missile testing was detected, no U-2 flights had occurred in over a year to confirm the Soviet claims of a growing missile gap.

Pressured by his own Defense Department officials, Eisenhower authorized a U-2 flight over Tyuratam on July 9, 1959. Despite its photographs of an enlarged missile test range, the U-2 flight provided no definitive answer to alleged Soviet missile program advancements. Eisenhower did not want to antagonize the Soviets with additional U-2 flights, but pressure continued to mount as Khrushchev made more unsubstantiated claims of producing upward of 250 missiles per year armed with thermonuclear warheads. Soviet technical problems that had delayed tests of their R-7 (NATO designated this vehicle the SS-6 Sapwood) were fixed and test launches occurred with greater frequency. Eisenhower authorized more U-2 flights in February 1960.

New U-2 missions proceeded in April. A mission on April 10 inspected Saryshagan and detected two radar sites there, found a nuclear testing facility at Semispalatinsk, and flew over Tyuratam. Over Tyuratam, the U-2 pilot photographed a two-pad launch site that intelligence analysts believed was built for a new missile. The U-2 flight was a success, but concerns about radar detection and reports of a new surface-to-air missile, the SA-2 Guideline, caused CIA officials to seek a flight path that might avoid air defenses. Demands from intelligence officials for more information about the SS-6 mounted from the U-2 flights. CIA analysts wanted photographs from operational SS-6 configurations to use as model to search for other sites. Eisenhower relented and authorized another flight, but it had to take place no later than May 1. The United States had agreed to a Paris summit with the Soviets on May 16, and the president did not want to endanger the meeting with a protest from Moscow over a U-2 mission.

Weather delays caused cancellations of the proposed U-2 flight. The mission was to fly south to north across the Soviet Union. On May 1, flying from Peshawar, Pakistan, CIA pilot Francis Gary Powers flew over Tyuratam and had turned toward Sverdlovsk. Powers was unaware that Soviet air defense radars had detected his aircraft fifteen minutes after crossing the Soviet border from Afghanistan, and thirteen interceptor aircraft attempted to shoot him down. All failed. However, a previously unknown SA-2 site let loose a three-missile volley that brought down Powers' aircraft at 70,500 feet. The U-2 suffered a near miss, but the attack damaged the aircraft sufficiently to force Powers to bail out. Soviet officials later recovered the plane's wreckage. Khrushchev used the Paris summit as a means to embarrass Eisenhower. Khrushchev demanded an apology; Eisenhower refused. The president only promised no more aerial missions above the Soviet Union. Despite the problems with this U-2 incident, the Soviet ballistic missile threat did not seem as massive as once thought. No operational bases were found.

Intelligence demands spawned further development of other resources. The U-2 was not the only means to gather information. The United States could also use radar sites in Turkey, electronic listening posts in Iran, and satellites. Air force and CIA officials again collaborated to investigate using space vehicles to detect Soviet ballistic missile capabilities. This effort included early warning satellites that used infrared technologies to detect the hot exhaust gases from a launch. Similarly, a wide system of communications for secure command and control activities, electronic signal gathering, weather, geodesy, and mapping for targeting strategic sites were being planned or explored. More important, the photoreconnaissance mission was highlighted as a way to watch the Soviet Union. In the late 1950s, no country had an effective antisatellite capability that could down a space vehicle. U-2 flights were also limited to selected areas within the Soviet Union. A photoreconnaissance satellite could sweep the entire country without fear of being shot down. Satellites offered a more robust intelligence-gathering system for the nation to investigate areas of the Soviet Union and other nations fairly easily and routinely. Strategic intelligence would enter a new era from space.

One of the longest-serving and most successful satellite intelligence programs was Project CORONA. Originally conceived as a television camera–based system, CORONA evolved into a high-resolution still photographic satellite. The U.S. Air Force and CIA requirements for the satellite were issued on March 16, 1955. By 1956, the Lockheed Missile and Space Company started to work on the system. CORONA was based on a simple concept. Using a Thor booster and Agena second stage, the CORONA satellite would launch from Camp Cooke (later renamed Vandenberg Air Force Base [AFB]) on the central California coast and enter a polar orbit. The satellite, once over its targeted area, would start taking images. Film would return through reentry and parachute recovery by a modified U.S. Air Force C-119, later C-130, over the Pacific. As a cover story, CORONA was billed as a scientific satellite named Discoverer. Lockheed was required to test the first satellite by early 1959. The first launch, on February 28, 1959, was a failure. No one knew what exactly happened to Discoverer I; analysts speculated it landed in Antarctica. More tests failed as satellites failed to go into orbit, recovery problems surfaced, Agena mishaps occurred, or other mistakes appeared. Finally, on August 10, 1960, Discoverer XIII returned its cargo, an American flag, safely to earth. Originally designed as an interim photoreconnaissance satellite system, CORONA would serve the United States until 1972 as one of the key strategic intelligence assets in America's arsenal.

Project CORONA provided a wealth of information for the United States. The first operational mission lifted off eight days later, on August 18. The satellite took photographs throughout the Soviet Union. This one mission took more photographs than all U-2 missions combined. The mission provided photographs of the Kapustin Yar Missile Test Range and its missile impact area. Still, the CIA could not detect any major ICBM or IRBM launch site.

CORONA satellite models were designated KH (Keyhole) -1 to KH-4. The joint U.S. Air Force–CIA CORONA program included 121 launches. The original KH-1 camera had a ground resolution, smallest discernable image, of an item forty feet in size. New technology and techniques improved this capability. KH-2 and KH-3 cameras made great strides in imagery by reducing ground resolution to only ten feet. The improvements allowed the air force and CIA to examine areas with greater clarity and regularity. KH-4 used two and three cameras, photographing the same subject at different angles, to gain a three-dimensional view of the target. These evolutionary advancements pushed the state-of-the-art imagery to new heights by increasing ground resolution to five feet. Project CORONA provided a foundation for further photoreconnaissance satellites that would produce even greater results. U.S. presidents could conduct national security policy with the confidence provided by the information from Project CORONA.

The missile gap seemed to have no basis. U-2 and CORONA missions indicated that by 1960 and 1961, the Soviets did not have a growing ICBM or IRBM force. Khrushchev was all bluff and bluster regarding nuclear armed

ICBMs. A 1961 CIA National Intelligence Estimate regarding Soviet ICBM activities sharply reduced the ICBM force to ten to fifteen ICBM launchers with possible growth to upward of 125 launchers by 1963. The missile gap, like the bomber gap, seemed to be fiction. Unfortunately, Eisenhower could not release any of these results in 1960 despite demands for public accountability over the missile gap. Eisenhower knew that the United States still maintained strategic superiority, but he could not compromise the intelligence sources from the U-2 and the CORONA.

The president had earlier formed several committees to study the missile gap allegation. These efforts resulted in an awkward position for Eisenhower when the Gather Report (1957) and the Killian Report (1958) claimed the Soviet Union would have an ICBM advantage. The U-2 and CORONA information would later contradict these findings, but in the late 1950s through 1960, the public and Congress wanted action. Despite the buildup of SAC nuclear armed long-range bombers, Congress wanted to authorize and build more ballistic missiles based on the fear of the Soviets' apparent military gains. No one seemed to question whether the Soviets had faced technical problems similar to the United States' missile programs. The SS-6 Sapwood required extensive and lengthy support to operate. Railroad operations to bring in fuel and other support were essential to the SS-6 Sapwood, unlike the Atlas or other missiles. However, the public, the Congress, the CIA, and the military services did not know about these extensive requirements.

Eventually, the missile gap became an election issue between presidential candidates John F. Kennedy and Richard M. Nixon. Democrats painted a Republican administration that was soft on defense issues. Kennedy claimed that the Eisenhower administration, including Vice President Nixon, had failed to expand America's ballistic missile programs to forestall a missile gap. Despite Eisenhower's emphasis on nuclear force development, deployment, and dependency, critics rushed to argue that the nation was left without an adequate defense. Eisenhower defense officials had reshaped the military to depend on nuclear weapons based on a massive retaliation strategy. This approach, called the New Look, offered a way to structure a slimmed down military that would use nuclear weapons and save funds. Conventional forces, like the army and tactical air forces, suffered. Eisenhower now was hit with questions about the failure in the ballistic missile race and inadequate conventional weapons as well.

BRINGING BALLISTIC MISSILES ON LINE

For the struggling ballistic missile programs, the successful Sputnik launches were actually a shot in the arm. Funding and national priority were advanced for their development efforts. Technical glitches had frustrated the Atlas program, but testing continued and the missile soon found some promise. Efforts on Titan also progressed and seemed to offer more potential than Atlas in terms of range and payload and as a future space system booster. Other systems were introduced as the public called for more defense capability, in terms of nuclear delivery activities. This included a new system, Polaris.

The navy had pressured Congress for development of their Jupiter S system, Polaris. The Polaris IRBM offered a way to secure a strategic advantage over the Soviets. By December 1956, the navy had dropped out of the army's Jupiter program to pursue independently Polaris with their contractors, Lockheed and Aerojet. Higher-yield, smaller-sized thermonuclear warheads helped promote the development of Polaris, since these missiles were now small enough to fit in a submarine. The first versions of Polaris would have a 500-kiloton-yield warhead. The navy also had nuclear submarines and could tap other technologies, such as miniaturized electronics, to develop Polaris.

In December 1957, Secretary of Defense Neil H. McElroy authorized the navy to build an operational Polaris A-1. Navy officials believed that a Polaris system could launch a missile from a submarine by 1960. Navy, Lockheed, and Aerojet engineers launched test vehicle from Point Mugu, California, in January 1958. Subsequent launches proved that a crew could perform an underwater missile launch, and the navy showed that the missile would reach its intended 1,380-mile range. On July 20, 1960, the USS *George Washington*, a nuclear submarine, initiated a launch sequence of a Polaris A-1. The missile performed to specification. The *George Washington*'s crew began its first operational cruise with nuclear armed weapons on November 15, 1960. The nation now had a mobile, stealthy nuclear capability that would continue to this day.

Eisenhower administration officials still wanted a limited force of Titan and Atlas ICBMs, no more than four squadrons apiece. Under public pressure and in response to the Gather Report, the air force expanded the planned missile forces. By early 1959, the air force asked for a total of seventeen Atlas and twelve Titan ICBM squadrons. Congress looked favorably on any missile program. Funding did not seem a major problem. The U.S. Air Force asked for more funding to develop another advanced ballistic missile program, the solid fueled Minuteman.

Atlas development continued. Throughout 1958, the test Atlas program expanded and started to show signs of credible advances in range and better accuracy. Still, missile technical glitches created concerns among SAC officials. Atlas was a stage-and-a-half missile that used a two-engine booster system with a smaller sustainer rocket along with two side vernier engines. By 1959, the first operational version, Atlas D, was ready for deployment. April 1959 was the planned date for the Atlas D to go on initial nuclear alert at Vandenberg AFB. Air force and contractor launch teams tested the Atlas D, but technical problems with the missile delayed its operational date. The first successful Atlas D test shot took place, however, on September 9, 1959. A month later, the Atlas D achieved operational status. Atlas D had some drawbacks; it had radio-inertial guidance that could be jammed. Additionally, a support radio system was required. If each missile had a different target, then each missile required separate frequencies or guidance information that might interfere with another missile if more than one missile were launched at the same time. So, the Atlas D might not be able to launch at the same time as other Atlas missiles. The long-awaited arrival of an American ICBM was finally met, but improvements were needed.

Rushing to meet an operational Atlas ballistic missile deadline required concentrated effort by the U.S. Air Force. This resulted in areas that were planned hurriedly and created some interesting problems. One concern was the shelters designed for the Atlas D. For example, Vandenberg, having the first operational capability, used open-air gantries to launch the missiles but would later receive environmental shelters. Atlas D vehicles stood on a launch pad ready for operations and had to withstand all weather conditions. Air force and contractor crews could operate the weapons. Later, these missiles served as training devices and had an emergency war fighting capability. Vandenberg had two complexes of three launchers. Each complex was controlled by a single launch control center. An attack on the launch control center would also disable launch operations to the three Atlases.

Future Atlas crews had to prepare a missile from a "coffin" launch shelter. Similar to the Thor shelters, this type of facility allowed protection from the weather and environment, but not from a nuclear attack. The launch crew had to move the missile from a horizontal to vertical position onto the launch pad and then fuel the vehicle. This effort was time consuming, subject to the weather, and vulnerable to enemy attack. A crew would take about fifteen minutes to launch an Atlas. The first operational base was F. E. Warren AFB in Wyoming when SAC took command on August 8, 1960. The squadron became operational with six Atlas D missiles on September 2, 1960. Soon nine other Atlas bases sprang to life.

Kennedy won the 1960 election and acted immediately on the missile gap allegations. His new secretary of defense, Robert S. McNamara, started to examine the nation's ICBM and other military programs. Kennedy approved plans for a thirteen-Atlas and twelve-Titan squadron force. Additionally, Kennedy wanted to modernize the force by allowing expanded development of Minuteman and Polaris. McNamara added 160 Polaris missiles (ten submarines) and sixty Minuteman ICBMs. Although Titan offered more capa-

Trident. U.S. Navy SSBNs could launch SLBMs from below surface. This Trident SLBM's stealth and mobility provided a difficult target to counter. The navy produced a series of SLBMs beginning with Polaris, then Poseidon and Trident. (Courtesy, U.S. Navy)

bility than Atlas, McNamara reduced the planned number of Titan missiles. Advances in solid propellants and continuing problems with liquid fuels drove McNamara to reduce reliance on Atlas and Titan.

Air force officials realized that Atlas was vulnerable. Atlas E did offer some improvement in terms of a more accurate RV and a better "hardened" shelter. Additionally, each launcher would have an assigned crew that would allow the system to improve its capability to withstand an attack on any command and control structure. The final version, Atlas F, made a major improvement to basing. It was stored in an underground silo. Once the ICBM was fueled, an elevator system lifted it to a launch position. The Atlas allowed ICBM development to continue, and U.S. Air Force officials learned from their experience. The first Atlas D shelters could withstand overpressures of 5 pounds per square inch (psi). Typical buildings fall apart at 6 psi. Later, Atlas D shelters were protected with 25-psi overpressure capacity. The Atlas F silo improved protection to 100 psi.

Atlas test and operational problems continued to underscore concerns about America's first-generation ballistic missile. Flight test failures continually plagued Atlas. Problems such as test missiles failing to hit their targets, mishaps in which missiles blew up on their launch pads, corrosion, and construction delays forced engineers to make changes. A propellant loading accident that destroyed an Atlas missile and its launch facility at Vandenberg in March 1960 also forced delays. SAC officials urged ARDC teams to institute more rigorous testing, but the additional tests did not help. Only three of ten Atlas E and F test flights met their objectives by June 1961. The reliability of Atlas as an operational weapon systems was debatable; the nation needed to look elsewhere for its future nuclear capability. From December 1960 to May 1961, the U.S. Air Force directed that Atlas D squadrons have their missiles stand down from nuclear alerts and have facilities and the missiles retrofitted with certain improvements. Engineers hoped to improve reliability of a successful launch and target destruction to between 50 and 75 percent, still a questionable weapon system. The initial rush to get a working system in the post-Sputnik era had created an inadequate system.

Similarly, the Titan program was now pushed toward operational capability. Atlas's days were numbered. Titan's proponents claimed that their missile was more cost effective and reliable and performanced better than the first-generation Atlas. Like the Atlas, Titan had a radio-inertial guidance system, shared similar nuclear warheads, used liquid fuel, could reach about the same range, and suffered the same inaccuracies in its CEP. Unlike the Atlas, Titan was a two-staged missile that was designed to be emplaced in an underground launch silo. The air force would only fully develop and deploy Titan if Atlas development failed. The Glen L. Martin Company was awarded a contract to

Atlas three engines. The Atlas was America's first ICBM. The liquid fueled first stage-and-a-half missile used three main engines, shown here. Atlas required extensive support systems to pump fuel and oxidizer into the missile's propulsion system. (Courtesy, Department of Defense)

develop Titan on October 27, 1955. The Sputnik launches changed this plan, and Titan I became an essential ingredient to a mix of ballistic missiles pushed by Congress for production and operational use. Martin delivered the first test missile to the U.S. Air Force on June 17, 1958.

Testing for Titan was more successful than testing for Atlas. Through June 1961, the U.S. Air Force counted about two-thirds of its thirty-five tests as fully successful, while three were failures. The rest of the tests met some objectives and were counted as partial successes. Testing for Titan I was complete by January 29, 1962. Construction crews had already started to build underground silos to hold Titan I missiles at Lowry AFB near Denver, Colorado. Six Titan I missile squadrons were made operational between April 18 and September 28, 1962. Lowry would have two squadrons, and the other squadrons would be located at four other bases. Each squadron had nine launchers, a force of fifty-four Titan I's ready to defend the nation.

Titan I crews still faced challenges. Titan I missiles did not contain storable fuels within the missiles. This meant the crews took time to fuel the missile, which would then be lifted by an elevator system above the silo for launch. Fueling mishaps occurred. A silo was destroyed in one accident, and another fire damaged a missile. Still, Titan I's development helped transition the ICBM force to multiple-staged systems. Despite this advance, Titan I was a first-generation ballistic missile and expensive to operate. Martin engineers returned to the drawing board to design a better system, Titan II.

Concerns about liquid fueled missiles beset the air force. Cost, reliability, readiness, and capability demands forced the air force to consider another option. Advances in solid fuels had moved air force officials to start another missile study in 1955. Weapon System Q, later Minuteman, was conceived as a three-staged solid fueled system. Air force leadership believed that it would field up to 100 missiles by 1964 and a total of 500 by 1965. Competition for limited funds between Polaris, IRBMs, and liquid fueled ICBMs slowed Minuteman's development. Like other ballistic missile programs, the Minuteman program was pushed into action after the launch of Sputnik. On October 9, 1958, the Boeing Aircraft Company signed a contract to build Minuteman. Less than a year later, Secretary of Defense McElroy elevated the Minuteman program to the nation's highest priority. By April 1959, McElroy proposed that 150 missiles, organized under three squadrons, become the initial force. This total would rise to over 445 missiles by January 1965 and 800 missiles by that June. General Thomas D. White, chief of staff of the air force, foresaw a possible missile force of 3,000 Minutemen by 1970.

Testing of the Minuteman began in September 1959. Boeing engineers had designed a superior missile. Testing was advanced and proceeded quickly. Air

Titan II silo. ICBM silos are nondescript, simple structures. This Titan II missile launch site was based near Davis-Monthan AFB close to Tucson, Arizona. The site only had visible antennas, limited support structures, and the missile silo door. Titan II was deactivated by 1987. (Courtesy, U.S. Air Force)

force concepts included both a fixed silo–based system and a rail-mobile missile. The rail version would reduce vulnerability and counter the U.S. Navy's arguments for more funding of its submarine-based Polaris missiles. Some air force plans envisioned three rail squadrons. Each squadron would have ten trains that would carry three Minuteman missiles each. This option would be an expensive one. Additionally, the logistical support and operating questions highlighted debate about the railroad option. SAC officials, concerned about the vulnerability of silos to a Soviet nuclear attack, held out hope for the mobile missile.

The Kennedy administration had inherited the Atlas, Titan I, and Polaris ballistic missile programs. It also had the Thor and Jupiter forces to supplement the burgeoning ICBM. The air force also operated and maintained its extensive SAC bomber programs. The B-52 program continued in production, the new supersonic B-58 was entering service, and the air force still had the B-47. McNamara also had to rebuild the conventional forces after Eisenhower's New Look, which focused primarily on nuclear forces while conventional ones atrophied. Kennedy started to rebuild the neglected conventional forces. He could not afford another expensive program. He would cancel the XB-70, a supersonic replacement for the B-52, and other defense programs came under his scrutiny. The rail-mobile Minuteman program would also fall victim to Kennedy's budget ax. The Kennedy administration chose to configure the Minuteman with the less expensive, fixed silo basing. The first base was already under construction in Montana at Malmstrom AFB.

Minuteman testing accelerated and showed great advances. Although there were testing failures, the replacement of the first-generation Atlas and Titan I force was possible by 1965. Testing proceeded from components to a complete underground silo. Minuteman's launch operations did not require the time-consuming, dangerous liquid fueling or an elevator to lift the missile up to the surface for launch. A single underground launch control center would control ten geographically separated weapons. Each control center could withstand a 700- to 1,000-psi strike. Each vehicle carried a one-megaton warhead, but the original version, Minuteman IA, had a smaller nuclear payload than either Atlas or Titan I. Minuteman IA's rail-mobile design had reduced its carrying capability and range. Because of its relatively poor performance, the missile was based only at Malmstrom while a more capable Minuteman IB was designed. Minuteman IA emplacement in silos at Malmstrom began on July 23, 1962.

Titan II replaced Titan I and became the United States' largest liquid fueled ICBM. However, it never numbered more than fifty-four missiles, compared with the 1,000 fielded Minuteman ICBMs. Nuclear retaliation would

Titan II launch. Titan II, like later ICBMs, launched from its silo. One can see the combustion chambers and extensive pumping systems that feed the rocket engines. (Courtesy, U.S. Air Force)

now be counted in minutes, not hours, away. A combined SAC force of bombers and missiles was built to ensure that the United States had a combination of weapons to complicate Soviet defenses. Coupled with the U.S. Navy's SLBM (submarine launched ballistic missile) program, this triad became the foundation of nuclear force structure during the cold war.

4

The Cuban Missile Crisis

THE UNITED STATES AND the Soviet Union competed politically, militarily, and economically around the globe during the cold war. They never initiated a major open military confrontation, but both sought ways to gain an advantage over their rival. A defining moment of the cold war about the use of nuclear weapons occurred during October 1962 over the question of Soviet positioning of MRBMs (medium-range ballistic missiles) in Cuba.

Cuba, once ruled by strongman Fulgencio Batista y Zaldívar, was a nation with increasing ties to the Soviet Union. Fidel Castro orchestrated a revolution against Batista, a corrupt and dictatorial leader, and eventually overthrew him in January 1959. Batista had protected American business interests during his reign and was not a communist. The Soviet Union started to court Castro by offering aid to Cuba. Castro slowly accepted socialism. The Soviets had gained a foothold at the doorstep of the United States. Castro would nationalize American business interests and turn east for support. U.S. businesses would lose vast holdings in agriculture, tourism, and other industries. Eisenhower reacted strongly by imposing economic sanctions that stopped Americans from purchasing Cuba's main export, sugar, and from selling petroleum products to Cuba. Soviet leadership was mindful of the United States' Monroe Doctrine, which considered the Western Hemisphere in Washington's sphere of influence and viewed any foreign incursion as a threat. Moscow courted Cuba very carefully. Khrushchev offered to buy Cuban sugar at above-market prices and to sell Castro products such as oil at subsidized rates. These moves pushed Castro firmly into the Soviet camp. The United States now had a socialist country ninety miles from Florida.

The Eisenhower administration, through the CIA, attempted to overthrow Castro. A socialist Cuba could spread revolution throughout the Americas.

Atlas launch sequence. Atlas crews had to lift their weapons from a coffin storage facility into a firing position. These images demonstrate a typical Atlas launch sequence that could take at least fifteen minutes for fueling, guidance, and other operations. (Courtesy, U.S. Air Force)

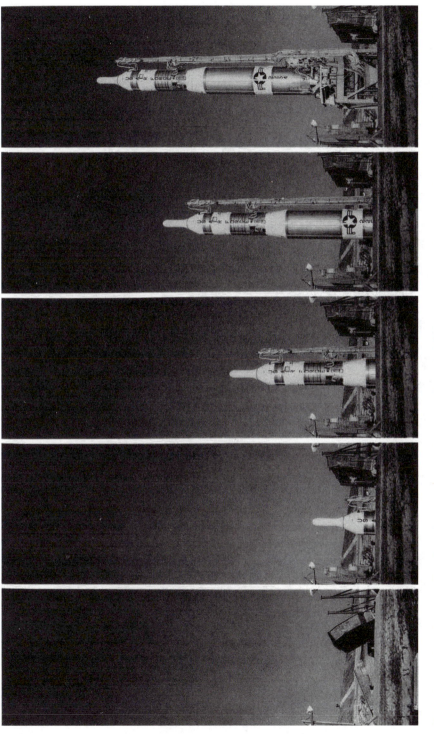

Titan I launch sequence. The Titan I, a first-generation liquid fueled ICBM, used an elevator system to move it from its silo to a launch position. This capability improved its survival from a near nuclear explosion. (Courtesy, U.S. Air Force)

Other corrupt governments, although friendly to the United States, might fall just like Cuba. Soviet influence would spread in the United States' own backyard. Castro had to fall. The CIA offered options to end Castro's control over Cuba. One elaborate scheme that gained momentum was a Cuban invasion by exiles supported covertly by the United States.

The CIA's plan involved several intricate parts. Cuban exiles, under CIA support, trained in Guatemala. Expatriate Cuban pilots would provide air support against Castro's military forces. The CIA assumed that once the exiles landed, the Cuban people would arise and boost the counterrevolution. CIA operatives had conducted a similar operation in Guatemala against a left-wing elected government in 1954. This operation succeeded in toppling the government and installing one that had stronger ties to the United States. Eisenhower was not able to execute the Cuban plan. Kennedy was elected, and it was up to his administration to see the CIA plan through. Eisenhower had briefed the president-elect about the plan, and Kennedy did not object to the planned invasion or stop it.

Unfortunately, the invasion was a disaster. On April 15, 1961, the CIA-trained Cuban exiles conducted their invasion at the Bay of Pigs and failed. Although the CIA and Joint Chiefs of Staff had assured Kennedy that the plan would succeed, the uprising of Cuban dissidents did not surface. Kennedy had earlier ordered no direct American military action to be taken in support of the attack. Most of the Cuban exiles were captured. The Bay of Pigs fiasco embarrassed Kennedy and the U.S. government. It also strengthened Cuban ties to Khrushchev and the Soviet Union. This event also highlighted the Soviet need to protect its new client state in the West and put pressure on Khrushchev to demonstrate his devotion to protect struggling socialist nations.

During this period, the Soviets had developed several ballistic missiles. They ranged from copies of the V-2 to smaller, conventional weapons to support field operations. Like its superpower rival, the Soviet Union had a crash program to produce longer-range MRBMs to ICBMs. Sputnik launches demonstrated to the world that the Soviet Union had the technical skill to produce an ICBM. However, the Soviet Union still did not have the production or support facilities that would deploy a large force. The U-2 and increasingly the CORONA satellite imagery indicated that the Soviets did not possess a large operational ICBM force that could threaten the United States. Soviet leadership was concerned about the public deployment of Thor IRBMs (intermediate-range ballistic missiles) in Britain and the Jupiter systems, under NATO, in Italy and Turkey. The United States had succeeded in putting IRBMs on the doorstep of the Soviet Union. Additionally, the Americans were pressing ahead with full-scale production of not only Atlas and Titan I but also newer systems like Titan II and Minuteman. The Soviets were losing the race for strategic superiority despite many American opinions to the contrary.

Khrushchev, faced with several strategic challenges, started to explore ways to not only protect Cuba but also improve the Soviet nuclear position relative to the United States. Although the Soviets had the SS-6, they would also develop the R-12 (SS-4 Sandel) and R-14 (SS-5 Skean), which had sufficient range to strike large portions of the United States. The SS-4 and SS-5 could not reach major targets in United States (except Alaska) from the Soviet Union or from its client states in eastern Europe. Instead, Khrushchev proposed, under Operation Anadyr, to deploy first the SS-4 and then the SS-5 on Cuban soil. An SS-4 could strike many areas of the southeastern United States, while a nuclear armed SS-5 had sufficient range to threaten all major urban areas in the United States except in the Pacific Northwest. The SS-4 and SS-5 carried one-megaton warheads and were liquid fueled missiles. The SS-4 had a range of about 2,000 kilometers (1,250 miles), and the SS-5 doubled Soviet reach to 4,100 kilometers (2,550 miles). Military planners could count on their SS-4s with a CEP of 2.4 kilometers (1.5 miles), while the SS-5 later cut CEP to a kilometer (0.62 miles). Soviet ballistic missile crews could now strike almost all military facilities in the continental United States including SAC bomber and missile bases. This capability offered the Soviet Union an instant strategic advantage.

KHRUSHCHEV MOVES FORWARD

Why did Khrushchev decide to pursue Operation Anadyr? No single reason appears to explain his actions. Risking a nuclear confrontation with the United States seems foolish at best and suicidal at worst. By April 1962, Soviet leadership believed that the United States had four times as many ICBMs as Moscow. The Soviets' new R-16 ICBMs (SS-7) were in testing, and it would take ten years of production to match SAC's arsenal. These one-megaton yield delivery systems could reach the United States, but Soviet military forces, despite a conventional advantage, could not match American nuclear superiority. A 1962 U.S. national intelligence estimate came to the same conclusion. The Soviets had only fifty ICBMs. By the end of 1962, SAC would have twelve Atlas squadrons, excluding the squadron at Vandenberg, with 132 operational missiles. Additionally, six Titan I squadrons would add their fifty-four missiles. The U.S. Air Force would also introduce Minuteman by 1962. The Soviets were losing the nuclear race with the United States.

One motivation for Khrushchev was simply to defend Cuba from any future U.S.-supported invasion. The Bay of Pigs invasion demonstrated clearly that Washington did not want a communist state on its border. The CIA also encouraged covert Cuban exiles to plan for the uprising against Castro and continued sabotage around the island under its Operation Mongoose. Cuban security was still at risk from the Americans. The Soviets' credibility around the world would suffer if they allowed the United States to push them out of the Western Hemisphere. Within the communist sphere, a divided camp between a more liberal Khrushchev and the more hard-line Stalinists led by China's Mao Zedong fought for leadership. If Khrushchev lost Cuba, fractures within the communist world would appear. Similarly, what revolutionary movement would look to Moscow for protection after what had happened in Cuba? Soviet assurances of mutual support would mean nothing. Standing up to the United States would aid the socialist image internationally and give a boost to other revolutionary movements.

Defense of Cuba, by emplacing twenty-four SS-4 MRBMs and sixteen SS-5 IRBMs, would provide a Soviet umbrella to Castro's regime. Soviet missile crews would have a stock of thirty-six SS-4 and twenty-four SS-5 ballistic missiles to send north into the United States. The Soviet Defense Ministry decided to relocate the ballistic missiles from operational units in the Ukraine and western Russia. Along with these weapons, the Soviets would add six nuclear-capable short-range IL-28 bombers, twelve SA-2 surface-to-air missile batteries (each battery had twelve launchers), eighty tactical cruise missiles, patrol boats, MIG-21 fighters, smaller tactical missiles with a nuclear capability, other weapons, and 42,000 Soviet ground forces (four motorized infantry regiments and two tank battalions) to act as a deterrent against an invasion. The cruise missiles would protect Cuban waters from an American naval force. These systems also had a smaller nuclear warhead. Any invasion would thus ensure that a conflict between the United States and Soviet Union could result in an attack on Washington.

Adding conventional forces alone to Cuba would help deter an American invasion. Why would Kennedy risk an open conflict with Soviet forces that could escalate into a nuclear confrontation? MRBM and IRBM forces could also strengthen the Soviet strategic position by instantly adding the equivalent of forty missiles to an ICBM force without rushing the SS-7 into production. These missiles would also reduce American reaction time to an attack. Although more vulnerable to an air attack, Khrushchev could launch a devastating attack on the eastern half of the United States. Soviet ballistic missiles could also intimidate Latin American and Central American nations. Just as the United States had positioned IRBM forces in Europe and Turkey, the Soviets could add a nuclear punch to their arsenal. MRBMs and IRBMs threatening America would put fear in the Kennedy administration and the American public. The Soviets could again regain parity in the balance of power with the Americans.

Defending Cuba and providing military aid was expensive. Khrushchev, despite the communist rhetoric about a worker's paradise, was being constrained by his World War II–ravaged economy. Supporting a large conven-

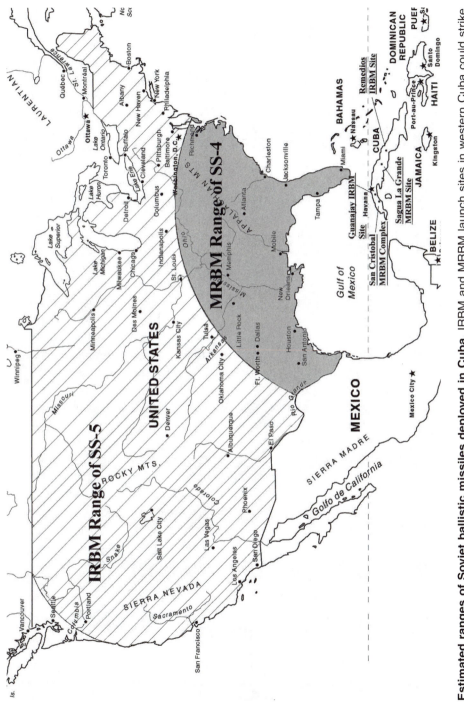

Estimated ranges of Soviet ballistic missiles deployed in Cuba. IRBM and MRBM launch sites in western Cuba could strike along the eastern seaboard. IRBM sites could strike targets throughout most of the continental United States. (Courtesy, Mapcraft)

tional force required costly personnel. Khrushchev believed that nuclear weapons and missiles were the wave of the future. They were fast, devastating, and cheap. The Soviet economy had to support a growing population and demands for nonmilitary programs. Nuclear weapons and their delivery systems could provide a means to substitute defense requirements for conventional forces, just as Eisenhower attempted to do in the United States. Providing MRBMs and IRBMs in Cuba would go a long way to reduce Cuban military aid and support the Soviet strategic position at a lower cost.

IRBMs in Britain, Italy, and Turkey may also have provided the Soviets with a motivation to introduce ballistic missiles into Cuba. Missiles in these NATO countries directly threatened Moscow. Removal of these squadrons could not only reduce the threat to the Soviet Union, but also reduce the American nuclear umbrella that protected her European allies. Soviet leadership was unaware of movements to reduce these squadrons and rely on the growing ICBM force and the SLBMs. Moscow would also have known about the public debate and Congressional approval of the ICBM, Polaris, and continued fielding of a large SAC bomber fleet. However, the Jupiters had just started to become operational in early 1962, and withdrawal of the missiles might offend the Turkish government and might appear to Khrushchev to be a sign of weakness by Kennedy. Still, Kennedy wanted the Jupiters out of Turkey. Turkish Jupiter IRBMs also served another strategic purpose for Khrushchev. Since the Americans had put nuclear missiles on Khrushchev's border, how could the United States argue that he could not do the same in Cuba?

Moscow and Washington's relationship appeared strained before Cuba. The Kennedy administration had embarked on an active foreign policy that included foreign and military aid in Southeast Asia. Washington started to strengthen its conventional forces as Kennedy moved from the New Look to a more balanced approach to force structure. Kennedy also refused to back down in Berlin. Khrushchev had wanted those areas of Berlin that were under American, British, and French control to be returned to East Germany. American defense exercises in the Caribbean during the spring of 1962 also heightened the tensions between the United States and the Soviets. These exercises included a mock amphibious invasion by U.S. Marines. Kennedy also continued the economic sanctions against Cuba that had been emplaced by Eisenhower, which started to impoverish Khrushchev's client state. Kennedy stated his intention to resume nuclear testing in April 1962. The United States and the Soviet Union had stopped nuclear testing, but Khrushchev had already broken the agreement a year earlier. The United States engineered the removal of Cuba from the Organization of American States. Kennedy compared Cuba to Hungary. He would not tolerate a socialist Cuba under the heel of a Soviet boot. Cuba was getting more isolated politically, militarily, and economically from the Western Hemisphere. Perhaps Khrushchev's deployment of ballistic missiles in Cuba could force Kennedy to give Khrushchev some respect. Cuba's socialist experiment might come to an abrupt halt without Khrushchev's quick, decisive action.

Soviet missiles in Cuba could help pressure Kennedy during the upcoming November congressional elections. More weapons in Cuba could deter Kennedy from attacking Cuba in order to "get tough" with the Soviets and support Democratic congressional aspirants in November. Likewise, MRBMs in Cuba could embarrass the young president and force him to comply with Khrushchev over certain issues.

Khrushchev could have avoided placing SS-4 and SS-5 missiles into Cuba. Protecting Cuba from invasion required only putting a conventional force into the island nation. Similarly, Khrushchev could have delayed his moves to reduce military expenditures and expanded the ICBM program. Perhaps there is no single best explanation for Khrushchev's decision to gamble on extending the nuclear threat against America from Cuba. All of these factors probably played a role in helping Khrushchev take his stand. By pushing SS-4 and SS-5 missiles into Cuba, the Soviets could solve several problems—assuming the United States would allow these forces to stay in place.

Khrushchev planned to move missiles into Cuba by the fall. Not all of the Soviet government agreed. Several Soviet officials openly questioned the proposal. Deploying the ballistic missiles into Cuba might elicit an attack on the island. War could break out if a crew launched a missile by mistake. There were also concerns throughout the Soviet government about Castro's acceptance of the missiles into Cuba. Cuba would become an instant target for United States. Locating a large conventional force was one issue; situating nuclear weapons that could destroy cities like New York or Los Angeles was another matter. Still, the nuclear weapons and added Soviet military presence would deter American attempts to foment revolution against the regime in Havana. Soviet operations would continue if Castro agreed to the plan.

Earlier, Moscow had rebuffed Castro's efforts for additional military aid, but this new scheme offered a way to protect Cuba. Fidel Castro's regime could look forward to added protection not only from a large Soviet presence but also through a nuclear umbrella. Castro's view of the umbrella might have changed if he knew it was filled with holes and smaller than he had thought. Soviet political, military, and intelligence officials agreed not to disclose their strategic nuclear inferiority to Castro. If Castro had known about this inferiority, then he might have balked at becoming a cog in the Soviet strategic machinery to enhance Moscow's stature. A Soviet delegation had obtained initial approval to emplace the ballistic missiles from Fidel Castro in late May. The Defense Ministry approved Khrushchev's proposed movement on June 10, and soon thereafter, the Presidium permitted Khrushchev to proceed. Fidel's

brother Raúl, who came to Moscow on a state visit, made the final arrangements for the missiles' emplacement during a July visit. Soviet military forces
would soon embark to Cuba.

The Soviet navy had the task of shipping ballistic missiles, personnel, and
other equipment from Soviet ports to Cuba. Soviet officials maintained secrecy throughout the process. Khrushchev did not inform his ambassador to
the United States, Anatoly Dobrynin, nor did Khrushchev contact his representative in the United Nations. Dobrynin would later advance the idea that
his government had not installed offensive, nuclear missiles in Cuba. Dobrynin's lack of knowledge unwittingly supported Khrushchev's deception.
Soviet military personnel were restricted to ports once they reported for em-
barkation. From July onward, Khrushchev sent his military forces to Cuba.
Continued secrecy and duplicity could only hurt future dealings with the
United States and other nations. Questions arose within the Kremlin whether
Khrushchev and Moscow could be trusted for future agreements such as arms
control or creating a ban on future nuclear testing.

Although the military movements had proceeded with the utmost secrecy,
the United States maintained routine photoreconnaissance missions over
Cuba by U-2 aircraft. The CIA and other nations had human intelligence
sources on the island to supplement a U-2 reconnaissance flight over Cuba.
The U-2 flight results were troubling. CIA photographic intelligence analysts
would soon discover the fixed SA-2 and ballistic missile sites before they became operational. Kennedy and his advisors were sure to notice the sudden
increase in Soviet military personnel and equipment. The shipment, assembly, and operation of aircraft on Cuban airfields were especially vulnerable to
detection. Still, Khrushchev moved forward.

Soviet military forces first started construction on air defense facilities. SA-
2 units, capable of shooting down the high-altitude U-2, were deployed. Creating an effective air defense system for the ballistic missiles was a priority. If
Moscow made the SA-2 units operational, then they could shoot down a U-
2 or other American reconnaissance aircraft. They could also destroy any attack or bomber aircraft. Soviet air defenders were no different from other
military forces worldwide. They deployed the SA-2 units according to approved military procedures and doctrine. Engineers built SA-2 layouts around
the ballistic missile sites like others in the Soviet Union. Unfortunately for
Moscow, U.S. intelligence agencies had identified these patterns through the
U-2 and CORONA programs. They would link these deployments to MRBM
and IRBM sites. The active U.S. reconnaissance program was a serious problem in Khrushchev's plan. Khrushchev tried to camouflage his move to Cuba
by bringing up other issues such as a new nuclear test ban agreement, Berlin,
and other political diversions.

If the United States detected the plan before Soviet engineers deployed the SS-4 and SS-5 missiles, then Khrushchev might have to retreat publicly from Cuba. Building fixed SA-2 and ballistic missile launch sites would take resources and time. If an SA-2 did shoot down a U-2 or other military reconnaissance aircraft, that could precipitate a retaliatory air strike or full-scale invasion that would endanger Castro's government. Typically, the CIA launched U-2 flights that would fly through western Cuba to its eastern half, turn around, and exit through its west coast. U-2 flights over Cuba had started in April 1961. Most pilots started their missions from Laughlin AFB in Texas. Eventually, the United States authorized flights over Cuba twice a month beginning in May 1962, after the CIA received reports of increased Soviet activity on the island.

The United States might react unexpectedly to a new adventure inspired by Moscow with the planned task force of eighty-five ships leaving from Black Sea, Baltic, and Murmansk ports to Cuba. Equipment would be loaded in holds, but larger pieces of equipment and crates were subject to visual identification. American and NATO navies in the Mediterranean and Atlantic would note the ships' direction toward Cuba.

OPERATION ANADYR

Soviet forces started to arrive in Cuba during the last week in July. By the first week in August, construction teams started to build seven SA-2 sites around western Cuba that included Havana. Through August, Soviet armored units began to appear. Another SA-2 site in the central section of the country was built by late August. The CIA had ordered two U-2 flights over Castro's island on August 5. The August 5 mission did not detect any finished construction, but analysts did note a substantial increase in weapon deliveries. This flight plus the increased shipping and reports from observers in the country of Soviet military forces arriving in Cuba startled CIA Director John A. McCone.

On an August 10 meeting with Vice President Lyndon B. Johnson, Secretary of State Dean Rusk, McNamara, Chairman of the Joint Chiefs of Staff General Maxwell Taylor, and others, McCone warned about the increased level of Soviet military aid to Cuba that might include MRBMs. McCone, at another meeting on August 21 with the same attendees, indicated clearly that Cuba probably had new SA-2 sites and pushed the idea that the Soviets would start MRBM emplacement soon. McCone reasoned that the Soviets would not build SA-2 sites in areas with no strategic value unless they were preparing the site to protect a highly valuable asset, like an MRBM site. SA-2 sites also concerned McCone since the vulnerability of the U-2 became evident when

Powers was shot down in May 1960. If the Soviets downed a U-2 over Cuba, then another diplomatic crisis or worse would ensue.

The next day, McCone provided the same information to Kennedy. McCone's MRBM theory depended on questions about the need for additional SA-2s above their requirement to defend Cuban airspace, their configuration, and the recent buildup of Soviet aid. The enhanced secrecy surrounding the arms buildup and SA-2 deployment also concerned McCone. If Cuba's defense was Moscow's aim, then the Soviets did not have to hide their effort by building a defensive force unless the real reason was the introduction of offensive weapons. McCone pressed the military services for additional low-level aircraft photoreconnaissance missions to search for more details. On August 29, another U-2 flight photographed eight SA-2 sites in western Cuba. McCone was afraid that the Soviets would make ballistic missiles operational and present a fait accompli to Kennedy. Ineffective economic sanctions, sabotage, and reliance on Cuban exiles had not seemed to force the Castro regime to make any change. Cuba seemed, in McCone's opinion, to get stronger militarily, becoming more difficult to overthrow.

The new threat from more Soviet military aid and the continued presence of a communist state on the border created much debate in the Kennedy administration. McCone and Robert Kennedy, the president's brother, supported an aggressive policy that included direct military action against Cuba. Providing SA-2 missiles to defend Havana was serious, but a nuclear ballistic missile threat that could destroy major American cities was an unacceptable risk. Rusk and others disagreed and were concerned about Soviet retaliation against American interests around the world, like Berlin, if the United States took aggressive action. Besides, the U-2 flights did not indicate proof of an MRBM or IRBM presence. The president was now aware of the missile debate. He would try to deter Khrushchev through a public statement about Cuba and the use of diplomacy. Washington needed more information about the precise threat posed by Cuba. Kennedy did not want any information released about the presence of SA-2 missiles or any speculation about MRBMs made public. An information leak at this time might cause an unwarranted demand for action within Washington circles. Additionally, political criticisms of weakness toward Cuba would hurt the president and Democratic congressional candidates in the upcoming November election.

Kennedy took action on September 4. He called a bipartisan congressional delegation to the White House to explain the buildup in Cuba of defensive weapons. Republican congressional members had already found out about Soviet military shipments to Cuba and had demanded answers. Kennedy also released a statement about the SA-2 presence in Cuba and tried to reassure the American public that the administration would provide more information as quickly as possible when it could verify it. The public statement also sent a direct message to the Soviets that explained the Kennedy administration's concerns and the conditions in Cuba deemed critical to U.S. national interests. These conditions included Soviet introduction of ground forces, creation of a Soviet military base, the threat to the U.S. naval station at Guantánamo, deploying offensive surface-to-surface missiles, and introducing any new strategic offensive capability on the island. Operation Anadyr had already introduced or planned to introduce Soviet ground forces, Soviet military bases, MRBM and IRBM systems, and IL-28 bombers. Khrushchev's plan was now beginning to unravel quickly. Stepped-up U-2, U.S. Air Force RF-101, and U.S. Navy F-8U aerial photography flights would soon catch Khrushchev. Predictably, Havana issued a statement that indicated the military aid was for defensive purposes only. Moscow stayed silent.

Operation Anadyr continued in earnest. The construction programs went on a crash course to complete facilities and make the missiles operational. By the first week in September, an SS-5 site was under construction in Guanajay, western Cuba, and workers started to assemble more SA-2 missile sites. By the middle of September, MRBM sites at San Cristóbal and an IRBM site near Remedios started to take form. The final MRBM launching location at Sagua la Grande broke ground at the end of the month. Each of the ballistic missile sites had SA-2 coverage. Construction began on additional SA-2 launch sites, but the Soviets built them to protect other targets. Despite these efforts, the MRBM sites required additional work and could not become operational until mid-October at best. The IRBMs might become capable of launching by November. Khrushchev was in a bind. Concern mounted that the Americans had decided to invade Cuba. Khrushchev could not stop Castro's downfall or threaten the United States.

Kennedy, on September 7, started to prepare for the worst. He requested that 150,000 reserve personnel be mobilized to active duty for a year. The callup shocked Khrushchev. An earlier American practice of an amphibious invasion, warnings about the discovered Soviet arms deliveries, Operation Mongoose, and other activities complicated Khrushchev's position. In reply to the American mobilization, the Soviet government released a press statement on September 11 that reiterated it would defend Cuba against any American aggression. Events simmered.

Concern about U-2 vulnerability to SA-2 missiles forced changes. Instead of flying the length of the island, Washington ordered pilots to fly over areas outside SA-2 range. Pilots conducted missions quickly, making their intrusions at the narrowest widths of the island along a north-south axis. These changes would slow intelligence gathering about the additional missile sites. U-2 crews found no signs of MRBM sites in September. Ground observers in

Cuba, however, reported MRBM construction in the western half of Cuba. Analysts believed they were SS-4 missiles. Since the CIA had avoided the area because of the SA-2 presence there, Washington could not tell if the construction of MRBM launch sites was in progress. McCone pressed for a U-2 flight that would pass over western Cuba with its known operational SA-2 missiles.

AMERICAN U-2 FLIGHTS MAKE A DISCOVERY

Soviet secrecy and deception had paid off. The Soviets had secretly transported MRBM and IRBM units into Cuba. Previously, American politicians could only accuse Moscow about the potential missile placement. Vague reports of construction and some sightings of ballistic missiles would raise eyebrows, but there was no concrete proof of any operational weapons. An air force SAC-piloted U-2 on October 14 made an important find. Photographic evidence indicated that MRBM sites were under construction in west central Cuba near San Cristóbal. The sites included canvas-covered missile trailers. The trailers had the size and configuration that could contain MRBMs. Other support vehicles and construction activities indicated that the location was an MRBM launch site. The Soviets only needed the systems' liquid propellants, nuclear weapons, and storage facilities to make the site complete. CIA officials believed the site could launch their weapons in about two weeks.

Within two days, the president and his National Security Council had the information about the MRBMs. Unfortunately, McCone's prediction had come true. Debate raged about what they should do about the ballistic missiles. Options ranged from conducting an instant air strike to destroying the missiles before Moscow made them operational to a complete invasion of the islands. Another alternative was to make the information public and pressure the Soviets to withdraw from Cuba. All agreed that the missiles needed immediate removal. Questions remained. How many missiles had Khrushchev sent to the island? Their locations were still unknown. How would the Soviets react if the United States invaded Cuba? Would they attempt to take Berlin? How would NATO allies respond to this move? Kennedy requested more information and ordered that the entire island be photographed by U-2 and other flights. Unfortunately, the nation did not have an available CORONA satellite to help with reconnaissance. Building a satellite, ensuring it was on a launch pad, getting the satellite into orbit, and retrieval of the satellite would take time.

Kennedy had given the approval to SAC to fly as many U-2 flights as possible to gather information about MRBM construction. Multiple missions crisscrossed Cuba daily throughout October. U.S. Navy and U.S. Air Force crews added low-level coverage to the U-2s. Intelligence analysts discovered new MRBM and IRBM sites, which fueled concerns in Washington about Soviet motives. The information allowed Kennedy to make several key decisions.

KENNEDY DECIDES

On October 16, Kennedy had formed EXCOMM, the executive committee of the National Security Council, which included the top foreign policy, intelligence, military, and his own personal advisors. EXCOMM provided the president with a forum to make and carry out a decision about the Cuban issue. The president was visibly upset about Khrushchev's move and deceptions about the MRBMs. EXCOMM members received information about the MRBM sites. Kennedy and EXCOMM members debated four alternatives to remove the new threat from Cuba. The only unanswered question was whether the MRBMs were ready to operate and if they possessed their nuclear warheads. Unbeknown to Kennedy and the CIA, the Soviet freighter *Indigirka* had arrived in Cuban waters on October 4 with a cargo of nuclear warheads.

The first alternative was that the United States could conduct a surgical air strike on the ballistic missile sites only. Unfortunately, intelligence analysts did not know if the three sites were the only ones on the island, nor could Kennedy's military advisor guarantee that aircrews could destroy all of the sites with certainty. The second alternative was that the nation could plan a broader air strike on all Soviet MIG-21s, SA-2 sites, and any ballistic missile support activities. The third alternative was that the president could order the attacks on the MRBM site and the broader air strike and conduct a naval blockade. A naval blockade would stop all future missile deployments, but not the existing MRBM sites. The fourth alternative, proposed by Robert Kennedy, was an invasion, which was an extensive option that would also solve the question of a communist Cuba. An invasion would take time. Army airborne forces could land on the island and seize key military objectives while naval forces gathered to transport U.S. Marine and army forces to Cuba. The United States did have some invasion plans on the shelf and military forces in Florida.

The president ordered no release of any information about the MRBM discovery to anyone outside EXCOMM. If Khrushchev knew about the American discovery, then he could speed up construction of the San Cristóbal site and any other possible ballistic missile locations. The initial round of debate produced three viable steps that involved attacks on Cuba. Kennedy had to decide on an attack only on the missiles, a strike on the MRBM and IRBM sites and other Soviet military installations, or the invasion. A military option seemed to Kennedy like the only way to go.

EXCOMM reconvened later that evening to discuss the options presented. Kennedy leaned toward a general air strike, but other options soon arose. McNamara kept advocating a naval blockade. Another choice revolved around a more diplomatic focus that involved trading the Jupiter missiles in Turkey for removal of those in Cuba. The diplomatic case seemed too weak to Kennedy; it would appear that Moscow had blackmailed the nation into submission. Kennedy still wanted a military response. He believed that a surgical air strike could solve the problem. The U.S. Air Force chief of staff, SAC's Curtis LeMay, countered that the strikes would have a great probability of success if he could unleash a large-scale bombing campaign. Civilian casualties might result. Meanwhile, McNamara pressed for the blockade as a measure between a military action and a diplomatic one. If the blockade did not work, then Kennedy could always order further military action. A preemptive attack might make the United States appear to be the aggressor. Robert Kennedy gave his brother a note that speculated, "I now know how Tojo felt when he was planning Pearl Harbor." Debate continued for days between air strike and blockade.

On October 18, with no clear EXCOMM decision, Kennedy met with Soviet Foreign Minister Andrei Gromyko. Gromyko wanted to attend a U.N. General Assembly meeting. Gromyko, who had questioned the decision to put missiles in Cuba, accused the United States of trying to overthrow Castro and stated that the Soviet Union would not accept this situation. The president raised the question about Soviet military aid to Cuba and the seriousness of the creating a "dangerous situation" between the two nations. Kennedy was ready to show Gromyko the U-2 photographs in the Oval Office, but decided to wait. Gromyko left the White House convinced that Kennedy did not know about the ballistic missiles.

Kennedy started to have second thoughts about an air strike. He and EXCOMM members began to shift from a military stance to the blockade. A blockade was a more flexible policy. The president could announce his decision and conduct action without being accused of launching his own Pearl Harbor. Creating a Cuban quarantine also did not seem as threatening to Soviet forces on Cuba. This action would probably not force a military response like a ballistic missile strike. If the Soviets did try something, then the blockade also allowed Kennedy to escalate action to the air strike or an invasion. Kennedy had some concerns about the credibility of the military and CIA officials who advocated an air strike or invasion. They had assured him of success in the Bay of Pigs that had injured his foreign policy earlier. Still, the EXCOMM membership was not unanimous about a decision on Cuba.

Adlai Stevenson, Kennedy's ambassador to the United Nations, continued to seek a diplomatic solution. Stevenson again proposed withdrawing the Jupiter missiles, exiting Guantánamo, and promising not to invade Cuba.

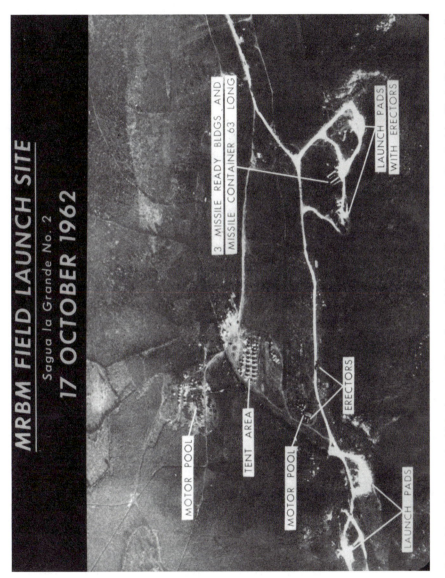

Cuba U-2 photograph. U-2 photography allowed U.S. intelligence agencies to identify ballistic missile sites. These photographs allowed Kennedy to expose Khrushchev's efforts to emplace IRBM and MRBM assets into Cuba. (Courtesy, U.S. Air Force)

Stevenson believed that mutual concessions would solve the crisis. Some EX-COMM members characterized this position as appeasement. Choosing between blockade and appeasement, air strike supporters would rather select a blockade. Kennedy was ready to select an option; he chose the blockade. The president wanted to give Khrushchev a way to get out of Cuba without firing a shot. Kennedy did want to have an alternate plan in case the blockade was not achievable. Additional ground forces, a tactical fighter-bomber squadron, and navy ships started to deploy to Florida as an invasion backup to the blockade. By October 21, U.S. Air Force officials could not guarantee that an air strike would destroy all of the missiles, and the specter of nuclear retaliation reinforced Kennedy's selection of a blockade. The blockade would serve notice to the Soviets that America had serious concerns about the missiles and Cuba. Kennedy would also start mobilizing American military forces throughout the world for future action. He would announce his decision to the American public the next day.

KENNEDY EXPOSES KHRUSHCHEV'S MOVE

Kennedy scheduled a national address on Cuba for October 22. The Kennedy administration had earlier notified allied nations about the situation and the proposed blockade. SAC officials put on a nuclear alert with bombers and ballistic missiles readied for any potential Soviet reaction. Navy submarines armed with Polaris missiles deployed to firing positions. The president also met with members of Congress before making his public statement. Congressional leaders complained that the blockade might not be enough. Some wanted more action, like an air strike or invasion. Kennedy and McNamara admitted that they did not know if the Soviets, once the Americans revealed the information, would fire their MRBMs into the United States.

The president also wanted to notify the Soviets of his policy before going public. Secretary of State Rusk notified Ambassador Dobrynin about the MRBM discovery and Kennedy's reaction. Dobrynin denied any previous knowledge about the MRBM deployment. Khrushchev had earlier heard rumblings about Kennedy's public statement. In the Kremlin, questions arose about what the United States might do in response to Khrushchev's gamble. Although the Soviet leader believed the United States would not invade Cuba, he was concerned. If the U.S. Marines landed on Cuban soil, then Khrushchev's ground forces and any Cuban military units would face the possibility of defeat. Khrushchev authorized Soviet commanders in Cuba to use tactical nuclear weapons in the smaller-range missiles on any invaders. Although the tactical nuclear weapons were smaller than the MRBMs, their use might act as a catalyst to the Americans to heighten the crisis. Khrushchev had to support Castro, and he had invested too much of his personal and political credibility on this decision to withdraw. Any miscalculation, however, could bring the United States and the Soviet Union into a nuclear war.

Kennedy now told the American public and the rest of the world about the MRBMs in Cuba. He colored the missile deployment as a clear offensive nuclear threat to the entire Western Hemisphere. The U.S. government was going to take action. The U.S. Navy would stop any ship trying to put offensive military equipment into Cuba. Washington would allow ships bearing food and other goods into Cuba. The president also ordered the increased use of reconnaissance assets to watch Cuba. Kennedy promised that he would view any Soviet MRBM or IRBM use in the Western Hemisphere as a direct attack on the United States. American nuclear and conventional forces would then conduct a full retaliatory attack on the Soviets. Kennedy warned the American people that the Cuban situation might turn into a more severe crisis. Kennedy asked Khrushchev to step back from his path. Khrushchev's plan was in tatters.

CONFRONTATION BETWEEN THE TITANS

The U.S. Navy had about 140 ships in the area around Cuba to enforce the blockade. Long-range antisubmarine aircraft supplemented the effort. Kennedy would refer to this action as a "quarantine," which sounded less ominous than a blockade. The quarantine would allow naval personnel to stop and search ships for illegal items that appeared to threaten the public good. Navy officials had existing rules of engagement to conduct quarantines from established regulations and tradition. The only questions arising from implementing the policy involved Soviet reaction.

Expectedly, Khrushchev protested that the American quarantine amounted to high seas piracy. Despite the president's disclosure of offensive ballistic missiles in Cuba, he had no shown no proof of their existence. Kennedy had not released or referred to the U-2 photography. Khrushchev's counter was to stand firm. Khrushchev believed that the American move was a pretext to invade Cuba and that Kennedy would back away from this move if Khrushchev stayed firm. Still, Khrushchev could not guarantee that the Americans would allow the missiles to stay without taking further action.

The blockade started to have some success, but Soviet ships did try to reach their destination in Cuba. Many of the ships just stopped. Khrushchev took some actions to avoid escalating the situation. He ordered a Soviet ship that contained nuclear warheads for the SS-5 systems to return to the Soviet Union. If the U.S. Navy had captured the cargo in a blockade inspection, events might again spiral out of control. On October 25, a U.S. Navy boarding party searched the *Bucharest,* an oil tanker, and allowed it to go on to Cuba. Tensions started to rise.

On the same day as the *Bucharest* incident, in a U.N. session, Soviet Ambassador Valerin Zorin pressed Stevenson for proof of the ballistic missiles in Cuba. Support for the United States' blockade would increase if Stevenson could demonstrate that the Soviets were hiding the deployment. Stevenson tried to get Zorin to simply confirm or deny the presence of the MRBMs and IRBMs; Zorin refused to answer. In front of the world, Stevenson finally released the U-2 photographs. The photographs exposed the Soviet government as engineering the crisis by their ballistic missile deployment.

The U.S. and Soviet governments publicly appeared to have locked horns about the issue. Fortunately, the fear of mutual nuclear destruction forced both Kennedy and Khrushchev to seek back door negotiations and open communications between the respective countries. Robert Kennedy and Dobrynin met secretly to discuss issues. Khrushchev started to look for a way out of the crisis by suggesting, through his representative, that if Kennedy made a pledge not to invade Cuba then Khrushchev would dismantle the Soviets' missiles. If Khrushchev could get the United States to accept this proposal, then he would have at least protected Castro's government.

A second proposal to end the crisis from Khrushchev added the demand to remove the Jupiter missiles from Turkey. This proposal presented some problems for Kennedy. How could the president deny a seemingly equal trade of weapons for Turkey and Cuba? Conversely, the United States had to ensure it maintained NATO security requirements. In addition, the president would have looked weak by agreeing under pressure to negotiate. Public perception might show that the president had buckled when he had already decided to remove the Jupiters. Kennedy administration advocates for invasion or air strike were livid. They demanded immediate action since the blockade had not persuaded the Soviets to remove the missiles. More bad news followed with the shoot-down of an SAC U-2 over Cuba. The pilot died. The hard-line EXCOMM advocates wanted a retaliatory air strike on the SA-2 site immediately, as a minimum action, and possibly invasion.

Within EXCOMM, unanswered questions revolved around what was Khrushchev's real proposal. Was it the first or second option? Some of Kennedy's EXCOMM advisors believed that Khrushchev's sudden reversal to a harder line in the second proposal was due to the Kremlin's coercion of the Soviet leader to get more demands. Others thought Khrushchev had been overthrown. The president would base his future dealings on the first proposal, but he was flexible enough to concede that the Jupiter removal was not out of the realm of consideration. The president faced increased pressure to reevaluate the invasion option. The United States and the Soviet Union again seemed destined for war.

Kennedy and Khrushchev had to reconsider their positions. Robert Kennedy and Dobrynin met to consider the proposals. The president's brother told the ambassador that military and other national security advisors who supported an air strike or invasion of Cuba in order to take out the missile sites had besieged the president. Robert Kennedy underscored the idea that the withdrawal of the missiles, under U.N. observation, would result in a pledge by the United States not to invade Cuba. Other EXCOMM members, such as Rusk, had also realized that the Jupiter removal could help solve the crisis. Turkish missile dismantlement was possible, but Moscow could not release publicly this part of the agreement. Any linkage between Cuban and Turkish systems was not possible. The United States would remove the Jupiters in four or five months after the Soviets dismantled their ballistic missiles in Cuba. Time was vital; every day without an agreement might create a situation like the Powers U-2 incident or worse.

Khrushchev was concerned about the increasing risk of war. He had miscalculated badly about using the MRBM and IRBM placement. He could not risk an invasion or escalation to a nuclear confrontation with the United States. The Soviet Union would agree on the ballistic missile removal in exchange for the United States' assurance that Cuba would not be invaded and an end to the blockade, but economic sanctions would remain in place. Khrushchev's dream of a Cuban nuclear deterrent melted. He could claim a victory over Cuban independence, but the Soviet Union appeared to have retreated under pressure from the United States. On October 28, Radio Moscow announced that Khrushchev had agreed to the withdrawal of Cuban missiles for the promise of no Cuban invasion. Secretly, Washington and the Kremlin also accepted an understanding on Turkey.

The Cuban Missile Crisis ended. Both sides claimed victory. The deployment of ballistic missiles and the threat of their potential destructiveness was a novel way to gain strategic advantage. Without the firing of a single shot, the Cuban Missile Crisis had escalated into a vital international fight. Both nations had now realized the potential for nuclear destruction. Out of the crisis came a mutual awareness that the two nations had to step back from direct nuclear confrontation and that arms control negotiations might solve many problems caused by attempts to gain nuclear superiority in the future. The crisis also highlighted Soviet ICBM inferiority. This weakness forced the Soviets to expand their ICBM development while seeking to limit American strength through arms control measures.

The public realized the power and capability of nuclear armed ballistic missiles for the first time during the Cuban Missile Crisis. The ballistic missile now had a new respect and fear. The nation had suffered through a potential full-scale confrontation that would have been on a grander scale than World War II. Despite the ninety-mile proximity of Cuba to Florida, the threat was wider. Most of the continental United States was threatened from Cuba, even though the Soviets had the same capability from thousands of miles away. Coercion and threat created a new calculus for national leaders and strategists to examine that would permanently become etched in developing national policy.

5

Ballistic Missiles at War: The Case of Iraq

THE UNITED STATES AND Soviet Union backed away from a nuclear showdown. Although the two nations continued to build weapons, the countries agreed to reduce certain types and quantities of nuclear weapons, along with ballistic missiles ranging from the MRBM to a number of ICBMs. Unfortunately, other nations had witnessed how these weapons provided an avenue to strike strategically and to coerce or affect a rival's behavior. These weapons also became a symbol of national pride so that their mere existence allowed states to demonstrate their resolve in the face of regional disputes or to gain domestic cohesion in the guise of protecting the nation. The Soviet Union and other countries sold technologies and complete systems to bolster client states and earn hard currency from foreign military sales. Two nations that acquired these systems were Iran and Iraq, traditional enemies, but both supported through arms sales by the Soviet Union. Iraq would use its missiles against Iran and would later use them against the United States.

THE MIDDLE EAST ERUPTS: IRAN AND IRAQ

In the late twentieth century, Middle Eastern conflicts had normally revolved around the Arab world and Israel. However, the picture of a unified Islamic world against Israel was not clear. Tensions between secular governments and others, dominated by Islamic fundamentalists, spilled over borders. Different Islamic sects vied for control over nations. Ancient claims over territory did not distinguish between countries that were Arabic, Persian, or Israeli. Other concerns involved economic ones, influence over oil fields and their potential wealth. These problems erupted between Iran and Iraq in 1980.

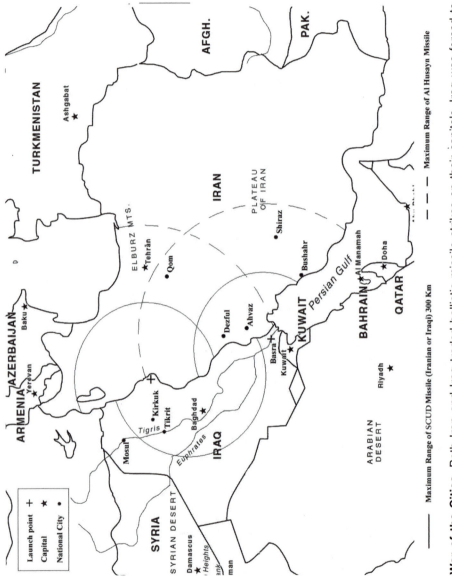

War of the Cities. Both Iran and Iraq traded ballistic missile strikes on their capitals. Iraq was forced to modify SCUD missiles to strike Tehran. (Courtesy, Mapcraft)

— Maximum Range of SCUD Missile (Iranian or Iraqi) 300 Km

– – – Maximum Range of Al Husayn Missile

At the end of the conflict, some experts claimed that the two Islamic countries exchanged over several hundred ballistic missile attacks.

Iranian revolutionaries had overthrown a government friendly toward the United States and the West in January 1979. Islamic fundamentalists had created a revolutionary government intent on creating a state that would replace many non-Muslim influences with their fundamentalist Muslim thought and philosophy. Tehran illustrated clearly its focus on removing Western influence by seizing the U.S. embassy. Although the United States gained release of these hostages, the effect was chilling for many nations around the Persian Gulf. One of the goals of the Iranian government was to transform other nations' governments and societies around the region to mirror its image. Iran tried to export its revolutionary movement west into Saudi Arabia to wrest control over many holy Muslim religious sites. The fundamentalist Islamic Iranians viewed the Saudi monarchy as a decadent group that had betrayed Islam by its continued dealings with the "Great Satan," the United States and the rest of the West. This same country had supported the former corrupt Iranian government until the revolution. Iraq was also a target, since it had subjugated its Islamic Shiite sect majority; Shiite members dominated Iran. Saddam Hussein and his Sunni sect seemed at odds with the Ayatollah Khomeini by dealing with the godless Soviet Union. Iraq was also a secular state that came into confrontation with the ideals of an Islamic state like the Iranian government. Iran had already deposed of its Shah, who had tried to develop an Iranian secular state.

Iraq was another country subjugated by a single voice. A secular government formed by Saddam Hussein had turned a former monarchy into a socialist government, at least in name. The nation became a threat to surrounding nations such as Kuwait, Saudi Arabia, and other Arab emirates, with the potential to spread political instability. These countries feared that Iran and Iraq would spread political unrest in their societies. A powerful Iraq could also threaten Israel directly or through its oil-funded support of its northern Marxist neighbor, Syria. Syrian and radical terrorist groups pressured Tel Aviv's northern borders and Lebanon. The United States and other nations feared disruptions of oil supplies that could wreck their economies and throw their political futures into disarray.

By 1980, the collision between the Iranian Islamic government of the Ayatollah Khomeini and Saddam Hussein seemed inevitable. Iran had depended on weapon purchases and training with the United States. This relationship all changed significantly when Islamic fundamentalists took control of the country and held the U.S. embassy personnel hostage for over a year. The United States refused to sell weapon systems and spare parts to Iran. Similarly, economic problems continued as the United States maintained sanctions, including the refusal to buy oil from Iran. Iranian air power, once a top regional force, had fallen into disrepair. Political will was strong, but Iranian military capability was lacking and had limited sustainability.

Iraq had access to the Persian Gulf through the Shatt al Arab area. Iran and Iraq had forged an uneasy agreement in 1975 over the vital property that allowed Hussein to ship oil from his country to sea lanes for export. Hussein's government, like those of other countries around the Gulf, depended on oil for its economy. Hussein wanted the Iranian government to allow him expanded access to the Persian Gulf by allowing Iraq to control some islands in the Shatt al Arab. Hussein threatened the Iranians to comply with his demand. The Iranians refused.

Hussein decided to launch an attack on his neighbor. Although Iraqi artillery units had conducted some shelling along the border, Hussein ordered no major attacks conducted on Iranian military units. Through early September 1980, Iraq started to prepare for war. Hussein could achieve many of his objectives if he could defeat Iran. He could preempt a possible Iranian-supported revolution that might topple the Iraqi government. Since Khomeini had threatened to topple secular states like Hussein's, removing this menace was paramount. If Iraq pushed Iran back from the Shatt al Arab, then Iraq would have a secure border. A military victory had the potential to make Iraq the regional military and political power in the Gulf. Hussein could also encourage counterrevolutionary forces in Iran to break Khomeini's power in Tehran. Hussein had strong motivations to feed his growing economy by taking Iranian oil fields. These motivations helped convince Iraq to take Iranian territory on September 10. Iraq demanded that Iran cede the captured area; Iran again refused and started to mobilize. The Iranians and Iraqis soon found themselves in a long war of attrition that would last until 1989.

Iraq's military had been supplied by the Soviet Union. Iraq did not have to conduct a major military rebuilding program due to any open conflicts with Israel, previous border conflicts, or revolutions before its fight with Iran. On paper, the Iraqi military had a great advantage over the Iranians. The Iranian military was half the size of its prerevolutionary self. The government in Tehran suffered internal problems as the revolution made radical changes. Iraqi government officials believed that taking the islands in the Shatt al Arab would result in some international debate and minor skirmishing but that eventually the territory would remain in Baghdad's hands.

Iraq tried to knock the Iranians out of the war early, but it could not. On September 22, the Iraqi air force bombed major western Iranian airfields to destroy aircraft on the ground. If the Iraqis could eliminate the Iranian air force, then any danger of Khomeini bombing major industrial or military sites or Baghdad would be remote. Iraqi aircraft also attempted to annihilate the

Iranian navy to ensure it would not interfere with its access through the Persian Gulf. Iraqi failure to remove the air and naval threats would encourage the Iranians and allow them to expand the conflict by striking the source of Iraqi wealth and power, oil. Iranian patrol boats, aircraft, and other forces would later attack shipping and oil terminals. Iranian and Iraqi air forces were roughly equivalent in size and strength. Iranian aircraft could bomb Baghdad, Kirkuk, and a key transportation site, Basra.

The Iraqis also misjudged Iranian will to continue the ground war. Despite the material and training advantages, Iran continued to attack Iraqi positions, and it would not cede any lost territory. Iranian Revolutionary Guard forces would conduct human wave attacks against the Iraqis. Soon, the conflict resembled World War I, with fighting between trenches and movements measured in yards, and it lasted for years. Control over areas around the Shatt al Arab and the borders was traded between the two sides. The Iraqis needed a new strategy to break the stalemate.

IRAQI MISSILES FALL SHORT

Saddam Hussein's arsenal contained some rocket and missile systems before 1980. Hussein authorized his nation's weapons inventory into operation against the Iranians. These systems focused on supporting battlefield operations. Iraqi systems were a supplement to artillery, not designed for strategic effects. The Iraqis did gain some experience by building and modifying these missile and rocket systems. Iraqi military commanders used multiple rocket launchers and missiles that had ranges of less than 100 kilometers (about sixty miles). The Soviet Union had sold the Iraqis some Free Rocket Over Ground (FROG)-7s (their Soviet designation is R65A or Luna), also deployed in the Cuban Missile Crisis, that had a limited range of sixty kilometers (thirty-seven miles). The FROG-7 was a development from the 1950s that was widely sold abroad. These rockets could not lift a sizeable conventional warhead in lieu of its designed twenty-five-kiloton yield nuclear payload. The FROG-7 had a 450-kilogram (about 1,000 pounds) conventional warhead capacity.

Iraqi military commanders started to use the FROG-7 in its early campaigns against Iran in 1980. The weapon had a single-stage construction powered by a solid propellant engine. This relatively primitive ballistic missile did not have a guidance system but was spin stabilized. The missile had limited usefulness and was very inaccurate, especially against entrenched Iranian forces. The FROG-7 had less capability than a German V-2, but it did possess a key advantage: it was launch capable off a single wheeled transporter/erector/launcher (TEL). An experienced crew could launch a missile every twenty minutes. Normally, another vehicle carrying three additional missiles followed the TEL. The Soviets had improved the FROG-7 by 1980, but it was still a primitive weapon.

Limitations of the FROG-7 forced the Iraqis to reconsider the FROG-7's use against other targets, cities, or larger urban areas. Early Iraqi missile operations focused on two locations, Ahwaz and Dezful, that had limited military value. The strikes concentrated on supporting Iraqi ground movements into Iranian territory. These FROG-7 attacks were sporadic and of limited value, however. Crews used ten missiles in 1980 and then fired fifty-four missiles the next year. Iraqi military commanders later phased out the missile from a direct combat role with only a single missile in 1982 and two missiles in 1984. Even against relatively large targets like cities, the FROG-7 was ineffective. Some missiles, just like the earlier V-2s, missed the target entirely. Baghdad needed a new missile to strike Iranian cities with more punch and accuracy.

The Iraqi government sought to increase the yield and range of its ballistic missile inventory. It turned to its R-17 (NATO code named SS-1C SCUD-B) missiles that the Soviets supplied to Iraq in the early 1970s. The SCUD-B was a single-staged, liquid fueled ballistic missile that used storable hypergolic propellants. A fully fueled and maintained ballistic missile could hit a target at an extended range of 330 kilometers (180 miles) with a CEP of about 450 meters (1,500 feet). SCUD-Bs could carry a 985-kilogram (2,175-pound) warhead. The missile had an inertial guidance system that used three gyroscopes to improve the accuracy of the missile over the FROG-7 despite the fourfold increase in range. Signals to the control vanes on the tail assembly would help correct the flight path of the missile in flight as long as the engine was operating.

The SCUD-B provided added capability to the Iraqis. Soviet engineers designed the SCUD-B to deliver nuclear, conventional, or chemical warheads. The warhead detaches from the missile's body. This capability provided the Iraqis with an ability to select an appropriate yield with either a conventional or a chemical weapon. The SCUD-B was also a very mobile weapon, like the FROG-7. Crews launched it from a TEL that would raise the missile from a horizontal to vertical position, ignite it, and move to another position to fire another missile. Still, the SCUD-B had problems. Its range was not sufficient to hit Tehran or other key targets. Unless Iraqi forces could take more Iranian territory, the SCUD-B could do little against Tehran. The Iraqis needed improved capabilities since the ground war was a stalemate.

Hussein now faced the prospect of acquiring new longer-range SCUD-Cs which had a range of 600 kilometers (or 373 miles), which still could not reach Tehran. Another option for Baghdad was purchasing advanced ballistic missiles from the Soviet Union (like the OTR-22 IRBM or SS-12 Scaleboard) or

Al-Husayn. Iraq extended its SCUD missiles by decreasing its payload and increasing the size of its propellant tanks. These Al-Husayn missiles allowed Iraq to strike Tehran in Iraq's War of the Cities; Iraq also later used them in the 1991 Persian Gulf War. (Courtesy, Department of Defense)

building its own ballistic missiles. Soviet sales or deployments of IRBMs were not possible due to ongoing arms reduction negotiations with the United States. Sales of an SS-12 and a SCUD-C might also widen an ongoing arms race within the Middle East that could have long-term consequences for the Soviets. Expectedly, the Soviets declined to sell more advanced and more accurate weapons to Iraq. Saddam Hussein would have to gain ballistic missile superiority by modifying Iraq's existing stock of SCUD-B missiles or by building variants of the delivery system. Iraqi missile engineers and designers would work on two variants of the SCUD-B, the Al-Husayn and Al-Abbas.

Modifying the SCUD-B into a delivery platform with an extended range required resources. Although the Iraqis had experimented with modifying some missiles, this was very different from extending the range of a relatively large ballistic missile. This effort required additional time, expertise, and funds. The ground war had slowed with no major effective offensive actions that had directly threatened either nation's capitals. Expertise to improve Baghdad's missile designs from other countries, such as the Soviet Union, would take time to find and then employ. The continued war on the ground, disputes in areas around oil terminals in the Shatt al Arab, and Iranian attacks on oil shipping lanes affected Iraqi finances. Trading off ballistic missile development against purchasing weapons to fight the war on the ground, air, and sea was a gamble. Still, Hussein started a program to modify the SCUD-Bs.

Iraqi launch crews would use SCUD-Bs and modified variants to attack some cities. Hussein directed these attacks against the cities to break the will of the Iranian population. These operations amounted to terror raids to force the Iranian government to either fail or negotiate an end to the war. On October 27, 1982, Hussein's missile crews began to replace FROG-7s with SCUD-Bs. The crews would still launch a limited three SCUD missiles in 1982. SCUD-B crews began ramping up: to thirty-three launches in 1983; twenty-five firings in 1984; a huge barrage of eighty-two missiles in 1985; no launches in 1986; attacks in 1987 to match their record in 1984; and 193 attacks in 1988. There is some dispute about the actual number of missile launches, but most estimates place the number of launches at no more than 251. Iraq focused many of its early SCUD attacks on border cities such as Ahwaz, Borujerd, Dezful, and Khorramabad. Even with their greater range and improvement in payload, these missiles did not provide sufficient damage. Unless the missiles hit a large factory, school, or area where people gathered, they became merely terror devices.

Iraqi efforts to expand the SCUD-B's capabilities resulted in development of the Al-Husayn missile. This missile had an increased range of 650 kilometers (400 miles) and was thus capable of striking central Iran. Iraqi engineers reduced the payload to 500 kilograms (1,100 pounds) and increased the amount of propellant carried by the missile by about 25 percent. Engineers extended the missile's fuselage to carry five tons of additional liquid propellant to power it for a seven-minute flight. Launch crews could reload and fire an Al-Husayn within an hour.

Defense experts believed that the Al-Husayn had the capability to carry a high explosive or chemical warhead. As for its earlier SCUD-B cousin, launch crews for the Al-Husayn used a locally produced wheeled TEL for operations. There is some debate whether the Al-Husayn was solely of Iraqi design. Several nations, such as the Soviet Union, China, Egypt, France, East Germany, Libya, and North Korea, had the technology or experience with these ballistic missiles to provide Saddam Hussein's engineers with sufficient information, components, or designs to modify the missile. Hussein also sought technical and component support from two unlikely allies, Argentina and Brazil. Hussein had offered financial help to these nations to develop their own ballistic missile programs. The Iraqis purchased 350 SCUD-Bs in 1984 and 300 more in 1986. These acquisitions provided additional systems for components and flight testing. Additionally, the Soviet Union may have supplied advanced SCUD-C components to allow the Iraqis to expand their weapons' capabilities.

Iraq now had the capability to strike targets around Tehran. The missile's seven-and-a-half-minute flight gave Iran little hope for warning its populace to take cover. Additionally, the Iranians had no active defensive capability to shoot down these vehicles, nor did they have a means to identify launch sites for attack by aircraft or artillery. These weapons provided a simple way to threaten cities and attack them without warning, a perfect terror device.

Iraq began to test the Al-Husayn in August 1987. Although flight tests proved the missile could work, there were some concerns. Iraqi engineers had to strengthen the airframe to compensate for larger fuel and oxidizer tanks. Fabrication teams had to extend internal tanks and provide additional air tanks to give adequate pressurization for the increased volume for the propellants. Iraq could use spare SCUD-B components for some assemblies, tanks, electronics, wiring, and other parts. However, they would have to weld them together, always a questionable proposition. In Iraq's case, the welding quality would eventually affect the missile's capabilities. Iranian forces witnessed many of these missiles that crashed, without warhead impact, due to welding problems. Pressurization or fuel leaks could have hampered the missile's operation. Iraq also tried to improve guidance systems to increase the missile's accuracy. Hussein's government claimed that the missiles now had a

CEP of 500 meters (1,640 feet). Some CEP estimates place the true accuracy at 2.6 kilometers (about 1.9 miles). The Al-Husayn missile effort was still a great strategic leap forward for Iraq. Even so, Iraq wanted even greater ranges.

The other major SCUD modification by the Iraqis was a more radical change to the missile to ensure it struck deeper into Iraq and potentially into other Middle East countries. Iraqi military officials tried to build on the success of the Al-Husayn by further reducing the SCUD-B's payload and increasing the propellant capacity. Iraqi engineers christened this modified Al-Husayn vehicle the Al-Abbas. Engineers reduced the missile's payload to only 300 kilograms (660 pounds), but it could strike a target at 900 kilometers (560 miles). Iraqi launch crews could now reach Tehran with ease and many parts of the Middle East as well, including all of Israel. Despite the greater range, the accuracy of the missile proved suspect. The CEP was about the same as that of the Al-Husayn, but official claims credited the Al-Abbas with a CEP of 300 meters (980 feet), less than a short-range unmodified SCUD-B. Iraqi missiles never met these capabilities in flight testing or apparently in the field. However, if crews launched the missile at large urban areas like Tehran and the purpose was to conduct a terror attack, then accuracy might not be necessary.

Iran was not helpless; it could respond to Iraqi missile attacks. Under Iranian air force control, launch crews fired SCUD-Bs against the Iraqis in March 1985. Libya first sold SCUDs to Iran, and then North Korea shipped about 100 missiles to Iran in 1988. News reports named Syria as a source of SCUDs for Iran. Curiously, these same countries may have provided components, technology, and assistance to Baghdad during the war. Iranian missile crews bombarded Iraqi positions and cities in retaliation for ballistic missile strikes. Iran first used fourteen missiles in 1985 launches; decreased to eight the next year; increased to eighteen in 1987; and spiked at eighty-eight missiles in 1988.

The Iranians did not have to modify their missiles. Iranian SCUD missiles did not have to traverse as great a distance to strike major cities as their Iraqi counterparts did. The distance between Baghdad and the border, less than 250 kilometers, or about 150 miles, was closer than Iraqi missile ranges to Tehran. As long as the ground war did not alter the battlefield, Iranian SCUDs could hit their targets. However, the Iranians did have an advantage over the Iraqis. Iranian revolutionary military forces held control of Iranian territory with vigor and wanted to avenge the unprovoked attack on their nation. Religious zeal allowed Iranian commanders to trade blood for territory through human wave attacks against prepared defensive positions. Time was on Iran's side, as they could use attrition against the Iraqis. Tehran had to just push back the Iraqis and use its unmodified SCUDs. Iran was not motivated to extend its ballistic missiles' range.

Superficially, Tehran had a tremendous advantage over the Iraqis in terms of missile range. However, several mitigating circumstances limited Iran's ability to take advantage of this situation. Iran, under economic sanctions from many nations, had problems selling its main export commodity, oil. The constant fighting in the Persian Gulf between Iranian and Iraqi air and naval forces reduced the flow of oil to both countries and affected their ability to gain hard currency to purchase weapons or support. The Iraqis, however, had outside financial support to wage their war against Iran. Islamic fundamentalism threatened Saudi Arabia, Kuwait, and other countries that were supported by the Iranian religious and political leadership. These countries started to provide loans and direct financial support to Saddam Hussein in his effort to fight Iran. The Iranian air force was also running out of resources, and its capabilities diminished slowly with time. Iraq could supplement missile attacks with aircraft raids to strike the larger cities. Iran could not do the same with its aircraft and had to rely on ballistic missile strikes that came from a decreasing pool of available weapons. One option for Tehran was to try to build SCUD-B systems. Instead of focusing on ballistic missile modifications, Iranian engineers concentrated only on production capability, but they failed to make operational improvements. The production centers allowed Iranian military forces to launch forty-kilometer-range (25-mile) Oghab vehicles. Oghabs supported ground operations and limited attacks on Iraqi cities. Iranian military commanders used these unguided missiles like artillery.

WAR OF THE CITIES

The conflict between Iran and Iraq dragged on. There was no sense of any negotiations or efforts to end the conflict. Ground operations continued with horrendous casualties. Both sides were bled white with losses. The conflict focused on urban and economic targets to inflict sufficient pain to force one side to capitulate. Iraq would have to rely on aircraft strikes until its engineers and production capability could make the Al-Husayn or Al-Abbas system operational or push Iranian ground forces back. Iran could reply by its limited aircraft, but its SCUD-Bs had sufficient range to respond immediately. By 1987, attacks on cities started in earnest.

When Hussein finally gained the capability to launch his Al-Husayn missiles, a new strategy emerged. Iraqi military forces could now hit Tehran without effect. On February 29, 1988, the Al-Husayn demonstrated its operational capabilities when Iraqi military missile crews launched five vehicles into Iran. This capability breathed new life into the Iraqi scheme to change the nature of the war. A new fifty-two-day "War of the Cities" erupted in the theater that would force both sides to the negotiating table.

From February 29 to April 20, both sides traded ballistic missile and air strikes on their capitals and other targets. While the missiles were inaccurate, Iraqi and Iranian SCUDs and their derivatives still produced massive physical damage and some casualties. Like their forebear, the V-2, and its attack on London, the missiles' purpose was to strike terror on the population. Some analysts believed that the Iraqis' missile inaccuracies approached several magnitudes above their stated CEPs. However, there were reports of Iraqi missile attacks conducted in salvos that landed around defined targets. Iraqi missile attacks appeared to gain in accuracy as the campaign continued. Even with the missiles' improved accuracy, cities became the attack's focus. Conducting a psychological attack on cities was easier than trying to destroy a specific military site like an airfield.

The greater Tehran and Baghdad urban areas sprawled for hundreds of square miles and had populations counted in the millions. Given each side did not have a warning system or a missile defense system, the population could do little except to prepare bomb shelters or leave the area. The only indication of an incoming missile strike was at warhead impact, as the vehicle attained speeds of Mach 1.5. The psychological impact of a missile that could kill many people quickly and allowed no defense terrorized the population. Ultimately, few died from these attacks, but their psychological effect created more impact than physical ones. Iran lost approximately 2,000 casualties and Iraq suffered only 1,000 losses in these attacks. These casualties were minor relative to the size of both capitals and major cities. Crowds could witness the destruction of a block or homes or large craters that forced people to speculate where the next Al-Husayn would land.

Iraq redoubled its efforts to panic the Iranian population. During the period, Iraqi air force pilots conducted over 400 sorties against urban and economic targets. Al-Husayn launch crews fired from 160 to 190 missiles against Tehran and Qom. Additionally, the Iraqis could use their SCUD-B stock to strike other border targets. The Al-Abbas was not ready for operation, but its flight testing and Iraqi propaganda statements continued to spew information about its future capabilities. The rate of Al-Husayn missile attacks was relatively low, about three per day during the "War of the Cities." News reports concerning the possible Iraqi use of chemical weapons, however, chilled the Iranian population. The Iranian people became convinced that Baghdad had the will and capability to use chemical weapons against them, as reports surfaced about how Hussein authorized battlefield employment of his chemical munitions against Iranian military forces and later the Iraqi Kurdish population. Iranian military forces understood that the Al-Husayn and Al-Abbas also had the ability to carry chemical warheads. These fears forced Iranian populations to consider leaving Tehran and other cities. As the ballistic missile campaign intensified, people started to depart. Khomeini himself evacuated the capital. After news reports made his departure public, millions followed him. Approximately a third of Tehran's population left for safety. While Iranian morale wavered, Iraqi confidence started to rise. The Iraqi strategy was starting to work.

Iran responded to the Iraqi attacks with its own SCUD-Bs. Iran launched about sixty-one ballistic missiles. These missiles represented most of Iran's remaining SCUD stocks. Given the quantitative disadvantage in missiles and Iraq's seemingly large production capability, Tehran needed to evaluate its position. Unlike the failed German V-2 campaign to pressure the British to negotiate, the War of the Cities had succeeded in forcing Iran to consider ending the war. Khomeini could not face a continued bloody war with his neighbor, economic atrophy, and a panicked population. Tehran considered the potential for continued Iraqi attacks with ballistic missiles and aircraft, and the Iranian government decided to accept a ceasefire with Baghdad in July 1988. The Iran-Iraq borders did not change appreciably; Hussein had gambled and received little for his nation's sacrifice.

Al-Husayn missile attacks helped end the conflict. Given the prospects for peace, the growing discontent for additional casualties, fears of additional attacks, and no capability to win the war, the missile strikes took their toll. The United States had also entered the conflict by protecting commerce and ensuring security for oil deliveries in the Persian Gulf, one of the main weapons Iran used against Iraq. Given the crumbling military, political, and economic conditions in Iran, the ballistic missile launches created conditions that caused a faster unraveling of Tehran's strategic position. Conventionally armed missiles and strategic bombardment proved a capable weapon against populations that were already in a fragile state to capitulate. Fortunately, Hussein did not arm the Al-Husayn with either a chemical or a biological weapon. With this success, Iraq would continue to develop advanced weapons programs. This lesson was not lost to Tehran, as that government also worked to develop long-range missile systems. Each side would later seek to arm these vehicles with an ultimate weapon, a nuclear device.

OPERATION DESERT STORM

Ballistic missiles would play another significant role in the Middle East three years after the Iran-Iraq War. A dispute over ownership of land between Iraq and another neighbor, Kuwait, would expand into a major conflict that would involve a coalition led by the United States and Saddam Hussein. The Iran-Iraq War was the first conflict where participants exchanged ballistic missile attacks. Fighting between Iraq and this coalition would feature a new aspect of missile warfare, active defense against attacks, and a campaign to eliminate mobile missile launchers. Although the United States had a large ICBM inventory, it had eliminated all of its IRBMs through an arms control treaty with the Soviet Union, and so the United States could not respond in kind. The American and coalition militaries would instead use their massive advantage in conventional air forces and cruise missiles to conduct an air campaign to paralyze Iraq. Iraq would rely on its proven ballistic missile force to fight. It had rebuilt and expanded its inventory of SCUD, Al-Husayn, Al-Abbas, and other missiles after its war with Iran.

Hussein and the Iraqi government had continued to suffer after their conflict with Iran with financial loans and economic reconstruction. Kuwait and other nations that had supported Iraq continued to prosper by selling oil and watching two major petroleum-producing rivals fight for eight years. Hussein would claim that he had repaid his financial obligations by stopping the spread of Islamic fundamentalism, which spared many of these nations, through the blood from their massive casualties. Hussein stated that he did not have to repay loans and suggested those countries provide him more financial aid in compensation.

On August 2, 1990, Iraqi ground forces invaded Kuwait. These forces occupied the country within a day. Hussein had captured his neighbor's wealth and valuable oil fields. Saudi Arabia feared that Hussein would continue south and seize its oil fields and possibly force its royal family to flee like Kuwait's monarchy. The United States acted quickly to defend Saudi Arabia by positioning airborne units and F-15 fighter units to protect the monarchy. Eventually, President George H. W. Bush would gather sufficient political support and Congressional approval to deploy American military forces to push Saddam Hussein's military forces out of Kuwait.

The United States' Central Command (CENTCOM) became the focal point to plan and execute operations to force Iraq out of Kuwait. Although the United States fought the war with a coalition, CENTCOM had the experienced personnel, equipment, and training to provide an organized planning function for military operations. Actions would include ground operations to eliminate not only Iraqi ground forces in Kuwait but also other Iraqi units that threatened Saudi Arabia on its Iraqi border. Naval forces were available to ensure that the oil industry throughout the Persian Gulf would not be disrupted, as in the Iran-Iraq War. Air campaign planners believed that striking key centers of Iraqi political, military, and economic strength would cripple Hussein's forces in the field. This would help ground operations and make retaking Kuwait easier. In the back of CENTCOM's planning minds was uncertainty about Iraq's ability and will to respond.

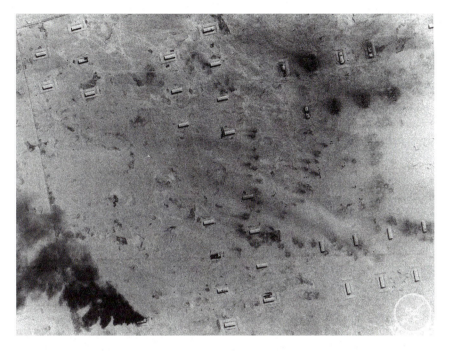

Iraqi missile sites. During the 1991 Persian Gulf War, coalition air forces at-tempted to destroy fixed Iraqi missile sites. Unfortunately, the air strikes failed to remove these sites, but Baghdad used mobile missile launchers instead. (Courtesy, Department of Defense)

Since the end of the Iran-Iraq War, Hussein sought advanced capabilities like weapons of mass destruction (WMD). Iraqi military commanders had shown that they would use chemical weapons against Kurdish populations who had tried to seek autonomy in Iraq. Western intelligence sources specu-lated about Iraqi importation of equipment and efforts to seek biological and nuclear weapons as well. Some sources indicated that the Iraqis had tested their SCUD-Bs to use chemical warheads. Iraq had already demonstrated its ability to build and use Al-Husayn and SCUD derivatives against Iranian pop-ulation centers and that these missiles could carry chemical weapons. Carry-ing biological weapons, however, was another matter. Placing biological weapons on a ballistic missile requires extensive support and special handling, but U.S. intelligence sources did not know the extent of Baghdad's progress.

Nuclear weapons development was another question mark. An Israeli force of American-made F-15 and F-16 fighters had bombed Iraq's Osirak nuclear plant on June 6, 1981. The Osirak nuclear plant was allegedly a part of a secret nuclear weapons plant that would have soon produced weapons-grade plutonium. How Hussein might use these WMD devices was a question raised in the planning process. Military planners did not know what Hussein had or was going to do. Potential for great destruction was present if the Iraqis could use a nuclear weapon. Analysts believed chemical weapons to be the most likely weapon for Hussein. Iraqi missile crews could use them against major troop concentrations or seek another way to create problems within the coalition.

The United States was successful in recruiting many nations to the coalition. Several of these nations included Arabic nations such as Egypt and Syria. These nations faced some internal debate due to supporting a war against a fellow Islamic country directed by a non-Muslim state. Hussein believed that he could capitalize on this concern. Iraq could exploit this seam in the coalition's fabric by attacking Israel with a missile strike. If Israel responded by a military attack, then the Arabic countries would be seen as helping Israel defeat a brother Islamic nation, despite its earlier attack on Kuwait. The coalition would dissolve with the United States failing to gain political and military support to conduct operations. Hussein had other motivations to strike at Israel. The Israeli raid on Osirak had humiliated him, and he could not retaliate since he was at war with Iran. Hussein had dreams of taking a position of leadership against Israel, and a direct attack against the Israelis would improve his standing in the Arabic world. The Israelis had demonstrated that they were a threat to Hussein's regime and were a true enemy to Baghdad. Any attack on Israel would benefit Hussein, whether Tel Aviv decided to respond or not.

Iraqi SCUD and other ballistic missile sites became key targets to eliminate by any air campaign. Attacking these missile and WMD sites allowed coalition forces to remove an immediate threat to their military forces, friendly capitals, and Israel. The destruction of these targets also reduced long-term strategic problems with Iraq within the region. Fixed sites in western Iraq became an important focus for pilots, because these fixed sites presented a highly identifiable target to attack. The air campaign would concentrate on the fixed missile launch locations, WMD production and storage sites, support facilities, and suspected mobile launch bases. Coalition air forces had not devised an effective means to locate and destroy mobile missile TEL launchers. Unfortunately, mobile TEL launchers would demonstrate an elusive target for CENTCOM planners and coalition pilots. Pilots believed that they could destroy these fixed sites easily. Unfortunately, the mobile SCUDs and their derivatives were harder to destroy. Iraqi launch crews would continue firing throughout the campaign.

During the period between Iraq's war with Iran and conflict over Kuwait, Hussein had continued efforts to build longer-range accurate missiles. The

Al-Husayn strike. The most deadly Al-Husayn attack on U.S. forces in the 1991 Persian Gulf War was on Dhahran in Saudi Arabia; it killed twenty-eight soldiers and wounded ninety-seven others in transient quarters on February 25, 1991. Fortunately, this scene was not repeated during the conflict. (Courtesy, Department of Defense)

Al-Abbas development was completed, but continual problems with poor workmanship crippled the missiles. When fired, the Al-Abbas would disintegrate in flight. A modified Al-Abbas would now be renamed the Al-Hijarah. Iraqi engineers continued to work on the vehicle, but could not solve many of the issues that had plagued the Al-Abbas.

Rapid Iraqi TEL movement to firing locations or drivers moving the TELs to hidden locations negated efforts by aircraft to destroy them. Although infrared satellites detected missile launches, aircraft could not catch them in the open. Missile teams could use prepared missile sites for rapid launch operations. Instead of a typical Soviet SCUD missile launch that took forty to ninety minutes, the Iraqis reduced launch times to only ten minutes. Even if an infrared detection by satellite had occurred, responding to it would take time. The United States had years of experience observing Soviet ballistic missile launches through early warning satellites and other sources. Different sizes and temperatures of its rocket engine's exhaust characterized different types of missile launches. Detection, analysis, communications, making a decision, and taking action took time. Destroying the TEL would be an afterthought; military commanders would have only a few minutes to warn a civilian population or to launch an anti–ballistic missile interceptor.

Western intelligence sources had some ideas about the Iraqi ballistic missile program. By February 1990, analysts had concluded that five fixed ballistic missile sites were under construction in western Iraq. Some reports indicated that there were twenty-eight missile launchers at the location. Their probable mission was to launch ballistic missile attacks against Israel, but they could also strike into Turkey, Syria, or parts of Egypt. This information provided some credence to the idea that Hussein could launch Al-Husayn missiles against Tel Aviv, Jerusalem, Haifa, or other cities to weaken Arab support for the coalition. Some prewar estimates of Iraqi ballistic missile inventory claimed that Baghdad had no more than 1,000 missiles. CENTCOM estimates, by December 1990, had projected that Hussein had 500–700 SCUDs and modified ballistic missiles. Intelligence sources believed that Iraqi missile commanders could count on sixty-four fixed launch sites in western Iraq. Considering that they had an independent production capability, albeit they still needed foreign-made components, and a WMD program, the threat seemed a potent one.

Fixed launch sites did provide some level of certainty to CENTCOM air campaign planners. Iraqi military commanders allegedly built launch locations in not only Baghdad, but also Taji and Dura. These sites allowed Iraq to hit targets at all points of the compass and reach out against many coalition partners. Iraq also had several SCUD-B fixed launch locations at H-2, a western airfield, with six to nine sites that could strike into Israel or Syria. If war

SCUD. The Soviet Union could operate SCUD missiles from wheeled TELs. Iraqi forces used mobile TELs in their conflict with Iran and the United States. Despite a concentrated air effort, U.S. and Coalition aircraft failed to stop SCUD launches in their Great SCUD Hunt in 1991. (Courtesy, U.S. Air Force)

did come, then these launch positions would become prime coalition targets. This was not lost on Hussein's military staffs. A sudden air strike would destroy valuable missiles and crews. The best option might be to launch the weapons early, if Iraqi defense systems detected a coalition attack. Conversely, knowing that an air attack was possible, ballistic missile operations could switch to the more difficult mobile operations.

THUNDER AND LIGHTNING: OPERATION DESERT STORM

The United States and coalition nations could not act immediately to remove Saddam Hussein from Kuwait. The closest large U.S. ground combat units were in Germany. Unfortunately, the U.S. Army had trained, organized, and equipped these forces to fight mostly in the forests and plains of central Europe, not in a desert environment. Likewise, air and naval units would take time to transition from their peacetime status to an active war footing. The president would need to mobilize reserve component forces to provide added combat and support forces. Building up, training, and equipping a large coalition force would take time. The coalition initiated Operation Desert Shield to protect Saudi Arabia and other Gulf nations but also to allow an orderly and relatively long buildup of forces in Saudi Arabia and other Gulf countries.

Operation Desert Shield proceeded smoothly. American military units grew from 82,806 on September 1, 1990, to 341,754 on January 1, 1991. On the eve of combat operations, the coalition would have well over 545,000 ground and air personnel in the theater. Facing this force, Hussein could count on about 1,140,000 military personnel. Coalition forces were in a tenuous position as the buildup continued from August to January. Iraqi forces close to home could launch an attack south and then push the small 50,000-strong Saudi army out of the way. Hussein allowed an orderly coalition expansion into Saudi Arabia. Hussein's forces were composed largely of conscripts who pushed out the small Kuwaiti defense force when it took over the country. The Iraqi ground forces, although rebuilt, had not recovered from eight years of bloody conflict with Iran.

The United States used many means to force Iraq to leave Kuwait. Diplomatic means through bilateral talks dialogue within the United Nations, and international pressure failed to move Hussein. Economic sanctions, boycotts, seizure of financial assets, and other actions pressured Iraq but did not force a retreat. Hussein hoped that the coalition forces would back down as Iraq absorbed Kuwait. By January, a coalition ultimatum was given to the Iraqi government to leave Kuwait; it was rejected. The only option left to the coalition was to initiate military action. It would begin with an air campaign and an extensive effort to destroy or disable Hussein's ballistic missile force.

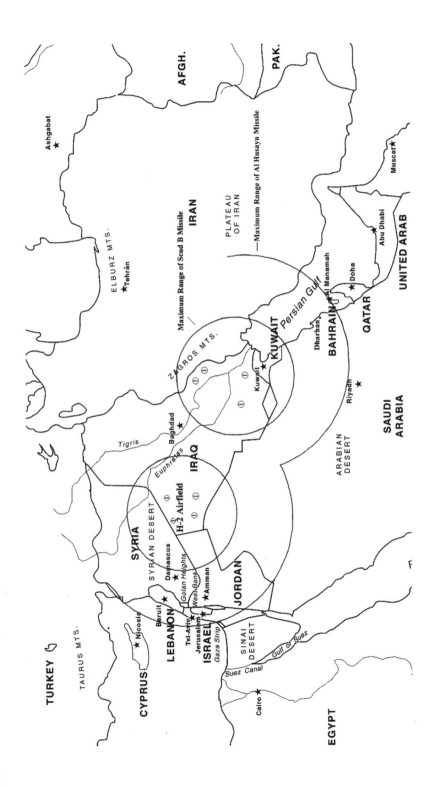

Estimated ranges of Iraqi missiles during the 1991 Persian Gulf War. Launch sites in western Iraq (H-2) could strike into Israel. Launches from southern Iraq could hit locations in Saudi Arabia. (Courtesy, Mapcraft)

Air campaign planning staffs realized there were a growing number of targets in Iraq's missile program. A June 15, 1990, preconflict CENTCOM target estimate identified only seven Iraqi launch or support sites. By December 20, the list had grown to thirteen facilities. These targets included not only the fixed launch sites but also liquid fuel production facilities. Intelligence analysts recognized the difficulties of gathering information on one of Hussein's most secret programs. Still, there was debate on CENTCOM's Central Tactical Air Forces (CENTAF) staff about the value of SCUD and other missiles relative to other targets. CENTAF was responsible for directing a large portion of the air campaign and other aspects of aircraft operations within the theater. Lieutenant General Charles Horner, responsible for CENTAF, initially believed that the SCUDs, as a military weapon, were insignificant. Horner believed these missiles had relatively small payloads and limited range and were inaccurate. Horner considered the missiles a nuisance. Horner would later realize that these weapons would have significant political value if they were used to force Israel into the war or if Hussein armed the missiles with a chemical or biological weapon.

Since intelligence and CENTAF planning staffs would face difficulties finding and destroying mobile TELs, a strategy was developed to reduce this threat. Coalition air forces had to reduce the threat. CENTCOM military actions had to reduce the opportunities for SCUD mobile operations by attacking support facilities and keeping TELs from moving. CENTAF ordered extensive aerial attacks on Iraqi ballistic missile logistics and maintenance facilities. Another option was to ensure that SCUDs and other missiles could not hit their targets. The U.S. Army had deployed a modified surface-to-air missile, the Patriot, to defend locations against missile attacks. Unfortunately, engineers designed the missile primarily to shoot down aircraft, not ballistic missiles, and so the Patriot needed technical modifications. The Patriot's target acquisition radar had difficulty distinguishing individual targets from a salvo launch or decoys to direct an appropriate interception. CENTAF air attacks also had to destroy any chance of Iraq using WMD warheads on its delivery vehicles. This requirement forced planners to seek out and obliterate any WMD production or storage sites. Horner had realized, however, that he could not guarantee destruction of all ballistic missile launch sites or support facilities during the first air attacks. Iraqi SCUDs and their derivatives would probably hit some targets during the campaign.

Concern about SCUD attacks on Israel took on a greater urgency as planning for the air campaign proceeded. Mobile missiles launched from western Iraqi airfields could strike Israel despite the massive air campaign that was planned against operational launch sites, logistics, and support facilities. Despite the ease of attacking fixed sites, there was a danger. If Baghdad detected the air campaign early and the fixed sites were not attacked immediately, then Iraqi launch crews could at least ignite any missiles on their pads to lessen potential losses. A communications link between the Pentagon and the Israeli Ministry of Defense provided shared intelligence and warning information. This would at least provide some warning to the Israelis of an impending SCUD or other missile strike. The United States had offered the Israelis two Patriot batteries to protect Israel's major cities, but the Israelis rejected the offer.

In the early morning of January 17, 1991, coalition forces began Operation Desert Storm. These forces initiated the campaign with air and naval forces hitting many key Iraqi targets. Aircraft and long-range cruise missiles launched from surface ships and submarines struck a host of military targets. These targets included logistics sites, airfields, air defense, command and control, naval, coastal defense, suspected WMD production and storage locations, equipment sites, and troop concentrations. Aircraft commanders and their pilots struck Iraqi missile launch and support sites throughout the night. Coalition pilots flew 2,759 sorties that included reconnaissance, refueling, air superiority, and strategic bombing missions.

Air attacks against early warning and surface-to-air missile sites would become the first targets destroyed. Ground special forces would aid the aircraft in their missions that would leave the Iraqi military commanders blind about the direction of aircraft flights. A combination of aircraft and cruise missiles would also strike Baghdad to remove the top Iraqi leaders' ability to communicate with their forces. This would help delay their ordering of a missile attack on Israel.

Attacks against western Iraqi missile sites took precedence over all other SCUD, Al-Husayn, or Al-Hijarah locations. The H-2 attack and other missile locations proceeded on time. Coalition air strikes hit targets throughout Iraq. Despite the intelligence gathered by the coalition, some from Israeli defense and intelligence sources, they did not destroy the fixed launch sites. The attack failed to accomplish its mission. Although the Iraqis did not use their fixed sites throughout the war, the coalition assigned aircraft to continue patrolling western Iraq. The Iraqis, however, had switched to mobile missile operations.

THE GREAT SCUD HUNT

Iraqi TELs moved quickly into action in the early hours of January 18. From 2:59 to 3:27 a.m., Al-Husayn launch crews sent their weapons toward Israel. Seven missiles fell on Israel, two in Haifa and five in Tel Aviv. There were only a few casualties—three died from suffocation due to putting on their gas masks improperly, and twelve had injuries. Israel did not implement its normal policy of immediate retaliation. The United States had promised more intelligence and military information. The coalition air forces also put more emphasis on attacking these Iraqi missiles. Still, the Israeli government had put their aircraft on alert to conduct a strike on Iraq and demanded certain identification codes to allow their aircraft to fly within coalition air space as friendly forces. If they did not receive these codes, then coalition aircraft and air defenses might shoot them down, or the Israelis might do the same to coalition forces. Israeli officials also wanted the coalition to get approval from Jordan and Saudi Arabia to allow Israeli combat aircraft to fly through their airspace. The United States refused to grant Israel either request.

Hussein launched more missiles on the following day. Four ballistic missiles headed toward Tel Aviv. Only three landed in the city, causing minor damage. The attacks did not kill anyone, but the attack forced the Israeli government to change its position on accepting the Patriot system. Israel accepted four Patriot batteries. CENTAF faced greater pressure from Washington to find and destroy missiles in western Iraq. The added emphasis on the "Great SCUD Hunt" for mobile missiles was not costless. CENTAF planners had to divert valuable air assets that had been destined to bomb Baghdad and other targets to the hunt for the SCUDs. This movement delayed the overall air campaign that would affect the ground offensive to liberate Kuwait.

The Iraqis still maintained the inaccurate Al-Husayn missile systems. Launches against Israel were mainly against major population centers concentrated along its Mediterranean coast. Perhaps motivated by Iraq's War of the Cities campaign, Hussein concentrated his attacks on Tel Aviv and Haifa. Most accounts of the missile campaign note that no more than forty Al-Husayns were destined for Israel. The first week saw about fifteen vehicles landing in Israeli territory, followed by twelve missiles in a second week. The coalition forces identified fewer daily missile launches in the next four weeks. Similarly, Iraqi missile launches focused on Saudi Arabia in the first two weeks and then dropped significantly to only a few random attacks during the six-week Operation Desert Storm campaign. Bahrain also received three strikes in the last weeks of the campaign. The most deadly attack against U.S. forces was a SCUD launch conducted against soldiers staging for deployment in the theater. On February 25, a SCUD hit a warehouse in Dharan, Saudi Arabia, that killed twenty-eight and wounded ninety-seven. Some of the reduction in missile launches may be attributable to reduced missile stocks. Other reasons included destruction of support facilities that provided fuel and air attacks and roving patrols looking for TELs. Ground advancement forced launch crews to operate further east, which reduced their missiles' range and relia-

Patriot launch. During the 1991 Persian Gulf War, the United States operated the Patriot ballistic missile defense system. Although its interception rate was debatable, it provided a welcomed psychological boost against the SCUD and Al-Husayn Iraqi missile attacks. (Courtesy, U.S. Army)

bility. Coalition ground operations started to push north from Saudi Arabia, and the Iraqi military concentrated on Kuwait.

Coalition air forces hunted and tried to destroy mobile TELs. U.S. and other coalition forces believed that Iraqi crews would follow established but time-consuming Soviet launch procedures. Additionally, Western intelligence sources had developed techniques to measure infrared signatures from vehicles such as the TEL or ballistic missiles from Soviet weapons. Intelligence analysts might also locate the mobile missiles by detecting electromagnetic emissions from radar or infrared signals during launch procedures or other uses of equipment. The infrared launch plume from a satellite would also provide a telltale sign of a launch location.

Since the Iraqis had changed equipment and operating procedures and used previously surveyed positions, locating these positions was problematic. For example, even if a Defense Support Program (DSP), American early warning ballistic missile satellite could detect a launch, analysts had to verify it. Analysts and control personnel had to pinpoint the location, communicate warnings, and assign a plane to attack the target. This took time and effort. Despite Iraqi night launches, about 80 percent of attacks, which created a stark infrared contrast with the cold sky compared to the missile's exhaust plume, the detection process was slow. This delay allowed Iraqi missile crews to drive away from the launch sites to hide under bridges, underpasses, garages, or buildings so that the search for them stalled. The coalition would only be able to destroy the TEL and its crews; Iraqi launch crews could still fire the weapon.

The Great SCUD Hunt relied on flying air patrols over western and southern Iraqi territory to detect missile launches. Pilots had to search hundreds of square miles and rely on airborne sensors to detect the TEL before it launched its weapon. The Iraqis also knew about the size and quality of the coalition air forces. They realized that American air power had a decided qualitative edge in speed, lethality, range, and precision. Iraqi military commanders used many decoy TELs and launch support vehicles to trick the coalition. Additionally, the airborne sensor had to distinguish the TEL from other similar vehicles, terrain, or debris. Another unpredictable factor, the weather, also affected air operations. During the first week of coalition air operations, low clouds and fog limited the pilots' visibility and canceled many missions, up to 15 percent of planned flights. Despite having all-weather-capable aircraft, pilots had problems identifying and bombing targets. These weather conditions limited the coalition's assessment of the bombs' damage to targets, which hampered efforts to plan future missions against SCUD preparation or storage supporting mobile operations. Coalition air forces would fly over 2,493 sorties hunting for TELs throughout the war.

Despite the coalition air forces' initial failure to destroy Iraq's mobile ballistic missile threat, Hussein's forces did not launch the maximum number of weapons on any given day. Most of the missile attacks occurred as single launches. At most, Iraqi forces lobbed six weapons within three minutes during the second week of Desert Storm. Iraqi SCUD crews conducted multiple missile salvos throughout the conflict. Many of these salvos included five to six ballistic missiles launched simultaneously against Israel or Saudi Arabia. Despite these salvos, the SCUDS could not overwhelm Patriot defenses or warning systems.

ANTI–BALLISTIC MISSILE DEFENSES BECOME OPERATIONAL

Allied commanders late in World War II were powerless to defend against V-2 attacks. Instead of providing a means to shoot down the V-2, they had to rely on ground forces to destroy German missile sites and support facilities. Eventually, ground operations that pushed Hitler's forces east eliminated the threat. During the cold war, scientists and engineers tried to develop an effective means to intercept an ICBM before it could deliver its nuclear cargo. An anti–ballistic missile (ABM) system had to detect, launch, and successfully intercept the incoming missile or warhead. This process took split-second timing to calculate an interception point and precision to destroy the enemy. Early in the cold war, computing power and precision were limited. Early ABM systems required nuclear devices to destroy ICBM components such as warheads.

By the 1980s, however, science and technology had advanced sufficiently to explore means to intercept missiles without a nuclear device. Computer hardware, software, radar, electronics, sensors, and a host of other devices allowed ABM systems to become more reliable, precise, and field mobile. Additionally, the fear of theater ballistic missiles used on the battlefield weighed on the minds of commanders. The United States and other nations had already solved many problems of developing surface-to-air missiles to destroy supersonic aircraft. Engineers and scientists turned their attention to the problem of creating a system that could do the same to theater ballistic missiles as they proliferated in Europe.

For the first time in warfare, military forces had the ability to intercept enemy missiles without the use of a nuclear warhead and under extreme time constraints. This breakthrough offered field commanders the ability to respond if they came under attack from theater WMD-armed weapons. Coalition forces were able to use the MIM-104 Patriot Air Defense System in an anti–theater ballistic missile (ATBM) defense role. Patriot missiles are seventeen feet long (over five meters) and weigh about 2,000 pounds (over 900 kilograms). The Raytheon Corporation designed and produced the Patriot originally to counter airborne threats flying from medium to high altitudes and flying no greater than 1,500 miles or 2,400 kilometers per hour. The Patriot could also handle aircraft or cruise missiles.

Engineers designed the Patriot to protect areas over a limited range. The U.S. Army deployed this ATBM system to defend point targets such as an airfield or headquarters, not an area target such as a population center. Radar coverage and limited range of the interceptor would force commanders to stretch missile coverage in wide areas. Unlike targets in Saudi Arabia, which has more land over which to disperse military forces, Israeli targets were concentrated densely. If a delivery vehicle did slip through Patriot defenses, damage would occur. Conversely, in Saudi Arabia, little damage would result from an errant missile due to the relative lack of urbanization.

Army commanders first fielded the Patriot in 1982. Patriot operations revolved around the workings of its lowest organizational structure, the battery. Each battery had a phased-array radar unit, control, and electrical power plant stations that monitored up to eight launchers with four missiles apiece. A Patriot battery would use its surveillance radar to first identify a target. If the target resembles a hostile aircraft or missile, a computer calculates a potential location given direction and speed of the radar image. The Patriot systems' computer, given other information about objects in the vicinity, then starts to track the target to gain information for an interceptor missile. If the target appears in the predicated location area, then a commander can decide to fire the interceptor missile. A Patriot crew could detect a SCUD or missile, in theater, about 4.5 minutes after its launch. Given that an Al-Husayn's total flight time was about seven minutes, crews had only a few minutes to react to incoming weapons. An Al-Husayn's warhead would hit the surface at speeds in excess of Mach 8 (about 5,300 miles, or 8,530 kilometers, per hour). Closing speeds for interception of the faster warhead with the much slower Patriot were a concern.

Patriot launch crews fired 158 interceptors at SCUDs and Al-Husayn missiles. There is much controversy over the interception rates for the Patriot. Some critics charge that the Patriot did little to counter the Iraqi missile threat. A U.S. General Accounting Office study measured the effectiveness of the Patriot to intercept warheads in the Persian Gulf as only 9 percent successful. Israeli officials were less charitable and claimed their batteries may not have hit any warheads. Some Patriots may have had difficulty distinguishing the warhead from the vehicle's fuselage once the RV separated. Al-Husayns also disintegrated in flight because of faulty welds or poor construction that created problems. However, the Patriot did boost the morale of populations under an attack. Stationing Patriots in Israel helped allay fears that Israel would strike Iraq, playing into Hussein's hands and destroying the coalition despite the missile's questionable operational capabilities.

Space assets greatly supplemented ATBM operations. The Patriot ATBM's phased-array radar unit could detect an incoming warhead, but it needed support. Patriot radar operators provided only general surveillance and target tracking for the interceptor missiles. If Iraqi missile crews launched several SCUDs or Al-Husayn vehicles, however, then the warheads, separated fuselages, or debris might deluge the Patriot radar crew. Missile defense operations would improve if intelligence or other sources could broadcast the information about an enemy launch to the Patriot crews instead of detecting the warhead as it was reentering the atmosphere. Reaction time would improve the interception analysis and the ability to decide to launch specific Patriots. The United States was able to use DSP satellites to first identify a missile launch from anywhere in Iraq. This process would include verification of the launch. Analysts would calculate where the launch originated and possible locations where the warhead would land. CENTCOM command and control elements had to authorize an interception, and then the Patriot crews would have to take action quickly. CENTCOM officials would also use the launch information to enable CENTAF to search for the TEL.

Operation Desert Storm demonstrated a major use of space assets. Space satellites allowed the coalition forces to increase their communications, intelligence, weather, navigation, and early warning. DSP satellites were originally not a part of the coalition's missile warning system. However, space experts had proposed using this resource to improve Patriot operations. Air force space operations personnel sought a way to demonstrate the value of timely, accurate information to military operations. These actions would become a key element in this operation and into the future. Providing more time to the Patriot's launch crews would aid interception by allowing the interceptor to catch an incoming SCUD or Al-Husayn earlier in flight. A Patriot battery could fire more than one ATBM weapon against a target if it were given more warning time.

The U.S. Air Force's Space Command had assigned three DSP satellites to help track ballistic missiles from western and southern Iraq. DSP satellites have an infrared telescope that can track the earth every ten seconds for a launch plume. Weather conditions such as clouds or humidity can slow down the detection. Once a missile broke through a cloudbank, if the weather was not clear, then the DSP satellite could detect the weapon. If a satellite detected a possible Iraqi launch plume, then data networks routed that information to a ground station and transmitted the information to a satellite control facility at Buckley Air National Guard Base near Denver, Colorado, and other stations in Europe. Analysts forwarded the information to the North American Aerospace Defense Command (NORAD) facility in the Cheyenne Mountain Complex near Colorado Springs.

NORAD was responsible for strategic missile warning to protect the United States and Canada and had the experienced staff and resources to analyze the satellite data to determine if the launch information was valid. NORAD officials also had to segregate the theater ballistic missile threat from its main objective of protecting the United States and Canada from an ICBM or SLBM attack. Despite the lack of Iraqi ICBM capability, an independent focus on national missile warning had to maintain a credible vigilance. Theater ballistic missile warning required specialized training and detection techniques. SCUD and Al-Husayn missiles had less powerful rocket engines than did ICBMs or SLBMs. These missiles produced a smaller, less intense infrared exhaust signature that burned in a shorter time than an ICBM and thus required much closer attention and specialized tracking in order to be detected and analyzed.

DSP operations allowed Patriot commanders extra time to prepare an interception. Although U.S. Air Force space operators did not have the training or equipment to handle theater ballistic missile warning, Operation Desert Storm allowed them the experience to improve warning time. At the beginning of operations, DSP warning time required over five and a half minutes from launch plume detection to warning in the field. Patriot surveillance radar would have already started to track the missile. Through training, improved communications, and streamlined processes, analysts reduced the warning time significantly, by two minutes. This extra time allowed the appropriate Patriot battery to prepare for launches instead of requiring all Patriot batteries to maintain constant surveillance, which would reduce combat effectiveness over time.

IRAQI BALLISTIC MISSILE OPERATIONS IN REVIEW

Saddam Hussein's efforts to break up the coalition over attacks on Israel failed. Unlike in the War of the Cities, a concentrated missile attack did not weaken the coalition's resolve. The Iraqi air force was unable to supplement attacks on Tel Aviv or Riyadh. Coalition air attacks destroyed launch sites and support infrastructure. The United States and other nations started a massive ground operation to push Iraqi forces out of Kuwait and parts of southern Iraq. This move pushed the SCUD launch crews out of range to attack many targets, like German V-2 crews in World War II. ATBM operations also allowed the coalition forces and regional populations to provide some protection from Iraqi missiles.

Iraqi missile operations provided valuable lessons for other regional powers. Ballistic missile operations provided a long-range power projection to strike outside the immediate battlefield. If the SCUDs or Al-Husayns had longer range and better guidance, then targets in Europe or other coalition nations would have come under fire, which could have affected their participation in the war. Similarly, if the Iraqis had armed the missiles with WMD, then the consequences of the war could have changed. A chemical or biological attack on Israel would have triggered a potential nuclear response from Israel or the United States. The war's character would have changed considerably. Despite the United States' advanced technological advantage in air, space, and missile defense capability, coalition air forces could not find and destroy Iraqi TELs. If the United States could not find TELs in a desert setting, then Washington might not easily find mobile ballistic missile units in mountainous or urban areas. Countries such as North Korea that possessed more and better missiles and TELs could provide a more difficult challenge to an opponent.

6

Ballistic Missile Proliferation

BALLISTIC MISSILES WILL CONTINUE to be a threat to many nations in the near future. Unlike during the cold war era, now many nations possess and others seek these types of weapons. This proliferation of ballistic missiles and WMDs has created an environment that can threaten the United States itself and its forces overseas. Nations that demonstrate hostility toward the United States or have elements within their territory that might take over these systems can create a very difficult situation not only for the United States but also for the rest of the international community. Although the United States and Russia have reduced their stock of ballistic missiles through international arms negotiations or obsolescence, other nations have sought these weapons out for their own security.

These countries may want to build these weapons for a number of reasons. Once built, they are alternatives to fielding large standing military forces and provide a source of national pride. Conversely, because few missile defenses are available to most nations, ballistic missiles can strike with relative impunity against a nation that might have a military advantage over a rival. Nations that once disputed borders with conventional forces can now deliver a strike against their neighbor's capital cities, much like Iran and Iraq in their War of the Cities, with the possibility of deploying a nuclear weapon. Over two dozen nations possess ballistic missiles, and more states are actively seeking such capability. Some are nuclear armed with ICBM capability, while others maintain Soviet-era SCUD theater weapons that are not immediate threats to anyone other than their neighbors. Missile technology has spread throughout the world through several means.

Ballistic missiles also cause concerns for nations that adopt them. Instead of creating a stable source of security, nations could create a destabilizing arms race. Fears of a rival gaining an advantage may spark a rush to develop delivery vehicles or precipitate a conflict. One country could decide to go to war before its foes complete their missile development. Additionally, this type of development is expensive. Although operating costs might be low, the development and acquisition of complete systems might be a heavy financial burden. The substitution of ballistic missiles for conventional forces may open a nation up to border conflicts, and the only way to respond to the conflict might be through a like response.

Ballistic missile acquisition could spawn international repercussions. Some nations might treat missile developers as rogue or pariah states. Other nations might not want to involve themselves with these countries politically, economically, or militarily. Missile deployment may escalate military actions. Instead of using diplomatic means to settle a problem, nations could revert to using military means, including WMD-armed missiles, to achieve an end. Countries faced with attrition or stalemate with their conventional forces might decide to stop the fighting, not continue it. Nations could use ballistic missile acquisition to signal that a more devastating destruction level is an option. Another nation similarly armed could retaliate.

At the end of World War II, the Soviet Union sought to improve the German V-2. This technology led to the SCUD, a relatively successful tactical battlefield weapon that Moscow provided to its allies. The most common ballistic missile type that has spread around the world is the SCUD or its many derivatives. After the breakup of the Soviet Union, nations inherited stocks of weapons that included the SCUD and longer-range missiles. The United States sold similar systems, in the form of such missiles as the Lance and Honest John. These weapons no longer possess nuclear warheads, nor have they proliferated like the SCUD. Unfortunately, while the Soviet Union could control components and systems between nations that purchased directly from it, other nations soon received the technology from others. Egypt, as the first Middle Eastern nation to acquire Soviet SCUDs, sold this technology or funded research from countries such as North Korea to improve their own economic or military condition. Once this information was released to them, North Korea and others prospered by developing a domestic production base that further spread ballistic missiles to other nations that already had similar Soviet systems or others that did not have these vehicles.

The United States and the Soviet Union needed over a decade of dedicated effort to design, build, and deploy ICBMs. Both nations had started construction of missiles using an evolutionary approach. They built theater-level weapons first and then proceeded to MRBMs, IRBMs, and eventually the construction of ICBMs. Today, the pace of development among nations wishing to develop IRBMs and ICBMs has accelerated at a greater rate than did the pioneering U.S. and Soviet efforts. Some of the advancement is undoubtedly

SS-8. Soviet ballistic missile development and deployment demonstrated its commitment to match and exceed American capabilities. This SS-8 on a May Day parade in Moscow allowed Soviet officials to showcase its growing nuclear capability in the Cold War. (Courtesy, Department of Defense)

due to technological advancements in several areas unrelated to missiles, such as microprocessors. Conversely, the lure of space has increased the desire to acquire space launch vehicles which require a booster to put them into orbit.

Few nations pose a direct threat to the United States or its regional interests. Some countries may possess only a small force of missiles, but armed with a WMD warhead, they could create a devastating impact on overseas U.S. military bases, key allied nations, and sensitive economic targets and have the potential to escalate a regional conflict into a global one. Still, some nations have the capability to strike directly against the United States. Russia still maintains an active ballistic missile force that has the range and payloads to deliver a nuclear weapon. Similarly, the People's Republic of China maintains a relatively small force of ICBMs that can provide a retaliatory strike against the United States. North Korea and Iran are seeking to develop a capability to strike targets outside Asia. North Korea has tested a ballistic missile that might have the range to hit Alaska or Hawaii. Slowing the development of ballistic missiles in countries like North Korea and Iran is a challenge for future national security issues. Direct diplomatic efforts, placement of economic sanctions, regional political pressure, and direct military action are all tools available to discourage these nations from developing a nuclear threat to the United States and the rest of the world. India and Pakistan do not pose a direct threat to the United States, but a nuclear confrontation between these nations could enflame a region involved heavily in religious conflict, terrorism, and other issues.

Understanding nations and their ballistic missile capabilities is a start to realizing the magnitude of the problem. Although many of these nations may not build many nuclear-armed vehicles, they can blackmail another state or simply deliver a nuclear weapon against a foe that has little means to defend itself against this type of weapon. To gain a better understanding about threats to the United States, one should review current American strategic nuclear forces in order to understand the size and capability of Washington's ICBM and SLBM forces.

U.S. BALLISTIC MISSILE FORCES

The United States maintains the most capable ballistic missile forces in the world. Despite reductions due to arms control and reduced threats from Russia, the nation still controls a sizeable arsenal of silo-based ICBMs and nuclear-powered ballistic missile submarines (SSBNs) with Trident-class SLBMs. These systems fall under the control of the U.S. Strategic Command (STRATCOM). STRATCOM, based at Offutt AFB, Nebraska, controls all of the air force's ICBMs and nuclear armed bomber force and the navy's SSBNs.

Peacekeeper launch. The Peacekeeper ICBM could carry up to 10 RVs and was the latest ICBM produced and deployed by the United States. Due to arms control reduction agreements, the Peacekeeper was removed from service. (Courtesy, U.S. Air Force)

Once controlled by SAC, a post–cold war reorganization by the air force dis-established SAC and created other commands. Today, the U.S. Air Force's Space Command is responsible for organizing, training, and equipping the ICBM force.

The air force plans to maintain a force of 500 Minuteman III ICBMs. Although a Minuteman III can carry these three RV MIRVs, they will carry a single warhead due to treaty limitations with Russia. Minuteman III has served the nation since June 1970. The United States continues to refurbish the system for continued operational life. The Minuteman III has a maximum speed of 24,150 kilometers per hour (15,000 miles) that can send the RV over 8,000 miles (about 12,800 kilometers). The United States' sole ICBM will be the Minuteman III. These weapons will deploy RVs with yields of about 375 kilotons. Crews operate Minuteman missiles at F. E. Warren AFB, Wyoming; Minot AFB, North Dakota; and Malmstrom AFB, Montana.

The air force is removing its newer, four-staged, Peacekeeper, which can deploy ten RVs, because of strategic arms control agreements. The air force may use the Peacekeeper as a space launch booster. The air force removed all operational Peacekeepers in October 2005. At the height of the cold war, the air force deployed 1,054 Minuteman and Titan ICBMs.

The U.S. Navy maintains a force of fourteen SSBNs. The SSBNs are located at Bangor, Washington, and King's Bay, Georgia. The Ohio-class SSBNs carry twenty-four SLBMs apiece. These SSBNs carry the Trident SLBM, which can deploy MIRVs. Four submarines carry the older Trident I C-4, which carries eight RVs with 100-kiloton yields, while the Trident II D-5 can carry eight RVs with yields ranging from 100 to 475 kilotons. Trident C-4 missiles have ranges approaching 7,412 kilometers (4,600 miles). D-5 SLBMs can cover 12,000 kilometers (7,440 miles). The navy has converted several of its Ohio-class SSBNs to cruise missile carriers. The navy will carry up to 384 SLBMs, but may deploy more RVs than the air force.

The U.S. Army operates some tactical ballistic missiles. The Army Tactical Missile System (ATACMS) has a range of 150 kilometers (ninety-three miles), but some submunitions can double the effective range. ATACMS can carry 275 antipersonnel and antimaterial bomblets or thirteen infrared guided antitank weapons. These missiles cannot carry a nuclear or other WMD warhead. The army has 830 ATACMS launchers in service.

NORTH KOREA: A GROWING THREAT TO THE UNITED STATES

Russia and China have the largest nuclear inventories that can destroy major portions of the United States. North Korea, however, currently seems to have the attention of most countries, including China, Russia, and the United States, as a source of regional instability. North Korea has maintained a highly militarized society dominated by a virtual dictatorship since the end of World War II. The nation relies heavily on international aid to feed its population while spending most of its resources on an army of one million men and women and other military programs.

North Korea's top leadership is motivated to build and sell ballistic missiles. The Pyongyang government's fears of American military actions have led it to consider developing weapons as a deterrent. If the North Koreans can create a viable threat, then they can strike many targets in their region if the United States makes an aggressive move. They could strike targets in Japan, South Korea, or other Asian or Pacific areas. North Korean officials also have parlayed their nuclear power development into weapons-grade material programs as a source of aid in the past. These actions have led neighboring countries to provide financial aid in order to divert these programs to more peaceful means. Their extensive ballistic missile research and development only make the threat more credible. The North Korean government has not moved toward dismantling its nuclear weapons programs.

Pyongyang does not require foreign assistance for its missile force. North Korean scientists and engineers are largely self-sufficient in designing and building components and complete systems. The North Korean government can gain valuable hard currency through selling not only illegal drugs and counterfeit currencies but also missile components and complete systems to a number of countries around the world. North Korean scientists, engineers, and technicians also aid nations that want to develop their own systems or modify their domestic versions of the SCUD. Iran and Pakistan have collaborated with North Korean sources to build their own indigenous delivery vehicles, which has led to missile developments for all three nations. North Korea's development of nuclear-capable missiles with Iran and Pakistan has allowed North Korea to expand its production base with new processes.

Pyongyang has kept a tight rein on all information about its society, economy, and government programs. Other nations know little about North Korea's ballistic missile programs except about some publicized sales and missile tests. Most of North Korea's missile production sites are located in underground facilities. International intelligence estimates believe that the North Korean production facilities can build from 100 to 150 SCUD-B and SCUD-C weapons a year. Longer-range systems that require multiple stages or more complicated guidance systems would take much longer and take more resources to produce.

North Korea now has the capability to develop SCUD clones and potentially an ICBM that can reach into the continental United States. Pyongyang

Minuteman launch key. Instantaneous launch capability allows ICBM launch crews to react to a national emergency. For years, Minuteman ICBM crews monitored control panels like this at launch control centers throughout the Midwest. (Courtesy, U.S. Air Force)

Ohio SSBN. Ohio-class SSBNs hold up to twenty-four Trident SLBMs. An internal pressure system allows SSBN crews to push the SLBM through a breakable inner hatch. Once the SLBM breaks the surface, the rocket motors will ignite. (Courtesy, U.S. Navy)

fields a force of SCUD-B and SCUD-C systems. By the 1990s, North Korea started to build its MRBM, the No Dong. Like the SCUD, launch crews use this road-mobile missile to hit targets more than about 1,300 kilometers (800 miles) away. This single-stage, liquid fueled vehicle puts all of South Korea and parts of Japan, including American military forces, under threat. The North Koreans probably have hundreds of SCUD and No Dong systems that can strike into South Korea at a minimum. Seoul is less than forty-eight kilometers (thirty miles) from the Demilitarized Zone with North Korea. SCUD and No Dong attacks against Seoul would provide a potent weapon, especially if the missiles contain chemical or nuclear warheads.

North Koreans tested a space launch vehicle, the Taepo Dong I, on August 31, 1998. North Korean engineers attempted to use this two-staged rocket to put a satellite into orbit but failed. The No Dong serves as the first stage and the SCUD-C serves as the second stage of the Taepo Dong family. A third-stage solid fueled motor failed to ignite, but the main space booster worked well. Japanese officials became alarmed when the Taepo Dong flew over its territory. The launch only heightened fears of North Korean nuclear weapon development.

The most troubling recent activities involving the North Korean ballistic missile program are its effort to develop an deploy an ICBM. If the Taepo Dong II were deployed, it could reach areas from India to parts of the continental United States. The missile has an alleged range of about 6,000 kilometers (3,700 miles), and so it could send a warhead of several hundred pounds throughout Northeast Asia. The Taepo Dong II is a more powerful two-staged liquid fueled system. One concern about this weapon is the increased range and potential to add a third stage that can expand its range to include all of the United States. If the North Koreans add a third stage to the Taepo Dong II, then it could have sufficient power to launch strikes on New York, Boston, or Washington.

Pyongyang's desire to obtain hard currency and increase its international influence can also lead the country to sell the longer-range Taepo Dong II to nations like Iran or Pakistan. An effective ICBM can also hold the United States hostage if conflict erupts on the Korean peninsula. If the United States intervenes in a Korean conflict, then North Korea might launch a retaliatory strike on a city like San Francisco or Kansas City. Although the North Korean Taepo Dong launch crews, in underground sites, may have only a few vehicles, they can deploy a WMD warhead.

North Korea has active nuclear, chemical, and biological weapons development programs. North Korea has claimed that it has produced weapons-grade plutonium that it can turn into a warhead for its Taepo Dong system. No one knows, however, how many, if any, nuclear devices North Korea has produced. The North Koreans have not tested any nuclear weapons, but they may have received outside assistance from countries such as Pakistan that successfully tested the weapon. Pyongyang has stockpiled chemical weapons like mustard gas and nerve agents that would create a significant threat, and biological weapons are also possible. North Korea might create these threats in a conventional laboratory.

The North Korean ballistic missile program provides the most significant threat to the United States and many nations in the region. North Korea has the capability and will to use such weapons if threatened. North Korea has maintained its people, economy, and military on a war footing since the 1952 Korean War ceasefire. Despite its failing economy, it has built a formidable arsenal.

IRAN: ANOTHER POWDER KEG IN THE MIDDLE EAST

Iran started acquiring and using ballistic missiles during its war with Iran in the 1980s. Since that period, Tehran has continued to develop and research ways to expand the range, reliability, and capability of its weapon programs. The Iranian military boasts the largest inventory of missiles in the Middle East, which includes deployed MRBMs and SRBMs in the hundreds. Iran has relied on a combination of nations to expand its program. North Korea, Russia, and China provided technical and production support for Iran's efforts. Like its counterpart, North Korea, Iran has expanded its missile delivery program and sought to develop WMD. Armed with a strong economy from oil revenues, Iran has the ability to purchase much of its development program with available hard currency from nations that might not want to deal with North Korea. This has allowed Iranian national and military leaders to purchase hundreds of systems and hire foreign nationals to gain technical support for Iran's WMD programs. Purchasing and building missiles provide an opportunity to transfer information among many countries, allowing a toxic mix of players willing to spread these types of weapons.

Economic resources, political desire, an educated population, and willing partners have allowed the Iranians to continue its domestic missile production since 1987. With its rival Iraq largely disarmed in 2003, Iran has the opportunity to realize its dream of spreading its brand of fundamental Islam throughout the Middle East. Ballistic missiles can provide Iran a means to threaten governments within the region or even farther to attain this objective. Iran's possession of a precision WMD delivery system can also menace Israel, a longtime foe. The Saudi monarchy, the secular Islamic government of Turkey, and Russia's continued war against Chechnya's Muslim rebels and contentions on Caspian Sea oil provide ample motivation for Iran to continue its development of these weapons as a national priority.

Currently, Iranian launch crews can launch short-range SCUD-Bs and SCUD-Cs and a Chinese derivative, the M-7. Iran has also experimented with its own Fateh-110 system. The North Koreans have sold their No Dong MRBM to Iran. This missile has become the Shabab III. Shabab III missiles have sufficient range to reach Israel, Saudi Arabia, Turkey, and southern Russia. On October 20, 2004, Iran conducted a test flight of a new version of the Shabab III called the Ghadr 101, or Shabab IIIA. Experts believe that Iran modified No Dongs to create the expanded-range Shababs. Iranian officials have also hinted that they have added a solid fueled second stage. The weapon has a 1,500-kilometer range (900 miles). Iranian officials had claimed earlier that the missile has a maximum range of 2,000 kilometers (about 1,200 miles). Iranian engineers are developing vehicles with greater ranges and increased warhead capabilities to include the Shabab IV and V. Tehran touts the Shabab IV as a space launch vehicle but is reportedly using components from the Soviet-era SS-4 and is supported by Russian scientists. If built, this vehicle may provide an ICBM capable of striking targets within Europe and Asia.

Iran has publicly stated that it wants to extend the Shabab family. Although Tehran has proclaimed that it plans to use an extended Shabab as a space launch vehicle, the Shabab can also be used as a long-range ballistic missile. If Iran conducts a space launch, then it can use this experience to develop technology to build an ICBM or IRBM. Besides allowing Tehran to orbit satellites, fielding an ICBM could threaten all of Europe and the United States. Undoubtedly, the close connection with North Korean ballistic missile developments would capitalize on Taepo Dong advancements. Iran has also shown interest in creating a solid fueled system that would provide it with a more reliable set of weapons. Iran could produce an ICBM by 2015.

SYRIA: A MIDDLE EASTERN QUESTION MARK

Despite years of attention toward and conflict with Lebanon, Israel, and their supporting terrorist groups, Syrian military forces have managed to maintain a missile capability. This force can deliver several hundred SCUD, FROG-7, and SS-21 missiles. Since Syria borders Israel, Syria does not need an MRBM or a better vehicle. Syria's failure to oust Israel from the Golan Heights and its relatively weak conventional military capability relative to Israel have fed speculation about Syria's potential use of WMD-armed ballistic missiles. These weapons would allow Syria to gain an asymmetric advantage over Israel in the initial stage of a conflict. Syria has actively pursued a chemical and biological weapons program and probably developed a chemical warhead for its military forces. Syria's chemical weapons include a stockpile of the nerve agents Sarin and Mustard.

Syrian military forces have fielded FROG-7s in 1971 and SCUD missiles since 1974. Although Syrian launch crews operate up to eighteen FROG-7 launchers, they pose little danger to Israeli cities or major military targets. Damascus can use twenty-six SCUD and eighteen SS-21 mobile launchers. These systems present the most immediate danger. Progressive SCUD improvements have increased range and accuracy. Syria has tried to purchase the SCUD-D. SCUD-D systems have a reported fifty-meter (165-foot) CEP based on a digital scene-matching device, like the Pershing II. These improvements have come at the cost of reduced payloads. If Syria uses chemical or biological weapons as terror weapons, then this reduced capability might not matter. These missiles only have to hit a large Israeli city to be effective. Syria has not tried to develop a nuclear weapon.

North Korea, Iran, Russia, and China have cooperated and supported Syria's research and production capacity in developing ballistic missiles. Syria has built SCUD missiles under license with help from North Korea and Iran. Syria's purported ties to international terrorism, hatred of Israel, and relationship with North Korea have attracted intense attention to all of its military efforts.

PAKISTAN'S NUCLEAR DILEMMA

Pakistan offers another challenge to the United States and the international community. For years, this Muslim country has had problems with its Hindu neighbor India over the control of Kashmir and other border areas. Since the separation between India and Pakistan in 1947, the two countries went to war in 1965 and 1971. Today both stand ready to fight another war. Religious extremists and other groups have conducted or supported an insurgency within India and Kashmir. Terrorists escaping from Afghanistan have settled among Pakistan's western border areas, resulting in a Pakistani crackdown on antigovernment factions. Domestic questions about the economy and political freedom have created more pressure within the country for change.

Today, Pakistan has a nuclear weapons capability and continues to seek ways to deliver its weapons toward India. Pakistan has chosen to build a nuclear weapon and delivery system not for international prestige, but in direct response to Indian military superiority. Most likely, Pakistan will build sufficient nuclear capability to counter only India, which translates to fielding only an MRBM or IRBM capability. India and Pakistan detonated nuclear devices in May 1998. Tensions increased with a mutual test of ballistic missiles in April 1999. Pakistani and Indian diplomats have attempted to defuse problems.

They have tried to negotiate the Kashmir issue and solve several long-standing problems. If the Pakistani government falls or takes a more radical turn, however, these measures might dissolve. Given centuries-old hatred between Muslim and Hindu factions, a nuclear armed Pakistan might risk a more deadly conflict with India or provide these systems or technology to more radical states. Given the poor Pakistani economy, Islamabad has to purchase nuclear and missile technology from countries such as North Korea. Unlike Iran or North Korea, Pakistan has focused on creating delivery vehicles aimed solely at India. These MRBM-class vehicles pose little direct threat to the United States. A nuclear war between Pakistan and India would, however, result in millions of deaths.

Pakistan has gained technology and support from North Korea and China. Islamabad has focused on two approaches for weapons development. North Korean support has led to liquid fueled systems based on the No Dong and Taepo Dong systems. Pakistani engineers launched the Ghauri I on April 6, 1998. Islamabad can attack many targets within India by launching the Ghauri I. The Pakistani government wanted to expand its potential nuclear reach, however, with a missile like the Taepo Dong, the Ghauri II. Pakistan first tested its Ghauri II–class MRBMs in April 1999 and has continued this effort. The Ghauri is in the same class as the No Dong. Similarly, the Pakistanis want to build a longer-range system based on the Taepo Dong.

Chinese technology and support have allowed Pakistan to explore solid fueled ballistic missile development. Pakistan flight tested its Shaheen I–class SRBM for the first time in April 1999, along with the Ghauri I missile that was based on China's programs. A newly designed vehicle, the Shaheen II, is a two-staged, solid fueled missile with a range of approximately 1,250 miles (2,000 kilometers). Pakistan has the capability to strike all of India with the Shaheen II. Pakistan can deploy its Shaheen with a road-mobile TEL. If the country can develop a multiple-staged weapon system, then it can build an ICBM-class vehicle.

INDIA: A GROWING REGIONAL POWER THAT WANTS TO GO GLOBAL

India also does not offer a significant direct threat to the United States. India has continued to build its ballistic missile force and has proven that it can develop a nuclear weapon. Unlike Pakistan, India has a vibrant space program that has allowed it to develop an ICBM capability. The main threat to India and thus its rationale for developing nuclear-capable weapons is Pakistan. Conflict with Pakistan over borders and alleged terrorists coming from Pakistan and creating homeland security issues for New Delhi have heightened concerns about problems between the two countries. India has developed a very robust missile and nuclear program to counter any Pakistani use of similar weapons. India's development of a retaliatory strike capability against Pakistan allows it to conduct potential military operations against Pakistan over a number of issues, including Kashmir.

Although India's main threat is Pakistan, it has a growing regional rival to its north, China. Like its problem with Pakistan, India has had border conflicts with China in the past. Potential problems with China, given Beijing's close relationship with Islamabad, have forced India to consider building missiles capable of striking not only west, but also north. As China improves its military capabilities and projects its power throughout Asia, India must also become concerned about the potential for conflict with Beijing. A nuclear-capable force can create sufficient pause to the Chinese to respect Indian sovereignty. These weapons also provide a visible symbol of India's growing regional and global image as a self-reliant, independent power. New Delhi can claim not to side with a particular camp, but can rather choose its own path in world events.

India has built several classes of weapons, from an SRBM to an ICBM. The Indian navy has also explored the development of an SLBM. Indian army forces can rely on the Prithvi-class weapon. This limited-range weapon is a conventionally armed missile that does not threaten either Pakistan or China. Indian military forces can launch the liquid fueled Prithvi I or II from a TEL. India has modified the Prithvi to a naval version, the Dhaush. The limited-range Prithvi forced New Delhi, in 1983, to seek a more capable solid fueled missile, the Agni.

Future Indian delivery vehicles will probably rely on the liquid fueled Agni class of vehicle. Intelligence sources believe these missiles are IRBMs or MRBMs. In the past, India has taken great strides in developing its ballistic missile programs without foreign assistance. The Agni missile series, however, uses technology from several sources. Given the increased economic strength of India, advancements in communications, computer hardware, modeling and simulations, software, and advanced materials have allowed New Delhi to build an advanced space launch vehicle. Indian government press releases have indicated that an ICBM, the Surya, is in development from India's efforts to produce a space launch vehicle. The Indian navy also is trying to field an SLBM, the Sagarika. These vehicles, with sufficient modification and time, can undoubtedly become an ICBM or IRBM. `

CHINA: THE FIERY DRAGON AWAKENS

Since the late 1970s, the communist Chinese government has sought to improve its economy and raise its status from a large but weak underdeveloped nation to a global power. China wants to improve its international and regional prestige, gain rapid economic growth, consolidate its nation under one flag to include Taiwan, and ensure its access to energy to feed its economy and populace. Economic advancement has allowed the country to improve its people's standard of living and has provided the financial and technical resources to improve its military. Instead of relying primarily on China's ground forces to protect the nation, Beijing has focused on additional improvements in its ballistic missile force, air force, and navy. China's ability to project power is limited given its lack of naval and long-range aircraft. Instead, China has expanded its capability to conduct precision strikes by building more missile systems. This ability to achieve power projection allows the government to demonstrate its growing global power but also deter other nations from making any perceived aggressive movements against it.

China, like other nations, started its ballistic missile program with SCUD technology and systems. Chinese military forces acquired Soviet SCUDs in the late 1950s. These short-range weapons allowed scientists and engineers to build a modified version of the SCUD, the DF-1. China produced a longer-range DF-2 in 1964. These battlefield systems allowed China's forces to threaten to use or employ these missiles against a number of bordering countries, notably Taiwan. However, the desire for global reach against other nations, including the United States, has led to gradual improvements in China's ballistic missile force.

Increasingly, China has provided technical assistance to a host of nations that want ballistic missiles. One can speculate why China has done so: perhaps to gain international influence, acquire more hard currency, aid foes of potential enemies, or ensure friendly relations to nations that contain needed resources such as oil. Much of this technical sales assistance has involved the Middle East, which includes Iran. Saudi Arabia has purchased about sixty DF-3 IRBMs from China. China has also aided Pakistan, Syria, Egypt, and North Korea in the past.

China's ballistic missile development has included both land-based and submarine-based systems. Chinese land-based systems have focused on mobile systems and building extensive underground silos. Protecting the few ICBM classes from a potential preemptive strike is important to China's ability to conduct a retaliatory capacity. Also troubling is the use of mobile missile systems. Chinese military officials viewing the 1991 Persian Gulf War were highly impressed with American precision attacks on Iraqi targets. Fear of having this capability used against their limited ballistic missile capability forced the Chinese to develop more underground facilities and TELs. Despite the extent and quality of the coalition attacks against Iraqi SCUD and Al-Husayn sites, TELs were able to operate. Still, Iraqi operations were limited by these attacks. If China used mobile nuclear ICBM or hardened silos, however, then its survival against an attack by American aircraft or ballistic missiles might allow for a nuclear response.

Chinese national leadership now relies on liquid fueled ICBMs based in silos. China's DF-4 (an IRBM) and the DF-5, two-stage, liquid fueled ballistic missiles have sufficient range to strike throughout Asia. The DF-5, a true ICBM with a five-megaton nuclear yield, can deploy its payload to any target within the continental United States. This weapon can also provide a potent capability to attack in reprisal for any perceived threat from Europe or Russia. Chinese scientists and engineers have sought ways to reduce the size of the nuclear payload and develop smaller, more numerous MIRV weapons with penaids. If successful, the Chinese could multiple their nuclear capability severalfold and complicate missile defense and warning efforts. The DF-5 has an estimated range of over 12,875 kilometers (8,000 miles). Chinese launch crews operate very few of these missiles, less than fifty.

The next generation of ballistic missile is China's DF-31 series. This solid fueled ICBM class is a road-mobile missile that will complicate potential targeting and destruction in case of a conflict. Road mobility allows China to create a survivable strategic deterrent against the United States or Russia. Observers have noted that the Chinese have tested the DF-31 with multiple RVs that include decoys that can target separate locations. This MIRV capability, with its reported road mobility, offers the Chinese the ability to reduce the number of deployed weapons. Beijing can use these resources to build other military systems while maintaining a potent nuclear capability against potential foes. Still, China faces many technical challenges to building an accurate guidance system and significant expense to deploy a MIRV system in a road-mobile or SLBM force. The DF-31 has a limited range of about 7,240 kilometers (4,500 miles). China also has experimented with an expanded-range DF-31, the DF-31A, that will increase its range to 11,260 kilometers (7,000 miles). China's military leaders have not deployed either missile.

China operates SLBMs. Chinese navy forces have a single Xia-class SSBN that operates twelve solid fueled JL-1s. The JL-1 has a limit of less than 2,000 kilometers (1,200 miles). These medium-range JL-1s, unless patrolling off shore to the United States, do not have sufficient range to hit the United States. However, China has continued to develop a longer-range JL-2 that is supposed to quadruple the range of the JL-1. This three-stage weapon will carry a single RV. The Chinese development of MIRV capability could turn these SLBMs into multiple RV carriers that create a much larger strategic force than the few SLBMs that China would probably field.

SRBMs are not a threat to American bases. However, China's desire to re-unify Taiwan under its control poses a different threat. Hundreds of conventional SRBMs can saturate Taiwanese military bases and key economic or political targets. These missiles avoid the international scrutiny of their longer-ranged, nuclear armed brethren. If the United States decides to aid Taiwan during an invasion by China, then American forces might not be able to defend Taiwan if the Chinese army uses hundreds of SRBMs. Chinese forces operate road-mobile SRBMs that can complicate efforts to search and destroy these TELs.

RUSSIA'S STRATEGIC BALLISTIC MISSILE FORCE

The Russian Federation continues to have the largest nuclear-armed ballistic missile force that threatens the United States. Russia has the only nuclear-capable force that could destroy this nation. The Russian nuclear force is a shadow of its former self, however. The Soviet Union dissolved in 1991, which reduced the need for some ballistic missiles; Belarus and Ukraine received some of the force. Economic problems, arms control treaties, old systems, failed missile programs, and other issues forced reductions in these weapons. Russia still possesses several hundred ICBMs and SLBMs, to threaten the United States. Russia maintains less than 500 ICBMs and about a dozen SSBNs that carry over 200 SLBMs. Like the United States, Russia does not field IRBM or MRBM systems due to arms control agreements. Russia has the technical capability, experience, production facilities, and desire to continue to expand and build new ICBMs. Russian military units still field a number of SRBMs, like the SCUD, that support battlefield operations.

Russia also faces a significant problem with its ICBM production base. When the Soviet Union dissolved, Ukraine became an independent nation. Ukraine's industrial east was the site for the former Soviet Union's ballistic missile production. As the Ukraine turns to the West and possible NATO membership, the Russians face problems finding a secure source for new and current weapon systems. This issue has forced Moscow to choose its new developments carefully and maintain its force with a limited source of spare parts and components.

Although the Russian Federation has deployed hundreds of silo-based and rail- and road-mobile missiles, it faces a more serious threat. The lack of funding has forced the Russian military to reduce security and protection of its ballistic missile force and nuclear material. This situation has raised questions about an accidental launch or loss of these types of vehicles to parties willing to make an unauthorized launch. Russia's past economic difficulties have created a situation where scientists and technicians with delivery vehicles and nuclear weapons can sell their services to other countries. Crime and corruption have led to charges of pilferage of nuclear materials at less secure facilities and have created problems as nations seek these materials to use as a nuclear or radiological weapon for ballistic missiles or delivery through other means. Poor economic conditions and the cost of maintaining an aging force have caused Russia to question the reliability and readiness of its missile force. As parts fail, Russia's maintenance crews and resources will have limited options to keep their missiles operational.

The Russian government is also wary of NATO expansion on Russia's European border. Russia's traditional fears of containment by potential enemies add to the concerns about maintaining a large ICBM and SLBM force. Like other nations in the post–cold war era, Russia wants to maintain an image of a global power and needs visible signs to illustrate this status, such as ICBMs and SLBMs. Given the expense of keeping a large conventional or a smaller ballistic missile force, Moscow must balance keeping a well-trained army to fight possible terrorists from Chechnya with sustaining its nuclear armed missile force.

Russia maintains a force of aging Soviet-era ICBMs. Eventually, these ICBMs will need replacement. Russia's Strategic Rocket Forces is forced to extend the life of older liquid fueled, silo-based RS-20 (named SS-18 "Satan" by NATO) and RS-18 (SS-19 "Stiletto") missiles. The Russian Strategic Rocket Forces also fields a few rail-mobile SS-24 Scalpel systems. The aging single-warhead RS-12M Topol (SS-25 "Sickle"), a three-staged, solid fueled, road-mobile system, is also being maintained as an operational system. Russia now fields the SS-27, a modification of the SS-25. This weapon has an interesting capability, the ability to use a maneuvering RV that can change its ballistic path. This ability has a tremendous effect on missile defense efforts. For example, a missile defense system might not be able to track an RV to intercept it. Predicting the SS-27's flight path is critical for early warning, tracking, targeting, and interception of a warhead.

Russia's submarine force maintains an SLBM force, but it has been in decline for years. Russian naval forces have shed ships and submarines to preserve a limited number of operating vessels. The Russian Pacific fleet maintains aged Delta III and IV submarines. Russia's SLBM fleet counts over a dozen boats, but it once deployed over sixty submarines. Even its most current submarine class, the Typhoon, has maintenance and training problems. Russia may decide to decommission the Typhoon. Poor maintenance and training programs are common among the Russian navy and submarine force. In August 2000, the Russian cruise missile submarine *Kursk* sank with all hands on board. Reduced SSBN patrols due to a lack of funds have brought into question the future of Russian SSBNs.

Russia's SLBM force operates from its Northern and Pacific fleets. Russia operates a combination of liquid and solid fueled ballistic missiles at sea. These weapons all have MIRV capability. They operate the RSM-50 Volna (SS-

N-18 "Stingray"), RSM-52 (SS-N-20 "Sturgeon"), and RSM-54 "Shetal (SS-N-23 "Skiff") systems. Russian navy officials have tried to improve their force by improving the SS-N-23 and a modified SS-27 Topol M solid fueled SLBM. Additionally, the Russian navy wants a new SSBN class to carry these new missiles and improve the navy's ability to increase its operational capability.

Russia's economic difficulties and aging of equipment have not slowed all efforts to improve the Strategic Rocket Forces. Russia's fears of having its ballistic missile force become obsolete have intensified since the United States' abrogation of the 1972 Anti–Ballistic Missile (ABM) Treaty. This treaty limited ABM development, testing, and deployment for the United States and the Soviet Union. Questions about the United States developing a limited ABM system, to counter accidental launchings or launchings by rogue states, have not dissuaded Moscow from trying to modernize its ballistic missiles and penaids to overcome the system and ensure Russia's vision of an effective nuclear force.

BALLISTIC MISSILE PROLIFERATION CONCERNS

After the Cuban Missile Crisis, the United States and the Soviet Union almost came to nuclear blows, but the two nations avoided a nuclear conflict. Later, throughout the cold war, both nations sought ways to reduce the potential for a nuclear conflict from an accidental launch and to reduce the ballistic missile and nuclear warhead inventory. Today, Russia and the United States still maintain a nuclear armed missile force, but more nations have nuclear capable forces. The United Kingdom and France field nuclear ballistic missiles that provide a deterrent against any nation attacking them. Other countries, such as Iran or North Korea, however, have questionable motives regarding their systems.

The United States and other nations can approach the proliferation of ballistic missiles with several options. Countries may voluntarily agree to arms control and disarmament measures to reduce the possibility of their use. Arms control advocates have a menu of approaches that include limiting the types of weapons, quality or particular operating capabilities, or when the weapons are used. Arms control agreements can allow parties to keep certain weapons or even increase some given the accord's specifics. Disarmament agreements can include many possibilities to reduce the number and types of weapons or eliminate them. Nations can also take a more active role in countering a missile expansion, building more weapons to survive an attack, or a state can develop a defensive capability. Building more weapon systems may provoke an uncontrolled arms race, and building a missile defense system may motivate a rival to build more weapons, but a missile defense system does offer a nation the chance to protect a particular site, whether it is a capital city or troops in the field. Recently, the explosion of SRBMs and development of potential ICBMs have focused much attention on national and tactical ballistic missile defense.

The United States and the Soviet Union largely used arms control to reduce certain capabilities and inventories. Arms control agreements recognized that both nations would continue to keep these weapons and not fundamentally change their relationship as adversaries. Washington and Moscow agreed to increase secure and rapid communications via the 1963 Hot-Line Agreement to reduce the threat of miscalculating a potential action that could lead to nuclear war. This agreement led to further agreements to limit nuclear testing, deployment of nuclear weapons and use in space, and other measures.

One key action was the 1972 Strategic Arms Limitation Treaty (SALT). SALT I was an agreement to impose some limits on land-based ballistic missile deployments, SLBMs, and ABMs (later a separate agreement). The SALT I agreement allowed the Soviet Union to expand its inventory to a certain ceiling, but the agreement did fix the number of weapons, which curbed the arms race from spiraling out of control. The Soviet Union could increase certain missile characteristics, however, such as MIRV capability and improved guidance systems. Still, arms control was the beginning for future negotiations. This led to agreements to make drastic cuts in nuclear weapons and ballistic missiles. Washington and Moscow signed the SALT II treaty in 1979, which laid the groundwork for more reductions. Other agreements, such as the December 1987 Intermediate-Range Nuclear Forces Treaty, allowed for the elimination of MRBM and IRBM forces in NATO and the Warsaw Pact.

Cold war arms control agreements allowed the nations to make some significant inroads toward reducing inventories. Elimination of weapons was in some cases secondary to the ability to negotiate with a rival and achieve some level of confidence with a potential adversary. Both the United States and the Soviet Union made agreements about a number of issues. Some success in arms control between the United States and the Soviet Union does not necessarily translate to success today. Nations that do not seek or are unwilling to abide by such treaties to reduce deployment or use of these weapons may make arms control measures obsolete. North Korea and Iran have continued to build chemical, biological, and nuclear weapons despite repeated international pressure and scrutiny.

North Korea and the United States signed a 1994 Agreed Framework to stop Pyongyang from producing nuclear fissile materials that could lead to nuclear weapons. This agreement allowed North Korea to close certain nuclear reactors in exchange for funding from the United States and other nations to build other reactors that would not produce weapons-grade plutonium. The United States allowed oil shipments to North Korea to ensure it an energy supply while the nuclear reactors were off line. The agreement called for substitute nuclear plants to be built that would not produce nuclear fissile materials. North Korea abrogated the treaty and claimed to have built several nuclear weapons. They want to reopen the closed nuclear plants. North Korea allows limited international contact within its borders, and so there is little certainty about this claim or others, including its ballistic missile force.

Arms control agreements with nations like those with North Korea may not work. In some cases, an agreement may provide false expectations and even allow countries like North Korea or Iran added time to develop their weapons programs. One method to limit their capability is to ensure those states do not receive economic or technical aid to further their proposed programs.

Agreements between nations do not have to limit missile systems or their capabilities just between the signatories. Countries may decide to limit certain actions with other nations that are not a party to these agreements. A state could decide, along with others, not to sell ballistic missile systems, components, or technology to third parties. A nonproliferation agreement can help stop the spread of certain weapons. The 1987 Missile Technology Control Regime (MTCR) tries to limit the spread or proliferation of missiles to countries. Unfortunately, in limiting certain technologies it is not easy to determine what solely affects ballistic missile development. For example, microchips that legitimate computer users could apply to industrial processes can also be used to miniaturize or improve guidance or other systems for ballistic missiles. Additionally, the 1987 MTCR tries to shape an environment that may change at any time. International relationships between countries can change rapidly. Since the 1987 MTCR signing, the Soviet Union is no longer a sovereign nation. New allies, economic demands, and other considerations may force a signatory to sell technology. Once an agreement has been breached, other nations may decide to sell technology, since another party may get the missile technology anyway. Still, signing such agreements may put international pressure on possible sellers of such weapons and build trust between parties.

Countries may not wish to depend on others for their security. These nations may use counterproliferation means to ensure their security by creating systems to defend themselves against a rival's ballistic missile force. These measures normally center on creating a defensive capability to reduce the effect of a ballistic missile attack. Defensive measures can include passive or active means. Passive measures might include building a civil defense system. These activities attempt to protect citizens and infrastructure from a nuclear

Delta III. The Soviet Navy copied the United States' SLBM introduction. While the U.S. Navy focused on solid fuel missiles, the Soviets choose liquid fuel missiles. Delta III class SLBMs continue to serve the Russian Federation's Navy. (Courtesy, U.S. Navy)

attack and include warning, mass evacuation, constructing shelters, making components impervious to the effects from a nuclear explosion, and other activities. Active defenses involve measures to defeat a missile attack by trying to disable or destroy the system in flight. ABM deployment is an example of an active defense. Military forces can try to shoot down a missile, as the United States did with Patriot vehicles during the 1991 Gulf War. Many of the active defense measures against missiles have centered on developing ABMs, directed energy weapons that are land based or airborne, and space defense efforts.

Active defense measures are the more contentious of the two types of actions. A nation may wish to develop a nuclear force to deter a nation from taking an aggressive stance. The presence of an effective ABM that might mute the deployment of a country's powerful, nuclear armed force might put pressure on a country to build even more missile systems and precipitate an arms race. An ABM's presence could thus send countries that have a delicate balance of power into a destabilized relationship that has broad implications for their region. Nations might build other types of weapons in lieu of a ballistic missile force, such as chemical or biological weapons, or might build up larger conventional forces. Likewise, a nation that has an effective ABM system to shield it against a ballistic missile attack might be emboldened to take an aggressive move. Since the opponent's missile force would not be an effective deterrent, a foe could launch an attack, especially if the nation with the missile force had relied primarily on those weapons for its defense. For example, two missile-armed countries might not attack one another for fear of retaliation. If one of those nations develops the capability to defeat significantly its foe's nuclear response with its ABM system, however, then that nation could feel confident enough to launch a preemptive nuclear strike.

ABM development falls under two categories: national and theater missile defenses. Most concerns focus on national missile defenses, which protect a country from nuclear devastation and thus help to ensure the country's survival. ABM systems that can neutralize a nuclear ballistic missile force can strike fear in countries that are trying to keep their weapon systems in parity. Conversely, tactical missile defenses that are emplaced to protect battlefield forces from conventionally armed missiles are not as contentious. Protecting large troop concentrations from such attacks or even attacks that may contain a WMD would not entirely disarm a nation like a national missile defense system. However, this determination is relative. One nation that uses SRBM or MRBM forces to threaten a neighbor might view the use of an effective ABM shield as a disarming move, forcing the nation to build more missile systems to overwhelm the defensive shield or attack its rival before the ABM system becomes effective.

There are three windows to intercept a ballistic missile in flight. An ABM system can try to destroy the missile just after launch in its boost phase, during the RV's midcourse phase, or in the terminal phase. A missile defense system does not have to be located near an enemy launch point. If a nation locates its defensive system near the launch point, however, then it can increase warning time and possibly its ability to intercept the missile. Some ATBM systems may intercept missiles effectively. Other systems, like a space-based or airborne laser or ship-based system located near the enemy launch site, could also be effective. In the midcourse phase, an ABM system could attempt to destroy the RV in its ballistic flight to its target. Many of today's ABM systems, like the Patriot, try to annihilate the RV while in flight. The final approach is to try to catch the RV after it has entered the atmosphere. This last chance effort is time sensitive and requires much detailed information for interception.

Countries can use many types of ABM weapons. They range from nuclear-tipped interceptors to kinetic energy vehicles that ram a warhead to obliterate it or a directed energy system. The United States and Russia possessed nuclear-tipped systems designed and built in the past. These nations had nuclear weapons to compensate for inaccurate guidance systems during the period. Advances in technology and issues such as concerns about high-altitude nuclear effects that would affect civilian and military activities made these systems questionable. Improved guidance allowed development of kinetic vehicles that could strike an RV directly. Countries made lasers, another science fiction dream, an operational reality. A directed energy weapon would heat portions of an RV to destroy critical components.

There are several limitations toward building an effective ABM shield. In the 1991 Persian Gulf War, the United States used the Patriot missile in an ATBM role. Questions about its effectiveness to track and intercept SCUD and Al-Husayn missiles created doubt about using tactical ballistic missiles. Technical issues about the ability to track and intercept many ballistic missiles, in a relatively short time, and their decoys dogged efforts to employ an effective ABM system. These ABMs used a number of nuclear effects (e.g., electromagnetic pulse, radiation, and blast) to damage the incoming RV. Unfortunately, using such weapons would also damage sensitive satellites in orbit and disrupt electronic systems on the ground and had the potential to spread radioactive material that would enter the atmosphere and land on the surface. Instead, ABM systems have evolved to use a kinetic system. A high-speed interceptor would ram the RV and obliterate it. Other systems could use an explosive device that creates fragments to damage the warhead.

ABM systems face a host of problems that involve penaids. A nation must first identify a valid launch and track the missile's launch point. Countries that have access to a dedicated on-orbit satellite warning system could provide sufficient warning and enable them to do this. Once identified, the warning system must distinguish where the RV is located to help with targeting the warhead. A nation could design a system that has electronic countermeasures that affect detection. Similarly, the warhead might contain decoys or imitations to the RV that could confuse a targeting system. The RV itself could use materials that reduce its detection to avoid targeting or delay its identification. Engineers could also devise means to deploy components and debris around the warhead so that it is difficult to detect. Finally, a country could design its ballistic missiles to dispense chaff or radar-reflective material around the RV to confuse satellite and ground radars by creating a massive radar image.

Once identified, the ABM system must quickly react to incoming RVs by launching interceptors. An enemy's ballistic missile force could overwhelm an ABM's interceptor force or targeting system by sending many weapons or having the system devote limited interceptors to decoys. Because the defending nation wants to ensure destruction of the incoming warheads, it might send several interceptors to destroy them. Depending on where the ABM intercepts the warheads—in boost, mid-course, or terminal phases—the ABM system might consist of a layered missile defense for both long-range and short-range interceptor capability to protect a certain area, like a major city.

Nations can also use airborne, space-based, or surface-based directed energy weapons. States can use directed energy weapons to destroy an incoming warhead at the speed of light. Normally, these weapons involve lasers that can engage multiple targets. Lasers may have a longer range than interceptor missiles. However, there are also some problems with using this type of ABM. Inclement weather, such as clouds and rain, can affect the operation of the laser. Directed energy weapons also require much energy to operate. Large chemical lasers may need huge quantities of fuel that can affect their mobility on airborne, spaceborne, or shipborne carriers. Stationary land-based systems could store sufficient fuel or use their own electrical power generation in terms of a nuclear reactor. Aiming lasers, getting sufficient power, forming the beam to proper shape, and other issues are difficult technical challenges to use against a fast-moving target. Technical challenges limit the ability to field operational systems. Adding lasers on space platforms may also force other countries to deploy weapons in space.

These systems are quite expensive. ABM design, development, testing, and production require years of effort and funds. Limited defense budgets may not allow the creation of an ABM and other vital programs. Once built, countries with offensive ballistic missiles would seek less expensive means to circumvent the ABM system. For example, maneuvering RVs, having more and better decoys, and saturating the defense by large missile salvos could overwhelm an ABM system. The continual improvement to missile defense requires a sustained effort to stay current with these countermeasures. Because tactical missiles have smaller payloads, tactical missile defense efforts are less prone to these problems than national defenses. Countries can still build many more and cheaper systems, such as the less capable SRBMs, instead of the larger, costlier ICBMs. For both tactical and national missile defense, there are difficult problems to overcome.

Today, the United States operates a host of ABM systems. America still operates the Patriot ATBM. It has sold this system to its allies. The U.S. Air Force has developed and experimented with an airborne chemical laser built on a modified Boeing 747 airframe. A shipborne missile interceptor is also in development that will allow destruction of a vehicle near its launch point, assuming it is from a coastal power, and great mobility like the airborne system. The United States has also decided to build a limited national missile defense. The system has interceptors located at Fort Greely in Alaska and Vandenberg AFB. This system uses a kinetic vehicle that will hit an RV in mid-course. The system protects the nations from countries that may posses a few missiles or from an accidental launch.

Building an effective ABM system would also expand a potential weapon against another lucrative target, satellites. Today satellites route much of the world's communications through low orbiting systems. RVs traveling to their targets share altitudes that approximate these orbital dimensions. If an ABM system can track an RV, then it might be able to target a satellite in a known, predictable orbit. A kinetic kill vehicle or laser could damage the relatively fragile satellite in orbit. With this capability, another arms race might occur that would include space control efforts to damage or destroy military and civilian space satellites.

7

Ballistic Missiles Reinvent National Strategy and Policy

WHY DID THE UNITED States develop a ballistic missile force? These weapons were intimately bound with the introduction and expansion of nuclear weapons and the growing cold war competition with the Soviet Union. As the Soviet Union became a military and political threat to the United States, Washington examined several ways to ensure that its national interests were met. Building a large and powerful ballistic missile force was an element of U.S. national security policy to provide a retaliatory force against the Soviet Union. This policy was based on deterrence; deterrence became an integral part of American foreign policy for decades to assure that the United States reached a level of stability in an apparently unstable nuclear world.

Deterrence was a goal for national survival for much of the cold war. This national security concept was quite different from the security measures that had been adopted before World War II. While the nation survived Pearl Harbor and the early days of Axis victories, the nation sought ways to mobilize and deploy a force to defeat Germany and Japan. The introduction of nuclear weapons changed everything. A single atomic bomb could destroy Washington, New York, or another major city in minutes. Fear of massive civilian casualties and destruction of whole cities caused the nation to seek ways to prevent such an occurrence. World War II had demonstrated the power of strategic bombardment, especially with atomic strikes on Hiroshima and Nagasaki. The Soviet Union soon developed a nuclear capability and seemed to have the political will to use it.

The concept of deterrence is simple. A nation or state can threaten another country with retaliation for an act, or it can prevent a foe from achieving an objective. For example, suppose a nation has the capability to launch a massive ballistic missile attack on another. The threatened country can simply state as its policy and build as its defense a credible force that promises to launch a punishing retaliatory attack. The nation that promises to conduct the counterattack makes the aggressor face a cost or risk greater than any benefit they would incur from launching an attack. Conversely, the state under threat could build a means to ensure any aggressive action taken by another would fail. A nation could have a ballistic missile aimed at its neighbor. If the neighbor creates an effective defense program to protect itself, then its rival's missiles might be rendered useless as a threat. Deterrence rests on the idea that national leaders see the logic of these arguments and create a stable environment. These national leaders must believe that their foes are rational and that they will realize the release of nuclear weapons would not result in an optimal solution. Nations would realize that any benefit of a nuclear attack was outweighed by its cost. Unfortunately, communications differences, values, internal issues, personalities, and other issues may affect rationality and thus interfere with deterrence.

A nation that wants to deter another country has several options. First, the defending country could retaliate against military targets after an attack, such as by striking ballistic missile or military bases. Second, national leaders can use counterforce capabilities to destroy another country's military capability to deny the aggressor the ability to strike. This would require a preemptive strike in most cases, however, and requires convincing evidence for a country to initiate. Third, nations could punish a transgressor by hitting more vulnerable targets that are not related to military capability, like a civilian population. This option, countervalue targeting, may create more damage to an aggressor than any initial attack on military capabilities and hold the aggressor hostage to massive destruction. Selecting any of these alternatives depends highly on the values of the opposing country and its leaders.

During the cold war, effective means to deter the Soviet Union's rapid employment of nuclear weapons amounted to punishment. Building offensive nuclear forces to counter Soviet ballistic missiles and bombers appeared odd to many. However, both countries would soon accept this tenuous stability created by mutual fear of nuclear destruction. Similarly, acquiring an effective defensive force to deny a foe's ability to use its bomber and missile force seems questionable. The cost, reliability, and technical feasibility of creating the capability to shoot down ballistic missiles proved unrealistic at the time. Protecting millions of individuals through evacuation or building underground shelters also appeared impractical. The only option available to the United States was to use punishment.

The United States used deterrence as a basis of its national policy along with its desire to contain the expansion of the Soviet Union. The combination of deterrence and containment of Moscow's expansion of global communism became the cornerstone of strategy. Ballistic missiles became a visible sign of deterrence theory. Developing, testing, and deploying more powerful weapon systems and maintaining a high level of readiness helped to expand the idea that the nation had the capability to conduct a nuclear retaliatory mission successfully. American foreign and military leaders also had to demonstrate their will to conduct operations. Highly observable and publicized actions to convince the Soviets that the nation had credibility also added to this image.

Post–World War II activities centered on military demobilization and a return to peace. The world and many nations had faced six years of global war, and most countries wanted to rebuild from devastation. The United States fortunately had escaped physical destruction, though it had suffered thousands of casualties. The nation had a nuclear monopoly in 1945 and the only potential ability to deliver the atomic bomb over long ranges. The Soviet Union had not appeared initially to be a threat to America; the Soviets had been allies in the defeat of Nazi Germany and had suffered millions of casualties. This relationship would quickly change as Josef Stalin started to expand the Soviet Union's sphere of influence in eastern Europe and continued to boast about spreading communism around the world.

THE UNITED STATES DEVELOPS A NUCLEAR POLICY

The United States' nuclear security blanket would soon unravel. By 1949, the Soviet Union had shattered the United States and the Western powers' idea of nuclear monopoly by exploding a test weapon in September. The Korean War erupted in 1950, and it demonstrated the Soviets and their communist allies were willing to confront openly the United States in an armed conflict. In 1953, the Soviets surprised the world by conducting a successful detonation of a thermonuclear, or hydrogen, bomb. Although the Soviets had an apparent nuclear arsenal, they did not have a means to deliver it.

Soviet weapons development was still a mystery to U.S. intelligence and military analysts. However, in their May Day 1954 celebrations, the Soviets had unveiled a new strategic bomber, the MYA-4 Bison. The Eisenhower administration started to take notice. Despite these events, the United States maintained its nuclear superiority. U.S. Air Force bomber bases had been built around the globe that could strike into the Soviet Union; long-range cruise missiles had the capability of delivering a nuclear payload; and a national air defense system that included surface-to-air missiles and interceptors was surfacing. If the nation had to conduct nuclear operations, it would prevail with SAC leading the retaliatory attack. However, a nuclear war would not be costless; millions would die, and physical destruction would be horrendous.

The nation could not stop the Soviets from building a large nuclear force. An arms race seemed inevitable between the two superpowers. Eisenhower had attempted to forestall an arms race with proposed international cooperation under the United Nations' auspices by December 1953. The policy floundered. Instead, Eisenhower's secretary of state, John Foster Dulles, argued that the nation should follow a deterrence policy dubbed "massive retaliation." Deterrence was based on creating the fear of a nuclear response to any strike on the United States or its allies. If the Soviet Union or its minions launched a military action, then the United States could unleash a larger and sustained nuclear attack that would destroy the nation. This stance allowed the United States to replace expensive conventional forces with a nuclear armed force of aircraft and a growing force of ballistic missiles. Unfortunately for deterrence advocates, credibility of massive retaliation was at issue. Would the United States actually launch a nuclear attack in response to a minor confrontation? As conventional forces declined, how would the nation fight minor scraps with the communists or others? Launching a nuclear confrontation against a small nation that crossed America also seemed out of proportion and would appear as if the nation were fighting an unjust war. Millions of casualties might occur; both military and innocent civilians would be killed.

The strategy of massive retaliation allowed the United States to provide a nuclear umbrella to western Europe, allowing it to base its military forces around the borders of the Soviet Union, especially in NATO and other countries. Instead of concentrating on protecting only the United States, Washington chose to extend deterrence to other nations. This approach allowed the United States to aid containment of the growing Soviet Union and its allies. If the Soviets or the Chinese decided to support another bloody Korea, then the United States would launch a nuclear attack at its choosing. Security was provided to NATO and other allies worldwide. However, officials started to question the strategy of massive retaliation. The United States could afford to use massive retaliation as a centerpiece, but it also depended on nuclear superiority and a viable force.

By the mid-1950s, the growing Soviet nuclear arsenal caused American national security experts to pause. Could the nation promise a massive retaliation but sustain a nuclear attack in return? Would the nation now put itself at nuclear risk if western Europe came under attack? Conversely, would western European countries want to be a nuclear target? SAC bomber forces were vulnerable to attack by being based in Europe, North Africa, and the Pacific. Perhaps other weapon delivery systems, like ballistic missiles that could launch at a few minutes' notice, were better. Strategic bombers and missiles might provide a more secure option to support the massive retaliation policy. Missile development proceeded.

Doctrine changed under the Kennedy administration. Military and diplomatic officials had raised credibility issues and moral concerns about unleashing nuclear weapons that had dogged massive retaliation as a national policy during the Eisenhower administration. The United States tried to inject more capability into the military by diversifying its military forces with more conventional forces and smaller-yield nuclear weapons under a policy called flexible response. Nuclear weapon release was possible, but would be used in response to a battlefield situation instead of striking into the heart of the United States or Soviet Union. Instead of relying largely on nuclear weapons and their delivery systems, the nation would adjust its response as appropriate to the situation. It was hoped that such a limited nuclear response would not expand to a larger-scale exchange of ICBMs. Still, the United States had to maintain its range of strategic options, and Kennedy had charged Eisenhower with allowing a "missile gap" to appear between the United States and the Soviet Union. Despite the expansion of conventional forces, Kennedy had to expand land-based ICBMs and maintain a modern SLBM fleet. The United States could still maintain a deterrent effect with all forces.

The country was secure, but the strategic calculus changed between the United States and the Soviet Union. Through the 1960s, Soviet engineers and scientists had perfected several ballistic missile technologies that the United States had experimented with: MIRVs, solid fueled propellants, and mobile launchers. Moscow was building more and improved missiles that seemed to overtake the United States. Washington started to fall from a position of nuclear superiority to one of inferiority. To maintain deterrence, the nation had to look at a new policy. How could Washington prevent Moscow from using its nuclear superiority to launch a preemptive nuclear attack? Soviet national leaders might believe that they could destroy the United States' nuclear capability in a quick, massive, surprise strike. If the Soviets could build an adequate defensive system that included ABMs, dispersing industry and populations, and other measures, then Moscow might win a nuclear war despite a weakened American military response.

MAD RULES NUCLEAR WEAPONS

In reaction to growing Soviet strength, the United States had to change strategies. How much the Soviets would be willing to suffer occupied the minds of strategic decision makers. Would Moscow risk losing 40 to 50 percent of its population if the United States could respond with a successful retaliatory attack? Robert McNamara pushed the concept of assured destruction: a few nuclear weapons would threaten to destroy a foe's highly valued targets if that foe initiated a nuclear attack. Although McNamara oversaw the expansion of the ballistic missile force under Kennedy, the process was expensive, and the flexible response doctrine required funds for a host of other systems and conventional forces. The Kennedy administration also had other priorities, which ranged from a lunar landing to social programs.

The United States soon refined its deterrence strategy to include the concept of mutually assured destruction (MAD). MAD could sustain strategic stability by creating the capability to launch a nuclear response that would destroy the Soviet Union. The counterforce strategy in place during the United States' nuclear superiority offered ample opportunity to destroy the limited number of targets that could strike the United States or its allies. Since the Soviets had not fully developed and dispersed a large number of ballistic missiles, submarines, and bomber bases, the United States could afford to limit its attacks to military targets. However, as the Soviet Union's nuclear arsenal expanded, the U.S. Air Force and U.S. Navy had a difficult time accomplishing its counterforce strategy. Trying to reduce significantly civilian or military targets in the United States became expensive and difficult. Older weapon systems, like the SAC bomber fleet, faced major challenges to deliver their nuclear cargoes in Soviet territory given the Soviet Union's expanded air defenses.

Despite a large force of ICBMs and SLBMs that would make air defenses irrelevant and the presence of relatively precise weapons delivery, problems were still apparent with the counterforce strategy. Titan II carried a nuclear RV that would deliver a yield of over nine megatons. Given the size of the blast and residual radiation, any nearby civilian areas would suffer casualties despite the best efforts to target only military areas. Soviet attacks against ballistic missile bases and SLBM facilities would similarly produce large amounts of collateral damage. Many ICBM and SLBM bases were located near major metropolitan areas that would only add to massive civilian casualties. Nuclear war would bring destruction to countervalue targets regardless of the original intent of destroying counterforce ones.

The assured destruction of civilian targets might be a way out of this dilemma. Holding hostage another nation by ensuring the destruction of a large number of military and civilian targets might deter the Soviets from launching nuclear weapons. The United States could use its existing ICBMs, SLBMs, and bombers without major modification or expense. It could destroy economic sites that would affect reconstruction or the nation's well-being. If both countries had the ability to destroy one another, then neither country would have any motivation to conduct a first strike. MAD would create strategic stability by allowing the fear of a second strike to deter a foe.

The United States maintained a policy of flexible response from the 1960s onward. The United States deployed and used military forces from simple humanitarian missions to open warfare. The Vietnam War involved the nation's military from the early 1960s to the fall of South Vietnam in 1975. During the heyday of military operations throughout the 1960s, the United States defense budget stripped funds from ballistic missile modifications and further development. The nation just maintained its ICBM force while the Soviet Union improved and expanded its ballistic missile force.

Existing ICBMs and SLBMs did not require precision guidance systems; they had to only deliver a large-yield nuclear weapon to achieve MAD. Such weapons would destroy large, unprotected areas. Hardened sites, like command and control centers or ICBM silos, might survive, but factories and residential areas would not. MAD allowed the nation to create a deterrent force that gave security through a change in ballistic missile use and technology. Building more nuclear weapons or delivery systems would not appreciably increase the value of MAD.

In the late 1960s, advanced technical developments involving ballistic missiles and strategic defenses started to worry Washington and Moscow. MIRV technology improvements allowed both countries to increase their nuclear capability without building more delivery vehicles. Operational ABM systems became possible as radar, computing, and guidance technologies matured. If the United States and the Soviet Union could deploy these systems, then one nation might be tempted to disarm the other with a nuclear strike and limit the damage from a second strike with an ABM shield. Arms control initiatives started to address these apparent destabilizing advancements. These actions culminated in the SALT I agreement in 1972 that limited the number of nuclear weapons possessed by each side.

MAD was not universally accepted. Fears arose in Washington circles that the Soviet Union might use the United States' pause to build more and better ballistic missiles. If successful, Moscow could develop a capability to limit damage to the Soviet Union and destroy any American nuclear retaliatory capability. MAD assumed that both sides would accept the concept that each nation would be so horrified at the potential for nuclear warfare and its results that they would not launch a nuclear attack. What if one state believed that nuclear warfare was winnable? Some Soviet military writers expressed the idea that a nuclear weapon was a viable option for a commander to use on the battlefield and, by extension, on a national level. If Warsaw Pact forces invaded NATO countries, then either side could use nuclear weapons. Soviet military commanders might throw tactical nuclear weapons at NATO forces to destroy major troop concentrations or air bases. In response, the Americans would release tactical nuclear weapons. Additionally, the United States' policy of protecting NATO members and other allies with a nuclear umbrella could extend to the launch of ICBM and SLBM forces. Even the idea of extending a nuclear umbrella was deemed questionable by America's allies. Would Washington knowingly risk nuclear destruction of Washington or Boston for London? The United Kingdom and France, despite their protection under the nuclear umbrella, opted to deploy their own nuclear forces, including ballistic missiles. Britain's experiment with Thor evolved into nuclear membership and the desire for an SLBM force. France took the same approach. The MAD concept started to unravel.

The United States adjusted its policies through the 1970s and the 1980s. Switching from a counterforce to countervalue strategy raised questions about targeting civilian populations. Killing millions of innocent civilians was abhorrent to many civilian and military leaders. Under President Richard M. Nixon, Secretary of Defense James Schlesinger greatly modified MAD. In January 1974, Schlesinger expanded the options that the president could use to include not only civilian population centers but also a return to counterforce targets. The Schlesinger Doctrine emphasized escalation control so that a nuclear exchange would not be automatic. Additionally, Schlesinger emphasized a range of alternatives that were capable of conducting global nuclear war to a limited exchange that would allow the survival of sufficient weapons to maintain a deterrent force against any further military attacks. Schlesinger advocated survivable nuclear forces, ICBM capability to rapidly change targeting, RVs that could penetrate hardened sites, and other missile improvements. Ballistic missile technologies, such as electronics and computer design, became more affordable, and technological advancements allowed the United States to improve accuracy and MIRV applications. The increased use of electronics and other technologies by commercial firms, together with consumer demand, stimulated advances in several technologies used in missile development.

Nuclear strategy changed in emphasis during the late 1970s under President Jimmy Carter. Carter believed that the United States maintained sufficient nuclear forces to deter any Soviet threat. However, Carter saw a "window of vulnerability" because Moscow's strategic weapon advancements would exceed those of Washington in the 1980s. Carter believed arms control agreements might reduce the threat to the nation by finding common ground with the Soviets. He unilaterally scrapped several strategic programs, including the B-1 bomber and other nuclear programs. Soviet political and military leaders took advantage of these conditions and expanded their strategic forces.

Many events forced change. A rapid Soviet military buildup, Moscow's invasion of Afghanistan, and expansion of military and diplomatic activities in Africa and other locations convinced Carter to modify national policy. Détente, a relaxation of tensions that started under Nixon's attempts at arms control and SALT I, was not working.

Carter abandoned the concept of MAD and increased defense budgets to include improving ballistic missiles. Carter's secretary of defense, Harold Brown, unveiled a new strategic concept, countervailing strategy, in 1980. This strategy would allow the United States to fight a protracted nuclear war that could endure for months. The nation would target top Soviet command centers to take aim at political and military leadership. This strategy expanded its targets to include nuclear, conventional military, leadership, communications, and economic areas. Some critics believed this countervailing strategy was an attempt to develop a strategy that would allow the United States to win a nuclear war.

REAGAN REVERSES AMERICA'S MILITARY DECLINE

By November 1980, a new mood swept Washington and the nation with the election of Ronald Reagan. Reagan would change the nature of nuclear strategy. Reagan believed that the United States should conduct relations with the Soviet Union from a position of strength, not vulnerability. Reagan authorized production of several strategic systems that would challenge previous nuclear policy. Reagan ordered the B-1 back into production and added military programs. He also used arms control. His arms control efforts initially centered on a phased mutual reduction in delivery systems, particularly ICBMs. Reagan believed that ICBMs were the most destabilizing element of the United States' and Soviet Union's inventories. To get the Soviet Union to make meaningful cuts, however, Reagan had to appear credible.

The Reagan administration's reversal of previous administrations' allowance of ballistic missile forces to atrophy was a key to getting the Soviets to make meaningful reductions. Reagan allowed the deployment of IRBMs and ground-launched cruise missiles, despite massive protests in Europe and domestic disagreement, which forced the Soviet Union to agree to the 1987 Intermediate-Range Nuclear Forces treaty that eliminated a whole class of ballistic missiles from both inventories. Reagan also allowed the new Peacekeeper ICBM and Trident SLBM development to flourish during his administration. Both weapon systems replaced older ones, giving the United States more capability to hit hardened targets and improved accuracy. Larger and more capable Ohio-class SSBNs that carried the Trident would become more survivable. The Soviets would have to negotiate new, more comprehensive arms control treaties.

Reagan also challenged the widely accepted concept that strategic defenses would be difficult to achieve. Although the nation had operated a single ABM system that defended the ICBM silos at Grand Forks AFB, North Dakota, that system was withdrawn by Nixon due to cost, technical concerns, and questions about the limited number of interceptors. That system was abandoned, but the Soviets continued to operate an active ABM site near Moscow. Given the lack of an effective ABM shield to protect its cities, the United States lay vulnerable and depended on its expanding retaliatory nuclear capability to achieve stability. The Reagan administration sought to deny the Soviets the ability to conduct a nuclear attack by proposing the Strategic Defense Initiative (SDI). SDI would include a combination of ground-based and space-based systems to intercept incoming ballistic missiles and warheads. SDI (also euphemistically called "Star Wars") was intended to protect the United States and render strategic-range missiles impotent.

SDI would include a massive investment in finding ways to intercept and destroy incoming ballistic missiles that ranged from interceptors, directed energy weapons, nuclear devices, and associated space support systems. The introduction of these systems would have violated several arms control agreements, such as the 1972 ABM treaty and its later revision in 1974. The Soviet government declared that the system was reckless and would destroy any sense of stability. If Washington could intercept their missiles, then the Soviets feared that the United States would contemplate a first-strike capability. Washington was not concerned solely about the growing Soviet ballistic missile threat, but also about a possible deployment of directed energy weapons in space. Although the Soviets had also tried to create an ABM system, they did not have the resources that the United States did to devote to the system.

By the late 1980s, the Soviet Union was crumbling. Despite a large nuclear ballistic missile force, the Soviet Union's military had significant problems ranging from obsolete equipment and poorly trained and equipped military personnel to a costly, attritional war in Afghanistan. Warsaw Pact countries yearned for more freedom and independence from the Soviet Union's control. New political leadership in Moscow under Mikhail Gorbachev started to open the once-closed Soviet Union to new political and economic initiatives. Moscow's economy was a failure, and it could not support its military. Gorbachev allowed a limited amount of free markets, which spread calls for new freedoms. After decades of supporting an archaic socialist economy, the Soviet Union was not capable of feeding its own people, nor could it compete with Western technological advances, except for military systems. SDI and

Reagan's military expansion forced Moscow to devote increasing resources from a constrained economy to a new arms race. These problems and other issues were too much for Gorbachev, despite his changes, and the Soviet Union eventually dissolved in 1991.

DETERRENCE SINCE THE COLD WAR

During the cold war, the United States and Soviet Union accepted deterrence and lived with a semblance of strategic stability. The application of deterrence policy evolved from massive retaliation, MAD, and Reagan's policies. Today, the United States and Russia have decreased their nuclear arsenals. However, other nations have improved and increased their ballistic missile forces. Could deterrence theory work with other nations to reduce the threat of a nuclear, biological, or chemical attack? During the War of the Cities between Iran and Iraq, neither side was concerned about the release of ballistic missiles on their capitals and other civilian targets. Fortunately, neither side released a chemical agent or other WMD.

Since the Soviet Union's demise, the United States tried to extend its policy of deterrence against nations that possess ballistic missiles. However, seeking a common deterrent policy against a rising number of nations proved difficult. The Clinton administration considered nuclear weapons and these delivery systems as waning instruments of military capability. Ballistic missiles were important to attaining a credible deterrent, but other military capabilities provided options.

President George W. Bush has reversed much deterrence policy by choosing another option, preemption. This policy allows the nation to launch a military attack if it believes that it is under imminent threat, thereby avoiding a devastating attack. Assuming that an imminent attack could be proven without doubt, the country could use a range of weapons against its foe. The fear of a potential nuclear strike might prevent the enemy from preparing or contemplating an attack. Building a large force of ballistic missiles might not only bring a country's leadership national pride but also signal a potential military action against it. Critics might argue that developing a preemption policy might force an enemy to attack early or hide its capability. Still, adding more uncertainty to a foe's calculation on the United States' reaction to a massive ballistic missile deployment or attack may cause a nation to pause and think.

The United States still faces several potential foes armed with ballistic missiles. Some nations, such as North Korea, may have only a few weapons but could strike a host of targets, from Asia to the United States. Regional powers that have missile forces that can strike American interests abroad may not pose a threat to a vital target in America but may hit a military base overseas

Pershing II launch. The Pershing II mobile ballistic missile provided an extremely accurate, long-range delivery system that could hit targets in western Soviet Union from Germany. This and other weapons were eliminated from Washington and Moscow's arsenal in the Intermediate-Range Nuclear Forces Treaty in 1987. (Courtesy, U.S. Army)

or a key ally. Before the end of the cold war, although many nations started building delivery vehicles with potential WMD capability, the United States' focus was squarely on the Soviet Union. After the cold war, countries with different national interests and motivations than the Soviet Union appeared as threats not necessarily to the existence of the United States but to U.S. regional interests. Russia and China maintain a nuclear strike capability that could conduct a significant attack directly on the United States. So far, deterrence strategies have worked with these nations.

The most important assumption about deterrence is the presence of rational actors. Is this assumption a valid one for nations like North Korea and Iran? Do national leaders act rationally, at least in the eyes of leadership, or do they have other motivations or influences acting upon them? One needs to consider why nations possess a ballistic missile inventory. The rationale for such a force can come from several avenues that include national defense, trying to establish a capability to bargain, a source of national pride, the desire to create a less expensive means of defense, and other reasons. Deterrence may not be as easy for the United States today compared to the era of the cold war. "Rational" leaders who fear their loss of position from an oppressed population are fueled by religious zeal, are influenced by historic hatred, or are motivated by some other rationale may not be deterred by the idea of a counterstrike of ballistic missiles. Deterrence policies that worked for Washington against the Soviet Union may find little in common against all the parties today that have these systems. Unfortunately, the number of nations that have the capability to launch an attack against the continental United States will grow.

Many nations today can use their ballistic missile force to counter American military strength in a region. These nations present a threat of massive damage against an ally, but little threat to America herself. Washington may not want to risk releasing ICBMs or SLBMs against a regional power. However, if a regional power has few vital targets within its borders or its leadership is willing to lose much of its population, then it could deter the United States by threatening to destroy a major American city with a single ICBM carrying a nuclear warhead. The nation with the less capable military force can now hold Washington hostage against taking action. Ballistic missiles have allowed nations that once relied on a policy of defense to switch to one of an offense. Offensive capabilities can allow countries to become more aggressive and bring nations closer to open warfare.

Other nations may be harder to evaluate, and discerning their nuclear strategy may be more difficult. Iran is led by a fundamentalist Islamic government. If Iran's motivation is to unify all of the Middle East under its brand of Islam and destroy Israel, then deterrence may not be an appropriate policy to attempt with Tehran. The Iranian government's motivation and incentive to develop nuclear-capable systems might not be solely to protect Iran against an attack.

Finding out why leaders want ballistic missiles may provide insight into the rationality of these leaders. The United States could then establish an appropriate strategy or policy that might influence a leader not to use a ballistic missile force except in self-defense. Unfortunately, Washington may not be able to maintain a single, all-encompassing deterrent policy as it did during the cold war, when it could concentrate its diplomatic and military efforts against a single player. The United States may face a more complex environment that calls for a set of individual policies crafted for particular cases. This will require blending a range of military, economic, diplomatic, and other means to reduce the chance of a ballistic missile release.

8

Ballistic Missiles and the Impact of Technology

BALLISTIC MISSILE OPERATIONS IN World War II were noticed by the Allied powers as a potential weapon. However, missile development by Washington languished for lack of funds and technical issues through the early 1950s. After the Soviet Union launched Sputnik on October 4, 1957, the United States rushed into a program to develop these weapons. Not only did the nation develop ICBMs, but it also developed commercial technology as a side benefit. Space development, electronics, and a host of civilian applications were created. Today, ballistic missiles still require specialized military development, but commercial technology can be used by nations that do not possess the capability to design delivery vehicles independently. Globalization and the availability of information by the Internet and other sources can make commercial technology and components widely available to purchasers. These developments have also made commercial technology and components a weapon to be used against the United States.

Weapon system development depends heavily on technology. Technology, the application of science or knowledge to overcome a problem, can result from a focused effort by design to solve a particular problem. Weapon development may be costly and time consuming because much of the necessary technology may be unknown and scientists might have to overcome many obstacles by solving complex problems. The arrival of new devices or weapons can require existing technology to solve a problem. This approach has an opposite evolution: commercial development or existing technology leads engineers to adopt it as a weapon. Frequently the emergence of technology has come as a surprise and military applications are then discovered. Today, ballistic missile development has elements of directed military technology and the application of available commercial products.

DOUBTS ABOUT BALLISTIC MISSILES

After World War II, the U.S. military believed it had a monopoly on atomic bombs and delivery systems. This advantage included not only the number of weapons, but also the technology that would enable the military to replicate and improve their capability. The U.S. economy had provided a great edge to the Allies in World War II by its massive industrial mobilization and undisturbed production of weapon programs. Military planners believed if the Soviet Union dared to attack the United States, Washington could replicate sufficient military capability to defeat the Soviets.

This attitude prevailed through 1950. Although the V-2 demonstrated the ballistic missile's technical feasibility, it still had its scientific critics. The field of guided missiles was in its infancy. Lack of technology to create guidance systems to ensure accuracy was an impediment to acceptance. German failure to send V-2s within miles of London echoed the criticism of many that future ballistic missiles would not hit their targets and was a waste of limited funds. Additionally, the missiles available in the 1940s were small. Scientific and engineering pitfalls regarding rocket propulsion systems seemed to limit their size and corresponding range. Dreams of an ICBM appeared limited to science fiction. Other concerns centered on the lifting capability of future missiles and its ability to carry and safely reenter a nuclear payload.

The basic technical feasibility of building a ballistic missile had been demonstrated, but scientists faced challenges to create more and improved technologies. A ballistic missile by itself does not constitute a weapon. The delivery vehicle is only a part of a system of components that has the objective of delivering a payload to a target. In this case, a nuclear weapon was the goal in the 1950s. Although the missile was a transportation system, it was a key element of the system. Within the missile are system components that need to operate together. Each component requires specialized technologies.

The story of ballistic missile development depended on several events and discoveries, many based on technology. For example, the U.S. government's assumption of having to use large nuclear weapons limited ballistic missile capability. Technical advancements in guidance technology, smaller nuclear weapon size, and the demonstrated ability to lift a large nuclear payload over intercontinental ranges were great enhancements. By 1950, Atomic Energy Commission's scientists had made lightweight nuclear weapons with improved yields. Other activities involved political events. The Soviets exploded an atomic bomb in 1949 that dashed the United States' nuclear monopoly and supported Moscow's claims that it was going to produce many nuclear weapons to challenge Washington. The Berlin Blockade and Korean War showed the determination of the Soviet Union to challenge the free world.

New technology involving electronics had evolved to make many of the components feasible for long-range missiles.

Ballistic missile development did not stop after 1945. Despite the technical challenges about its potential, missile development continued. Instead of a crash program, an evolutionary approach toward building missiles took place. A slow advancement from the single-stage V-2 to the larger three-engine-powered Atlas seemed possible. The United States and its air force had time to build a ballistic missile while the nation basked in its nuclear superiority. Similarly, the U.S. Air Force could reduce technical risk and save funds by this slower development effort. This technical development path could also allow the air force to await a firm requirement for the ICBM before it applied its efforts to build the vehicle.

The United States' land-based ballistic missile development was aided by many concurrent technological efforts. Cruise missile engine development, SRBM tactical missile advancement, nuclear weapon yield, miniaturization progress, and other related ventures slowly helped build technology for the ballistic missile. One aspect that further mobilized American science and technology was information coming from German scientists returning from the Soviet Union. Moscow had, at the end of the war, forced technical personnel to work on Soviet missile programs. Soviet military authorities had uprooted whole factories, components, and people to the east. Returning German scientists, after years of forced labor, claimed that the Soviets were concentrating on long-range ballistic missiles. These advancements created some concern among the missile research and development community in 1953. Within three years, after Sputnik, this concern would turn into panic.

NEW CONCEPTS FOR BALLISTIC MISSILE DEVELOPMENT

The U.S. Air Force and the U.S. Navy viewed ballistic missile development unlike the development of previous weapons. The air force and the navy had to ensure that a number of systems would operate to create a working nuclear delivery system. The height of a systems approach involved the navy's development of a nuclear-powered SSBN that enclosed a SLBM to transport it to a launch point. Similarly, technologies that involved communications, security, guidance, nuclear devices, and a host of systems needed design, research, development, production, and maintenance. These functions created special relationships that the services did not have to consider before. These relationships involved a wider list of participants, new management techniques, and a realization that a change in technology can significantly change a new weapon.

These complex systems depended on a host of technologies and scientific support that neither service controlled. Despite the presence of laboratories, test ranges, and arsenals, the air force and navy had to rely on private industrial contractors to develop many of the key technologies and components for missiles and other programs. Previous weapon development had relied on a single contractor, or the government conducted development and production at an arsenal or laboratory. The sheer size and reliance on new technologies that were unfamiliar to government agencies forced changes. Research and development organizations that focused on technology became prominent. The air force used the Western Development Division in Los Angeles, which later became the Ballistic Missile Division. The creation of these organizations centered on the growing aircraft and defense industry in California, especially around Los Angeles. The air force even encouraged private firms to enter the ballistic missile field. WDD air force officers also relied increasingly on contractor support to actively manage subcontractors and other activities for missile development.

Technical risks and development became a shared responsibility between government leaders, military officers, scientists, and contracting officials. All parties involved had to ensure adherence to multiple designs, production schedules, testing, and development. The air force and the navy used applications of organizational behavior, optimal planning techniques, and other techniques to maximize production while minimizing time and cost for these systems. The navy introduced its program evaluation and review technique (PERT) that revolutionized program management of large, complex acquisitions or activities. PERT allowed managers to find critical pathways, shift activities without loss of scheduled completion, and perform other actions. Applied science and technology were managed through a new lexicon of efficiency and effectiveness.

The reliance on contractors and schedules also forced air force and navy managers into tighter control over development. Scientists and engineers needed a more focused path to document changes in design to ensure accountability and to better track system failures for repair. Still, the rush to complete ballistic missiles, the size of the programs, and the complexity of integrating components created problems. In the early period of ICBM development, scientists and engineers in the Western Development Division attempted to meet schedules by building systems without adequate controls over technical and contractual matters. Development was slowed by mistakes in design and testing. Later efforts by Ballistic Missile Division personnel that instituted better program management oversight allowed for more control over activities, which reduced design flaws and cost overruns.

One of the most important technical changes that shaped ballistic missiles was not a deliberate air force or navy design. The Atomic Energy Commission's development of lighter nuclear weapons was an unforeseen technical advantage. Aside from Soviet fears of similar missile development, the reduction in weight of nuclear weapons energized the debate about the future of the ICBM. Building a huge missile was possible before this discovery, but the relatively heavy nuclear warhead would limit range or would force designers to build very accurate systems to put a much smaller nuclear yield on target. The unexpected technical advancement of reduced-size nuclear weapons allowed scientists to expand range while keeping a relatively large-yield weapon on the vehicle. Accuracy was not as important if the air force or navy could deliver a warhead that weighed less but delivered the same nuclear yield near the target. This unexpected discovery changed the face of ICBM and other weapons development.

The navy had attempted to push SLBM development in the mid-1950s. However, the relatively heavy nuclear warheads would force the use of large liquid fueled propellant ballistic missiles that made SLBMs problematic for safety and operational use in submarines. Instead, the smaller-yield nuclear weapons allowed a new missile technology to be considered, solid propellants. Solid propellant technology was in its infancy, but acquired a new emphasis. The air force, seeing the navy's success in solid fuels, encouraged its use on Minuteman.

Other ballistic missile concepts flourished. The navy accomplished the same mission as a larger land-based ICBM with its mobile SSBNs and multiple reentry vehicles (MRVs). MRVs could place several small RVs near a target to ensure its destruction. This development gave new muscle to the navy's fleet. An SLBM's MRV payload would spread out in a pattern, and it exploded on or around the target to create blast and heat effects that could provide an impact similar to that of a large warhead. Multiple RVs complicated enemy early warning and possible defensive measures. Additionally, scientists and engineers started to examine the possibility of using separate RVs against different targets. SLBMs also allowed the navy to hit targets deep within a nation. This capability allowed navy leadership to provide additional strategic options for the nation. Later air force ICBMs would also use this technology.

TECHNOLOGY AFFECTS DEFENSE PLANNING

Ballistic missiles provided a new way to strike an enemy quickly with relative precision and with few effective defenses. This type of delivery system caused profound changes in strategy. As with the atomic bomb, the United States had new weapon system that would force new changes to strategy and national policy. The advent of nuclear armed missiles raised many questions about how warfare would be conducted in the future. The horror of war, fighting face-to-face on a battlefield, would be replaced with "push-button" conflict that could ease the start of a war. Similarly, the technical nature of ballistic missiles and nuclear devices introduced more scientific and academic interest in the development of strategy. Military leaders, shaped by their World War II experience, had to accept single-use, unmanned weapons that had replaced manned aircraft systems as the primary delivery system of long-range strategic bombardment.

Some critics feared ballistic missiles would replace armies. Questions arose about how the nation could select a proper mix of forces. Washington could not afford to pay for all military forces. The rise of missiles allowed a change in defense planning; cost became a key ingredient to determining national strategy. Although questions arose about how many tanks, airplanes, and ships could be maintained with limited resources, this change in forces was a major transformation for the United States.

The nature of war had evolved from one of massive industrial production to one dominated by science and technology. One might argue that World War II had advanced science and technology so that they became an integral part of warfare. Germany had introduced the V-2, radar was used for the first time, and the atomic bomb was used in combat. The United States' industrial base and unscathed economy allowed it to produce large amounts of war materials for the Allies. The Americans and Allies used massed forces to deliver bombing raids over Berlin and Tokyo. Ground forces slowly advanced onto the Normandy beaches or the Pacific islands to capture the enemy's capitals. Now, the nation did not have to expend as many resources, nor did an attack require the time to mobilize or conduct operations. If nuclear armed ballistic missiles had to be used, then the nature of war would change. No longer could nations afford to mobilize, fight, and reconstruct the country after the conflict. Nations had to fight a war with whatever resources they had before the war. Nuclear weapons could destroy all means of industrial and economic activities within the country within minutes.

The destruction from nuclear weapons might include massive civilian casualties. Fear of many casualties or great destruction might stop potential aggressors from using these weapons; in effect, weapons would be built that would never be used except as a threat to intimidate foes. National leaders could point to chemical weapons as an example. Chemical weapons were used extensively in World War I. Their horror, forever etched in the minds of national leaders, provided a deterrent against their use in World War II. Nations were afraid to use poison gas or other chemicals in combat for fear of retaliation. Nuclear weapons could provide the same deterrent.

The United States still had reasons to develop nuclear weapons. These in-

cluded moves to replace expensive conventional forces with less expensive nuclear ones; air force objectives to demonstrate the power of strategic bombardment and its future as a separate service from the army; and use as an
insurance policy against the rising Soviet Union. After World War II, ballistic
missiles were a mere idea for scientists to tinker with. These vehicles would
have to compete with an air force dominated by bomber pilots, limited budgets, and some organizational resistance to new weapons. Manned bombers
could deliver nuclear bombs and were the mainstay of American strategic projection. This was demonstrated twice in August 1945 over Japan. Still, ballistic missiles offered new ways to think about warfare. Instant reaction, speed
of delivery, ability to penetrate defenses, and low maintenance cost forced the
nation to consider many questions. Bombers, due to their limited range and
vulnerability to air defenses and attack, were forced to share their role of providing nuclear forces in the United States. SAC bombers, while they offered
relatively fast nuclear reaction, were subject to enemy bombardment or were
at the mercy of foreign approval for use on foreign bases. American strategic
bombers, due to their vulnerable location on overseas bases, were forced back
to the continental United States. Bombers appeared capable of attacking their
targets at a snail's pace relative to an ICBM despite aerial refueling, ability to
recall and change targets, bomber dispersion, and hardened hangars.

Civilian scientists, academics, and firms became the focal point for creating new capabilities. Scientists and engineers created ICBMs with an extensive and methodical improvement program on existing technology and
advancements. Civilians occupied key roles in the design, development, production, use, and strategy of ballistic missiles. Military officers had to share
their once exclusive realm with many.

Ballistic missiles and nuclear weapons forced the top minds in the nation
to focus on the use of these weapons. The military had dropped the atomic
bomb, but the larger-sized nuclear yields and ballistic missiles pushed uniformed and civilian strategists to consider strategies to use these systems.
American military officers had never used ballistic missiles in any extensive
role, especially missiles with intercontinental or nuclear capabilities. The debate on nuclear weapons became complicated after the Soviet Union attained
similar capabilities. Organizations like the think tank RAND Corporation
began to study complex problems that faced the nation, which included ballistic missiles. At first, RAND examined technical issues and later advanced to
other issues. RAND was instrumental in using rational techniques to select
weapons such as systems analysis to compare options and solve problems.
RAND analysts viewed ballistic missiles as an effective, less costly option to
defend the nation as technical issues were solved. Still, systems analysis could
not actually predict cost growth on untested technology. RAND did evaluate

why ballistic missiles were a viable solution, but scientists and academics also commented on how to use the missiles.

Systems analysis started to make inroads into strategy development. Military and civilian strategists had to compare competing options to meet common objectives. A rational system to compare different weapons became a key component in justifying them to a cost-conscious government and public. Money, time, and technological advances became more intertwined with strategy development. Although RAND and other similar think tanks examined weapons concepts, the birth of systems analysis fundamentally changed weapons development and opened the once-closed world of military strategy to new eyes, those of scientists and engineers. Systems analysis and comparisons of dissimilar weapons and strategies became the norm for weapons use and budgetary comparisons of systems.

As new technologies developed, Washington had to devise ways to incorporate them into a strategy. Solid fuel propulsion, MIRV advances, greater accuracy, ABM development, and other new devices added capabilities and challenges to the strategic environment for the United States and the Soviet Union. During the 1960s and through the 1970s, computer and electronics technology greatly expanded in depth and scope. Information was processed at the speed of light, allowing a ballistic missile guidance system to store data and improve its performance by correcting and improving its RV delivery. Launch crews could make targeting changes quickly, giving the nation more flexibility to react to an unexpected attack. Radar and computer advances created conditions where ABM systems could make the detailed tracking processes and discrimination of RVs and their decoys possible to intercept ballistic missiles and their nuclear cargoes. These technological advances forced the United States and Soviet Union to change their national strategies. Arms control, nuclear strategy, and relations between the nations evolved as the United States developed many new advances, some produced specifically for ballistic missiles and others adapted for other military uses.

SPACE: A NEW FRONTIER

Ballistic missile requirements changed many other technologies that would affect the future of key capabilities. National leaders required rapid, accurate, and global information to detect, decide, communicate, and execute a retaliatory response to an attack by the Soviet Union. Using ground-based radars located around the Soviet Union's periphery might be time consuming and was limited to locations that might not detect a launch against the United States. Space-based early warning detection systems, communications, and other intelligence gathering systems were devised and deployed for the strategic nuclear force. The United States' desire to push manned and unmanned space programs demanded new capabilities to lift objects into orbit, especially after Sputnik and later when Moscow sent a man into orbit. Large booster systems that could deliver relatively large nuclear payloads thousands of miles away could also send a satellite or manned space capsule into orbit. Thor, Atlas, and Titan were only a few of the missiles that evolved from a weapons delivery system into a space booster system. These advances allowed the nation to venture into a new environment, space.

Missile development fired the imagination among individuals to look beyond the skies. Although scientists, engineers, visionaries, and the public dreamed about space travel, early rockets were too small and incapable to reach outside the atmosphere. Before and after World War II, people's interest spiked about the possibilities of expanded space exploration. During the 1920s and 1930s, rocket technology was immature and space travel was only a dream. After 1945, the V-2 and other German rocket designs had indicated the possibility of advancing space travel. However, federal government budget cuts reduced American dreams of an active space program at the time.

The only practical avenue for United States space interests seemed to involve the U.S. Air Force. The service had a dedicated budget, albeit a small one, to explore rocketry and potential military satellites. RAND had already completed several studies on the feasibility of orbiting satellites. The studies indicated that satellites would also provide a valuable military service. RAND envisioned the use of satellites to provide surveillance and other activities, like weather reporting, for the nation. The United States had an apparent nuclear monopoly over the Soviet Union in the late 1940s, but this advantage started to erode by the 1950s. Demands for accurate intelligence about the Soviet Union led to calls for new ways to gather information to gauge Soviet efforts and activities. Without precise intelligence data, the nation could face total destruction if the Soviets launched a surprise nuclear attack. Nuclear strategic forces required precise target information and early warning; space satellites gave the United States almost unfettered capability without fear of being shot down.

The burgeoning ICBM and missile programs provided scientific, technical, and industrial support for space activities. The U.S. Air Force's Western Development Division would develop both ballistic missiles and the service's initial space efforts. Space launch booster capability was tied directly to missile advancements. Many activities became linked, such as the establishment of missile launch and test centers at Cape Canaveral and Vandenberg AFB. Military space activities also led to a host of technological innovations that would in turn lead to communication, information, weather, navigation, and other civilian uses.

Technology to support ballistic missile and space activities became intertwined. Space satellites' requirements to support the burgeoning missile developments created the opportunity to expand on existing technologies. For example, ballistic missiles designed to lift a certain payload might not be able to put an astronaut into orbit. The capsule and extensive life support system might need a larger booster. Air force and civilian scientists and engineers started to build larger space boosters from existing missiles. The National Aeronautics and Space Administration (NASA) began a relationship with U.S. Air Force missile and space experts in their quest to develop a manned space program and other projects, such as planetary exploration.

Military and civilian advanced technology was shared by several common threads. Experts shared propulsion, fuel, electronic, and other technical activities in the scientific community. Space created another opportunity for the air force. While ballistic missiles extended the speed and range of strategic bombardment, space offered other incentives. Like ICBMs, space was a new mission for the air force and other services. Spacecraft allowed the service to fly faster, farther, and higher, themes air force officials would appreciate. Early air force space efforts included missions to support terrestrial activities but also extend several traditional ones above the atmosphere. Manned air force space efforts would later include designs for a manned orbiting laboratory that could be used for intelligence gathering and a pre–space shuttle orbiting vehicle, like the X-20 Dyna-Soar. These opportunities could lead to a host of military missions from antisatellite to strategic bombardment operations. Unfortunately for the air force, technical and cost issues stopped many early space programs.

Today, space technology has grown into its own expanding field. Ballistic missile technology provided the basis for present and future space activities. Now, the two operations have matured sufficiently to allow many independent paths of development. Space activities would have had a difficult road to follow, however, without the initial advances in ballistic missile propulsion and the requirement to support particular functions to protect and warn from a surprise Soviet nuclear attack.

BALLISTIC MISSILES, TECHNOLOGY, AND CHANGES TO ORGANIZATION

The rise of ballistic missiles provided new missions and roles for the U.S. Air Force and U.S. Navy. Government leaders and military officers that once understood the application of force, from World War II, were now faced with new challenges that they barely could comprehend. Service components that did not have a visible or important role now took center stage in the development of American strategic military power. The air force expanded its role of strategic bombardment to include the possibility of offering the nation a means to end an entire conflict through strategic-range missiles. The navy extended its reach from the blue water and littoral zones to the heartlands of continents. Both the air force and navy expanded their influence and prestige against the once-preeminent army as the primary guardians of the American security.

By the end of 1945, demobilization among the services had forced active competition among them for limited budget authority. Each service sought ways to preserve its organization's roles and missions. As nuclear weapons became the Eisenhower administration's tools to economize and secure military capability, each service sought ways to include these weapons into its force structure. Army units created cannons capable of firing nuclear armed shells and single-crewed rockets. The air force concentrated on manned bombers, cruise missiles, and ballistic missiles. Naval leaders advocated nuclear armed carrier aircraft and cruise and ballistic missile armed submarines. New programs in the 1950s normally had to have some connection to fighting a nuclear conflict to survive budget hearings.

The U.S. Air Force, and its predecessor the AAF, debated its future before the advent of nuclear weapons. Air force leadership pondered the question about the proper role of air power. Many air force officers extolled the role of strategic bombardment that, according to their claims, significantly degraded German and Japanese military capability. Others disputed the claim and argued that a more effective role of air power was in support of ground forces rather than strategic bombing. As the nuclear weapon became the primary means of achieving security, SAC's strategic bombardment role rose to prominence. Even tactical aircraft absorbed a limited nuclear mission to fight on a battlefield. The traditional fighter pilot was fast becoming a nuclear weapons deliveryman, an SAC appendage. As the air force developed and deployed ballistic missiles into SAC, the role of strategic bombardment advanced further, and a gap between it and tactical air power widened. This difference would create a shortage of tactical aircraft during the Vietnam War.

Ballistic missiles provided SAC another avenue to cement its position as the dominant provider of firepower within the U.S. Air Force and for the nation. Early SAC IRBM and ICBM advocates were met with skepticism by the bomber pilot–dominated SAC leadership. The Atlas, Thor, and early Titan had a host of operational deficiencies and readiness concerns. As second-generation Titan and the new solid fueled Minuteman systems overcame many of these concerns to become operational, they gave the air force a greater nuclear capability than strategic bombers in terms of speed, readiness, and destructiveness.

Soviet air defenses improved greatly through the 1960s, and questions arose about the viability of bomber survival. SAC had acquired a string of strategic bombers through the early cold war. SAC had its B-52, but it too seemed vulnerable to modern Soviet advanced radar and surface-to-air missiles. Air force bomber development also became erratic. Several bomber programs were canceled or curtailed due to cost and technical concerns. During the Vietnam War, SAC B-52 units were pressed into service to conduct conventional bombing missions over Southeast Asia. Although SAC commanders protested the diversion from their strategic nuclear deterrent mission, B-52s operated from 1965 to 1973. Bombers were losing their clout and SAC had to rely on ICBMs to carry more of the nuclear retaliatory burden.

The United States came to rely on ballistic missiles for the majority of its land-based strategic nuclear deterrence. The weapons' low operating cost and high degree of readiness convinced advocates to move them from a position that supplemented the manned bomber to one of arguable preeminence. SAC was still ruled by the bomber pilot, but the influence of missiles within the organization grew. SAC flying officers sought opportunities to command ballistic missile units. ICBMs and events transformed the U.S. Air Force into a more technologically focused organization.

The U.S. Navy, as an organization, had different impacts on its structure as SLBMs entered its inventory. At the end of World War II, the U.S. Navy ruled supreme over the seas. Naval leaders had seen the power of surface and air actions on the outcome of the war in the Pacific and Atlantic. Submarines had played a major role by isolating the Japanese home islands from critical resources, but they were largely unseen as the "silent service." German U-boats, effective early in the war, had turned from the hunter to the hunted after the U.S. Navy developed effective countermeasures. Battleship and aircraft carrier officers controlled the navy. The navy became the expeditionary force for the nation and used its combined aircraft carrier, surface fleet, and Marine Corps amphibious forces to conduct global expeditionary operations. Despite increasing challenges by the Soviet navy, the American forces had an almost insurmountable lead in weapons capability, strategy, bases, experience, leadership, and support to conduct operations. SLBM operations provided a foot into strategic nuclear operations, but the U.S. Navy did not want the new capability to challenge its traditional naval role, sea control.

Ballistic missile developments had an effect on the navy, but not to the extent that they had on the air force. Despite their new ability to strike deep against a foe, surface and naval aviation communities continued to control the service and dominate its operation. Control of the seas was still the service's desired primary mission. Surface, submarine, and aircraft carrier forces also had to contend with the growing Soviet navy that challenged the Americans through the cold war as Moscow sought ways to expand in the Atlantic, Mediterranean, Indian, and Pacific areas.

Still, the U.S. Navy strove to develop its capability to attack the enemy in other ways. Nuclear propulsion offered a way to reduce support requirements and expand the operating range for its surface vessels and submarines. Nuclear powered vessels could operate for relatively long periods of time; the only constraints were the human crews and logistics. This capability would allow the navy to operate at sea for longer deployments to contain the Soviets. Early experiments with submarines showed great promise. SLBMs provided a major motive to support nuclear propulsion. Submarines could stay underway without fuel replenishment, which would allow them to stay at sea undetected. Additionally, SSBNs would continue on patrol for unprecedented long periods that could reduce any logistical requirements. SSBN development demonstrated that nuclear propulsion safety and operation could be applied further to surface ships and aircraft carriers. This achievement revolutionized naval warfare.

Nuclear strike capability also allowed the navy to get funding and keep at least the submarine industry in operation. Organizational survival in the late 1950s helped push the development of the Polaris SLBM and a stake in the nation's nuclear retaliatory forces. During the early 1960s, the Kennedy administration's emphasis was a flexible response and a balanced force. The combined conventional and nuclear naval forces allowed the service to strike literally from land, sea, and air against a host of targets in the cold war. This capability provided a mix of war fighting elements that could support this new strategy. Unlike the air force's concentration on strategic bombardment, the navy was able to use technology to not only extend its primary goal of sea control but also extend its mission in other directions. This allowed the navy to adapt from one strategy to another throughout the cold war and beyond.

The air force and the navy had changed their organizational structure, mission, and force structure with the rise of ballistic missiles. These systems enabled the services to seek new abilities that changed the nature of warfare and the nation's security policies. New technologies today have forced countries to seek new capabilities to attain their national interests much like the United States in the 1950s. How nations deal with these issues can seriously affect not only how they organize and fight wars, but also how the United States will develop and use future weapons against them.

BLUNTING AIR POWER

The rise in ballistic missiles has added several complications to potential U.S. military actions. Aside from nuclear armed systems, conventional missiles have complicated American military planning. Greater missile capabilities and availability have allowed countries to extend their military reach to destroy or threaten targets once thought invulnerable. This problem heightens Washington's concerns about using expeditionary forces where the nation might have problems gaining access to key areas for military action. Ballistic missiles could strike American and allied airfields and deny the nation its use of one of its preeminent military instruments, air power.

As the nation reduces its permanent military bases overseas yet expands its commitments, the certainty about deploying military forces around the globe is questionable given the spread of SCUDs and longer-ranged derivatives around the world. In the 1991 Persian Gulf War, the United States and its coalition partners had an uninterrupted buildup of military forces. Today, with the Global War on Terror and potential flashpoints in areas never before considered in its national interests, the United States may not have the ability to build up forces rapidly without being attacked. A foe could delay a U.S. response and cost the nation its ability to access or defend key ports, airfields, cities, or other geographic areas.

The United States has a great advantage in the use of air power; few nations could challenge it in an air confrontation. However, aircraft do have a great vulnerability, when they are on the ground. In the future, nations that have ballistic missiles could destroy airfields or make them unusable for periods of time that could halt aircraft operations. An enemy would not need to challenge the United States directly in the skies to control them. An enemy could eliminate airfields and aircraft by using MRBM or IRBM systems. These weapons might not even need any WMD release. Instead, they could replace their warheads with a series of small bombs or cluster munitions that are dispersed along a particular track. If the enemy could launch a salvo of these vehicles, they might overwhelm any ATBM efforts.

This cluster bomb technology is not new, but increased precision could make cluster bombs more deadly. Today, the desire for improved accuracy can be met through the use of widely available Global Positioning System (GPS) receivers. GPS is a constellation of navigational satellites that requires only a handheld receiver to gather accurate location and timing information. If a ballistic missile has a system to correct its flight path, then it could deliver a relatively accurate set of munitions on a target. The weapons might not need to carry a large amount of munitions.

Cluster bombs (or other weapons like a single warhead or mines) use a container holding hundreds of bomblets. A SCUD could carry more than 100 cluster bomblets and release them over a target at an altitude of sixty kilometers (about thirty-seven miles). Launching several cluster munitions–armed ballistic missiles would complicate ATBM efforts. When over a target, the cluster bomb releases its bomblets, which spread over a wide area and can damage personnel or aircraft on a runway. Small bomblets could easily damage thin-skinned aircraft, support vehicles, or personnel. An enemy could use a salvo of several missiles to dispense the cluster munitions in a pattern or use a high explosive warhead to crater the runway and limit the use of American air power. A hostile power could do the same against a major port, transportation, logistical base, troop concentration, or other key target.

Two countries, North Korea and Iran, offer situations where ballistic missiles could endanger American and allied forces in a conflict. Both countries could encourage open conflict in their regions that could involve U.S. forces. North Korea has been in a virtual state of war since the 1953 armistice ended open warfare between North Korea and the United Nations. As the nation becomes more entrenched and economically starved, North Korean leadership might take the opportunity to strike south to gain territory or divert its populace's suffering against the current regime. The United States operates two major air bases in South Korea, Osan and Kunsan. The U.S. Air Force also operates bases in Japan and Guam. Marine Corps and U.S. Navy facilities in the Pacific are also vulnerable. These facilities are well within range of North Korean MRBM and IRBM systems.

Iran may decide to take action against a previous foe, Iraq, or attempt to spread its version of fundamentalist Islam. Conflict in the Persian Gulf would not only create problems for peace in the region, but would also affect the ability to supply oil and natural gas to the world. Iranian forces may wish to strike aircraft based around the Persian Gulf from Iraq to the United Arab Emirates. U.S. air forces operate from major air bases in Qatar, Bahrain, Kuwait, and Turkey. These airfields are vulnerable to potential ballistic missile attack.

There are several countermeasures that the United States could take to reduce the possibility of these attacks on airfields. Like other missile defenses, these activities include active and passive measures. Active measures normally include the defeat of enemy missiles before they hit their targets, like additional ATBMs. Another measure that the United States could actively pursue is jamming or encrypting the GPS signal in certain quadrants. Military units could still receive encrypted navigational signals to operate, but commercial and other users would be denied the use of the system. However, Iranian or North Korean users could use a complementary civil, unencrypted space navigational system, the European Space Agency's Galileo or the Russian Federation's GLOSNASS programs, that are similar to GPS.

Passive defenses can take several roles. The most notable is to protect aircraft and personnel from an attack. Perhaps the best possible option is to have fixed, hardened shelters. However, the United States would have to convince a host nation that this is a wise investment. Additionally, building fixed hangars at one or a few locations might create less flexibility to locate aircraft at particular locations. Another alternative is using mobile shelters that personnel can construct quickly. Air forces could create dummy airfields to draw attention away from actual operating runways.

Another method to reduce ballistic missile attacks on airfields is to change the use of air power. This would include reliance on more long-range aviation assets or putting aviation assets at sea to create a more difficult mobile target. Longer-range aviation assets or stand-off weapons would need to be placed well out of reach of ballistic missiles. This will affect the number of aircraft sorties generated and responsiveness to any enemy actions. This alternative would require more support aircraft, such as tankers, to conduct operations or carry more fuel tanks that would displace the number of weapons carried. In this way the United States could reduce its vulnerability but would trade off certain operational capability to reduce the missile threat.

Denial of allied air power by nations like North Korea and Iran could significantly alter the strategic equation in a conflict. If the North Koreans or Iranians faced American air power with their own meager air forces, they would probably fail. A new approach, however, using ballistic missiles to attack airfields, despite ATBM efforts, could reverse any air power advantage that the United States enjoys today. Using conventional weapons, a relatively poor nation like North Korea could challenge the United States and its allies to thwart a large-scale invasion.

Appendix: Tables

Soviet/Russian Submarine Launched Ballistic Missiles[1]

Designation[2]	Type	Fuel	Maximum Range (miles)	Weight (lbs)	Warhead[3]	CEP (miles)[4]	Entered Service
SS-N-4 (R-13)	MRBM	Liquid	740	57,460	5mt	1.9	1960
SS-N-5 Sark (R-21)	MRBM	Liquid	740	39,780	800kt	1.7	1963
SS-N-6 Serb (R-27)	MRBM	Liquid	1,860	31,380	2×350kt	1.2	1967
SS-N-8 Sawfly (RSM-40)	ICBM	Liquid	5,640	73,590	2×800kt	1.0	1973
SS-N-17 Snipe (RSM-45)	IRBM	Solid	2,420	59,450	1mt	0.8	1974
SS-N-18 Stingray (R-2S)	ICBM	Liquid	4,960	78,010	7×200kt	0.6	1968
SS-N-20 Sturgeon (RSM-52)	ICBM	Solid	5,155	185,560	10×100kt	0.3	1982
SS-N-23 Skiff (RSM-54)	ICBM	Liquid	5,145	89,065	4×100kt	0.3	1986

[1]This table includes operational ballistic missiles deployed by Soviet or Russian forces.
[2]NATO designation is used to identify the ballistic missile. Soviet/Russian designation is in parentheses.
[3]Indicates largest nuclear yield carried by ballistic missile. Yields are measured in kiloton (kt) or megaton (mt). Multiple RV capability is indicated by the number of RVs × maximum yield.
[4]Nominal CEP is in miles. Some ballistic missiles are extremely accurate, as indicated by >0.1 miles.

Major U.S. Land-Based Ballistic Missiles

Designation	Type	Fuel	Maximum Range (miles)	Weight (lbs)	Warhead[1]	CEP[2]	Service Dates
Corporal M-2	SRBM	Liquid	75	11,000	20kt	n/a	1954–1964
Honest John M-31	SRBM	Solid	23	5,820	40kt	1.1	1954–1979
Redstone SSM-A-14	MRBM	Liquid	200	61,350	2mt	n/a	1958–1966
Sergeant MGM-29	SRBM	Liquid	87	10,000	60kt	n/a	1961–1979
Lance MGM-52	SRBM	Liquid	75	2,850	1kt	0.2	1972–1992
Pershing I/IA MGM-31A	MRBM	Solid	460	10,275	400kt	0.2	1962–1985
Pershing II	IRBM	Solid	1,100	16,540	50kt	>0.1	1983–1989
Thor SM-75	IRBM	Liquid	1,500	110,280	1.44mt	2.0	1958–1963
Jupiter SM-78	IRBM	Liquid	1,500	110,245	1.44mt	0.9	1960–1963
Atlas D SM-65D	ICBM	Liquid	9,000	265,640	1.44mt	2.5	1960–1965
Atlas E SM-65E	ICBM	Liquid	9,000	270,660	4mt	2.3	1960–1965
Atlas F SM-65F	ICBM	Liquid	9,000	270,660	4mt	2.3	1961–1967
Titan I HGM-25A	ICBM	Liquid	6,300	220,000	4mt	0.9	1961–1966
Titan II LGM-25C	ICBM	Liquid	9,300	330,000	9mt	0.5	1963–1987
Minuteman IA/B LGM-30A/B	ICBM	Solid	6,300	65,000	1mt	0.5	1962–1969
Minuteman IB LGM 30B	ICBM	Solid	6,000	65,000	1.2mt	n/a	1965–1974
Minuteman II LGM-30F	ICBM	Solid	7,021	73,000	1.2mt	0.3	1965–1994
Minuteman III LGM-30G	ICBM	Solid	8,083	78,000	3×375kt	0.1	1970–Present
Peacekeeper LGM-118	ICBM	Solid	6,000	192,300	10×300kt	>0.1	1986–2005

[1]Indicates largest nuclear yield carried by ballistic missile. Yields are measured in kiloton (kt) or megaton (mt). Multiple RV capability is indicated by the number of RVs × maximum yield.

[2]Nominal CEP is in miles. Some ballistic missiles are extremely accurate, as indicated by >0.1 miles.

Major U.S. Submarine-Launched Ballistic Missiles

Designation	Type	Employment	Fuel	Range	Weight	Warhead	CEP	Service Dates
Polaris UGM-27 A-1	MRBM	Strategic	Solid	1,380	28,800	600kt	1.1	1960–1965
Polaris UGM-27 A-2	MRBM	Strategic	Solid	1,700	32,500	800kt	0.7	1961–1974
Polaris UGM-27A-3	IRBM	Strategic	Solid	2,880	32,700	3×200kt	0.5	1964–1981
Poseidon UGM-73 C-3	IRBM	Strategic	Solid	2,880	64,400	10×100kt	0.3	1971–1994
Trident I UGM-96 C-4	ICBM	Strategic	Solid	4,600	72,600	8×100kt	0.2	1979–Present
Trident II UGM-133 D-5	ICBM	Strategic	Solid	7,440	130,600	8×100–475kt	>0.1	1988–Present

Chinese Ballistic Missiles[1]

Designation[2]	Type	Fuel	Maximum Range (miles)	Weight (lbs)	Warhead[3]	CEP (miles)[4]	Entered Service
Land-Based							
CSS-1 Dong Feng[5] 2A (DF-2)	MRBM	Liquid	775	70,720	20kt	1.8	1966
CSS-2 Dong Feng 3/3A (DF-3)	MRBM	Liquid	1,735	141,440	3mt	0.6	1971
CSS-3 Dong Feng 4 (DF-4)	IRBM	Liquid	2,945	181,220	2mt	0.9	1980
CSS-4 Dong Feng 5 (DF-5)	ICBM	Liquid	8,000	404,430	5mt	0.3	1981
CSS-5 Dong Feng 21 (DF-21)	MRBM	Solid	1,200	32,490	250kt	n/a	1987
CSS-6 Dong Feng 15 (DF-15/M-9)	SRBM	Solid	370	13,260	90kt	0.2	1991
CSS-7 Dong Feng 11 (DF-11/M-11)	SRBM	Solid	175	8,400	90kt	0.4	1992
CSS-8 (M-7)	SRBM	Solid	93	5,855	C, CH	n/a	1992
CSS-9 Dong Feng 31 (DF-31)	ICBM	Solid	4,500	44,100	3×100kt	0.2	2004
SLBM							
CSS-N-3 Ju Lang 1 (JL-1)	MRBM	Solid	1,200	32,490	250kt	n/a	1988
CSS-N-5 Ju Lang 2 (JL-2)	ICBM	Solid	4,960	92,820	3×150kt	0.2	n/a

[1]This table includes operational ballistic missiles deployed by Chinese forces.
[2]NATO designation is used to identify the ballistic missile. Chinese designation is in parentheses.
[3]Multiple RV capability is indicated by the number of RVs x maximum yield. Yields are measured in kiloton (kt) or megaton (mt). Missile warheads carried are shown as conventional (C) or chemical (CH).
[4]Nominal CEP is in miles. Some ballistic missiles are extremely accurate, as indicated by >0.1 miles.
[5]Dong Feng translates to "East Wind," and Ju Lang means "Great Wave."

Selected Ballistic Missiles

Designation	Type	Fuel	Maximum Range (miles)	Weight (lbs)	Warhead[1]	CEP (miles)[2]	Entered Service
India							
Agni I	MRBM	Solid/Liquid	1,550	41,990	200kt	0.1	1997
Agni II	IRBM	Solid	2,170	35,360	200kt	>0.1	2000
Prithvi I (SS-150)	SRBM	Liquid	93	9,725	C	0.2	1998
Prithvi II (SS-250)	SRBM	Liquid	155	9,725	C	0.2	1999
Dhanush (SS-250 SLBM)	SRBM	Liquid	155	9,725	C	0.2	2003
Iran							
Shabab III	MRBM	Liquid	900	35,915	C, CH, N	1.5	2000
Iraq							
Al-Husayn	SRBM	Liquid	400	14,145	C	1.9	1988

Pakistan

Hatf-1	SRBM	Solid	62	3,305	C, CH	n/a	1992
Hatf-2A (Shardoz)	SRBM	Solid	186	12,125	C, CH	0.1	1992
Hatf-3	SRBM	Solid	496	14,365	C, N	n/a	n/a
Hatf-4 (Shaheen-1)	SRBM	Solid	372	20,995	35kt	0.1	2000
Hatf-5 (Ghauri-1)	MRBM	Liquid	930	35,030	35kt	1.6	1998
Hatf-5A (Ghauri-2)	MRBM	Liquid	1,435	39,340	35kt	n/a	n/a
Hatf-6 (Shaheen-2)	MRBM	Solid	1,550	55,250	35kt	0.2	n/a
North Korea							
No Dong 1	MRBM	Liquid	806	35,910	C, CH, N	1.6	1994
No Dong 2	MRBM	Liquid	930	n/a	C, CH, N	0.2	n/a
Taepo Dong 1	MRBM	Liquid/Solid	1,240	47,960	C, CH, N, B	1.9	n/a
Taepo Dong 2	ICBM	Liquid	3,720	141,440	C, CH, N, B	n/a	n/a

[1]Indicates largest nuclear yield carried by ballistic missile. Maximum nuclear yield is indicated. Missile warheads carried are shown as conventional (C), chemical (CH), biological (B), or nuclear (N).

[2]Nominal CEP is in miles. Some ballistic missiles are extremely accurate, as indicated by >0.1 miles.

Soviet/Russian Land-Based Ballistic Missiles[1]

Designation[2]	Type	Fuel	Maximum Range (miles)	Weight (lbs)	Warhead[3]	CEP (miles)[4]	Entered Service
SS-1 SCUD A (R-11)[5]	SRBM	Liquid	112	9,700	50kt	1.8	1955
SS-1 SCUD B (R-17)	SRBM	Liquid	180	14,100	70kt	0.3	1965
SS-1 SCUD C	SRBM	Liquid	373	14,100	C, CH, N	0.4	1965
SS-1 SCUD D	SRBM	Liquid	186	45,000	C, CH, N	n/a	1952
SS-3 Shyster (R-5)	MRBM	Liquid	744	63,200	40kt	n/a	1956
SS-4 Sandel (R-12)	MRBM	Liquid	1,250	92,800	1mt	1.5	1958
SS-5 Skean (R-14)	IRBM	Liquid	2,550	77,350	1mt	0.6	1961
SS-6 Sapwood (R-7)	ICBM	Liquid	4,900	552,000	5mt	6.1	1961
SS-7 Saddler (R-16)	ICBM	Liquid	7,130	311,390	5mt	n/a	1962
SS-8 Sasin (R-9)	ICBM	Liquid	7,750	176,800	5mt	n/a	1964
SS-9 Scarp (R-36)	ICBM	Liquid	7,440	117,800	4.5mt	n/a	1966
SS-11 Sego (RS-10)	ICBM	Liquid	6,500	110,720	3×200kt	0.7	1966
SS-12 Scaleboard (OTR-22)	SRBM	Solid	560	20,770	500kt	>0.1	1962

206

SS-13 Savage (RS-12)	ICBM	Solid	5,830	112,710	750kt	1.1	1969
SS-16 Sinner (RS-14)	ICBM	Solid	5,580	97,240	1mt	n/a	1965
SS-17 Spanker (RS-16)	ICBM	Liquid	6,820	157,130	3×200kt	0.2	1975
SS-18 Satan (RS-20)	ICBM	Liquid	6,820	466,530	10×500kt	0.2	1975
SS-19 Stiletto (RS-18)	ICBM	Liquid	6,200	233,375	6×500kt	0.2	1975
SS-20 Saber (RSD-10)	IRBM	Solid	3,100	79,560	3×150kt	0.2	1975
SS-21 Scarab (OTR-21)	SRBM	Solid	43	4,420	100kt	>0.1	1976
SS-23 Spider (OTR-23)	SRBM	Solid	310	10,365	100kt	>0.1	1980
SS-24 Scalpel (RS-22)	ICBM	Solid	6,200	230,945	10×500kt	0.1	1987
SS-25 Sickle (RS-12M)	ICBM	Solid	6,510	99,670	550kt	0.1	1985
SS-27 Topol M (RS-12M2)	ICBM	Solid	6,525	77,160	550kt	0.2	2000

[1] This table includes operational ballistic missiles deployed by Soviet or Russian forces.

[2] NATO designation is used to identify the ballistic missile. Soviet/Russian designation is in parentheses.

[3] Indicates largest nuclear yield carried by ballistic missile. Yields are measured in kiloton (kt) or megaton (mt). Multiple RV capability is indicated by the number of RVs × maximum yield. Missile warheads carried are shown as conventional (C), chemical (CH), biological (B), or nuclear (N).

[4] Nominal CEP is in miles. Some ballistic missiles are extremely accurate, as indicated by >0.1 miles.

[5] There are many derivatives of the SCUD missile built under license or developed from the system. North Korea, Iraq, China, and others have modified the SCUD for their purposes.

Selected Bibliography

Baylis, John, et al. *Strategy in the Contemporary World: An Introduction to Strategic Studies.* Oxford: Oxford University Press, 2002.

Bergquist, Ronald E. *The Role of Airpower in the Iran-Iraq War.* Maxwell AFB, AL: Air University Press, 1988.

Blight, James G., and David A. Welch. *Intelligence and the Cuban Missile Crisis.* London: Frank Cass, 1998.

Brodie, Bernard. *Strategy in the Missile Age.* Princeton, NJ: Princeton University Press, 1965.

Campbell, Christopher. *Nuclear Weapons Fact Book.* Novato, CA: Presidio Press, 1984.

Cordesman, Anthony H., and Abraham R. Wagner. *The Lessons of Modern War Volume IV: The Gulf War.* Boulder, CO: Westview Press, 1996.

Davis, Richard G. *On Target: Organizing and Executing the Strategic Air Campaign Against Iraq.* Washington, DC: Air Force History and Museums Program, 2002.

Freidan, David R. *Principles of Naval Weapons Systems.* Annapolis, MD: Naval Institute Press, 1985.

Friedman, Norman. *The Fifty-Year War: Conflict and Strategy in the Cold War.* Annapolis, MD: Naval Institute Press, 2000.

Fursenko, Aleksandr, and Timothy Naftali. *"One Hell of a Gamble": Khrushchev, Castro, and Kennedy, 1958–1964.* New York: Norton, 1997.

General Board. *V-2 Rocket Attacks and Defense Study #42 File R 417.6/1.* United States Forces, European Theater: U.S. Army, 1945.

Gruen, Adam L. *Preemptive Defense: Allied Air Power Versus Hitler's V-Weapons, 1943–1945.* Washington, DC: Air Force History and Museums Program, 1998.

Helfers, M. C. *The Employment of V-Weapons by the Germans During World War II.* Washington, DC: Office of the Chief of Military History, 1954.

Hiro, Dilip. *The Longest War: The Iran-Iraq Military Conflict.* New York: Routledge, 1991.

Hogg, Ian V. *German Secret Weapons of the Second World War: The Missiles, Rockets,*

Weapons and New Technology of the Third Reich. London: Greenhill Books, 1999.

Issacs, Jeremy, and Taylor Downing. *Cold War: An Illustrated History, 1945–1991.* Boston, MA: Little, Brown, 1998.

Johnson, David. *V-1 V-2: Hitler's Vengeance on London.* Chelsea, MI: Scarborough House, 1981.

Johnson, Stephen B. *The United States Air Force and the Culture of Innovation, 1945–1965.* Washington, DC: Air Force History and Museums Program, 2002.

Jupa, Richard, and Jim Dingeman. *Gulf Wars.* Cambria, CA: 3W Publications, 1991.

King, Benjamin, and Timothy J. Kutta. *Impact: The History of Germany's V-Weapons in World War II.* Rockville, NY: Sarpedon, 1998.

Knight, Michael. *Strategic Offensive Air Operations.* London: Brassey's, 1989.

Lee, R. G., et al. *Guided Weapons, 3rd ed.* London: Brassey's, 1998.

Lennox, Duncan, ed. *Jane's Strategic Weapon Systems.* Coulsdon, Surrey: Jane's Information Group, various years.

Lonnquest, John C., and David F. Winkler. *To Defend and Deter: The Legacy of the United States Cold War Missile Program.* Champaign, IL: U.S. Army Construction Engineering Research Laboratories, 1996.

McAuliffe, Mary S., ed. *CIA Documents on the Cuban Missile Crisis.* Washington, DC: History Staff, Central Intelligence Agency, 1992.

Miller, David. *The Cold War: A Military History.* New York: St. Martin's Press, 1998.

Neufeld, Jacob. *Ballistic Missiles: In the United States Air Force, 1945–1960.* Washington, DC: Office of Air Force History, 1990.

Neufeld, Michael J. *The Rocket and the Reich: Peenemünde and the Coming of the Ballistic Missile Era.* New York: The Free Press, 1995.

Pelletiere, Stephen C. *The Iran-Iraq War: Chaos in a Vacuum.* New York: Praeger, 1992.

Prados, John. *The Soviet Estimate: U.S. Intelligence Analysis and Russian Military Strength.* New York: Dial Press, 1982.

Putney, Diane T. *Airpower Advantage: Planning the Gulf War Air Campaign, 1989–1991.* Washington, DC: Air Force History and Museums Program, 2004.

Rosen, Stephen P. *Winning the Next War: Innovation and the Modern Military.* New York: Cornell University Press, 1991.

Schwartz, P. *USSTAF Memorandum No. 5-10a German V-2 (Long Range Rocket).* Headquarters, U.S. Strategic Air Force in Europe: Office of the Armament Officer, May 29, 1945.

Shubert, Frank N., and Theresa L. Kraus, eds. *Whirlwind War: The United States Army in Operations Desert Shield and Desert Storm.* Washington, DC: Center of Military History, 1995.

Spencer, Jack. *The Ballistic Missile Threat Handbook.* Washington, DC: The Heritage Foundation, 2000.

Steury, Donald P. *Intentions and Capabilities: Estimates on Soviet Strategic Forces, 1950–1983.* Washington, DC: History Staff, Central Intelligence Agency, 1996.

Welborn, Mary Catherine. *V-1 and V-2 Attacks Against the United Kingdom During*

World War II Technical Memorandum ORO T-45. Washington, DC: Operations Research Office of The Johns Hopkins University, 1950.

White, Mark J. *Missiles in Cuba: Kennedy, Khrushchev, Castro and the 1962 Crisis*. Chicago, IL: Ivan R. Dee, 1997.

Winnefeld, James A., Preston Niblack, and Dana J. Johnson. *A League of Airmen: U.S. Air Power in the Gulf War*. Santa Monica, CA: RAND Corporation, 1994.

Index

Accelerometers, 17–19, 35

Aerodynamic control surface, 10

Aerojet, 77

Aggregat (Aggregate or Assembly): A-1, 42; A-2, 42, 43; A-3, 43; A-4, 41, 43, 45; 46; A-5, 43. *See also* Dornberger, Walter; *Vergeltungswaffe*-2 (V-2); Von Braun, Wernher

Agni missile, 155

Agreed Framework with North Korea, 161–162

Ahwaz, Iran, 114, 116

Air Force Space Command, 137. *See also* Space

Air Research and Development Command (ARDC), 66, 80

Airframe, 6, 7

Al-Abbas missile, 116, 119, 122, 126; specifications, 118

Al-Hijarah missile, 126, 131

Al-Husayn missile, 115, 119, 121, 122, 123, 125, 126, 131–132, 136–138, 156, 165; modified from SCUD-B, 116–117; specifications, 117–118

All-inertial guidance, 15, 19, 20, 68

Amatol, 51

Anti–ballistic missile (ABM), 135, 160, 167, 173, 175, 178, 190; national missile defense, 164, 165–166. *See also* Anti–theater ballistic missile (ATBM); Strategic Defense Initiative (SDI)

Anti–Ballistic Missile Treaty, 160, 178

Anti–theater ballistic missile (ATBM), 135–138, 196–198. *See also* Anti–ballistic missile (ABM); Patriot MIM-104

Antwerp, Belgium, 50, 54, 55

Apogee, 4, 21

Ardennes offensive, 54

Army tactical missile system (ATACMS), 146, 165

Arnold, Henry "Hap," 59, 60

Assured destruction, 174

Atlas ICBM, 23, 62–63, 66, 68, 88, 90, 185, 191, 193; development and deployment, 77–78, 80; parallel development with Titan, 64; problems with development, 80. *See also* Cold war; Consolidated Vultee Aircraft Corporation (Convair); MX-774 (Hiroc); Titan ICBM

Atomic Energy Commission (AEC), 62, 184, 187. *See also* Nuclear weapons

Attitude, 5, 17, 18, 21

Azimuth, 2

B-1, 177
B-47, 84
B-52, 84,194
B-58, 84
Baghdad, 112, 113, 114, 118, 120, 121, 126, 131, 132
Ballistic missile: characteristics, 1–2; components, 6; conventional counter-measures against, 197–198; flight path, 2, 4, 6; guidance system, 15, 17–20, 21, 35; problems with develop-ment, 35–36; proliferation concerns, 160–162, 164–167; propulsion sys-tems, 6–7, 8, 10, 12, 15; reasons to build, 141–142, 144; technology changes warfare, vii, viii, 187–190; threat to airpower, 195–197; trajec-tory, 33–34. *See also* All-inertial guid-ance; Radio-inertial guidance; Reentry vehicle (RV); Trajectory
Ballistic Missile Division, 186
Bangor, Washington, 146
Basra, Iraq, 113
Batista Zaldívar, Fulgencio, 87
Bay of Pigs Invasion, 90, 102
Becker, Karl, development and control of V-2, 41, 42
Beijing, China, 155, 156
Berlin, Germany, 43, 57, 98, 188
Boeing Aircraft Company, 82
Boost phase 2, 15
Borkum, 42
Borujerd, Iran, 116
Boston, Massachusetts, 150
Bucharest, 106
Buckley Air National Guard Base, Col-orado, 137
Bush, George H. W., 122
Bush, George W., 179

C-119, 75
C-130, 75
Camp Cooke, California, 75
Cape Canaveral, Florida, 70, 191

Carter, Jimmy, 176, 177
Castro, Fidel, 87, 89, 95, 102
Castro, Raúl, 96
Central Command (CENTCOM), 122, 124, 126, 130, 137. *See also* Operation Desert Shield; Operation Desert Storm; Persian Gulf War
Central Intelligence Agency (CIA), 67, 72, 91, 96, 97, 100; attempts to over-throw Castro, 87, 90; 1961 National Intelligence Estimate, 76. *See also* Cuban Missile Crisis
Central Tactical Air Forces (CENTAF), 137; diverts air resources to Great SCUD Hunt, 132; plans attacks on Iraqi ballistic missiles, 130. *See also* Operation Desert Shield; Operation Desert Storm; Persian Gulf War
Centripetal force, 17
Cherbourg, France, 52
Cheyenne Mountain Complex, Col-orado, 138
Chinese ballistic missile programs: aid to other countries, 156; current sys-tems, 157–158; rationale to build, 155–156
Chiswick, England, 52
Chrysler Corporation, 70
Cigli, Turkey, 70
Circular error probable (CEP), 23, 24, 69, 80, 91, 118, 120, 153
Clinton administration, 179
Cluster bomb, 196–197
Cold war, vii, 87; arms race, 66–67; early efforts to build ballistic missile pro-grams, 60–65; operational United States systems, 68–72, 76–78, 80, 82, 84, 86; rationale to build ballistic missile forces, 57–60; United States government demands increased intel-ligence programs, 72–76. *See also* Cold war; CORONA; Cuban Missile Crisis; Kennedy, John F.; Khrushchev, Nikita; U-2

Colorado Springs, Colorado, 138
Combined Bomber Offensive (CBO), 44, 45
Combustion chamber, 7–10
Consolidated Vultee Aircraft Corporation (Convair), 60. *See also* Atlas ICBM; MX-774 (Hiroc)
Containment, 170, 172
Coriolis Effect, 15
CORONA, 74–76, 90, 100; availability in Cuban Missile Crisis, 96
Counterforce strategy, 170, 174, 176
Counterproliferation efforts, 162, 164
Countervalue strategy, 170, 174, 176
Cuban Missile Crisis, viii, 39–40, 113; background, 87, 90; Kennedy takes action, 101–102, 104–105; naval blockade, 105; negotiations between Kennedy and Khrushchev, 106–107; Soviet strategic position, 90–91; United States intelligence gathering efforts, 100–101; United States suspects Soviet motives in Cuba, 97–100. *See also* Kennedy, John F.; Khrushchev, Nikita; McCone, John A.; Operation Anadyr; U-2

Damascus, Syria, 153
Defense Support Program (DSP), 134, 137, 138
Delta SSBN, 159, 163
Deterrence, 169–172, 173, 174, 179, 181–182
Dezful, Iran, 114, 116
DF missiles, 156–157
Dhahran, Saudi Arabia, 125, 132
Dhaush SLBM, 155
Directed energy weapons, 165, 166, 167
Discoverer program, 75. *See also* CORONA
Dobrynin, Anatoly, 96, 104, 107
Dornberger, Walter, 44, 45, 46, 47, 48, 49, 59, 61; development of early German missiles, 41–43. *See also* Vergel-

tungswaffe-2 (V-2); Von Braun, Werner
Douglas Aircraft Company, 70
Drag, 1, 4, 22, 34
Dulles, John Foster, 65, 172
Dura, Iraq, 126

Eisenhower, Dwight D., 59, 63, 66, 76, 90, 94, 172; decides ballistic missile production is a nation priority, 65; expands intelligence programs, 72–76; missile gap, 75–76. *See also* Cold war; U-2
Electromechanische Werke (EKW), 48
Executive Committee (EXCOMM), 101, 102, 104, 106
Exhaust nozzle, 8, 10

F-8U, 99
F-15, 122,123
F-16, 123
Fateh-110 missile, 152
F. E. Warren AFB, Wyoming, 78, 146
Fort Greeley, Alaska, 167
Free Rocket Over Ground (FROG)-7, 113–114, 152, 153
Friction, 1, 22, 33

Galileo, 20, 197
Gather Report, 76, 77
General Accounting Office, 136
Ghadr 101 missile, 152
Ghauri missile, 154
Gioia del Colle, Italy, 70
Glen L. Martin Company, 80, 82
Global Positioning System (GPS), 20, 196, 197
Global War on Terror, 196
Globalization, viii, 36, 183
GLOSNASS, 20, 197
Gorbachev, Mikhail, 178, 179
Grand Forks AFB, North Dakota, 178
Great SCUD Hunt. *See* Operation Desert Storm

Gromyko, Andrei, 102
Guanajay, Cuba, 99
Guantánamo, Cuba, 99, 102
Guidance system, 6, 15, 17, 18, 19, 20, 21, 22, 32, 33, 34, 35. *See also* All-inertial guidance; Radio-inertial guidance
Gyroscope, 17–19, 35

H-2, 126, 131
Haifa, Israel, 126, 131
Havana, Cuba, 96, 97, 98
Heat sink. *See* reentry vehicle
Heereswaffenamt (HWA), 41, 42
Himmler, Heinrich: attempts to control V-2, 46–48; SS takes control of V-2, 49. *See also Vergeltungswaffe*-2 (V-2)
Hiroc. *See* MX-774 (Hiroc)
Hiroshima, Japan, 58, 62, 169
Hitler, Adolf, 42, 45, 46, 47, 48, 51, 54, 135; decides to transfer V-2 operations to SS, 49. *See also Vergeltungswaffe*-2 (V-2)
Honest John missile, 142
Horner, Charles, 130
Hot-line Agreement, 161
Hussein, Saddam, 111, 112, 114, 116, 119, 121, 122, 123, 124, 126, 128, 130, 132, 138; turns to missiles against Iran, 113; seeks ways to strike Tehran, 117. *See also* Iran-Iraq 1980 War; Persian Gulf War
Hypergolic fuel, 7

IL-28, 92, 99
[bj10]Indian ballistic missile program: current ballistic missile systems, 155; rationale to build, 154–155
Indigirka, 101
Intermediate-Range Nuclear Forces Treaty, 161, 177, 180
Internet, 183
Iran-Iraq 1980 War: Iran receives SCUD missiles, 118; Iraqi goals, 112; seeds of conflict, 109–112; use of ballistic missiles, 113–114, 116; War of the Cities, 119–121, 132, 141, 179
Iranian ballistic missile program: current ballistic missile systems, 152; help from North Korea, 151; rationale to build, 151–152
Islamabad, Pakistan, 154, 155

Jerusalem, Israel, ix, 126
JL missile, 157
Johnson, Lyndon B., 97
Jupiter IRBM, 64, 65, 67, 68, 90, 94; deployment, 69–70,72; NATO squadrons, 70, 72; specifications, 70; withdrawn after Cuban Missile Crisis, 106–107. *See also* Cold war; Polaris SLBM; United States Army; United States Navy

Kai-feng-fu, 39
Kammler, Hans: commands V-2 program, 49; construction of V-2 facilities, 48. *See also* Himmler, Heinrich; *Schutzstaffel* (SS); *Vergeltungswaffe*-2 (V-2)
Kansas City, Missouri, 150
Kapustin Yar missile test range, Soviet Union, 75
Kashmir, 153, 155
Kennedy, John F., 59, 76, 90, 92, 94, 95, 96; approves additional U-2 flights, 100; confronts Soviets over Cuba, 105–107; decision on actions in Cuba, 101–102, 104; evaluates Cuban options, 98–99; exposes Soviet missile programs in Cuba, 104–105; initial ballistic missile plans, 78, 80; modifies cold war strategy, 173–164; negotiates with Khrushchev over Cuba, 106; restructures strategic programs, 84. *See also* Cold war; Cuban Missile Crisis; U-2
Kennedy, Robert, 98, 102, 106, 107
Keyhole satellites, 75

Khomeini, Ayatollah, 111, 112, 121

Khorramabad, Iran, 116

Khrushchev, Nikita, 67, 73, 74, 75, 87, 90, 98, 100, 101, 104, 105; Cuban plan unravels, 99; decides to move missiles to Cuba, 95–96; motivation to emplace missiles in Cuba, 91–92, 94–95; negotiates with Kennedy over Cuba, 106–107; political gain over Sputnik, 67. *See also* Cold war; Cuban Missile Crisis; Kennedy, John F.

Killian, James R.: 1958 Killian Report, 76; Science Advisory Committee's Technical Capabilities Panel, 64, 65, 68

King's Bay, Georgia, 146

Kirkuk, Iraq, 113

Kummersdorf, 42, 43

Kursk, 159

Lance missile, 142

Laughlin AFB, Texas, 97

LeMay, Curtis E., 65–66, 102

Liege, Belgium, 54, 55

Lockheed Missile and Space Company, 75, 77

London, England, ix, 52, 54, 55, 120, 184

Los Angeles, California, 186

Lowry AFB, Colorado, 82

Luftwaffe, 43, 44, 45, 46; starts V-1 campaign, 48. *See also Vergeltungswaffe*-1 (V-1)

M-7 missile, 152

Malmstrom AFB, Montana, 84, 146

Maneuverable reentry vehicle (MARV), 32

Mao Zedong, 92

Massive retaliation, 172–173, 179

McCone, John A., 97, 100; warns of ballistic missiles in Cuba, 97–98. *See also* Central Intelligence Agency (CIA); Cuban Missile Crisis

McElroy, Neil H., 77, 82

McNamara, Robert S., 69, 78, 84, 97, 102, 174; modifies Atlas and Titan programs, 80. *See also* Cold war; Cuban Missile Crisis

Mid-course phase, 4

Mig-21, 92, 101

Minot AFB, North Dakota, 146

Minuteman ICBM, 11, 14, 78, 87, 90, 92, 94, 95, 97, 98, 99, 100, 101, 104; development, 92–94; illustrated flight path, 25–30; Minuteman I, 84; Minuteman III, 10, 15, 16, 25, 26, 27, 146

Missile defense, 6, 21, 23, 24, 57, 66. *See also* Anti–ballistic missile; Anti–theater ballistic missile

Missile Gap, 59, 73, 78, 173; debunked, 75–76. *See also* Cold war

Missile Technology Control Regime (MTCR), 162

Mittlewerke, 48, 49

Monroe Doctrine, 87

Moscow, Russia, 65, 67, 72, 73, 74, 94, 95, 96, 97, 100, 102, 142, 143, 161, 173, 175, 178, 191

Multiple independently targetable reentry vehicle (MIRV), 21, 157, 159, 161, 173, 175, 190

Multiple reentry vehicle (MRV), 187

Murmansk, Soviet Union, 97

Mutually assured destruction (MAD), 174–175, 176, 177, 179. *See also* Deterrence

MX-774 (Hiroc), 60–61, 62, 63

MYA-4 (Bison) 65, 171

Nagasaki, Japan, 62, 169

National Aeronautics and Space Administration (NASA), 192

National Defense Education Act, 67

National Security Act of 1947, 61

National Security Council, 65, 100, 101

New Delhi, India, 154, 155

New Look, 76, 84

New York, New York, 150
Nixon, Richard M., 59, 76, 176, 177
No Dong missile, 150, 152, 154
North American Aerospace Defense Command (NORAD), 138
North Atlantic Treaty Organization (NATO), 70, 159, 172
North Korean ballistic missile program: current systems, 150; development, 150–151; rationale to build, 147–148
Norwich, England, 54
Nuclear weapons, viii, x–xi, 21, 31, 35, 36, 40, 57, 62, 63, 68–69, 84, 91, 92, 123–124, 174–176, 184; Chinese weapons programs, 157; Indian weapons programs, 154–155; lower cost alternative to other forces, 58–59; North Korean weapons programs, 147, 150–151, 161–162; Pakistani weapons program, 153–154; rationale to develop, 187–189; Russian weapons programs, 158–159; Soviet nuclear developments, 62, 64, 71, 72; United States develops lightweight weapons, 77, 184; United States monopoly, 184. *See also* Atomic Energy Commission (AEC); Cold war; Reentry vehicle (RV)

Offut AFB, Nebraska, 144
Oghab, 119
Ohio SSBN, 146, 149, 177
Operation Anadyr: implementation, 97–99; rationale to emplace missiles, 91–92, 94–96. *See also* Cuban Missile Crisis
Operation Desert Shield: defensive actions against Iraqi ballistic missiles, 135–138; objectives, 128; reasons for conflict, 122; start of military build-up, 128. *See also* Operation Desert Storm; Persian Gulf War
Operation Desert Storm: ballistic missiles become key target, 124; difficulty with mobile Iraqi missiles, 126; Great SCUD Hunt, 127, 131–132, 134; start of military operations, 131. *See also* Operation Desert Shield; Persian Gulf War
Operation Mongoose, 91, 99
Operation Paperclip, 61
Organization of American States, 94
Osrirak raid, 123–124

Pakistani ballistic missile program: Chinese aid, 154; rationale to build, 153–154
Paris, France, 52
Paris Gun, 40
Patriot MIM-104, 133, 164, 165, 167; deployment in Persian Gulf War, 130–131; Israel accepts deployment, 132; operations, 136–137; specifications, 135–136; use of space assets, 137–138. *See also* Operation Desert Shield; Operation Desert Storm; Persian Gulf War
Peacekeeper ICBM, 145–146, 177
Peenemünde, Germany, 43, 45, 47, 48
Penetration aids (penaids), 21, 157, 160, 165
Perforation, 10, 13
Pershing I missile, 9, 32
Pershing II missile, 32, 153, 180
Persian Gulf War, viii, 96, 164, 165. 196. *See also* Operation Desert Shield; Operation Desert Storm
Peshawar, Pakistan, 74
Pitch, 5, 17
Point Mugu, California, 77
Polaris SLBM, 77, 78, 79, 84, 94, 104, 195
Poseidon SLBM, 79
Powers, Francis Gary, 74, 98. *See also* U-2
Precession, 18
Preemption, 173, 179
Prithvi missile, 155

Program evaluation and review technique (PERT), 186
Pyongyang, North Korea, 147, 150, 151

Qom, 120

R-7, 66, 67, 72, 73. *See also* SS-6
R-12, 91. *See also* SS-4
R-14, 91. *See also* SS-5
R-16, 91. *See also* SS-7
R-17. *See* SS-1
Radar area guidance (RAG), 32. *See also* Pershing II missile
Radford, Arthur W., 65
Radio-inertial guidance, 15, 19–20, 78
RAND Corporation, 60, 191; impact on ballistic missile development, 189–190
Raytheon Corporation, 136
Reagan, Ronald, changes nuclear strategy, 177–179
Redstone Arsenal, Alabama, 70
Redstone missile, 64, 70
Reentry vehicle (RV), 27, 28, 29, 30, 31, 32, 35, 36, 167, 176, 187, 190; ablative RV, 22; attempts to defeat, 165–167; heat sink RV, 21–22; improvements, 23, 32; operation, 20, 24. *See also* Maneuverable reentry vehicle (MARV); Multiple independently targetable reentry vehicle (MIRV); Multiple reentry vehicle (MRV); Nuclear weapons
Remedios, Cuba, 99
RF-101, 99
Riyadh, Saudi Arabia, 138
Roll, 5, 17
Royal Air Force (RAF), 43, 44, 71; operates Thor, 69
RS-12M (Topol). *See* SS-25
RS-18. *See* SS-19
RS-20. *See* SS-18
RSM-50. *See* SS-N-18
RSM-52. *See* SS-N-20

RSM-54. *See* SS-N-23
Rusk, Dean, 97, 104
Russian ballistic missile program: current systems, 159; rationale to build, 158–159

SA-2 (Guideline), 73, 92, 96, 97, 98, 99, 100, 101. *See also* U-2
Sagarika, 155
Sagua la Grande, Cuba, 99
San Cristóbal, Cuba, 99, 100, 101
San Francisco, California, 150
Saryshagan missile test center, Soviet Union, 72, 73
Schlesinger, James, 176; Schlesinger Doctrine, 176
Schutzstaffel (SS), 46, 47, 49, 51, 52
Semispalatinsk, Soviet Union, 73
Shabab missile, 152
Shaheen missile, 154
Shatt al Arab, Iran, 112, 113, 116
Smith, Fredric H., Jr., 70
Space, vii, 12; ballistic missiles enable space launch capabilities, 190–192; military rationale to enter space, 191. *See also* CORONA; Defense Support Program (DSP); Keyhole satellites; Sputnik; Strategic Defense Initiative (SDI)
Speer, Albert, 44, 46, 47 48
Sputnik, 191; Sputnik I, 67, 68, 183; Sputnik II, 67
SS-1 (SCUD), 196; Chinese SCUDs, 156; Iranian SCUDs, 152; North Korean SCUDs, 147; popularity, 146; SCUD-B, 114, 116, 117, 118, 120, 123, 126; SCUD-C, 114, 116, 117; Syrian SCUDs, 153; use in Iran-Iraq 1980 War, 114–116
SS-4 (Sandel), 91, 92, 95, 97, 100, 152
SS-5 (Skean), 91, 92, 95, 97, 99, 105
SS-6 (Sapwood), 73–74, 90
SS-7 (Saddler), 91
SS-8 (Sasin), 143

SS-12 (OTR-22 or Scaleboard), 114, 116
SS-18 (Satan), 159
SS-19 (Stiletto), 159
SS-21 (Scarab), 152
SS-24 (Scalpel), 159
SS-25 (Sickle), 159
SS-27 (Topol M), 159, 160
SS-N-18 (Stingray), 160
SS-N-20 (Sturgeon), 160
SS-N-23 (Skiff), 160
Stevenson, Adlai, 102, 104, 106
Stalin, Josef, 57
Stalingrad, Soviet Union, 49
Strategic Air Command (SAC), 65, 66, 78, 80, 84, 86, 91, 94, 100, 102, 104, 106, 146, 171, 172, 174, 189, 193; controls RAF's Thor nuclear warheads, 69
Strategic Arms Limitation Treaty (SALT), SALT-I, 161, 175, 177; SALT II, 161
Strategic Command (STRATCOM), 144
Strategic Defense Initiative (SDI), 178
Strategic Rocket Forces, 159
Surya missile, 155
Sverdlovsk, Soviet Union, 74
Syrian ballistic missile program: current ballistic missile systems, 152; rationale to build, 152–153
Systems analysis, 190

Taepo Dong missile, 150, 152, 154
Taji, Iraq, 126
Taylor, Maxwell, 97
Technology: impact on warfare, 187–190; weapons development, 183. See also Cold war; Nuclear weapons
Teflon, 22
Tehran, Iran, 111, 114, 117, 118, 119, 120, 121, 151, 152
Tel Aviv, Israel, 124, 126, 131, 132, 138
Terminal phase, 4
The Hague, Netherlands, 52

Thor IRBM, 65, 67, 71, 191, 193; space booster, 75; specifications, 69; United Kingdom acquires, 68–69
Thorneycroft, Peter, 69
Thrust, 6, 7, 8, 10, 12, 15
Thrust-to-weight ratio, 6–7
Titan ICBM, 191, 193; development, 77, 80, 82; Titan I, 66, 78, 82, 84, 89, 91; Titan II, 7, 15, 31, 84, 88, 89, 174
Tokyo, Japan, 57, 188
Trajectory, 1, 2, 4, 24, 33–34. See also Ballistic missile
Treaty of Versailles, 40
Trident SLBM, 144, 146, 149, 177
Typhoon SSBN, 159
Tyuratam Missile Test Range, Soviet Union, 72, 73

U-2, 72–74, 76, 96, 97, 98, 100, 102, 106; discovers Cuban MRBMs, 100; vulnerability to SA-2, 99. See also Cold war; Cuban Missile Crisis; Kennedy, John F.; Powers, Francis Gary
United Nations, 172, 197
United States Air Force, ix–x, 61, 62, 64–65, 69, 79; 167, 185, 191, 192, 197; ballistic missile force, 146; ballistic missiles change organization, 192–194. See also United States ballistic missile programs
United States Army, 54, 61, 62, 65, 128; development of Jupiter, 68, 130. See also Jupiter IRBM; United States Navy
United States ballistic missile programs: cold war nuclear policy, 171–179; deterrence in the post–cold war era, 171, 181–182; deterrence policies considered, 169–171; questions about technical feasibility, 184–185; United States Air Force development, 185–187; United States Navy development, 185–187. See also Cold war
United States Marine Corps, 94, 104, 194

United States Navy, ix, 62, 65, 68, 185, 192, 197; ballistic missiles change organization, 194–195; blockade of Cuba, 105; development of Jupiter with United States Army, 68; SSBN force, 146. *See also* Jupiter IRBM; United States ballistic missile programs

Vandenberg AFB, California, 75, 78, 167, 191
Velocity, 1, 4, 6, 8, 10, 12, 18, 33
Verein für Raumschiffart (VfR), 42
Vergeltungswaffe-1 (V-1), 46, 48, 52, 54, 55, 58; rival to V-2, 45
Vergeltungswaffe-2 (V-2), viii, 41, 42, 50, 53, 61, 66, 113, 114, 120, 135, 142, 184, 185, 188, 191; effectiveness of operations, 55; launch operations, 51–52, 54–56; launch site development, 46–47; production concerns, 48; specifications, 49, 51. *See also Aggregat* (Aggregate or Assembly): A-4, Dornberger, Walter; Hitler, Adolf; Himmler, Heinrich; Kammler, Hans; Peenemünde, Germany; Von Braun, Wernher
Vietnam War, 175, 193
Von Braun, Wernher: develops German ballistic missiles, 42, 45, 46, 49; develops United States ballistic missiles,

59, 64. *See also* Cold war; Dornberger, Walter; *Vergeltungswaffe*-2
Von Fritsch, Werner, 43

War of the Cities. *See* Iran-Iraq 1980 War
Washington, D.C., ix, 132, 150, 161, 177, 181, 182, 184, 188, 190
Watten, France, 46, 52
Weapons of Mass Destruction (WMD), 123, 124, 126, 131, 135, 142, 144, 151, 152, 164, 179, 181, 196. *See also* Nuclear weapons
Weapon System Q. *See* Minuteman ICBM
Western Development Division, 186, 191
White, Thomas D., 82
White Sands, New Mexico, 63
Wilson, Charles E., 70; delegates missile responsibilities, 65; proposes changes to ballistic missile priorities, 66
Wizernes, France, 46, 52

X-20 Dyna-Soar, 192
XB-70, 84
Xia SSBN, 157

Yaw, 5, 17

Zorin, Valerin, 106

About the Author

CLAYTON K. S. CHUN is Chair of the Department of Distance Education at the United States Army War College, Carlisle Barracks, PA. He is a former Missile Launch Officer and Pentagon Officer in the Strategy Division of the Air Staff. His publications include *Aerospace Power in the Twenty-First Century: A Basic Primer, US Army in the Plains Indian Wars 1865–91;* and *The Doolittle Raid 1942.*

Contents

Foreword   ix

Acknowledgments   xiii

Introduction   1

1 The Marginalization of LGBT People   9

2 LGBT Identity   25

3 Sharing the Struggles: The Role of Allies   47

4 Family: From Exclusion to Nurturance   65

5 Inside the Classroom Walls   83

6 Outside the Classroom Walls   101

7 We Are Our Communities   119

Conclusion   137

Queerossary of Terms   141

Appendix: LGBT Resource List   151

Notes   161

Index   185

Foreword

As a professor of human development and the co-author with my husband Phil of *Development Through Life*, a lifespan text that is in its 11th edition, I have been reading, writing, and teaching about gender-related themes for quite some time. The field has been slow to consider the systematic unfolding of sexual orientation. Despite Freud's early theorizing about the sexual nature of children, research and theory about the emergent nature of sexual fantasies, desires, or behaviors, whether self- or other-focused, is far less developed than the research and theory about gender. Parents are famously uncommunicative about sexuality; educators are ill-prepared to teach children and youth about their sexuality; and political controversies swarm around communities, resulting in cautious, minimal teaching or deliberate exclusion of this topic altogether. Many children are left to figure things out for themselves through movies, websites, books they can find at the library, and gossip. Imagine if we had so little to say about which foods were safe to eat and how to prepare foods to make them taste delicious. Imagine if we had so little to say about dental hygiene and the importance of brushing and flossing. Yet here we are in the twenty-first century, tongue-tied about sexuality.

The culture is chaotically divided in its approach to sexuality. On the one hand, children and youth are exposed to media images of sexual encounters, ads for products intended to enhance sexual performance, music and videos from sexually suggestive performers, and erotic magazines, websites, and movies. On the other hand, there are relatively few environments where children and youth can talk freely about their own sexual experiences and learn about how to express their sexual impulses in ways that are pleasurable, physically safe, and, when appropriate, responsive to their sexual partners. As a result, many children and youth arrive at adulthood in a state of confusion: their personal identity is disconnected from their sexual selves. This leads to a variety of social harms, including self-loathing, vulnerability to sexual predators, unsafe sexual practices, sexual aggression, sexual stigmatization, sexual harassment, and prejudice against those who appear to have a non-normative sexual preference. In my opinion, we have failed to create a safe space for children to learn about their sexual natures and to be accepting of the diverse pathways and preferences of the sexual motivation and behaviors of others.

Annemarie Vaccaro, Gerri August, and Megan Kennedy shared a vision for a project that would address this failure with a particular focus on lesbian, gay, bisexual, and transgender youth. They recognized the need to support LGBT youth as they function in their everyday lives across time and space—that is, from childhood into the college years, and from family to school and community settings. *Safe Spaces* starts from where we are now—acknowledging the challenges that LGBT youth continue to face and the many voices in communities across the country that marginalize and vilify them and threaten their futures.

The book uncovers evidence of support, innovation, and power in LGBT youth themselves as well as their allies. As you read, you will hear many voices—voices of children, youth, college students, parents, teachers, community leaders, scholars, and politicians. The sense is that there is an active, dynamic dialogue taking place, sometimes openly in kitchens, classrooms, libraries (ever so quietly), youth organizations, and community centers; and sometimes in the hidden corners of bathrooms, locker rooms, parking lots, and websites. The book envisions a more secure, supportive, and accepting future for LGBT youth, and guides us as we strive to achieve this future by describing role models, sharing the courage of children and youth themselves, and giving us a wide palette of strategies for creating safe spaces wherever we can.

As a reader, I was reminded of my own reactions to the first couple who came out to me as lesbian partners many years ago. I disappointed them with my reaction; I was both surprised and shocked. But little did they know that in trusting me with their truth, they prepared me to be more accepting and encouraging when one of my sons and my daughter came out. Our childrearing philosophy was heavily influenced by the work on gender that was taking place during the 1970s, and if you could summarize our outlook, it was captured in the album *Free to Be You and Me*. We cherished creativity, individuality, and freedom of expression, and we saw each of our children blossom into a young person with tremendous talents, a generous spirit, and a love of life. Unfortunately, the album and the prevailing gender narrative left out some important ideas about sexual orientation, so we weren't as prepared for some aspects of *Free to Be* as we might have been. Nonetheless, communication was open, affection was deep, and we have a delightfully diverse family. We are hoping for at least one queer grandchild.

So it is with great relief and optimism that I welcome *Safe Spaces* and commend it to you as readers. If it is possible for a book to be a safe space in its own right, this is such a book. Despite the bigotry and discrimination that many LGBT youth and their allies face, the authors strike a hopeful tone. They ask us as readers to reflect on our thoughts, feelings, behaviors, and beliefs and to consider taking action in the domains where we may have an impact—home, school, university, and community. The book is inclusive, both in its consideration of the wide range of people who might serve as allies, and in its consideration of the diversity of LGBT youth. And the book is constructive, offering many ideas about how to enrich settings for young people so that they always experience a sense of belonging as they carry out the work of forming their sexual and gender identities. *Safe Spaces* is an important contribution to the construction of a more open, supportive environment in which all children and youth can address the cognitive, emotional, and social nature of their own sexuality and the sexuality of others.

Barbara M. Newman, PhD

Acknowledgments

We are indebted to many individuals who helped make *Safe Spaces* a reality. First, the wisdom of more than 100 lesbian, gay, bisexual, and transgender individuals and allies fills the pages of this volume. We are grateful to those who shared deeply personal and often painful life experiences with us. Their stories serve as inspiration to us. We are certain that parents, educators, community leaders, and LGBT youth will be equally moved by their powerful narratives.

Many friends, colleagues, and students offered us their expertise, enthusiasm, and encouragement. Their personal and professional support was invaluable to the creation of *Safe Spaces*. Specifically, we would like to thank Dr. Barbara Newman, who offered us guidance on the content and graciously accepted our invitation to write the foreword.

A very special thank you to Amy Tedesco, who became an expert on Chicago Manual Style—a task that far exceeded the scope of graduate assistant responsibilities. Amy's tireless work and attention to detail improved the look of the manuscript. Beyond mere technical detail, Amy offered an objective eye and thoughtful feedback, which made our message clearer and stronger.

Finally, we offer our deepest appreciation to our families who stood by us as we researched, crafted, and revised this book. Their emotional support and encouragement helped make this book a reality. We thank our families for being our greatest allies.

Introduction

Aiyisha Hassan, Asher Brown, Seth Walsh, Raymond Chase, and Tyler Clementi are just a few of the LGBT youth who committed suicide in 2010.[1] For each of these highly publicized deaths, scores more go undocumented. Youth who struggle with lesbian, gay, bisexual, or transgender identities (LGBT), or who are bullied for the mere perception of being different, often feel as if they have nowhere to turn. Death should never be an option. Unfortunately, for many young people suicide feels like a better alternative than living with rejection or abuse from peers, family members, or community leaders.

From our homes and neighborhoods to schools, athletic fields, and community organizations, LGBT youth often experience physical and psychological harm inflicted by peers and adults. While overt discrimination like bullying, harassment, and violence are clearly harmful, LGBT youth also encounter less overt forms of marginalization in family, school, and community settings. Throughout *Safe Spaces* we show how marginalization often comes in the form of messaging. No, we do not mean text or email messaging. Instead, messaging refers to the verbal and nonverbal communications that LGBT youth receive from family, peers, teachers, media, and community members. Overt verbal messages can include anti-LGBT slurs, jokes, or prejudicial comments. Messages, however, can also be delivered more subtly. Parents, teachers, neighbors, coaches, and peers need not use anti-gay language to communicate that it is unacceptable to be lesbian, gay, bisexual, or transgender. Refusing to talk about LGBT issues or showing discomfort when LGBT topics arise are nonverbal messages that tell youth that being LGBT is abnormal or wrong.

Unfortunately, many adults engage in subtle types of harm, sometimes without knowing it. For instance, most adults unconsciously perpetuate heterosexism; heterosexism is the assumption that everyone is or *should be* heterosexual. At the bus stop, soccer field, dinner table, or local grocery store, adults reinforce the messages of heterosexism. A well-intentioned adult's questions or comments about romantic interests often assume opposite sex attraction, leaving a lesbian, gay, or bisexual youth uncomfortable or, worse, ashamed. Casual comments on how happy heterosexual couples look can sound like indictments to LGB youth. Messages that pressure youth into heterosexuality, although often unintended, are far from rare. In fact, such messages surround us and create a heteronormative social reality that LGB youth must wade through. Two college students, Lisa and Christina, blog about the effects of heteronormativity: "A heteronormative perspective or bias is one that implicitly or explicitly believes that the only 'normal' perspective is one which is heterosexual, which understands gender and sexual identity as static concepts."[2] The implication? Heterosexuality is seen as normal while lesbian, gay, and bisexual youth are viewed as abnormal.

Safe Spaces, however, goes beyond the experiences of lesbian, gay, and bisexual youth with heterosexism to include young people who are transgender. Being lesbian, gay, or bisexual is about one's sexual orientation—a person's feelings of romantic or sexual attraction. Being transgender, on the other hand, has to do with an individual's sense of gender, not sexual orientation. In fact, transgender youth may identify as lesbian, gay, bisexual, asexual, or heterosexual. The term *transgender* is an umbrella term that encompasses a broad spectrum of individuals who feel and express their gender in ways that are considered outside the norm. Individuals who identify as transsexual, intersex, gender nonconforming, queer, genderqueer, or as a cross-dresser would be included beneath the transgender umbrella. Other youth whose gender identity or expression falls outside the typical bounds of societal normativity may also claim the label *transgender* as an identity. In short, transgender is both an umbrella term for many identities *and* an identity in and of itself.

In U.S. society, youth not only experience pressures to be heterosexual, but they also receive messages that suggest everyone is or should be cisgender. A cisgender person is someone who "possess[es] a gender identity or perform[s] in a gender role that society considers appropriate for one's sex."[3] In other words the term cisgender refers to someone who is not transgender. Our society, like most, codifies a gender binary in assuming that everyone is either male or female. We give little recognition to (or deem abnormal) individuals who are born with ambiguous genitalia (e.g., intersex people) or those who refuse to chose one of the two commonly accepted identities of male or female (e.g., queer, genderqueer, and gender-nonconforming people). We also teach young people that their birth sex (determined by their genitalia) should dictate their gender identity. Unfortunately, sex (biology) and gender (psychosocial sense of self) are not necessarily the same thing. For some transgender people, their birth sex may not align with the gender they believe themselves to be. Yet society normalizes anyone whose gender identity matches the biological sex they are born with and marginalizes everyone else.

Our society also teaches youth that they should *express* their gender (through clothing, hairstyles, makeup, etc.) in a manner that matches their biological sex. Adults reinforce "appropriate" forms of gender expression by praising youth when they behave or dress in ways that align with traditional gender norms. For instance, boys who want to wear nail polish and skirts are often reprimanded or ostracized by parents, neighbors, teachers, and sometimes strangers, while those who dress in more acceptable attire (i.e., jeans, t-shirts, athletic jerseys) are viewed as normal.

Another way our society restricts gender expression is through the strict use of traditional gender pronouns. We refer to biological males as "he" and females as "she" even if that is not how they identify. Some transgender or genderqueer youth even prefer gender neutral pronouns such as ze, hir, or hirself (instead of she/he, her/his, or herself/himself). Yet, our society frowns upon youth who ask to be called an "inappropriate" or uncommon pronoun.

LGBT youth seek out messages from family members, teachers, coaches, religious figures, and community leaders as they try to understand how they fit into the world. They want to know things like: "Do people think I am different, bad, or abnormal? Am I supported? Does my family love me the way I am? Will I be rejected or harmed if people find out about my sexual orientation or gender identity? Is this person or place safe?" Too often, the answers to these questions are inferred from negative messages received in homes, neighborhoods, and schools. LGBT youth are like sponges, absorbing all of the negative messages that surround them. *Safe Spaces* offers insight into the prevalence and power of messaging. We also provide suggestions on how to send affirming messages to the LGBT youth in your life.

Our Approach to Youth

Whether you are reading *Safe Spaces* with the intention of supporting a young child or a college student, this book has something to offer. Throughout the book, we use the terms *youth* and *young people* to describe individuals as young as five to as old as twenty-five. We believe it is myopic to read about what life is like for LGBT youth only by asking young children, preteens, teenagers, or young adults. To truly comprehend the realities of LGBT youth, a wide-angle lens is necessary. Here's why:

Ask any lesbian, gay, or bisexual adult about when they first knew they were *not* heterosexual. Many will admit they felt crushes on same-gender teachers and camp counselors as early as age five or six. Or talk with transgender people who can tell you tales about their desire to dress in or play with toys designed for the "other" gender. Some four- or five-year-olds secretly yearned to be a different sex. Then ask those same LGBT people if their journeys of sexual orientation or gender identity commenced during their childhood. The response will likely be no. Hence, the need for a wide-angle lens.

Often, before children can talk or walk, they learn that boys and girls are "supposed" to dress and act in certain ways. Through fairytales and cartoons and by observing adult behavior, young children also learn whom they *should* fall in love with—someone of the opposite sex. Intense socialization into heteronormativity and traditional gender roles pressure even the youngest of children to be like everyone else—even when they are not. Young children who do not know the terms *lesbian, gay, bisexual,* or *transgender* may nonetheless feel different—and they know that being different is bad. These early experiences are just the beginning of lengthy sexual orientation and gender identity journeys.

During adolescence, while hormones are raging, young people continue to wrestle with confusing feelings about identity and relationships. Most already know they are different. But by now they have heard terms for their difference—lesbian, gay, bisexual, or transgender. Or, worse: fag, dyke, homo, queer, or freak. For adolescents, early messages about whom we *should* be attracted to or what gender we are *supposed* to be have been deeply reinforced by family, peers, and the media. Young people know they *should not* be lesbian, gay, or bisexual, nor *should* they act upon their same-sex feelings. Out of fear of rejection, transgender youth may not explore a gender identity that is different from the one they *should* settle for. As adolescents grow into young adults, they continue to wrestle with the complexity of identity. The high-school and college years are a time when youth solidify an identity independent of their parents. During these years, emerging adults also engage in sexual experimentation.

Clearly, the experiences of a five-year-old are vastly different from those of a twenty-five-year-old. From initial awareness of difference, to experimentation, to identity solidification, young LGBT people have an array of experiences. By using a wide-angle lens, *Safe Spaces* captures them all. Despite the spectrum of LGBT youth experiences, many books about sexual orientation or gender identity focus exclusively on young children, high-school students, or college populations. We take a more inclusive approach, one that spans from kindergarten to college. By including the voices of children, preteens, teenagers, and young adults, *Safe Spaces* reflects the scope of what life is like for lesbian, gay, bisexual, and transgender youth.

About the Book

This book is dedicated to creating safe spaces for LGBT youth in our schools and local communities. In Chapter 1 we offer an overview of the many forms of prejudice and discrimination faced by LGBT people. This foundational chapter describes the complexity and pervasiveness of LGBT marginalization in society. Armed with this foundational knowledge, adults are best poised to support youth in their local communities. Chapter 2 provides readers with an overview of the psychological literature on lesbian, gay, bisexual, and transgender identity development. While no two human beings are exactly the same, research has shown that LGBT people experience similar milestones, challenges, and emotions as they make sense of their sexual orientation or gender identity. Chapter 3 is dedicated to allies, individuals who stand up for the rights of LGBT youth. In this chapter we define what it means to be an ally and offer indicators of ally behavior. Chapter 4 is about family. We explain how levels of connection, communication patterns, and adaptation within families influence in the lives of young people. Chapter 4 transcends the walls of our homes and offers suggestions about how readers can support LGBT families in their communities. In Chapter 5 we travel inside K–12 and university classrooms. From kindergarten through college, young people spend many waking hours inside classrooms. You need not be a teacher, however, to benefit from this chapter. Any adult can learn from inclusive teachers like Zeke to integrate and interpret LGBT topics in their home environment. Chapter 6 reminds readers that classrooms are not the only spaces that can be unsafe for LGBT youth. From locker rooms to hallways, playing fields to playgrounds, campus cafeterias to residence halls, young people often experience marginalization outside classroom spaces. While youth spend much time at school and home, they also navigate a variety of community spaces such as libraries, community centers, and outdoor public spaces. Young people may also be involved in community activities such as sports leagues, religious organizations, or scout troops. In Chapter 7 we summarize how community spaces and organizations can be made more welcoming for LGBT youth. In that chapter, and throughout this book, we contend that it is everyone's responsibility to make our schools and communities safe for LGBT youth. We are our communities. *Safe Spaces* concludes with our hopes for the future. In the Conclusion, each of the authors goes beyond safe schools and communities to envision what a utopia could look like for LGBT youth and families. We suggest that creating safe and welcoming spaces for LGBT youth should be a starting point, not an end goal.

The crafting of *Safe Spaces* was both a personal and professional endeavor for the three authors. As educators and members of the LGBT community, we saw the need for a book that could help everyday people make schools and communities safe spaces for LGBT youth. Each of us knows of friends, loved ones, and students who have been deeply harmed by LGBT prejudice and discrimination. We also know many LGBT individuals who exhibit strength and resiliency in the face of marginalization. It is those LGBT individuals who inspired this book.

This book has special meaning for Annemarie, who has worked with college students for almost two decades. One academic year, three LGBT students attempted suicide at her college; one died, while two survived. Countless other LGBT college students shared painful stories of marginalization in the safety of Annemarie's office—an environment that was often a stark contrast to a campus rife with heterosexism and homophobia. For Gerri, *Safe Spaces* imagines a world in which children of gay and lesbian parents are not ostracized and traumatized by the social stigma associated with their parents' sexual orientation. *Safe Spaces* cannot erase the painful moments her children and stepchildren experienced, but perhaps it can ease the passage of other children through similar experiences. As a former K–8 teacher, Megan witnessed the challenges and benefits of educators, parents, and volunteers collaborating to create safe school and community environments for LGBT children. In her faculty role, Megan educates preservice teachers about creating safe classrooms for LGBT youth.

Safe Spaces is not merely a book about facts, figures, and statistics. It was born out of the real-life experiences of LGBT youth. In fact, *Safe Spaces* gives voice to a population that has historically been marginalized. This volume is filled with stories of triumph and tragedy, love and loss, joy and sadness. Stories have power to teach us valuable lessons. Stories also move readers beyond easily forgotten facts and figures to narratives that can be forever etched into our hearts and minds. *Safe Spaces* contains narratives gleaned from personal interviews with nearly 100 LGBT people from a variety of geographic regions, ethnic backgrounds, religious and spiritual persuasions, and ages. Of course, 100 people cannot teach us everything there is to know about being a lesbian, gay, bisexual, or transgender youth, so we augmented these personal interviews with public narratives—news stories about LGBT youth from around the country. In combination, these individual and public narratives offer readers a snapshot of what it is like to be a lesbian, gay, bisexual, or transgender youth in contemporary U.S. society.

Safe Spaces, however, is more than a mere collection of stories. Narratives highlight powerful individual experiences and show how people make sense of life events. In essence, stories are about not only the events of our lives, but also how we think and feel about those experiences. By engaging in an analysis of individual stories *and* the collection of narratives from over 100 people, we can learn about the society in which we live. A method referred to as narrative analysis allows researchers to holistically explore a person's identity, relationships, and emotions, all within a larger cultural and social context.[4] Through the use of narrative analysis, we identified common themes of identity, family, school, and community from more than 100 seemingly unique stories. By locating people's stories within these common themes, we show how the experiences of LGBT people are not merely random, isolated incidents. Certainly, each individual has a unique history and set of life experiences. Those experiences, however, are situated in a social context in which being lesbian, gay, bisexual, or transgender is outside the norm. Our analysis helps readers see beyond the stories of youth like Laurie, Brian, or Alex to understand the larger social implications of what it means to be a lesbian, gay, bisexual, or transgender youth in America.* *Safe Spaces* is a cultural critique of sorts, one that exposes deeply entrenched marginalization of LGBT youth in America.

Narratives and our corresponding cultural critique have the power to inspire us to reflect and act. Thus, each chapter contains what we call *Reflection Points* and *Action Steps*. *Reflection Points* are designed to prompt your thinking about how social realities for LGBT youth apply to your life. We ask you to consider things like: "Who am I? What do I value? What

---

*With the exception of those who requested we use their real name, pseudonyms are used to protect the identities of our participants.

messages do I send to the youth in my life? How safe is my home, neigh-borhood, school, or community for LGBT youth?" Creating safe spaces for LGBT youth, however, requires more than reflection; it necessitates action. Throughout this book, *Action Steps* offer tangible suggestions about how to create safe spaces for LGBT youth in your home, schools, and com-munity. We offer an array of possible activities and behaviors. Some of the *Action Steps* require substantial time commitments, while others will take only a few moments.

Like many books, *Safe Spaces* contains a glossary. Our glossary, though, is unlike most. We call ours a "Queerossary." To queer something means to do it in a manner that is unconventional or nontraditional. Conventional glossaries offer one definition for each key term. Instead of providing a sin-gle definition for each LGBT term, we provide many. Why? Terms used to describe the lesbian, gay, bisexual, and transgender community can vary slightly from source to source. We believe the variation in the definitions is insightful. The multiplicity of definitions shows there is fluidity in the ways we make sense of LGBT realities. We suggest you visit the queerossary now. There are a few key terms we use throughout the book that you should become familiar with before you continue. Those terms include: heteronormativity, heterosexism, homophobia, transphobia, sexual orien-tation, gender identity, gender expression, ally, lesbian, gay, bisexual, and transgender.

Safe Spaces also contains a list of LGBT resources. For many readers, this book is one step on a long journey toward creating safe spaces for LGBT youth. We do not expect you to become an expert on all things LGBT after reading *Safe Spaces*. Instead, we provide a list of resources that provide you access to experts when needed. While the list is not exhaustive, it provides a variety of national organizations where you can find additional information.

Now that you understand how *Safe Spaces* came to be and how it is struc-tured, how will you proceed? Well, that is up to you. There is no one right way to navigate this book. By design, foundational ideas like social margin-alization, identity, and allyship come first. Yet we realize that not everyone has the luxury of reading a book cover to cover. Every chapter in this book was therefore written in a manner that allows it to stand on its own. Each can be read independently. So go ahead: turn to the chapter that is most rel-evant to you and begin reading. Or start with Chapter 1. No matter what approach you choose, you will find information, narratives, social analyses, *Reflection Points*, and *Action Steps* to help you create safe spaces for the LGBT youth in your home, school, and community.

Chapter 1

The Marginalization of LGBT People

What image comes to mind when you think about a safe or welcoming space? Is it an inclusive classroom environment, affirming community organization, or loving home? No matter what your image, it likely does *not* include fear, hate, or exclusion. Unfortunately, LGBT youth often experience schools, extracurricular activities, community organizations, neighborhoods, and homes that are anything but safe or welcoming. Lesbian, gay, and bisexual people young and old must navigate a world where it is difficult or downright dangerous to be themselves—a world permeated by heterosexism. Heterosexism is "the assumption that everyone is heterosexual and that heterosexual relationships are natural, normal and worthy of support."[1] Transgender people also face systematic marginalization because of their gender identity or expression—especially, when those identities or expressions fall outside the bounds of what our society considers normal. These systemic forms of inequality pervade all corners of society.

While this book is about creating safe spaces for LGBT youth, the experiences of young people cannot be discussed in isolation. We believe that readers who understand the scope of discrimination for *all* LGBT people are best poised to support youth in their communities. Consider this chapter a foundation for the rest of the book. As you read forthcoming chapters that highlight narratives of pain, violence, and exclusion (Chapters 3–7), the context provided here will help you see those stories not merely as isolated incidents experienced by unlucky LGBT youth. Instead, the stories represent systematic marginalization. In this foundational chapter, we first document a few of the many forms of LGBT discrimination inscribed in federal, state, local, and organizational policy. These systemic forms of marginalization impact all LGBT people, no matter what age. Next we provide an overview of the ways LGBT youth and their families face exclusion in our homes, schools, and communities. We show how policies and practices combined with interpersonal prejudice and violence touch the lives of LGBT youth.

The State of Equality for LGBT People in the United States

Prejudice and discrimination against LGBT people are harsh realities in all realms of U.S. society: the workplace, healthcare, media, education, and politics. Why discuss workplace issues, marriage equality, healthcare, or politics in a book about creating safe spaces for LGBT youth? First, these issues touch the emotional, legal, and financial lives of LGBT people. The inability to get married, work in a safe and equal environment, or obtain equal rights will impact the futures of today's youth. Second, creating safe spaces for LGBT youth requires an understanding of how LGBT people are treated. We believe that readers who understand the depth and complexity of LGBT discrimination on a national level will be better equipped to create truly safe spaces for youth in their schools and local communities. In the following paragraphs, we describe discrimination against LGBT people that occurs at a societal level. Documenting all of the inequalities faced by LGBT people in the United States is not possible in this single chapter. Instead, we offer a snapshot of some of the barriers to LGBT equality.

Some of the most overt forms of discrimination faced by LGBT people are those inscribed in law. Many are surprised to learn, for example, that in 30 states it is perfectly legal to fire an employee because that person is (or is perceived to be) lesbian, gay, or bisexual, or that in 38 states a person can be fired for gender expression.[2] Troubling, but true. Even model employees who have won productivity awards can be fired because they are believed to be lesbian, gay, bisexual, or transgender. How can such a miscarriage of justice be legal? One of the reasons discrimination persists is that many states lack legislation that explicitly prohibits discrimination based on sexual orientation and/or gender identity. When states include sexual orientation or gender identity in their statewide nondiscrimination clauses that prohibit discrimination based on social identities (such as race, national origin, or religion), LGBT employees enjoy some protection. LGBT people who live in states without nondiscrimination statements, however, have no legal recourse if they experience workplace discrimination. It should be noted that nondiscrimination statements protect against more than merely work-related discrimination. They can also protect people who are refused service or treated in a discriminatory manner by an organization.

Lacking protection from the state, some LGBT people may turn to the federal government for redress. What LGBT people discover, however, is that anti-discrimination protections offered under current federal legislation do not extend to them. Title VII of the Civil Rights Act of 1964 prohibits discrimination based upon race, color, religion, sex, and national origin.[3] Sexual orientation and gender identity are unprotected categories under Title VII. There have been efforts to pass federal legislation to protect LGBT people in the workplace. The Employment Non-Discrimination Act (ENDA) was first introduced in 1994 during the 103rd Congress.[4] Since then, LGBT activists and allies have made many attempts to pass ENDA legislation, which would give federal protections to LGBT people. Unfortunately, to date, none of the ENDA-related bills in the Senate or House of Representatives have made it into law. Thus, there is no federal protection for LGBT people who experience discrimination as an employee or consumer.

LGBT people in every profession are at risk not only for job loss, but also for lack of promotions, harassment, and other forms of unequal treatment. Teachers, coaches, and others who work with youth are especially vulnerable. Many people believe that lesbian, gay, bisexual, or transgender people pose a risk to youth. Such fear can have negative implications for LGBT people. Teachers who have been disciplined or fired for being LGBT testify to the ongoing struggle for LGBT equality. Quality teachers are fired for proof (or mere perceptions) of their sexual orientation. We talked to many K–12 and college faculty who feared losing their jobs if their sexual orientation were to be discovered. Too often, educators who live in states without statewide nondiscrimination policies are fired because of their sexual orientation or gender identity. Unfortunately, they have little legal recourse.

Some LGBT people find employment safety in nondiscrimination statements written by their employer. Many fair-minded organizations draft their own in-house nondiscrimination policies that protect employees from sexual orientation or gender identity discrimination. Eighty-five percent of Fortune 500 companies include sexual orientation in their nondiscrimination statements; thirty-five percent include gender identity.[5]

Many educational entities, including school districts, colleges, and universities, protect LGBT people against employment discrimination or other forms of unequal treatment. Until recently, school-level protections provided peace of mind to educators, coaches, and school administrators across the country. On March 4, 2010, however, Virginia Attorney General Ken Cuccinelli issued a letter to the presidents and rectors of Virginia's public colleges in which he advised them to remove sexual orientation, gender identity, and gender expression as protected classes in their school nondiscrimination statements.[6] He argued that since the State of Virginia did not protect sexual orientation or gender identity, schools had no right to offer such protections. Luckily, that letter has yet to be supported by official legislation. Nonetheless, it is a chilling prospect for LGBT people working in Virginia colleges and universities (and for LGBT people everywhere) who feel some safety in nondiscrimination policies crafted by their employers. LGBT people who live in Tennessee also have little hope for employment safety. Currently, Tennessee has no statewide nondiscrimination statement. While the absence of this protection is troubling, legislation signed in May 2011 by Tennessee's governor represents an act of overt marginalization. SB 632/HB 600 expressly prohibits cities and counties from offering local protections to LGBT people.[7] In effect, local municipalities are prohibited by the state from adopting nondiscrimination statements to protect LGBT people in their communities.

Beyond policy, workplaces can be unsafe spaces for a host of other reasons. Employees can receive implicit and explicit messages that being lesbian, gay, bisexual, or transgender is not okay. Explicit messages can include being exposed to heterosexist language or homophobic comments, or having one's office space vandalized. Covert forms of exclusion also plague work environments. For instance, LGBT people can be "kept out of the loop" or fail to receive important work-related information. Work environments, however, include more than the daily tasks associated with a job. Work-sponsored events like an employee barbeque or holiday party are often crucial to professional success. LGBT people (and their partners) can be excluded from or made to feel unwelcome at such events.

How are employment discrimination and unwelcoming work environments relevant to LGBT youth? First, many youth work part-time jobs to support themselves or their families. When applying for part-time work, it is not uncommon for LGBT youth to hear things like, "Sorry, we are out of applications" or "We are not hiring," even when a Help Wanted sign is posted in the establishment. Moreover, LGBT youth who are employed may experience harassment or discrimination at their part-time jobs. Without legal protection, working youth have little safety.

Youth are constantly reminded how important their futures are. We ask them, "What do you want to do when you grow up?" For LGBT youth, this question may raise anxieties unrelated to their capabilities or their vocational interests. They sense that they may not be accepted for who they are in many workplaces. Peter's career dreams were altered because of LGBT discrimination. All his life he had hoped to become an FBI agent. As a college student, however, he read a memoir of an FBI officer who was fired for being gay. Through the pages of that book, his career dreams were shattered. Or consider how transgender youth whose gender expression does not match the "sex" listed on their official documents contemplate how they will dress and present themselves for a job interview. Transgender youth wrestle with questions like, "Do I express myself freely or hide who I really am?"

One career path that has been particularly treacherous for LGBT people is the military. The military is one of the most accessible paths to upward mobility for young people, especially those without a college education. At the time of the writing of this book, the government repealed the military's "Don't Ask, Don't Tell" (DADT) policy, which was signed into law by former President Bill Clinton. That policy allowed LGB people to serve in the military only if they kept their sexual orientation a secret. Anyone believed to be lesbian, gay, or bisexual was subject to dismissal under DADT. While the discriminatory policy is no more, the military climate for LGBT people may still be hostile. Consider the training videos produced by Naval Captain Honors exposed in January 2011 that made fun of same sex individuals. Those videos were shared with hundreds of sailors for pure entertainment value.[8]

Sadly, Captain Honors's ship is not the only unwelcoming military space for LGBT people. After the passage of the repeal, one college military reservist told us that she would not be comfortable sharing her orientation with her fellow unit members. Even though she knew she could not be dishonorably discharged, she feared the emotional exclusion that could ensue if she came out of the closet. Policy can be changed by the stroke of a pen, but climate (or the feel of an environment) must be changed via people's hearts. Unsafe military climates, however, have more than emotional ramifications. Service to one's country has historically offered young people a path to college. The post-9/11 GI Bill offers benefits that vary by length of active duty. Veterans are eligible for partial-to-full tuition assistance, a housing allowance, and a stipend for books and fees.[9] For youth from lower socioeconomic backgrounds, joining the military might be the only way they can afford college. But if LGBT youth fear an unwelcoming climate, the benefits of the GI Bill may be inaccessible.

Besides the fear of losing a job, LGBT people face other work-related hurdles such as unequal employment benefits. Heterosexual people regularly enjoy employment benefits not afforded to LGBT people. Some employment benefits that are often unavailable to LGBT people include access to family leave, retirement benefit payouts, and healthcare coverage.

These benefits are just a few of the many instances of heterosexual privilege described in this book. Heterosexual privilege is the combination of advantages and benefits given to those who are (or are assumed to be) heterosexual. (See the Queerossary for more about heterosexual privilege.)

Access to healthcare for our families is a concern for most Americans, whether LGB or heterosexual. Yet many lesbian, gay, and bisexual people struggle to obtain quality healthcare coverage for their same-sex partner. Transgender people also experience unique challenges related to healthcare. Many transgender employees cannot obtain appropriate coverage for themselves, especially when health plans do not cover (or deem elective) services that some transgender people need, including hormones and surgeries. Of the thousands of colleges and universities in the United States, only fifteen were rated by the Human Rights Campaign as offering health benefits that meet or exceed the minimum for transgender-inclusive coverage.[10] Moreover, lack of medical studies and subsequent medical education often leave healthcare professionals unable to provide adequate care to transgender patients.

For lesbian, gay, and bisexual people with same-sex partners, obtaining healthcare for a partner can prove to be a challenge. Many healthcare plans cover only legally married spouses. In an effort to make work-related benefits accessible to their LGBT employees, some equity-minded employers offer benefits to domestic partners. A domestic partnership recognizes a personal relationship between two adults who reside in the same household, but who are not married or in a civil union. LGBT people who work for employers who offer domestic partner benefits can purchase coverage for a same-sex partner. While the details of domestic partner healthcare policies vary from employer to employer, one fact remains constant: same-sex couples pay an average of $1,069 more a year in taxes on the exact same healthcare coverage than their heterosexual counterparts.[11] In short, even those LGBT employees who work for LGBT-friendly employers and who receive domestic partner benefits still face financial inequalities.

As with healthcare, many work-related inequities stem from the inability of same-sex couples to marry. Six states (Massachusetts, Connecticut, Iowa, New Hampshire, New York, and Vermont) and the District of Columbia recognize same-sex marriage while the remaining 44 states do not.[12] Even though many people consider marriage a religious event, it is a legally recognized status. No matter what one's religious or spiritual beliefs, marriage benefits are civil and have legal and fiscal implications. The legal benefits of marriage are extensive. In fact, the U.S. General Accounting Office produced a document listing all of the federal laws in which the status of marriage is a factor. More than 1,000 U.S. policies offer particular benefits to legally married people.[13] It would be impossible to provide a detailed list of the nearly 1,000 benefits in this chapter. Instead, a few key examples highlight the vast inequalities same-sex couples face. Widows, widowers, and divorced spouses may be eligible to receive the social security benefits of a deceased husband or wife. Many elderly people are dependent on these payments for survival. Yet LGBT couples who have been in long-term, committed relationships (but cannot legally marry) are denied such benefits. Married couples also benefit from a number of tax policies, such as capital gains taxes, which can be avoided between spouses. Legally married couples can transfer property to one another without having to claim a gain or loss for tax purposes. Same-sex couples are often forced to pay large sums of money for similar transfers. In the case of bankruptcy, married couples can file one claim and pay only one filing fee, while same sex couples cannot. These examples are just a few of the many benefits (i.e., heterosexual privileges) available to legally married couples.

In addition to the hundreds of marriage-related benefits, other family issues have a differential impact on LGBT people. For instance, hospital visitation is sometimes limited to legally recognized "family" members. Historically, same-sex couples have been excluded not only from the legal right to make health decisions for incapacitated partners, but also, in some cases, from visitation privileges. In a presidential memorandum dated April 15, 2010, President Obama called for compassion and equity in hospital visitation policies. He suggested "that participating hospitals may not deny visitation privileges on the basis of race, color, national origin, religion, sex, sexual orientation, gender identity, or disability."[14] While the memorandum is not an enforceable law, it is a ray of hope for same-sex families who fear being separated from their loved ones at a time when they need them most. Sadly, since most visitation policies are created independently by each hospital, LGBT people in many communities continue to be kept from their loved ones.

The inability to visit a partner in the hospital is only one of the ways that LGBT families face discrimination. Since U.S. society assumes that parents are a heterosexual couple, many gay and lesbian parents have to go to extraordinary lengths to protect their families. Constructing a family is an act that lesbian, gay, and transgender people plan carefully. Some same-sex couples go through adoption procedures. Others chose insemination or surrogacy. Regardless of their path to parenthood, same-sex couples face unique hurdles.

Non-birth parents often lack the same legal rights as birth parents. While approximately half the states allow same-sex, second-parent adoptions, the other half do not. In some states lesbian and gay couples are discouraged (or banned) from adopting or serving as foster parents. Exclusionary policies also keep non-birth parents from obtaining legal status as parents. Lack of legal protection can compromise the parental rights of a second gay or lesbian parent in the event of a breakup or the death or incapacitation of a birth parent. On a more local level, youth are often allowed to be registered for a community event or picked up only by a legal guardian or parent. For many gay and lesbian families, lack of legal recognition can mean an inability to support their child in an emergency. Imagine being a gay or lesbian parent who is not legally recognized by a school or community agency. Your child is hurt on the playground and transported to the hospital. But you never receive a call because you are not considered a legal parent. Unfortunately, scenarios like this happen far too often for gay and lesbian families.

Transgender parents also face a host of legal hurdles and social stigmas. Our society has fairly rigid notions of what a mother or father is supposed to look like. Parents who identify as transgender or who have transitioned from one gender to another can face prejudicial treatment and logistical challenges from school systems and community organizations who require parents to document their status as a mother or father. If transgender parents do not "look the part" or if they are in transition, they may face discrimination. For instance, a transgender male who was born a biological female could have birthed a child before (or after) a transition. Thus, they could present as a man, but technically be considered the "biological birthmother" of a child. This is only one of the many logistical challenges that transgender parents can face. Devon, a transgender parent, constantly worries about how his son will be treated by those who learn or suspect that Devon was once a woman.

All of the exclusionary policies described thus far send implicit and explicit messages to LGBT youth: it is illegal, immoral, wrong, or abnormal to be lesbian, gay, bisexual or transgender in this country. Young people learn early on that if they want equal rights, they had better not be lesbian, gay, bisexual, or transgender. These messages crush the spirits of our LGBT youth. One way to create safe spaces in your local community is to fight inequality in all realms of society. Here are a few things you can do to help equality become a reality for LGBT people.

Action Steps

- Your vote counts! Familiarize yourself with issues of LGBT inequality. Vote on matters in your state and in the country that offer LGBT equality. Visit the Human Rights Campaign website to find out more about legislation in your state. http://www.hrc.org/laws_and_elections/state.asp

- Use the power of the pen (or electronic mail)! Write to your congresspeople. Tell them you support ENDA.
- Support Marriage Equality. Visit http://www.marriageequality.org/ for more information about the national movement and what you can do in your state.
- Find out if your employer offers domestic partner benefits or if your health-care meets the needs of transgender coworkers. If not, ask if there is a committee that reviews such policies. If so, volunteer to be a new member. If not, suggest the creation of an employee task force to review employee benefits.

The Marginalization of LGBT Youth

What happens on a national level is often mirrored in our local communities, schools, and homes. Throughout this book, we offer a multitude of examples of prejudice and discrimination faced by LGBT youth. While an in-depth discussion of unsafe spaces (schools, communities, and home) can be found in forthcoming chapters, a brief overview is included here. In the following pages, we explain how policies, practices, and interpersonal violence shape the lives of LGBT youth and families.

Just as adults have no federal protection against workplace discrimination, youth have little safety in many of our schools and local communities. In fact, they often face exclusionary policies and practices that make it unsafe to explore or be open about their sexual orientation or gender identity. In the previous section, we discussed how nondiscrimination policies protect LGBT employees. Nondiscrimination statements can also safeguard LGBT youth in our schools and communities. Youth can be refused services, excluded from programs and events, or treated poorly because they are believed to be LGBT. Libraries, schools, community centers, and local establishments that have inclusive nondiscrimination statements have the potential to be safe spaces for LGBT youth. Certainly, any staff member at a library, school, or community establishment can treat youth badly. The presence of a nondiscrimination policy, however, adds a level of protection for youth. California has led the way here. In 2000, legislators passed the California Student Safety and Violence Prevention Act (AB 537) which prohibits public and nonreligious private educational institutions from discriminating against LGBT youth.[15] The law makes it clear that educators have a duty to protect LGBT students from harassment and discrimination— a ray of hope for LGBT youth.

In this book you will read about widespread discriminatory school and community policies: prohibitions from attending school dances with same-sex dates, barriers to gay-straight alliances in schools, and exclusion from community organizations and religious communities. LGBT youth face these and other challenges, often in environments without nondiscrimination policies to protect them. While many youth feel powerless when they are excluded from full participation in school and community organizations, others have challenged the status quo. In Chapter 6 you will read about Ginger, a high-school student who appealed the denial of a gay-straight alliance to her local school board.

While the previous paragraphs are relevant to all LGBT youth, transgender youth can face additional forms of marginalization in our schools and communities. School documents, standardized tests, and forms for most community activities (e.g., soccer leagues, summer camp) require demographic information. One of the first questions that most forms ask: Are you male or female? Transgender youth who do not identify as either, or youth who self-identify as a gender that does not match their legally recognized sex, struggle with these documents. (See the Queerossary for definitions of sex and gender.) Another way transgender youth can be marginalized in schools and community organizations is through dress codes. Youth who want to wear clothing that is not designed for or considered "inappropriate" for their gender can be punished for breaking dress code policy. Even when school officials look the other way, transgender youth can face harassment from peers and adults for their appearance.

One of the most basic and pressing structural inequalities that LGBT students face in our schools and communities is access to safe spaces— namely bathrooms and locker rooms. Later in this chapter, we describe various forms of violence waged against LGBT people. Much violence perpetrated against LGBT youth in schools and communities happens in semi-private spaces away from adult supervision. Using the bathroom or a locker room are basic needs that all youth have. Many LGBT youth, however, are denied such basic needs. Many schools, libraries, and community organizations do not offer lockable unisex or single-stall bathrooms that offer safety for LGBT youth.

Rules, policies, and structures are just some of the ways that LGBT people are marginalized in school; another is by being treated as if they are invisible. When youth see themselves reflected in positive images, they feel included. Conversely, when there is an absence of positive images of LGBT people, feelings of invisibility can take hold. One of the most common ways youth see themselves represented is through literature. Even though positive images of LGBT people in literature have increased since the Gay Rights Movement of the 1970s, very few LGBT-friendly books make it to public schools or community libraries. In fact, many of books with lesbian, gay, bisexual, or transgender characters have been included in the American Library Association's list of frequently challenged books.[16] A book is considered challenged when a person or group tries to restrict or remove a particular book from a library. A banned book is one that has been removed from library circulation. While books are challenged or banned for a host of reasons (e.g., sexually explicit material, use of drugs, profanity, references to the occult), books with lesbian, gay, bisexual or transgender characters are often challenged. Community and school libraries may restrict access to copies of books such as *And Tango Makes Three*, *Luv Ya Bunches*, and *The Perks of Being a Wallflower* because they have "homosexual content." Sometimes the removal or restriction of a book is done officially through school board decisions. Other times, the restrictions are done informally, with questionable books placed behind the checkout counter. To access the book, youth must verbally request it from a librarian—a frightening prospect for many young people. Moreover, concerned parents or community members have been known to hide, steal, or destroy books that they do not want young people to see.

In some cases, teachers have been prohibited or strongly encouraged not to use books that contain any LGBT messages. Teachers who defy such suggestions often face negative repercussions. Two teachers in Massachusetts, where same-sex marriage is legal, were sued because they read age-appropriate books that featured LGBT characters.[17] The lack of books with LGBT characters sends a message to all youth. The message: it is not okay to be lesbian, gay, bisexual, or transgender. Young people who have questions about their sexual orientation or gender identity often do not know where to turn for support. Many youth fear talking to family, teachers, or religious figures about their feelings. Sometimes books can be the only safe place to learn about LGBT issues or to find role models. Brad, a young person who was born a woman but believed himself to be male, never had the opportunity to meet other transgender people. So he turned to books, notably transgender memoirs, as he searched for role models. In Chapter 7 you will read about Laurie, a lesbian who believes that access to LGBT literature "saved her life" when she was a child.

The removal of LGBT-friendly educational resources goes far beyond books. Many schools prohibit or frown upon teachers discussing any LGBT issues in their classrooms. In fact, as we were writing this book, the Tennessee State Senate passed a bill that would restrict K–8 teachers from introducing LGBT issues in the classroom.[18] Yet exclusionary policies like these are only part of the problem. In our schools, youth regularly receive hidden messages that exclude LGBT issues or demonize LGBT people. Frequently omitted from the school curriculum are the contributions of famous and influential LGBT people in history. Youth may learn about famous people like Langston Hughes and Walt Whitman, but they rarely are told they are gay. While being gay may not seem relevant to Whitman's accomplishments, the lack of positive gay role models teaches youth that no LGBT people ever accomplished anything noteworthy. LGBT exclusion from the curriculum happens at all grade levels, kindergarten through college. While some colleges and universities offer LGBT or queer studies, such programs are few and far between. In the educational world, the invisibility of LGBT people and issues is considered a form of hidden curriculum.[19] While the curriculum typically covers topics such as math, science, and spelling, the hidden curriculum includes the unofficial and less overt messages that youth learn on a daily basis. In the hidden curriculum, heterosexuality and gender conformity are the norm.

In our schools and communities, the hidden curriculum surrounds our youth and teaches them that being heterosexual or cisgender (not transgender) is normal and valued. While the number of gay-straight alliances is on the rise, there are still many schools where clubs or organizations for LGBT youth are officially (or unofficially) banned. The message: We do not want to provide a safe space for people like you. The lack of safe spaces for LGBT youth are in sharp contrast to the number of school and community events that promote heterosexuality and gender conformity. For instance, boys and girls are encouraged to bring dates of the opposite sex to school dances. School lesson plans and religious teachings are filled with positive messages about heterosexual courtship, marriage, and parenting. Community organizations that host programs and events for youth often encourage heterosexuality through activities such as kissing booths or chastity clubs. In fact, children are socialized from a young age to find a husband or wife. Children's books and movies are filled with stories of princes and princesses who exhibit gender identities and expressions that society deems normative. No matter the tale, cisgender princes and princesses always end up living "happily ever after" as heterosexual couples. The invisibility of LGBT people, coupled with the pressure to be heterosexual or cisgender, can have profound psychological effects on LGBT youth. As we describe in

Chapter 2, LGBT youth can experience shame and self-hatred. The pressures of the hidden curriculum can intensify these feelings.

In some cases, LGBT-friendly resources never make it to our schools, libraries, or homes because they are restricted by politicians with anti-LGBT agendas. In Chapter 5 you will learn how political influence was used to censor a positive media message about a healthy gay family on PBS. Sadly, it is one of many instances where LGBT people are made invisible in the media. Exclusion from pubic television is merely the tip of the iceberg when it comes to the ways the media exclude LGBT people. Youth, and the adults who work with them, are influenced by television, music, and the Internet. We live in a society dependent on multimedia gadgets. Most youth, and even young children, have access to iPods, cell phones, laptop computers, iPads, and tablets. Whether they are at school, in their homes, or in their local communities, youth of today are connected to these electronic devices that allow them round-the-clock media access. Youth spend significant amounts of time in front of a television set, with children between the ages of one and five watching thirty-two hours and youth ages six to eleven viewing twenty-eight hours of television a week.[20] Consider how often lesbian, gay, bisexual, or transgender people are shown on prime-time television or in blockbuster movies. While more LGBT people are being portrayed in the media, too often they are in secondary roles or play characters who are mentally ill, criminals, or live an "atypical" life. Overall invisibility combined with negative portrayal of the small numbers of LGBT characters can have profound effects on impressionable youth.

Youth are often drawn to media images because they contain pop icons. Whether they are television, movie, or music celebrities, famous people influence the thoughts and self-concepts of youth. When famous people engage in anti-LGBT behavior they send messages to youth that prejudice and discrimination against LGBT people is okay. For instance, a popular music star has a song in which she decides to get revenge on an ex-boyfriend. Her solution is to tell everyone he is gay. While the example may seem harmless, associating an LGBT identity with revenge suggests something negative about the LGBT community. Or consider the harm done when admired professional athletes use gay slurs.

Famous celebrities can influence the lives of youth, but local public figures can also have an impact. Local politicians, religious figures, school officials, business owners, and other community leaders can reinforce positive or negative messages about LGBT people. There are many positive role models in local communities. But there are also many community spaces where LGBT youth encounter adult figures who are poor role models—or worse, discriminatory. Through campaign speeches and public-policy stances, community leaders send messages that tell LGBT youth that there is something wrong with them. For instance, local leaders who refer to LGBT people as an "abomination," view same-sex marriage as a "sin," or vote against pro-LGBT ballot measures send negative and hurtful messages to LGBT youth. Moreover, youth in some religiously affiliated organizations are told that being LGBT is wrong and immoral. Receiving such messages can be damaging to impressionable LGBT youth.

Action Steps

- How much do you know about LGBT marginalization in your local schools and community? Bring together a group of parents, friends, and neighbors to discuss the issues raised in this chapter.
- Talk to the youth in your life about the power of the media. What images do they see and hear about LGBT people? What do those messages mean to them? How do celebrities influence their thoughts and behaviors?
- Talk to your community and school librarian about banned and challenged books. Find out what LGBT friendly resources are available to youth.

Discriminatory or non-inclusive policies and practices often make our communities and schools unsafe spaces for LGBT youth. In addition to structural issues, much LGBT marginalization happens on an interpersonal level. LGBT youth regularly face physical and emotional violence in our schools, athletic fields, neighborhoods, and community organizations. Ninety percent of transgender middle and high-school youth experience verbal harassment and more than half face physical violence because of their gender identity.[21] Lesbian, gay, and bisexual youth also report high levels of verbal harassment (86.2%) and physical abuse (66.5%).[22] Interpersonal violence doesn't end when youth go to college. LGBT university students experience derogatory remarks on campus, deliberate exclusion by peers, and harassment by university officials.[23]

Some might argue that taunts, derogatory terms, and mean-spirited jokes are just "kids being kids." We disagree. Verbal harassment is often the gateway to other forms of interpersonal violence. (For more information about bullying, see Chapter 6.) Even if verbal abuse doesn't turn physical, the effects can be profound. Almost a third of LGBT youth skip school because they fear for their safety.[24] Other youth forgo activities such as sports, clubs, and community events because they are afraid of being bullied. Bullying, however, does not stop when youth leave the school grounds. A study of LGBT youth from middle school to college found that more than half had experienced cyberbullying in the previous month.[25] Cyberbullying can include the posting of humiliating photos, threatening emails or text messages, and hateful information posted on social networking sites. Youth who experience bullying, taunting, or harassment in person or through cyberspace are at risk for depression, lowered self-esteem, and suicide. A recent study of 31,852 eleventh graders found that LGBT youth were significantly more likely to have attempted suicide than their heterosexual peers (21.5% versus 4.2%).[26] These harsh realities should cause us to pause and consider the importance of creating safe spaces for LGBT youth.

While harassment and bullying from peers is widespread, many youth also experience physical and verbal abuse from family members. Families have a profound impact on the lives of youth. Home should be a place of nurturance and support. Yet too many LGBT youth reside in homes that are unwelcoming or unsafe. Some youth live with parents, siblings, or other relatives who subject them to verbal abuse and punishment for being LGBT. Youth who experience negative reactions from their families about their sexual orientation are 8.4 times more likely to have attempted suicide, 5.9 times more likely to report depression, and 3.4 times more likely to cope by using illegal drugs than youth from more accepting families.[27] In Chapter 4 you will read about Jim, whose family rejected him for being gay. As a sophomore in college, Jim committed suicide.

Like Jim, many LGBT youth face shunning or outright rejection from family. One study estimated that 26 percent of youth who come out to their family are disowned and become homeless.[28] Youth who live on the streets or end up in the foster-care system face a variety of health and safety issues. Lambda Legal has documented some of the challenges faced by youth in foster care to include: disapproval by caseworkers, abuse by foster parents, harassment by foster siblings, violence in group homes, and prejudicial treatment throughout the system.[29] In Chapter 4, Mara, a foster care supervisor, relates her experiences with the foster system.

In addition to peers, family, and the foster system, some youth experience marginalization from adults in their communities who are supposed to be serving as role models—soccer coaches, camp directors, teachers, religious leaders, and principals. Many youth hear respected role models use derogatory terms like "fag" or "homo" in their presence. Other youth overhear adults in their communities tell jokes or stories that demonize or make fun of LGBT people. Transgender youth can be punished by coaches, troop leaders, and neighbors for not acting how a boy or girl should. These messages can have a profound and negative impact on LGBT youth. In fact, research has shown that witnessing bad behavior in non-parental adults inspires bad behavior in youth. Luckily, that same study also reinforced how influential positive role models can be.[30] The choice to read this book likely reflects your desire to be a positive role model for LGBT youth. In each of the forthcoming chapters, you will learn countless ways to serve as a role model to youth. Moreover, this book is filled with concrete suggestions on how you can make your home, neighborhood, schools, and community safe for LGBT youth.

Reflection Point

- In what ways do you already serve as a role model to youth in your community? How can you build upon those strengths to support LGBT youth?
- Have you talked to the youth in your life about the prevalence of LGBT bullying or harassment in school or community spaces? What are their perceptions of the issues faced by LGBT youth? Ask them how you can be supportive.

Chapter 2

LGBT Identity

Who am I? Am I different? Who do I want to become? How do I fit in to my family, community, and society? People exploring their identities ask many questions like these. Identity is a complex combination of our biology, personality, beliefs, and cultural backgrounds. Our identities are what makes us uniquely us. Identity also involves our sense of who we are and how we fit into larger society. For many young people, answers to questions of identity are strongly influenced by their sexual orientation or sense of gender. In this chapter, we discuss what it means to be lesbian, gay, bisexual, or transgender in a world where being lesbian, gay, bisexual, or transgender is not "normal." More specifically, we discuss what it means to have an LGBT identity. *Is* there such a thing as a "gay identity"? Decades of psychological research suggest there is. How then, do youth develop a lesbian, gay, bisexual, or transgender identity?

In the following pages, we share basic identity concepts that will help readers understand some of the psychosocial issues related to being a LGBT youth. We describe the experiences of youth from elementary school to college to show what LGBT identity journeys can look like in everyday life. Stories in the forthcoming pages offer parents, neighbors, educators, and politicians insight into how to create safe spaces where LGBT youth can grow and thrive—spaces where youth can develop a healthy identity. By understanding the complexity of identity, readers will be best poised to understand and support LGBT youth in their homes, schools, and communities.

In this chapter, we argue that identity formation is both individual and community work. Youth do not develop their identities in a vacuum. Sustained social interactions with other human beings shape an individual's sense of identity. Moreover, the identity struggles of LGBT youth are situated within larger societal issues of discrimination and prejudice. Lesbian, gay, bisexual, and transgender identities cannot be separated from a youth's everyday surroundings. Hence, this chapter provides an overview of the ways family, community, and school settings influence the identity development of LGBT youth.

Identity and Context

For decades, psychologists have grappled with the question of what it means to be gay.[1] Some researchers suggest that lesbian, gay, bisexual, and transgender people progress through a series of stages over the course of their lifetimes. Stage theorists believe that it takes a major life event or a transformative learning experience for someone to move from one stage to the next. Other research suggests that LGBT identity is not so linear, nor does every lesbian, gay, bisexual, or transgender person develop the same way. Scholars who resist stage theories suggest that there are developmental milestones or identity processes that lesbian, gay, bisexual, and transgender people can achieve across the lifespan.[2] Typical milestones include coming out to self, coming out to family, and immersing oneself in the LGBT community. Unlike developmental stages, milestones are less sequential and can be achieved at any time. A person does not have to experience a major life event to move from one milestone to another.

Whether they are based upon a stage or milestone framework, psychological identity models offer valuable information about the experiences of lesbian, gay, bisexual, and transgender people. Identity models tell us a lot, but not all we need to know about the complex identity journeys of LGBT youth. Because it is difficult to find research participants, LGBT identity studies are often completed with small numbers of lesbians, gay men, or bisexuals. Transgender youth are included in research studies with even less frequency. Therefore, findings from LGBT identity studies may not accurately represent the full spectrum of lived realities for LGBT people. Nonetheless, identity models offer insight into the ways youth make sense of being lesbian, gay, bisexual, or transgender. Because specific LGBT identity development theories should be used with caution, we have chosen not to present particular models of LGBT identity development. Instead, we provide an overview of three key themes that exist in almost every identity model.

The voices in this chapter illustrate both the commonality and the diversity of identity in the LGBT community. In the narratives, readers will note many similar themes, but will also recognize the uniqueness of each identity journey. Much of the uniqueness stems from the fact that every youth grows up in a unique environment. While LGBT youth may face common forms of exclusion in their homes, neighborhoods, and schools, no two lesbian, gay, bisexual, or transgender individuals grow up in identical environments.

Even people who were born in the same town were born into different families, and likely had different home environments, friends, and teachers and lived in different neighborhoods. It has been argued that "the developmental trajectory of a given person is similar to that of no person who has ever lived."[3] We agree: different environments influence our development into unique human beings. That is not to say that we believe that being lesbian, gay, or bisexual is a result of one's environment. Quite the contrary, most people would argue that they are born lesbian, gay, bisexual, or heterosexual. However, the process of coming to terms with, and having positive feelings about, a LGBT identity is shaped by the level of support and safety in our home, school, and community environments.

Erik Erikson, one of the classic scholars on identity, argued that identity is shaped by a person's experiences, reflections, and observations in society.[4] More specifically, identities are shaped by our observations of, interactions with, and reflections upon our surroundings. In essence, we are products of our interactions with our environments. Figure 2.1 offers a visual image of the environments that shape young people's sense of self. Those settings include their homes, schools, extracurricular environments, local communities, spiritual and religious organizations, virtual communities, and the media. In addition to places where development occurs, Figure 2.1 also includes people who influence development. Family members, teachers, classroom aides, coaches, community figures, peers, and others shape the identity journeys of lesbian, gay, bisexual, or transgender youth.

Key Themes in Lesbian, Gay, and Bisexual Identity Development

In this section, common themes from lesbian, gay, and bisexual identity development models are shared. We refer to the three key themes as identity beginnings, identity explorations, and identity integrations. You may note that the "T" is missing in this section. That is because the three key themes emerged from identity models specific to lesbian, gay, and bisexual people. We include identity development for transgender youth in a forthcoming section. Here, the voices of young people exemplify three themes prevalent in LGB identity models. We also describe how readers might use identity themes to better understand young people and to subsequently create safe spaces for lesbian, gay, and bisexual youth.

Identity Beginnings

A number of overlapping themes related to early developmental issues can be found in LGB stage models and milestone theories. Many of those

FIGURE 2.1   Environmental Influences on LGBT Identity

theories suggest that early realities for LGB youth include initial awareness of difference, confusion, self-hatred, and/or mere tolerance for being different. Why are such negative thoughts and emotions associated with early phases of an LGB identity? The answer is partially found in Chapter 1. All Americans are born into a society where LGB prejudice and discrimination are harsh realities. In Chapter 1 we described how U.S. culture teaches youth that being heterosexual is normal and valued, while being lesbian, gay, and bisexual (or transgender) is deviant and shameful. Further, the media and Internet can reinforce negative stereotypes and exclusionary practices. All of us—lesbian, gay, bisexual, and straight—are surrounded by heterosexual-affirmative (and LGB-marginalizing) environments from birth. Since young people spend most of their time in schools, local neighborhoods, and their homes, they are especially vulnerable to anti-LGB messages in those environments. Heterosexist messages from influential parents, teachers, coaches, neighbors, and peers certainly affect identity beginnings.

While LGB youth may experience some similar identity beginnings, the identity path of each individual is unique because each individual's surrounding environment is also unique. For instance, initial awareness of difference is a typical identity beginning. Yet *how* and *when* youth come to this awareness is different for each person. Most identity models suggest that lesbian, gay, and bisexual people engage in initial awareness at very early ages. Many of the LGB individuals who shared their stories for this book told us they were cognizant of their difference at very young ages, sometimes as early as five or six. By the age of six, Carl knew he was "different." However, as a six-year-old, he did not have the words to express his difference. It was only when he entered high school that he understood and could verbalize that his difference meant "being gay."

Other hallmarks of identity beginnings include confusion, self-hatred, or self-tolerance. The presence and intensity of these feelings are largely a result of the level of support and safety in a youth's home, school, and community environments. LGB-affirming environments help youth mediate negative thoughts, while unsafe spaces fuel self-hatred. As explained in Chapter 1, children learn early in life that same-sex feelings, attractions, and relationships are not "normal." Sometimes such messages are subtle; other times, they are overt. On school buses and on playgrounds, it is not uncommon for children to hear the derogatory terms "fag" and "homo." Many of the people who shared their experiences in this book were called those terms (and worse) as young people.

Nick grew up in suburbia with his parents. He started having same-sex feelings at a very young age. The feelings were confusing. He described how he learned from parents and peers that being gay was "bad." Nick did not want to be "bad." Negative messages were reinforced in middle and high school where he was called hateful names. He shared, "When I was little, I never totally understood what being gay was. I just knew it was bad. I remember being beat up a lot in sixth grade. I have been called a faggot, queer, homo, everything . . . and been brought to tears by it. But I've learned that words are just words."[5] Nick went on to explain that he never told his parents about the abuse he encountered in school and in the community. His parents were deeply religious people who believed "homosexuality was a sin." Thus, while Nick was wrestling with coming to terms with being gay, he was unable to find safe spaces in school, at home, or in the community where he could make sense of his emerging gay identity. Nick's conflicted feelings about the power of words can be seen in the juxtaposition of his conclusion that "words are just words" with his admission that these words had brought him to tears. Would that hateful words were all LGB people had to endure. As discussed in Chapter 1, LGB people can experience not only rejection, but outright violence because of their identity. Unfortunately, hatred and violence happen in all communities and schools. The people who contributed stories to this book grew up all over the United States—in small, large, and mid-sized towns. Whether in Mayberry or Manhattan, many of our participants experienced verbal abuse or physical violence.

Like Nick, all of the LGB people we talked to learned at a very young age that homosexuality was "a bad thing." Nick learned from bullies and unaccepting parents, but youth learn messages from all of the people and places listed in Figure 2.1. For instance, young people are bombarded by images in storybooks, films, cartoons, television, even fairytales that teach them that princes and princesses (i.e., boys and girls) belong together. In the vignette below, Nancy reflects upon her internal struggles as a young lesbian. Her story is a good example of how youth can internalize homophobia (believing negative messages about LGBT people and engaging in self-hatred). By middle school, societal images had taught her that beautiful women were those loved by men. She internalized subtle messages from magazines, television, and music that lesbians were somehow less attractive, on the outside and inside. Nancy described how she felt "good" about herself before she thought she was a lesbian. As soon as she started to recognize that she was "different" her self-esteem plummeted. In fact, she described feeling "horrible" about herself. Nancy had learned at a very young age that "pretty" was equated with girls being attractive to boys. In Chapter 1 we described how LGB people are marginalized by laws, policy, and the media. We also described how the power of everyday cultural norms and beliefs can inflict harm on LGB people by teaching them that they are not "normal." As a child, Nancy associated fitting in with physical beauty (another culturally derived norm). She struggled to accept her lesbian identity because she assumed that physical beauty (and social acceptability) was exclusive to the heterosexual world.

Youth who find themselves in dangerous or unwelcoming environments develop many coping mechanisms. Some avoid violence by "passing" as straight. Youth can pass as heterosexual by remaining silent and letting others assume they are not lesbian, gay, or bisexual. Others actively pretend to be heterosexual as a measure of self-protection. We argue, as many developmental experts do, that young people cannot develop healthy LGB identities if they feel like they must hide who they really are.

Anthony explained that as a fifth grader he felt the need to pretend to have "crushes" on members of the opposite sex so his peers would not suspect he was gay. Melody, a lesbian, also described how she had what she called "decoy dates" in high school to uphold the image that she was heterosexual. Both of these young people pretended to be heterosexual to protect their physical and psychological safety. Having to pretend to be something you are not can have profound psychological implications for youth. A positive sense of self and healthy self-esteem are paramount to identity development. Creating safe spaces where youth can "be themselves" is fundamentally important. Only when they are comfortable with who they are can they begin to more deeply explore what it means to have a lesbian, gay, or bisexual identity.

Reflection Point

- Have you ever thought about the identity of the youth in your life? Would your home be a safe place for a youth to talk about her, his or hir identity struggles?
- Consider the messages you send to young people. Do you unconsciously send messages to girls that beauty is equated with being attractive or desirable to boys? Or do you send messages that boys should find girls attractive? If so, you may be sending messages about heterosexuality as "normal." What more affirming messages can you send to youth?
- How can you ensure that you create safe spaces where youth feel like they can be smart, beautiful, and loved for who they are?
- What would you do if you suspected a youth in your life was "passing"?

Identity Explorations

Many identity models suggest that people move from being mired in self-condemnation to increasing self acceptance. Why is this? A simple answer is that it is hard to maintain an identity rooted in confusion, self-hate, and pain. It has been argued that one of the most motivating forces in human behavior is the search for self-worth.[6] It is a natural tendency to seek an identity rooted in self-worth and happiness. All of the people who shared stories for this book talked about moving from negative to more positive identity spaces. Some people moved through awareness, questioning, and pain quickly, while others lingered. Again, identity progression is largely the result of people's interactions with their environments. Positive environments, or safe spaces, help us learn to feel good about ourselves, while anti-LGB environments serve as obstacles to healthy identity development.

Jarrod reflected upon his transition from a negative to a positive self-image that happened between high school and college: He said, "I don't mind being seen with gay people anymore! I don't mind being seen as gay myself. I even find it sort of fun to make sure that people know that I'm gay. . . . It was probably six months after I came to this university that I found out that it's okay to be gay. Where I'd been living before in the deep, deep South just wasn't really the time or the place to be gay." And yet, Jarrod *was* gay in the deep, deep South. It wasn't until college that he discovered it was "okay to be gay." His choice of words is telling. Jarrod's early social experiences taught him that being gay was shameful. It took not only time, but also a positive college environment for Jarrod to unlearn the negative messages he had internalized about gay people, including himself.

While Jarrod lived in the deep South, he kept his identity secret. He allowed few people to know who he really was. Positive interpersonal relationships are essential for all people, including LGB youth. Yet it is difficult to establish meaningful and healthy relationships with others if we do not feel positively about ourselves. When youth engage in identity explorations, safe places and people (i.e., positive role models and supportive adults) are incredibly important.

As youth explore what it means to be lesbian, gay, or bisexual, it is essential for them to see examples of healthy and "normal" LGB adults in their local neighborhoods and in society. Youth are acutely aware of the presence (or lack thereof) of positive lesbian, gay or bisexual role models. Valerie, a college student, was exploring what it might mean to be bisexual. She explained that if she had positive role models, she "wouldn't be so lost and confused." As parents, educators, community leaders, and allies, we should pay special attention to youth who seem to be struggling with developing a positive sense of self. If you are lesbian, gay, or bisexual, being an active and out role model can mean the world to young people like Valerie. If you are heterosexual, take the time to introduce youth in your life to positive LGB role models through film, books, or interpersonal relationships.

In addition to safe adults, young people sometimes seek other lesbian, gay, or bisexual youth to find out answers to their burning questions. Am I really LGB? What does being lesbian, gay, or bisexual mean for me? How will my family react? Will I lose my friends? Some youth are lucky enough to have personal connections to other LGB youth in their schools or communities. Others, however, do not know any other LGB youth.

These young people have no one to talk to about their identity struggles. Sometimes, isolated youth look to the Internet to find connection with others. The Internet can be very helpful to youth who are isolated in unsafe environments. Young people can look up answers to their LGB questions and learn about gay-friendly organizations such as PFLAG, GLSEN, and HRC. There are also many safe sites where young people can connect with other LGB youth. However, there are also many predators on the Internet who will take advantage of youth. Additionally, there are many anti-LGB websites that promote hate. The messages on these anti-LGB sites can certainly hinder positive identity exploration for LGB youth.

Another milestone that often happens when youth are exploring their sexual orientation is that they "come out" to others. Coming out is an ongoing interpersonal process of admitting to oneself and others that one is lesbian, gay, or bisexual. For many young people, coming out happens once they have completed some identity exploration and feel somewhat confident claiming a lesbian, gay, or bisexual identity. Coming out can be a terrifying prospect for young people, especially those who live in unwelcoming and unsafe environments. Eduardo admitted that coming out to his father was "one of the scariest things I ever did." Even young people with relatively open-minded parents can fear coming out. The negative messages young people receive from *all* of the people and places in Figure 2.1 are powerful. The barrage of anti-LGB messages from those people and places can even overshadow positive messages sent from parents. Jackie described her parents as very accepting people. Her mother even had a gay friend. However, when she considered coming out to her parents, she still worried. Would they reject her? Would they love her any less? Would they be disappointed?

While many people believe that coming out happens once, the reality is that coming out is an ongoing and lifelong process. Every time a lesbian, gay, or bisexual individual meets a new person, they must decide whether or not to disclose their sexual orientation by coming out. Each time young people meet new classmates, teammates, or neighbors, they have to consciously think about coming out.

Action Steps

- Be a supporter and positive role model by learning more about the identity struggles of LGB youth. Identity exploration is often about unanswered questions. The more you know, the more helpful you can be.
- Realize when you may not be the most effective role model for the youth in your life. Refer youth to organizations where they can find helpful role

models. Become familiar with support organizations for students (such as GLSEN) and for families (such as PFLAG).

- If a lesbian, gay, or bisexual youth comes out to you, know they are seeking understanding and support. Listen intently. Don't be judgmental. Ask youth what they need from you. Don't assume you know what they need (i.e., counseling, resources, a listening ear).

- Keep the confidence of a young person who comes out to you. Do not share his or her identity with anyone else. The only exception would be if the youth indicated an intention to engage in self-harm.

- If you know a young person who is looking to connect with others, recommend sites like OutProud (www.outproud.org), a safe forum where LGBT youth can dialogue about their experiences. See the Appendix for other youth-friendly LGBT sites.

Identity Integrations

Many identity models suggest that people eventually integrate their LGB identity into a more complicated and holistic sense of self. While identity integrations often begin in adolescence, the process can last a lifetime. Identity models also suggest that LGB people have varying perspectives on the centrality or salience of their sexual orientation. People who shared their stories with us represented a full spectrum of possibilities about the level of significance of the LGB part of their identity. For instance, while some people said things like, "Being gay is just one small part of who I am," others, like Craig, argued that being gay was far more central to their identity. He said, "I think your sexual orientation is a huge part of who you are! I mean, a lot of people don't even realize it, what a huge part!" The significance of one's "LGB-ness" often evolves over a person's lifetime. For youth, however, understanding how being lesbian, gay, or bisexual fits into the rest of their lives can be paramount. Creating safe spaces for students to explore their identities is essential. Adults must be prepared to support youth as they struggle to figure out how being lesbian, gay, or bisexual fits into their world.

Unlike the negative feelings (such as confusion and shame) that can be associated with earlier identity themes, pride, empowerment, and self-love can often accompany identity integrations. While identity models from the 1970s and 1980s suggest that positive experiences happen in adulthood, many contemporary LGB high-school and college students express pride and self-love. Some of the college students we talked to said things like, "I am proud to be gay," "Being bisexual rocks," and "I wouldn't change who I am—I love me."

It is important to remember that the timing of people's movement to more positive thoughts depends wholly on safeness and support, or lack thereof, in their everyday environments. Social support has positive effects on a person's mental health, physical health, and overall quality of life.[7] Moreover, the presence of positive adult role models and supporters is key to identity integration, just as it is to other aspects of identity development. It is likely that young people who experience identity integration have had the good fortune of safe spaces and supportive people to help them along their identity journeys. Manny explained how the combination of encouragement from a loving mother, caring teachers, and supportive principal helped him develop a sense of pride in his gay identity during his junior year of high school. In fact, Manny was not just privately proud of his identity, he was an activist who shared his sexual orientation openly.

Many identity models suggest that once people feel good about their sexual orientation, they become committed to publicly identifying as LGB. They may also seek social and political connections to LGB groups. Many lesbian, gay, and bisexual youth join high-school or college clubs such as gay-straight alliances (GSAs) or diversity organizations where they can celebrate their identity and engage in activism. (More about GSAs in Chapter 6.) Youth also grow into adults who are actively involved in LGB book groups, choruses, arts groups, community activist groups, and civil rights organizations. Participation in LGB groups ebbs and flows over people's lifetimes as they need and desire more (or less) support, friendship, and connection with other LGB people. Such ebbs and flows are natural, as people's identities transform over time.

Action Steps

- Support the youth in your life who want to engage in LGBT communities such as gay-straight alliances or other local LGBT-positive youth groups.
- Don't fear activism. Support youth who want to be out activists in their schools and communities. Be a role model and join an LGBT activist group yourself.

Identity Beyond LGB

In the previous pages we focused on themes common to the lesbian, gay, and bisexual models of identity. In this section we go beyond lesbians, gays, and bisexuals to other identities. First we discuss identity issues related to being transgender. Next we explore the meaning of a queer identity. Finally, we share some thoughts on the complexity of multiple identities.

Transgender Identities

While LGB identity development is about sexual orientation, transgender identity journeys are about reconciling one's sense of gender, gender expression, and/or chromosomal makeup. So, while LGB youth struggle with attractions during their identity journey, transgender youth grapple with what it means to be a "boy," "girl," or no gender at all. Their identity journeys may include developing a healthy gender identity that may not "match" their assigned sex at birth. Transgender youth may also wrestle with how to express themselves with regard to their felt gender. Because transgender issues are about gender, not sexual orientation, transgender individuals can identify as heterosexual, lesbian, gay, bisexual, asexual, or queer.

While there are some individual transgender stories and memoirs[8], little research is available on transgender identity development. The word *transgender* is an umbrella term that encompasses a variety of different types of people with very different experiences. People who identify as transsexuals, drag queens, drag kings, gender queer, gender variant, and intersex are all included under the transgender umbrella. It is unlikely that people with such diverse identities share a common path of identity development. For instance, children who were born intersexed (with ambiguous genitalia) will likely have a different identity journey than those who were born a genetic male or female but "feel" like they belong to the other gender. People who dress (i.e., cross-dressers) or perform in clothes of the "opposite gender" (i.e., drag kings and drag queens) will likely follow a different identity path than those who want to change their sex through surgery. Even transsexuals who live as a sex other than the one assigned at birth may follow different identity paths depending on *if* and *how* they desire to change their bodies through hormones or sex-reassignment surgery.

While a unitary transgender identity theory is improbable, transgender people may experience hurdles that can be similar to lesbian, gay, and bisexual people. In fact, some researchers have suggested that transgender people may experience similar milestones to gay, lesbian, and bisexual people.[9] One of the few identity models available is restricted to transsexual people and suggests there are fourteen stages to identity.[10] That model encompasses many of the same themes found in LGB identity theories such as discovery, confusion, comparison, tolerance, acceptance, and integration.

Like LGB people, transgender individuals must develop an identity in a society where they experience discrimination and prejudice because of their difference. In this case, that difference relates to their gender, not their sexual orientation. One of the milestones for gay and lesbian people includes the decision to move toward adopting a healthy sexual identity. Transgender youth may experience a similar milestone. At early ages, transgender youth may have a first awareness that their gender identity or expression does not "match" their biological sex. Some studies show that very young children may want to dress like or *be* a boy or girl—even if they were not born as such.[11] A study with 16- to 20-year-old transgender youth found that first awareness of their gender differences happened at age 10.[12] Many young people who talked with us knew even earlier in life.

Another milestone is sharing one's identity with others. Like "coming out" for lesbian, gay and bisexual youth, telling others about one's gender identity can be stressful. Transgender youth receive messages from the people and places listed in Figure 2.1 that they should behave as, look like, and *be* the sex they were assigned at birth. Studies with transgender youth suggest that the age at which people first share their gender identity with others varies widely. Some youth who are lucky enough to live in supportive environments (or are bold enough to defy unsafe environments) might explore their gender identity in middle or high school. Other transgender individuals are adults by the time they are comfortable sharing their identity with others.

Nick began to consider taking on a transgender identity in college. Sometimes he felt more male than female, while on other days she felt more female than male. However, Nick had very few adults to talk to about these confusing feelings. Ricardo, on the other hand, had a mother who patiently listened and tried to understand how her biological son believed herself to be a woman. Ricardo loved having an identity that transcended gender boundaries. Ricardo also had the courage to go to high school dressed in drag, even when her peers called her names.

Another milestone for some transgender people can include openly living a lifestyle that is in line with their gender identity, not their assigned birth sex. This milestone can be especially difficult for youth. Some families respond negatively to, or expressly prohibit youth from living a life where their gender expression differs from their birth sex. For instance, family members may shame boys from wearing makeup, nail polish, or dresses. On the other hand, girls may be told that they look too much like a tomboy and be forced to wear pastel colors, dresses, and makeup. Certainly, not all families respond negatively to non-normative gender expressions—but many do. Even open-minded adults may encounter disagreements with partners about *how much* non-normative expression to support. Ed and his wife cannot agree about allowing their child to express himself by wearing nail polish. So Ed promises his son that he can paint his nails when mommy is out of town.[13] While we applaud Ed for supporting his child's gender expression, doing it secretly (while mommy is away) can send unintended negative messages to a child: It isn't okay to be yourself. You must hide who you are. Keep your gender a secret.

Beyond families, our social institutions limit the gender expression of youth. Dress codes in schools and gender-segregated activities (e.g., boys and girls athletic teams) are structural hurdles that many transgender youth cannot tackle. These hurdles are not just physical, they can also be barriers to healthy psychological development. When people cannot express themselves in a way that feels right, they are forced to hide their true selves. Developing a healthy and positive sense of self is difficult when we cannot express or share who we really are.

Because the transgender umbrella encompasses so many different types of people, Ricardo and Nick's experiences are not representative of the diverse experiences of transgender youth. While we talked to many transgender people for this book, we were unable to talk to people who self-identified as each of the following transgender statuses: transsexuals, drag queens, drag kings, gender queer, gender variant, and intersex. Thus, we cannot offer a comprehensive review of the ways all transgender youth develop a transgender identity. We strongly recommend that adults who know a youth struggling with gender identity learn more about that individual's specific experiences. A list of transgender resources can be found in the Appendix.

Claiming a Queer Identity

In the last 20 years, the term *queer* has been slowly reclaimed by part of the LGBT population. Queer can be used as an umbrella term under which lesbian, gay, bisexual, or transgender fall. It can also be a separate identity marker. For many youth, queer is seen as a preferable identifier as it represents an understanding of sexual identity, gender identity, and gender expression as fluid or flexible points on a continuum. Queer has come to be seen as a way to identify with the "other" and avoid confinements and stereotypes traditionally associated with labels, like lesbian, gay, bisexual, or transgender.

To *queer* something means to approach a topic/situation/text from a new angle that avoids traditional categorizations (gay/straight, male/female); unexpected interactions emerge once these categories are erased. This intentional removing of labels has even led other populations, such as individuals with disabilities, to adopt the term queer as a term of description.

It is important to note, however, that for many in the LGBT community, the word "queer" evokes memories of harassment, hate language, and bullying. In fact, many people still use the word in a derogatory fashion. Nonetheless, we are seeing a shift towards an intentional reclaiming of this word and corresponding identity, especially with the younger activist generation.[14] When working with youth, it is important to distinguish whether the term is being used in a hateful or emancipatory way.

The New Gay Teenager documents how contemporary youth reject traditional terms and identity labels like lesbian, gay, or bisexual.[15] Many of the high-school and college-age youth we talked to embody the positive notion of queer. Taylor, an 18-year-old undergraduate student attempted to explain her identity. She shared how she sometimes is pushed by lesbian or bisexual women to claim one of those identities, instead of a queer one. Taylor said, "I call myself queer . . . I'm not going to fight with [people] about who I am. I know what I am! Either they accept it or they don't. But, that is their problem, not mine!" Taylor could not explore her emerging identity in her rural hometown in Arkansas, as her high school offered no safe space to do so. Immediately upon arrival to college, she joined the Queer Student Group along with a host of other diversity organizations. In those clubs, she found friends who accepted her as a queer person.

I'm Not Just LGBT! I'm Also . . .

In this section, we touch upon the complicated nature of multiple identities. Books that address LGBT identities without considering other aspects of people's lives tell only part of the story. Lesbian, gay, bisexual, and transgender youth have a sexual orientation and a gender identity, but they also have many other social identities that make them whole. Sexual orientation, gender, race, age, social class, ability, and religious identities intersect to create unique and complex identities in every person. Figure 2.2 represents the variety of social identities that can influence a person's LGBT identity development.

In this section we have chosen to share just a few of the *many* possible identity intersections that LGBT youth can experience. First, one young man describes the ways his religion influenced his identity process. Second, three young people explain how their ethnicity shaped who they are as LGBT people. Next, we share two stories of gay and lesbian youth with disabilities. Finally, we explain how social class can intersect with sexual orientation and gender identity development. The youth described in this section (and throughout the book) aren't just gay, lesbian, bisexual or

FIGURE 2.2   Social Identity Influences on LGBT Identity

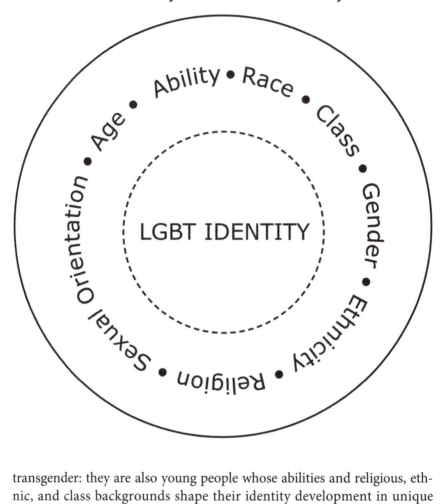

transgender: they are also young people whose abilities and religious, ethnic, and class backgrounds shape their identity development in unique
ways. By selecting stories that highlight the intersections of religion, social
class, ability, and ethnicity, we in no way mean to suggest that other identities are somehow less important. We cannot offer a comprehensive discussion of multiple identities in this short chapter. However, we want
readers to understand how an LGBT identity is not necessarily the only
identity young people have. For those who are interested in delving deeper
into the topic of multiple identities, there is research (mostly completed
with college students) available.[16]

Historically, religious identity and practice have been difficult (sometimes impossible) to reconcile with an LGBT identity. Many people who

shared their stories with us related that they learned early in life that their religion would not accept them as an LGBT individual. For instance, Stephen, grew up in a very conservative Southern Baptist household. He wanted his spiritual home to affirm his Christian and gay identities. But he learned from family and religious figures that he could not be both. Beginning at age 12, he spent most of his time "praying for Jesus to make me not be gay." Sadly, for many LGBT people, religion has been used as a tool of hate.[17]

Like religion, ethnicity can be a significant aspect of a person's identity. LGBT people of color who contributed stories to this book described cultural barriers to their attempts to create a positive LGBT identity. Yet they persisted. Each was determined to find an integrated identity, an identity that celebrated both their ethnicity and their sexual orientation. Interactions with peers, role models, and supportive adults influence how easily youth concurrently develop a healthy LGBT and ethnic identity. Some youth find safe spaces to explore the intersections of their ethnic and LGBT identities, while others do not.

There is no single way that families from any ethnicity respond to their children when they come out. They run the gamut from total acceptance to utter rejection. Alejandro shared his journey of being a gay Latino. Born to an immigrant mother and American father, he was raised in a lower-middle-class family in Texas. His family and local community members held what he referred to as traditional Latino values. He explained, "In the Latino culture, it's not good for [boys] to be gay . . . You have to be tough. You have to be manly. You have to be the man of the house. For a male to be gay is a big issue." These cultural mantras kept Alejandro in the closet during his middle and high school years. Because he perceived his home and community environments to be unsafe spaces to explore his gay identity, Alejandro was unable to engage in real identity exploration until he left for college.

Alejandro's experience was very different from that of Fernando, who also came from a traditional Latino family. Fernando, a transgender youth, was accepted by his Latino parents. Because he had a safe home space, Fernando was able to engage in identity explorations long before arriving at college. His mother supported his gender expression and even bought women's clothes and shoes for Fernando to wear.

Another young woman named Hua described how difficult it was to find words to explain her emerging bisexual identity to her Chinese family. Her parents were born in China and her extended family was still in that country. Even though she knew by grade eight that she was not heterosexual, she did not tell her parents about her sexuality until she was a junior in college.

During those years, she struggled to figure out what it meant to be both Chinese and bisexual. Eight years is a long time for a youth to keep a secret from loved ones and to have a positive identity journey stalled.

The tales of Alejandro, Fernando, and Hua show that no two youth will experience the same LGBT journey. Cultural backgrounds shape the home lives and identity processes of LGBT youth in unique ways. Despite cultural differences, adults have a responsibility to create safe spaces for youth. In these safe spaces, youth can work through the sometimes difficult journey of reconciling being LGBT with a particular cultural heritage.

Young people with disabilities face unique hurdles related to LGBT identity development. Tommy, a young man who uses a wheelchair, is attracted to men but has not yet had the opportunity to explore his emerging gay identity. One reason for this delayed gay exploration is that Tommy has expended much of his emotional energy coping with the fact that he has a progressive disability that will worsen as he ages. Once he came to terms with what it meant to identify as a person with a disability, he then wanted to explore what it meant to be a gay person with a disability. Yet he had no role models. One of Tommy's biggest challenges was integrating into the gay-straight alliance at his college. His peers saw him as the "guy in the wheelchair" instead of as a gay classmate who had a sexual identity. Some scholars have documented the ways people without disabilities assume those with disabilities do not have sexual feelings or desires; they assume they are asexual.[18] These assumptions can serve as barriers to interpersonal relationships and positive LGBT identity development in people with disabilities. Or consider Shandra, a deaf middle-school student who is questioning her identity. Is she a lesbian? What exactly does being a lesbian mean? All young people, especially those in early stages of LGBT identity development, need the support of advocates and allies. As we describe in Chapter 3, finding trustworthy adults in whom they can confide can be a challenge for LGBT youth. Shandra, however, faces an even greater hurdle—finding a trustworthy adult who also knows sign language.

Finally, many LGBT youth must navigate social class identities as they wrestle with their sexual orientation or gender identity. While we don't like to admit it, our society is largely segregated by social class. Children who grow up in the same neighborhoods and attend the same schools usually do so with others who share a similar social class (i.e., upper, middle, or lower class). These social class boundaries often influence the people we become friends with and whom we date.

Social class can also influence the exploration and expression of gender identity. Consider Edwin, who was born a biological boy but feels herself to be a girl. At as young as four, she begged her parents to buy pink shirts, dresses, and dolls to play with. Because they assumed (and hoped) their child was cisgender, they expressed disapproval of Edwin's requests. Even when they realized that their child would be *happier* expressing herself in attire typically reserved for girls, they just couldn't afford to honor the requests. Purchasing jeans, sneakers, and t-shirts for school was an economic hardship for Edwin's family. Often, they relied on hand-me-downs from older (male) cousins and neighbors to clothe their child. Buying skirts, dresses, and dolls was not just out of the question, it was out of financial reach.

Even middle-class transgender people may struggle to afford to express their gender in ways that feel right. Some transgender people (not all) need hormones or surgeries to align their physical bodies to their felt gender identities. Hormones and surgeries are very costly and are rarely covered by medical insurance. Imagine what it might be like to be unable to afford to express yourself in a way that felt right? What implications would that have on your sense of self?

Action Steps

- Be mindful of multiple identities when interacting with youth. Being LGBT may not be the only identity that youth are struggling with. Ask yourself how ethnicity, religion, social class, and ability might influence the identity development of the youth in your life.

- Find out if there are religious or spiritual organizations in your community that are LGBT-friendly. Introduce yourself to the religious leaders and determine how to best refer youth should you need to.

- How much do you know about your own cultural heritage? Other cultural backgrounds? Make an effort to learn more about the cultural backgrounds of the LGBT youth in your life so that you may offer support in a culturally sensitive way.

- Don't assume people with disabilities have no sexual identity or desire for romantic and sexual relationships. Visit DisabilityResources.org for more information. http://www.disabilityresources.org/GAY.html

The Complexity of Identity

In this chapter we grappled with the question of what it means to be lesbian, gay, bisexual, or transgender in a society where heterosexuality and gender binaries (i.e., male/female) are normalized. People's stories reveal many patterns and consistent themes in LGB identity development, including: identity beginnings, identity explorations, and identity integrations.

FIGURE 2.3   LGBT Identity

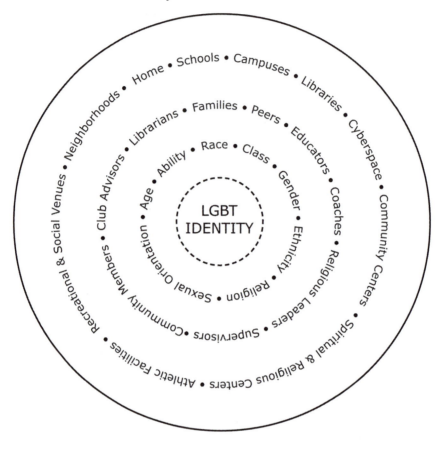

While there is far less research about transgender identity development, some argue that transgender individuals experience similar milestones and hurdles to those of LGB people.

The stories in this chapter reflect the uniqueness in each person's identity journey. We would like to end this chapter by reminding readers that we all have multiple social identities that make us whole, including our sexual orientation, gender, religion, race, ethnicity, gender, socioeconomic status, age, and ability. When people's multiple identities are situated in the unique environments where they live and learn, a complex picture of LGBT identity appears. Figure 2.3 represents the people, places, and other social identities that can influence LGBT identity development. Being LGBT doesn't happen in a vacuum, nor is being LGBT the only identity that shapes the lives of young people.

The voices in this chapter, and throughout the book, show how diverse the identity patterns of LGBT youth can be. Ultimately, we argue that while there are similar themes in identity development models, there is no *one way* to be lesbian, gay, bisexual, or transgender. To create safe spaces, adults must understand both the common patterns and unique issues related to healthy LGBT identity development.

LGBT identity shapes not only who we are, but also how we learn and grow. Moreover, educational, neighborhood, and home environments are paramount to lesbian, gay, bisexual, and transgender identity development. Many of the people who shared stories for this book mentioned how their familial, educational, and community experiences influenced the development of their LGB or transgender identity. They also shared how family and community settings were safe or unsafe which either helped or hindered their identity development. As we explained in the opening section of the chapter, LGBT identity cannot be separated from context. Forthcoming chapters explore key contexts of home, school, and community. First, however, in Chapter 3 we explore what it means to be an ally.

Chapter 3

Sharing the Struggles: The Role of Allies

Margo had a secret. Since middle school, when her friends' attention shifted to boys and her attention stubbornly refused to follow suit, she huddled in the closet. And there she remained throughout most of high school. Each anti-gay slur echoing in the hallway or scrawled on the bathroom wall was a gag order, silencing her. Now in her senior year, Margo had begun dating. Her girlfriend Grace was becoming increasingly important to her. Margo knew she needed to "come out," but how? She could hardly change her Facebook status or casually drop Grace's name when discussing weekend plans. She finally sought out her favorite teacher and mentor, Beth Clarkson. Her heart pounding, Margo confided, "I am finally happy. I am dating someone . . . and it is a girl." She held her breath. Ms. Clarkson smiled and asked, "So, when do I get to meet this lucky girl?" Margo breathed. Tears streamed down her face. Beth Clarkson had just thrown her a lifeline. Margo had an ally.

Through acts of solidarity, allies like Beth Clarkson empower LGBT youth and mitigate the effects of their negative experiences. They save lives. But their work can be as complex and risky as it is vital. Beth Clarkson's response to Margo could (most likely *will*) complicate her professional and personal life; she and other allies often need support as they engage in the struggle to make our schools and communities safe for LGBT youth. This chapter is dedicated to them.

Ally: Noun and Verb

In simplest terms, allies are *individuals* (noun) who *act* (verb) on behalf of the LGBT community. They take sides. Allies interpret social settings and media messages differently from those whose vantage points are dictated by heteronormative attitudes or assumptions about gender binaries. They recognize veiled discrimination where others see only business as usual.

Jill experienced this shift the moment her best friend Angie "came out" in high school. She supported her friend both privately and publicly—she listened as Angie catalogued her fears; she interrupted thoughtless anti-lesbian comments. And when she went to college, Jill expanded her ally work: she joined the campus gay-straight alliance. Through her experiences, Jill came to understand what it means to be an ally. Jill explained, "An ally is someone who advocates, speaks up, and stands behind the rainbow banner in solidarity with LGBT people . . . they stick their own neck out on the line." Advocate, speak, stand—all action verbs.

Jill's definition references the various behaviors associated with being an ally. It highlights the benefits extended to the LGBT community. The following definition couples this focus on activism with a personal dimension that is less obvious, but crucial to effective allyship: An ally is "a heterosexual person or non-transgender person who confronts heterosexism, homophobia, biphobia, transphobia, and heterosexual privilege *in themselves* and others *out of self-interest* and a concern for the well-being of lesbian, gay, bisexual, and transgender people" (emphasis added).[1] We like this definition because it draws attention to not only the public dimension of allyship but also the private dimension. This personal work entails two related aspects. First, allies acknowledge that their immersion in heterosexual and/or cisgender privilege has created assumptions and attitudes that cannot be dismantled on command. Privilege (i.e., unearned advantages conferred by one's membership in a socially valued group) does not speak its name—it masquerades as moral, cultural, or intellectual superiority. Peggy McIntosh describes privilege as an "invisible, weightless knapsack of special provisions, assurances, tools, maps, guides, code-books, passports, visas, clothes, compass, emergency gear, and blank checks."[2] Although she originally applied her invisible knapsack metaphor to white privilege, McIntosh goes on to discuss its relevance to heterosexual privilege: "[Heterosexual privilege] is a still more taboo subject than race privilege: the daily ways in which heterosexual privilege makes some persons comfortable or powerful, providing supports, assets, approvals, and rewards to those who live or expect to live in heterosexual pairs. Unpacking that content is still more difficult, owing to the deeper imbeddedness of heterosexual advantage and dominance and stricter taboos surrounding these."[3] Allies unpack the contents of their invisible knapsack of heterosexual (or cisgender) privilege and in doing so confront the various manifestations of heterosexism *in themselves*. Second, allies recognize that they themselves are diminished by living within the constraints of a heterosexist society or one where strict gender binaries dictate gender norms. Their work is not solely altruistic; they act *out of self-interest*. McIntosh points out that systematically conferred privilege, although closely correlated with social and economic power, does not translate into strength of character. She explains, "Those who do not depend on conferred dominance have traits and qualities that may never develop in those who do ... In some groups, those dominated have actually become strong through *not* having all of these unearned advantages, and this gives them a great deal to teach the others. Members of so-called privileged groups can seem foolish, ridiculous, infantile, or dangerous by contrast."[4] Thus, allies stand with the LGBT community against homophobia, heterosexism, and transphobia because they understand that participating in unexamined privilege stunts their personal and moral growth.

In this chapter, we discuss first the personal (noun) aspects and then the performance (verb) aspects of ally development. We begin with questions that explore ally identity development and end with where that identity work leads. Such is our outline. It is important to note, however, that ally development is a nonlinear process. Its dimensions overlap; the work ebbs and flows. Each experience drops a pebble into the millponds of our lives, shifting and transforming the nouns and verbs of our existence.

It's Personal

What separates allies from scores of bystanders who see no evil, hear no evil, and do no evil? What gives allies eyes to see, ears to hear, and the will to act? We looked to the statements of self-identified allies for answers to these questions. Out of the diverse stories that were shared with us, a pattern emerged: the allies that spoke with us described an inner or private dimension of their outward or public acts of solidarity with the LGBT community. In some ways, this finding is unsurprising. Most ally stories begin with a friend or classmate who was lesbian, gay, bisexual, or transgender. Seeing friends get teased, taunted, or assaulted for being LGBT can be a powerful motivator for young people to become an ally. Watching a friend, neighbor, or loved one struggle with negative emotions related to coming out can also inspire heterosexual people to work for LGBT equality. But not always. Not even usually. For allies, these experiences become personal—they work their way into their psyche, their worldview. *They* change, so their *actions* change. In short, they build an ally identity. Into their gender, ethnicity, religious, sexual orientation, professional, and political self-concepts, they integrate the notion that they are LGBT allies. Such a transformation might be mysterious, but it is not magical. It comes from real shifts in thinking, from intellectual and ethical commitments.

Possibly the most significant change is that allies abandon the appealing and ever-popular notion of personal or political neutrality. One student in the early stages of ally development put it this way: "LGBT issues are not just 'theirs.' As a human being, I have a responsibility to support LGBT communities because the problems they face are about humanity, social justice and equality."[5] This student recognizes that any violation of human rights diminishes us, collectively and individually; that silence equals complicity, not neutrality; and, finally, that neutrality in the face of oppression is a fiction. This awareness dramatically alters one's perspective and resets one's moral compass—it serves as the foundation of ally identity. Solidarity with the LGBT community, with any nondominant group, then becomes inextricably linked with our personhood—not something we do for "the other."

In their self-examination, allies come to recognize the privilege associated with their sexual orientation, gender identity, or gender expression. Beyond the legal and fiscal benefits described in Chapter 1, allies acknowledge the benefits associated with safety and comfort: holding hands or showing affection with a partner in public, speaking openly about relationships in work and community settings, and expressing their gender identity freely. To help build self-awareness, allies notice the many ways in which they reveal their sexuality or gender identity and imagine how it would feel to keep it hidden.

Zoie, a heterosexual ally, described her heterosexual privileges as the ability to talk about her boyfriend in classes, hold his hand on campus, and post pictures of them as a couple on Facebook without considering potential negative consequences. She has the freedom to be herself *and* be in a heterosexual relationship without fearing for her safety. As part of her ally journey, Zoie learned that it is a privilege to be heterosexual and enjoy a relationship that is deemed "normal" by society.

Steve, a middle-school teacher, reflected upon his cisgender privilege. In Steve's class was a child named Cal, a biological boy (by school records) who liked to wear his hair long and paint his fingernails. During recess, Cal also preferred to play with girls and toys designed for them (i.e., dolls). From students and teachers alike came comments and questions about why Cal's gender expression did not match his sex. They *should*, after all. Through his relationship with Cal, Steve learned many important lessons—

one of the most important lessons was about his cisgender privilege. Steve never had to think about if or how his gender identity or expression aligned with his birth sex. Nor did Steve ever have to fear snickers, jeers, or discrimination based upon his hairstyle and clothing choices. He had the privilege of expressing his gender and gender identity in a fashion that society deemed acceptable for a man.

For some, the personal dimension of being an ally is rooted in their own experience with discrimination and intolerance. Ava, a 32-year-old teacher, described how her lesbian childhood friend had initially inspired her to become an ally. It was her present-day relationships, however, that solidified her commitment to fighting for LGBT equality, especially marriage equality. Ava explained:

> I've had a lot of really close gay female friends—really, really close. One is a friend that I grew up with since I was a little girl. We've been able to talk about a lot of things. I learned a lot from her. Recently, I was telling my husband why I came to volunteer and do this LGBT ally interview. It is partly because we have an interracial, intercultural marriage. Sadly, every now and then, I'll read something that reminds me why I am an ally. Fifty years ago or a hundred years ago, I would have been lynched for being in my [interracial] marriage. I mean, things are different now but we still deal with a lot of discrimination—because of his color and who he is. I just really feel like being an ally for any minority group, especially because I have these close ties with gay friends. My social justice work and ally work is inspired by this. We all have the struggle, but it's just one more layer of fighting that LGBT people have to engage in.

Ava's story illustrates the personal dimension of the ally journey. While she began her ally journey supporting lesbian friends, her learning continued into adulthood, where she came to see all forms of hate and prejudice as intolerable.

Understanding the private dimension of public acts can aid aspiring and fledgling allies in their development. It can also help veteran allies recruit and train future allies. Linda Christensen is in the business of creating allies. Her laboratory is her classroom, where her students analyze historic and personal scenarios of human rights violations. Christensen explains:

> When I taught this unit to a sophomore class, I was astounded at how many students confessed to being perpetrators, targets, and bystanders, and how few acted as allies. One student offered that he was a "jackass" in middle school and regularly tormented other students. Many talked about making

fun of younger, weaker students. Sometimes their abuse was physical. Few students had stories of acting as allies. In our discussion, it was clear that students didn't feel good about their participation or their lack of intervention, but they didn't feel powerful enough to stop the racist, homophobic, or belittling behavior and comments.[6]

Christensen begins with historic accounts of injustice. She directs her students to identify each participant in a scenario as a target, a perpetrator, a bystander, or an ally. These young people confront their active and/or passive participation in anti-gay discrimination. The students analyze the strategies employed by allies and then imagine themselves using those strategies in their personal accounts of injustice. They practice being allies; they re-write (and pre-write) history. Christensen's students are preparing to act publicly through building an ally identity.

Peter Ji, a professor of clinical psychology at the University of Illinois, agrees that identity development is an important facet of allyship. He designed and taught an LGBT ally course in which college students considered salient LGBT topics (e.g., coming out, religious attitudes, and marriage rights), attended an LGBT-themed event, and conducted an interview with an LGBT individual or someone related to an LGBT person. The following reflection describes one student's transformation:

> Because being heterosexual is the social norm, I perceived any deviance from it to be weird and not normal. I knew homosexuals struggled to be accepted by others. The seriousness of such issues never impacted me directly, so I saw their issues to be theirs only. My passive, indifferent attitudes toward LGBT issues have changed since I began to learn about LGBT issues in class and when I participated in the LGBT activities. Once I was part of the seminar I realized I was not going to be able to sit around and just half listen and observe, I was going to have to take part. There was work to be done, more than I expected. I thought I was going to be on a team but just sit on the bench . . . I got put in the game without knowing it and now I enjoy playing and being part of the team.[7]

It's Public

In tandem with personal identity work, allies adopt a public stance in solidarity with the LGBT community. As noted in the two foregoing definitions, allies identify oppressive acts and confront prejudicial ideas and discriminatory behaviors. In fact, the act of confronting discrimination and bullying is the hallmark of an ally, but one that can be challenging. For new allies, the transition from "standing by" to "standing up" can resemble the coming out process that some LGBT individuals undergo. Peter Ji experienced this in his journey toward allyship:

> I lived in fear of proclaiming who I wanted to be. I wanted to be an ally and I was afraid of coming out as one . . . Gradually, I realized if homophobia and oppression did not exist, I would not be fearful or anxious about being an ally. This realization was an important step because I thought that my status as a heterosexual Korean male meant that I could not truly relate to the community. However, I could relate to the LGBT community because as an ally, I too am likely to encounter oppression and homophobia.[8]

Allies allow their personal transformation to work its way outward and in so doing exercise solidarity with the LGBT community. By confronting oppression, allies make spaces safe for LGBT youth. This public dimension further hones the personal, and on it goes.

While every individual has their own style of confrontation, the most effective allies confront oppression with humor, patience, and grace. In his role as a coach for his son's soccer team, Bill advocates for the rights of LGBT youth and confronts prejudice with both grace and age-appropriate language. One Saturday, Bill overheard the boys using the word "fag" to refer to a child on the opposing team. In a low and caring tone, he asked his team why they would use a hurtful term. He then asked them to consider how they feel when they are called hurtful names. He reminded them that "good sports" are also good people. They win fair and square and are never mean to others. He told the boys that he hoped he would never hear the word "fag" or any other hurtful term again.

Also, consider the story of Kate. She was 13 years old when her world was turned upside down. Her parent's marriage was beginning to dissolve because of her mother's sexual orientation. She was to be the child of divorced parents—a foreign and terrifying prospect. Kate's freshman year of high school was an academic and emotional hellhole. Kate's friends were forbidden to call her when she was with her mother. The message was clear: Your mom is not okay. She can't be trusted with the care of young teenagers—even though those same friends had practically lived at Kate's before learning her mother was a lesbian.

Two years later, her mother was surprised to overhear Kate on the telephone with her friend. Kate: "Yeah, my mom's a lesbian. You didn't know that? Yeah, I live with my mom and her partner." When Kate emerged from around the corner and saw her mom, she simply said, "That was Jamie. She's coming over tomorrow night." Kate was not a flag bearer, but she was an ally nevertheless. She reported her home life matter-of-factly, unapologetically. She aligned herself with her mom. Several years later, Kate developed a serious relationship with a young man whom her mother had never met. Kate's mother wondered if Kate had told Brian about her sexual orientation. The conversation went like this:

Mother: Does Brian know that I am a lesbian?

Kate: Of course. It's the first thing I tell guys that I might hang out with. I say, "My mom's a lesbian. You cool with that?" If not, why bother?

Kate's statements appear simple and straightforward. But it was clear that Kate had regular conversations with potential friends or romantic interests about her mother's sexual orientation.

Allies can engage in efforts, large and small, to support LGBT people. Small, everyday actions like role modeling inclusive behavior or asking a child how he, she, or ze is doing are important ally actions. Kate's and Bill's experiences are perfect examples of how small actions matter. Larger commitments may include taking a class, staging a protest, or serving as a mentor to LGBT youth. Everyday conversations are just as important as large activist endeavors. Both large and small efforts send a message to LGBT youth—we care about you and we want to support you.

In addition to being willing to intervene when they witness acts of marginalization, allies make an effort to learn about the LGBT community and the challenges faced by LGBT youth. Through self-education, allies learn how best to support LGBT people. Toby identifies as a bisexual. In college he enrolled in a political science class where he was required to engage in activism in his local community. By week four, Toby found the courage to "out" himself as a bisexual individual to his peers. He also mentioned that he was planning to attend an LGBT rally at the state capitol. He wondered if his classmates might want to join him. To his surprise, all but one of his peers decided to support him. None had ever been to a rally or protest, but they decided it was something they wanted to do for Toby. More than a venue for support, the protest offered heterosexual students an opportunity to learn about issues that their bisexual classmate faced on a daily basis. Most were amazed to learn that LGBT people experience discrimination in almost all realms of society.

These stories demonstrate that allyship is an equal-opportunity adventure. Children can be allies for parents in the same way that parents can be allies for children. Kate was an effective ally for her mom, and Toby's classmates stood in solidarity with him. They represent many young heterosexuals who stand up for the rights of their family, friends, classmates, and teammates. LGBT youth need the support and allyship of both peers and adults. Every day, LGBT youth must navigate unsafe spaces where there is little or no adult supervision. In these spaces, peer allies are essential. LGBT youth also need allies in their parents, neighbors, teachers, coaches and community leaders. If more youth and adults learned to be allies, the rates of bullying and verbal harassment in our communities would certainly decline, and our schools and communities would be safer for LGBT youth.

While allies are often described as heterosexual, LGB persons can act as allies to transgender individuals and transgender individuals can be allies for the LGB community. LGB people can also act as allies to one another. At one university, a small group of lesbian college students heard stories of gay and lesbian peers being bullied and harassed on campus. While this group of lesbians had not personally experienced acts of intolerance, they wanted to act as allies to their peers. They felt an obligation to make the campus better for their classmates, so they started an "It Gets Better" campaign on campus. Or consider the gay-straight alliance that wanted to be more inclusive of transgender members. First, they changed their name to the LGBT and Straight Alliance to include the "T." Members also began to use inclusive pronouns. Most of us are familiar with pronouns such as *she, her, herself, he, his,* and *himself* but there are other options. While their use is not yet widespread, gender neutral pronouns (*ze, hir,* and *hirself*) do exist. Being an ally, however, does not mean assuming that a transgender person prefers to use these pronouns. The best way to determine the appropriate pronoun is to ask. Students in the LGBT and Straight Alliance wanted to be respectful of their transgender members, so they instituted a standard introduction format called Preferred Gender Pronoun or PGP. At the beginning of every meeting, students had an opportunity to introduce themselves and to share their PGP with the group. This gave transgender students the opportunity tell their peers how they liked to be addressed. One cross-dressing student said, "Hi, my birth name is Felix, but my drag name is Flora. My PGP is ze." The next student said, "My name is Jennie and my PGP is she." With a quick exchange of names and a five-minute PGP activity, lesbian, gay, and bisexual students demonstrated allyship to their transgender classmates.

In the next section, we describe common ally behaviors in the context of ally development. As you read the indicators of ally development, consider your own experiences. What perspectives and behaviors do you exhibit? What new ally actions would you like to try? If you already consider yourself an ally, the following indicators may help you determine how to grow in that role.

Indicators of Ally Development

Being an ally is a journey, a way of life. The full spectrum of ally-related behaviors described in this section develop only with time and experience. Even experienced allies meet new challenges as their social contexts change—ally development is nonlinear, organic. Thus, we offer these indicators not as a rubric or grading system, but as descriptors of the range of ally behaviors. Descriptors follow each indicator. We invite you to consider the extent to which you identify with each descriptor.

Before delineating the indicators of ally behavior, it is important to clarify how allies should *not* act. The following behaviors create unsafe spaces for LGBT youth:

Anti-Ally Behaviors—Engaging in Active or Passive Oppression

- Laughing at/telling jokes about LGBT people.
- Mocking people that do not fit within traditional gender roles.
- Abandoning a friendship because of the person's sexual orientation/gender identity.
- Remaining silent in the presence of anti-LGBT language/jokes.

Readers will recognize the first two behaviors as obviously harmful. We argue, however, that the passivity described in the last points is just as harmful, in that it props up and perpetuates destructive social practices. Silence in the face of oppression makes our communities unsafe for LGBT youth. When we ignore derogatory jokes, hurtful language, or exclusionary policies, we become part of the problem. Moreover, inaction and silence send a strong message to both LGBT and non-LGBT individuals. When parents, teachers, coaches or other community leaders fail to address hate speech, offensive jokes, name calling, or violence, they send the message to LGBT youth that they are not valued. They also send the message to all youth that it is acceptable to use language to demean another individual. In short, hatred and exclusion of LGBT people are acceptable.

To become an ally, one must learn how to confront oppression. As explained previously, we contend that this work is rooted in personal transformation. Those unwilling or unprepared to confront oppression are often those who have spent little time thinking about why it is important to be an ally. They have not done the personal work described earlier. Aspiring allies must ask themselves questions like: What are my biases? Where does my fear or discomfort about LGBT issues come from? Why have I failed to "stand up" for LGBT youth? How have I created unsafe spaces for LGBT people? Once people acknowledge their own biases and assumptions, they can move toward becoming an ally and creating safe spaces for LGBT youth.

Ally Indicator One: Being a Safe Person/Confidant

- I am a person who cares about the stories of LGBT people.
- I listen to LGBT people without judgment and offer my unconditional support.
- I make it known that LGBT people can confide in me.
- I keep conversations with LGBT people confidential.*

While there are many indicators of allyship, being a "safe person" is an essential first step. Being a caring and open person to talk with is a simple way to begin establishing yourself as an ally. Like all young people, LGBT youth struggle with relationships, life decisions, and peer pressure. Unfortunately, LGBT youth often lack access to safe environments where they can discuss those challenges with a trustworthy adult. Many LGBT youth do not know any safe people, or allies, in whom they can confide. Being a nonjudgmental listener can be invaluable to LGBT youth who are desperate to talk to an adult who cares. Margo found a nonjudgmental listener in Beth Clarkson. Another student, Tao, found a confidant in his math professor. For years, Tao had struggled with his same-sex feelings, but it was taboo to talk about being gay in his household. Tao went to his professor for math help, but he found much more. Tao's professor had safe-zone signs and gay-affirming symbols posted on his office door. In the midst of getting help with a quadratic equation, Tao also found an ally with whom he could discuss his same-sex attractions and coming-out fears.

There are many ways that allies can show LGBT youth that they are safe people. First, allies consistently use inclusive terms when referring to romantic relationships, sexuality, and gender. By using terms such as *partner*, *companion*, *significant other*, and *main squeeze*, allies convey openness to

---

*Exception: Disclosures of intended harm to self or others require a confidant to seek professional assistance.[1]

different kinds of partnerships. By using gender neutral pronouns such as *ze*, *hir*, and *hirself* allies send messages of transgender inclusion. Second, allies can display symbols and signs on their cars or office doors. Bumper stickers and signs with LGBT affirmative messages can speak volumes about your intentions as an ally. They signify to LGBT youth that you are a safe person. For years, Annemarie displayed a safe-zone sign on her office door. She hoped it would send students a message of inclusion, but she never really understood how important the sign was until she met Chris. He had felt isolated and alone for the first two weeks of his freshman year. He searched the campus for signs that he was not the only LGBT person at the school. Surely he wasn't. When he saw the safe-zone sign on her door, he felt a sense of relief. Finally, someone like him. Finally, a safe space on campus.

Ally Indicator Two: Confronting Oppression

- When I hear an inappropriate joke, I refuse to laugh. I explain that anti-gay or anti-transgender jokes are hurtful.
- I question and/or object to derogatory terms used to refer to LGBT people.
- I make choices to participate in pro-LGBT activities regardless of what others might think of my sexual orientation or gender identity.
- I respond to acts of prejudice and discrimination with grace (i.e., without defensiveness, sarcasm, or threats).
- I challenge others who make assumptions that everyone is cisgender (i.e., not transgender) or heterosexual (i.e., everyone is married or should be seeking a heterosexual partnership).

If you identified with these statements, you actively confront oppression—an essential ally activity. To create safe spaces for LGBT youth, allies interrupt anti-LGBT actions and words. Confronting oppression is especially important in situations where LGBT people are not able to stand up for themselves. LGBT people can risk low grades, emotional abuse, or physical harm if they stand up to LGBT oppression. They can also risk their jobs. Katrina, a 16-year-old lesbian, was working her afterschool job when her boss decided to tell an anti-gay joke. A usually quiet, heterosexual coworker told the supervisor that she was offended by the joke. Katrina remarked, "I was so impressed that she did that, you know? I think those little things definitely count. I think when people are able to say they support [LGBT issues] that's great, but when people are able to speak out like that, it's even better!" When allies stand up to confront offensive language or jokes, they can make a real difference in the lives of LGBT youth.

Sometimes it is assumptions that need challenging. The assumption that everyone is heterosexual or cisgender discounts the lived realities of LGBT people—it makes entire groups of people invisible to society. A simple way to confront this form of oppression is by correcting people when they talk only about people's husbands, wives, boyfriends, or girlfriends and exclude non-heterosexual relationships. Allies also challenge the assumption that everyone identifies as a "she" or "he" and that people's gender identity can be assumed based on the way they look. An ally is ready and willing to explain why assumptions create unwelcoming and unsafe environments for LGBT people.

Ally Indicator Three: Educating Oneself and Others

- I read books and magazines by, for, and about LGBT people. I have listened to LGBT music and/or watched LGBT films.
- I have attended or participated in cultural events like a local pride parade, National Coming Out Day (HRC.org), or Day of Silence (dayofsilence.org).
- I educate myself; I do not rely on LGBT people to be the experts.
- I engage in self-reflection regarding my strengths and areas for ally growth.
- I am aware of individuals, organizations that support LGBT equality.
- I educate others about LGBT issues.
- I consider it my job to encourage others to become allies.
- I model allyship for young people in my life.

If you identified with these statements, you are growing and learning as an ally. At a minimum, allies have a basic understanding of and comfort with lesbian, gay, bisexual, and transgender terminology. This includes being comfortable with saying the words *gay, lesbian, bisexual*, and *transgender* and also having the language to describe what each term means. Allies realize that those terms represent differences in human experience but not differences in humanity. Thus, they see how they are different from and similar to LGBT individuals. This basic knowledge is enhanced as people grow as allies.

Allies seek ways to expand their knowledge of the issues faced by LGBT people. Allies acquaint themselves with statistics, laws, policies, and cultural practices that affect LGBT individuals. Enhanced awareness can be gained through conversations with LGBT individuals, reading about LGBT people, and by attending awareness-building workshops. Allies attend LGBT cultural and community events and encourage others to attend those events too. These experiences provide both social and educational opportunities.

Margo, the mother of a lesbian daughter, felt a little awkward at the annual gay pride event in her city, but she attended to show support for her daughter and to learn about the LGBT community. After the pride parade, Margo visited each educational booth in search of resources that could help her be a better mother to a lesbian daughter. She needed to learn. She wanted to learn. The more knowledge allies have, the more able they are to create safe spaces for LGBT youth. This education, however, cannot always be provided by LGBT people.

Allies take responsibility for learning and growing without expecting LGBT people to always be the "teacher." It can be tiring and sometimes painful for LGBT people to explain their experiences to others. Imagine how difficult it might be for LGBT people to recount painful stories of coming out, family rejection, experiences with discrimination, or other harsh LGBT realities. Jeremiah, a bisexual student, explained how much he appreciated having allies on campus. However, he sometimes grew weary of having to explain why a joke, campus event, or class lecture was heterosexist and thus offensive and hurtful. Jeremiah admitted, "Sometimes I don't want to be the gay educator, I just want to be me. Having allies who really understand my reality would be refreshing."

Allyship is rooted in relationships—professional and personal relationships with LGBT persons, with other allies, and with those who actively or passively create unsafe spaces for LGBT youth. Ally development entails reflection on those relationships. For instance, an ally may be an effective interpersonal support for LGBT youth, able to listen intently and communicate concern without condescension or judgment. That same ally, however, might not be skilled at confronting others with grace. Some allies harbor anxiety about confronting loved ones. Even allies who are comfortable confronting others may come across as aggressive when challenging oppression. As discussed earlier, allies can grow only if they are willing to take risks. And when we take risks, we sometimes make mistakes. Allies grow through reflection on their experiences—both positive and negative.

Allies must also reflect upon what motivates them to be an ally.[9] Do they want to be an ally so that they can feel like they are a "good person"? Do they want to be an ally to make a difference in the lives of others? The most effective allies understand that standing up for LGBT rights is good for themselves, LGBT people, and society in general.

Self-aware individuals are best poised to pass the torch and inspire others to become LGBT allies. The education of others is an extremely important role for an ally. But you don't have to be a teacher like Linda Christensen or Peter Ji to educate others about the importance of being an ally. Effective allies spread positive LGBT messages and education through everyday actions in their communities. Allies teach and share knowledge though direct and indirect modeling. Through their efforts and positive role modeling, individuals can inspire others to become allies. This inspiration is vital to creating safe spaces for all LGBT youth. The world can never have too many allies.

Ally Indicator Four: Challenging Oppressive Systems

- I challenge systems, rules, and policies in order to promote atmospheres of respect and support for LGBT people.
- I petition, protest, and fight for LGBT positive legislation (i.e., human rights, civil rights, marriage).
- I address LGBT issues through training in my professional or community organization, on my team, and/or in my home.

If you identified with these statements, you have already started to challenge unequal systems as a seasoned ally. Being an ally is more than just supporting LGBT people and confronting other individuals. Allies must work actively to challenge inequitable systems that keep LGBT youth from gaining equal rights. For instance, allies challenge oppressive systems (i.e., policies, programs, or services) in their schools and communities. They question why school dances are restricted to heterosexual dates. They ask community organizations why transgender youth are excluded from participating in "boys" or "girls" sports teams. Allies also work with local leaders to encourage and promote an atmosphere of respect within their local communities. Gina, a cisgender college student, worked tirelessly to be an ally to her transgender classmates. She petitioned her school to create gender-neutral restrooms on campus. By her count, there were only a few gender-neutral restrooms in classroom buildings and none in the residence halls. Her demands were heard by the administration and a transgender inclusion committee was formed. As a student representative on that committee, Gina helped bring gender-neutral restrooms to almost every building on campus.

Allies' transformative work expands beyond their local communities. They support state and national organizations that are LGBT-friendly or have pro-LGBT employee policies. Allies vote for positive change in local and national elections. They fight for change through a variety of venues, including protests, letter-writing campaigns, and petitioning. No matter what the form, allies understand that creating safe spaces for LGBT youth must happen everywhere—in our backyards and across the country.

Action Steps

- Identify three ally behaviors you would like to strengthen. What support do you need from other allies and LGBT individuals to do so?
- When has another individual been an ally or advocate for you? Consider how you can replicate their ally efforts in your interactions with LGBT youth.
- Begin a campaign to put a GLSEN Safe Space Kit in every school in your community (safespace.glsen.org).
- In what ways do the youth in your life demonstrate ally tendencies? How can you positively reinforce those tendencies?
- Conduct ongoing "ally audits" of the community, religious, or political organizations to which you belong. Challenge any policy, program, or service that excludes LGBT youth.

Benefits and Challenges of Being an Ally

Because allyship is rooted in relationships, it enjoys the benefits and faces the challenges of social interdependency. First, the benefits: Many allies we talked with believed allyship was an essential aspect of responsible citizenship. Most explained that standing up for LGBT youth was the "right thing to do." They believed that a just society does not wait for a community tragedy, such as an LGBT youth suicide, to take action. Allies see the creation of safe spaces for LGBT youth as an exercise of their democratic duty and an expression of their humanity.

Second, through their supportive actions, allies open themselves up to the possibility of close relationships with lesbian, gay, bisexual, and transgender individuals. Lasting friendships can blossom between LGBT people and their allies. When allies put themselves in harm's way to stand up for LGBT rights, it signifies to LGBT people that the allies care. We met many LGBT people who said their best friends were individuals who stood up for LGBT rights on a regular basis. Many LGBT people trusted those allies with their lives. What deeper relationships can you imagine than those founded upon such depths of trust?

Third, through interpersonal relationships, allies have an opportunity to learn and grow. Interpersonal relationships allow allies to get firsthand knowledge of harsh social realities that they will never experience. This increased awareness helps allies form a more complex worldview. Toby's peers certainly gained a new worldview by attending the LGBT protest.

Fourth, allies are inspirational. Allies who become impassioned to "make a difference" often teach their heterosexual peers about LGBT discrimination. Increased awareness and passion for human rights can be contagious. Allies have an opportunity to inspire others to support LGBT youth in their schools and communities. In short, some allies become teachers themselves. Through this teaching, they expand their connections with other like-minded people and help develop a community of support for LGBT people.

Along with benefits come the challenges of being an ally. We've mentioned that just as an LGBT person "comes out of the closet," an ally comes out as an ally by publicly acknowledging her, his or hir support for LGBT people and issues. This can be an uncomfortable experience for many people. Moreover, allies may be called hurtful names and be harassed just like the LGBT people whom they support. In high school, Faith became an ally to her best friend. Faith explained:

> My best friend from middle school and high school came out to me our freshman year. We grew up in Topeka, Kansas, which is home to Fred Phelps, very anti-gay, very anti-everything who pickets everywhere and supports godhatesfags.com. When someone comes out to you, it is a life changing moment. When she came out to me, that was a very big moment in my life and I started to research LGBT things. An ally really needs to be somebody that actually advocates and stands up and says something. An ally is someone who is willing to speak up in a class, even to a professor who says something offensive. Being an ally can mean that you lose people you thought were friends. After I sort of stopped talking to some conservative friends in high school, I met other good friends.

Faith shared some of the difficult realities of being an ally. By standing up for her LGBT friend, she ran the risk of becoming the target of hate and prejudice. While Faith was never physically harmed, she did experience the emotional hurt of losing friends who thought that being LGBT (or an ally) was a bad thing. Luckily, after losing anti-LGBT friends, she found a new peer group—one that was affirming of LGBT people.

The Road Ahead

The previous pages summarized some key indicators of allyship. Being an ally is not easy: it takes awareness, education, and action. The indicators may seem daunting to readers who have yet to begin their ally journey. We encourage readers to select realistic goals and work at a pace that feels right. Since allies are invaluable to creating safe spaces for LGBT youth, exhibiting just a few of the aforementioned indicators can make a real difference in the lives of LGBT youth.

The road to LGBT equality is long. Change will not happen overnight. Allies stay the course—no matter how long it takes. In the course of their efforts, they are bound to engage in efforts that are ineffective. Allies are human and, like all humans, they make mistakes. However, allies do not give up when they make a mistake or when they get discouraged. If you do become discouraged, we suggest you think of Jackson, a college student. When Jackson talked with us, he argued that neither he nor the LGBT movement would be successful without allies. He said, "I think allies play a role in letting the heterosexual society know that it's okay to support an issue, you know? It's okay to stand up for something that you believe in and rights for people in general. I think allies serve a huge purpose. I don't think the queer movement would be anywhere near as strong or as powerful without allies." How will you stand up for LGBT youth in your schools and communities?

Chapter 4

Family: From Exclusion to Nurturance

We all have families—by birth or by choice. These families come in all shapes and sizes—nuclear families, extended families, single-parent families, blended families, adoptive families, and foster families. Exploring every possible familial structure would be impossible in this chapter. Instead, we offer a snapshot of some of the issues that impact youth and their families. While some books focus solely on how parents react when their child comes out as LGB or T, we explore broader notions of family and kinship. Whether you are a parent, grandparent, aunt, uncle, or concerned citizen, this chapter has something for you. We offer tangible suggestions on how to support LGBT youth in your immediate or extended family. We also suggest ways you can create safe spaces for LGBT youth (and families) in your community.

The following pages contain stories of LGBT youth who experienced a range of responses from their loved ones—from extremely positive to extremely negative, and all points in between. In the first section, we share the journeys of LGBT youth from families who attempted to create safe familial spaces. Those stories show how creating safe spaces is a process— one that is easier for some families than for others. Just as youth must learn how to be lesbian, gay, bisexual, or transgender, families must also learn how to be an ally to LGBT youth. As we described in Chapter 3, becoming an ally is a journey. That journey can include: (1) being a safe person, (2) confronting oppression, (3) educating oneself and others, and (4) challenging oppressive systems. Many LGBT youth who shared their stories with us described parents, grandparents, aunts, or uncles as allies. Those family members offer hope and inspiration for anyone interested in creating safe spaces for LGBT youth.

In this chapter, we also offer less affirming stories—stories of family members who failed to act as allies to LGBT youth. We believe that most parents want to love and support their children. Unfortunately, there are some families who do not know how, or refuse to do so, when the child is lesbian, gay, bisexual, or transgender. This section of the chapter offers cautionary tales so that you may avoid the mistakes made by families who failed to create safe spaces for the young people in their lives.

Toward Safe Family Spaces

A family is a dynamic system, one with complicated relationships, roles, and structures. LGBT youth who come out to family members must navigate a complex family system. One of the most widely used models of family systems suggests that there are two key areas of family functioning—cohesion and adaptability.[1] Families with too much or too little cohesion or adaptability struggle to function well. Healthy families possess a balance of cohesion (or emotional bonding) and the ability to adapt to stressors. A stressor that can challenge cohesion and adaptability is a family member coming out as LGB or disclosing a transgender identity.

Adapting to having a child, grandchild, niece, nephew, or other relative who is LGBT can take time—but adaptation is a necessary step on the path toward creating safe family spaces for LGBT youth. Every family has a history of how they adapt to stressors. This history will likely repeat itself when a youth comes out. This is not to say that family history is unchangeable. Instead, history is a powerful force that can be changed by families who make the effort. Consider how well your family adapts to change.

Examining adaptability, cohesiveness, and other family dynamics *after* a youth comes out is myopic. Tensions, dynamics, and levels of trust that were present *before* a youth comes out play a role in how a family reacts. For instance, Jacob came out to his parents in high school. He explained how his relationship with his parents was "never really that close to begin with." Jacob described his parents as relatively neutral in their response to his sexual orientation. His prior relationship with them, which had contained little emotional bonding, certainly played a role in their response to his coming out. Luckily, Jacob had a gay uncle who lived across the country with whom he had a stronger emotional bond. He spent many hours on the phone with this uncle, who helped him learn to love himself for who he was.

There is no universal way that family members respond when a loved one comes out. Parents, grandparents, aunts, uncles, and other kin can display a range of initial emotional responses when learning that a family member is lesbian, gay, bisexual, or transgender. While responses vary from person to person, common feelings associated with learning that a loved one is LGBT include shock, anger, sadness, confusion, and acceptance.[2] Even the most open-minded of family members can respond with initial shock or disbelief. Yet families that adapt are able to move past these initial reactions to offer safe and loving long-term responses. Randy, a high school student, told his mother he was gay. He explained, "Even though she was very accepting, she still cried." But she moved quickly past her tears to offer him unconditional love and acceptance.

Creating safe family spaces for LGBT youth takes more than the efforts of *one* family member. All members must learn to adapt to a new familial reality. You may be reading this book because you want to support a young person in your life who has just disclosed an LGB or T identity. But you are not the only person whose response matters. Youth do not receive one reaction from family members when they come out. Over time, they receive multiple, and sometimes conflicting, messages from parents, siblings, aunts, uncles, grandparents, and other kin. Trae's and Lila's stories show that family dynamics are complex. Lila's parents were initially surprised when she told them, "I think I like girls." At first, they asked her things like, "Are you sure you don't still like boys?" Over time, they learned to accept Lila's sexuality. Lila had a less positive response from her adopted sister, who was more than a little "uncomfortable" in her presence. After she came out, Lila's sister no longer wanted to share a bedroom with her. To date, Lila's relationship with her sister remains strained.

Trae's mother was very loving and accepting in her response to his coming out. She tried to show her son that she was proud of him for being confident with his sexuality. One of the ways she expressed her support was by proudly proclaiming her support for Trae's sexuality in her holiday newsletter to the extended family. Unfortunately, there were many relatives who were far less supportive than his mother. His mother adapted quickly; others did not. Her newsletter unleashed some negative family responses that made extended family gatherings unsafe for Trae. Despite the unconditional love and support of a mother, Trae still had to contend with lack of support from extended kin.

In addition to adapting to a new reality that includes having an LGBT family member, adults must also learn to navigate the harsh realities of homophobia and transphobia. As described in Chapters 1 and 6, discrimination, bullying, and violence happen all too often to LGBT youth. Intense amounts of pain can be involved in hearing about or witnessing hurtful acts directed at loved ones. When instances of harm do occur, family members can respond with support or lack thereof. The former strengthens relationships, while the latter can cause tension.[3] Family members who ignore or downplay exclusion, name calling, or other forms of bullying are not only complicit in creating unsafe spaces, but they also run the risk of harming their relationship with LGBT youth. Conversely, family members who act as allies may strengthen the cohesiveness of their family. By standing up to those who use derogatory language or who engage in exclusionary behaviors, family members can engender trust and confidence in their relationships with LGBT youth. Scott, a female-to-male transgender individual, had his relationships with his parents strengthened when they fought for his right to play on the boys baseball team even though he was born a biological female. His parents did not have to stand up to discrimination, but they did and it meant the world to Scott. Their action also strengthened familial connections.

How families come to terms with discovering a youth is LGBT depends not only on cohesion and adaptability, but also on family interaction and communication.[4] Family communication can happen with or around LGBT youth. For instance, even when adults are not talking directly to youth, young people overhear, and try to make meaning of, those conversations. When youth hear parents, aunts, uncles, grandparents, or siblings talking about LGBT people in negative terms, they learn a powerful lesson: it is not okay to be LGBT. Youth may decide against coming out if their families speak negatively about LGBT issues or people. Conversely, LGBT youth may be comfortable talking about their sexual orientation or gender identity in family settings where positive talk about LGBT people and topics is the norm.

While positive family talk around children is important, positive talk *with* children is essential. Families that are open to and encourage talk about feelings can create safe home spaces for youth. Moreover, families that set a standard for healthy communication are more likely to engage in positive communication once a youth discloses her, his, or hir sexual orientation or gender identity. LGBT youth are more apt to discuss their identity struggles and successes in familial environments where positive family talk is the norm. In Chapter 2 we shared how LGBT identity journeys can be rife with negative emotions. Youth need safe family outlets where they can share their feelings—both positive and negative. Positive family talk is essential to the health and well-being of LGBT youth and family functioning.

Positive family talk is good practice for all families—those with LGBT youth and those without. This form of communication cannot begin once a traumatic or stressful event has happened. Instead, families must encourage children, young and old, to talk about their emotions in good times and in bad. Positive family talk should be a regular occurrence in every household. Too often, parents and other relatives are concerned about everyday topics such as undone chores, dirty rooms, loud music, or a child's focus on video games. While these are certainly important concerns, talking about mundane activities may preclude families from discussing important emotions and stressful life events. It is the role of parents and other relatives to help children figure out who they are and what they value. Adults should check in regularly with children about their feelings and sense of identity. Spending quality time engaging in positive family talk can help families create safe home environments where LGBT youth feel comfortable talking about tough identity issues, including being lesbian, gay, bisexual, or transgender.

Creating safe spaces where youth can talk about their feelings is as important as the *feel* of conversations themselves. *Connected conversations*[5] are those in which individuals are in tune with the tone, emotion, and inflection of others. When a family member asks a youth how she, he, or hir is feeling, the adult must be fully engaged in the conversation. Life is hectic. Adults are constantly distracted by ringing cell phones, double-booked schedules, and their own emotional challenges. It can be difficult to find the time and emotional space to really listen to a youth. But partially listening to a child sends a message that her, his, or hir emotions are not really important. One study found that lesbian and bisexual women who sought support from parents described those conversations as less than helpful.[6] This may be the result of lack of awareness on the part of parents, but it may also be a sign that those conversations were not truly connected.

Artie knew that he was gay in middle school. Throughout high school he really wanted to tell his mother and stepfather about his sexual orientation. They were loving and affirming parents who regularly encouraged him talk about his feelings. Yet those conversations were not always connected. Artie continually hinted at his sexual orientation, making comments that should have raised questions, but his parents never picked up on his efforts. Artie wished that they would simply ask, "Are you gay?" But they never did. Artie's story shows how disconnected family conversations can be. Artie's story also brings up two other important points. First, Artie's experience reflected his family reality. Other youth may not want family members to ask "Are you gay?"—preferring instead to disclose when they are ready. Second, there are many adults who have wonderful relationships with the youth in their lives. Even those with the most accepting and loving hearts may not recognize when a child is LGBT, no matter how many hints are dropped. What matters, however, is how family members react once a child comes out. It is never too late to engage in connected conversations. It is better for families to get a late start than never to begin at all.

Disconnected conversations may be the result of distracted adults, but such conversations may also be a byproduct of youth communication modes. Contemporary youth are accustomed to conversing via technology such as texting, tweeting, and e-mail. They can have entire conversations with friends without ever speaking a word. Youth may feel safe divulging personal information via technology because they do not have to see the emotions of the recipient. If a family youth shares her, his or hir sexual orientation or gender identity with you via email or text, we encourage you to follow up with a face-to-face conversation. It is impossible to show an LGBT youth your care and support through electronic media only. Reach out and have a face-to-face, connected conversation.

Whether it be via face-to-face communication or an electronic medium, coming out to family can be a big step for LGBT youth. In the not-too-distant past, educators discussed how young people often explored their sexual identity in college—in a new environment away from family. While collegiate exploration may be a reality for some youth, many LGBT people recognize and explore their sexual identities at much younger ages. In fact, studies suggests that some LGBT youth have same sex attractions at as young as age 10 or 12.[7] Many of those youth come out to family in middle or high school. Given these statistics, family members should prepare themselves to engage in age-appropriate, connected conversations with very young children.

No matter when youth disclose, the decision is rarely easy. Youth often weigh a range of factors before they talk to a family member about their sexual orientation. First they consider how cohesive the family is. They also consider ways their family has talked about LGBT issues. Do adults use negative terms to refer to LGBT people? Or do they have caring relationships with LGBT coworkers and friends? Finally, the history of family dialogue often signals to youth whether a conversation will be welcome and connected. We must note however, that no matter how adept family members are at connected communication, a young person may still be fearful about coming out to family. This fear can stem from many things, including confusion or shame about one's identity, discomfort with larger family dynamics, or societal pressures that normalize heterosexuality and gender conformity.

Adults who struggle to understand the lived realities of LGBT youth often worry that they may never truly connect with their loved one. Many heterosexual and cisgender adults worry that they live within a different world or reality from that of their LGBT youth. Communicating across those seemingly disparate worlds can feel impossible. Family members who feel this way must seek out information so that they can learn what life is like for LGBT youth. As we described in Chapter 3, education about LGBT issues is essential to being an ally. Such education is also foundational to ongoing, connected conversations between LGBT youth and their families. Studies have shown that families that seek LGBT resources are more likely to positively integrate LGBT youth into their family unit.[8]

By seeking out resources, family members show youth that they care enough to take the time out of their busy schedules to learn about not only who they are, but also their struggles and successes as LGBT people. Seeking educational resources can be done from one's own home. Family members can order LGBT-friendly books or visit websites where they can learn about how to support LGBT youth. Educating oneself can also include stepping outside the privacy of one's home to attend LGBT events or meetings. Consider the story of Jennifer. She explained how her older sister, Courtney, was learning about the LGBT community. Their family relationships were strengthened by her sister's efforts. Jennifer shared, "My sister wants to go to Pride Fest this summer and bring my nephews. She's willing to put herself out there and see people that she works with, or see whomever is going to be there, and is willing to have conversations with her kids when [LGBT] things come up." Jennifer's sister was acting as an ally by learning about the LGBT community. Her sister also saw the gay pride event as an opportunity to serve as a role model to her children. They needed to learn how important it was to be supportive of LGBT people—including their aunt Jennifer. Courtney also made a bold statement. She was proud to be seen at Pride Fest and she was not afraid to stand by her sister, publicly, as her ally. Through this event, Jennifer's family connections were enhanced.

Or meet Natalie, an educator whose career was filled with ally behaviors. As a white woman, she worked tirelessly for racial equality. She also infused multiculturalism into all of her classes. However, when her son told her he really wanted to be a girl, she was at a loss. While she was committed to diversity and inclusion, Natalie's knowledge about transgender issues seemed wholly inadequate. So she worked up the courage to attend local

LGBT events. There, she could listen to people's stories and learn about how to best support and connect with her transgender child.

Both Natalie and Courtney needed to increase their LGBT awareness before they could truly connect with their loved ones. Education was important to the changing relationships with their LGBT loved ones. Yet education about the harsh realities facing LGBT people can be frightening for families. Adults worry about their children when they hear stories of harassment, bullying, discrimination, and violence against LGBT people. All parents fear for the safety of their children. It is normal. But fear can make individuals act in ways they otherwise might not. For instance, family members who accept their LGBT youth may exhibit seemingly unsupportive responses which stem from fear. Trevor's mother worried for his safety. As a high school student, Trevor liked to dress in drag. On a day he was scheduled to address the entire student body at a pep assembly, Trevor wore a skirt, heels, and a wig. He recounted his mother's response. "My mother was terrified. She was like, 'You're doing what? You're wearing what to school? What are you thinking? You are going to die, they will hurt you!' And I'm like, 'Mom it will be ok.'" Out of fear, Trevor's mother attempted to convince him not to dress in drag for the assembly. Even though she typically supported his choice of dress, she changed her tune when she worried that Trevor's safety was at stake. Jeanette, a college student, also explained how her parents worried about her safety and success in life. Yet they were able to navigate their fear and remain connected to her. Through connected conversations, Jeanette's parents were able to express both their concern for her safety and their support of her sexual identity. She explained, "They're more worried about my career and what people would say about me rather than what I am. And they've always made that clear, so they support it, they just want me to be careful."

Action Steps

- Does your family engage in positive family talk? When was the last time you talked to your child about her, his or hir feelings or identity? Start tonight by asking the youth in your life the following questions: What was the best part of your day and why? Is there something you want to talk about? How do you feel today? Is there anything you are concerned about?

- How connected are the conversations in your family? Remain focused on youth during conversations and ask them to do the same. Take a "timeout" from technology and other daily distractions and talk with the youth in your life.

- As a concerned adult, yes, you can and *should* share your concerns about safety with the LGBT youth in your life. But instead of prohibiting youth from expressing themselves, help them draft a safety plan. Determine safe people (teachers, peers, neighbors, etc.) that an LGBT student can call if they feel unsafe.

Unsafe Familial Spaces

The road to creating safe spaces can be full of hurdles and detours. No two families are alike, so the journey toward creating safe spaces is also unique. What families in the previous sections had in common was a desire to create safe spaces for the LGBT youth in their lives. However, it is idealistic to believe that all families are interested in, or have the capacity to, create safe spaces. Sadly, many families do not.

When parents, aunts, uncles, or other relatives respond negatively to the sexual or gender identity of LGBT youth, there can be grave consequences. One study showed that LGBT youth from unsupportive family environments were 20 percent more likely to commit suicide than their counterparts in more supportive homes.[9] Another study suggests that LGBT youth whose families strongly reject them are three times more likely to use illegal drugs.[10] Overall, LGBT youth with more accepting families have lower risks of mental and physical health problems.[11] These sobering statistics speak to the need for families to create accepting and safe familial spaces for LGBT youth.

Some of the most negative reactions that LGBT youth can encounter from families include rejection and abandonment. It is estimated that 26 percent of youth who come out to their family are disowned and become homeless. We also know that a disproportionate percentage of homeless youth are transgender.[12] Youth who become homeless are forced to navigate unsafe streets and shelters. Homeless youth face higher levels of depression, substance abuse, victimization, and suicide than their LGBT peers who live in accepting and stable homes. Angel, a homeless youth, described what it felt like to be homeless. She explained, "You don't have any place to go, any place to take a shower, you don't know how you're going to eat. You really don't know who you can trust. It's terrifying, especially being young. It's really scary."[13]

While some LGBT youth end up on the streets or in shelters, some may become part of the foster care system. The foster system can provide safe options, but sometimes the system further victimizes LGBT youth. From the age of seven, Danny grew up in the foster care system. He was moved from home to home and encountered sexual abuse in a number of places.

Eventually, he became homeless.[14] Mara, a social worker with experience in the foster system, explained that the system is intended to support LGBT youth. However, it is not always successful. She shared, "Some youth don't feel supported by their families in regards to their sexuality, and that can be a huge barrier to reunification or permanency. Therefore, it is extremely important for the social workers to educate and address the barriers even though it can be a difficult topic—this is especially true if the social worker struggles with their own acceptance of LGBT issues." As a supervisor, Mara works with social workers to develop a sense of compassion and acceptance for LGBT youth. Her organization offers ongoing staff training about the unique needs of LGBT youth. She also helps her staff identify local services and support groups where youth, foster families, and biological families can find support and guidance.

Linda Dame, another social worker, recounted the story of a transgender youth whose chosen identity as a female was invalidated and disrespected by many child advocates. Social workers and child advocates have the potential to be wonderful allies to LGBT youth. Unfortunately, those who worked with this particular transgender youth refused to use the child's chosen female name or suggested she not wear girls' clothing or makeup.[15] While their profession required them to provide safety and advocacy, these professionals did neither. In fact, they participated in creating unsafe spaces in the very system designed to protect at-risk children.

Some LGBT youth may not be disowned by their families, but can be forced to live in negative or hostile home environments. In the most extreme of unsafe environments, LGBT youth are subjected to physical or verbal abuse from parents, guardians, siblings, or extended kin. The emotional effects of abuse can be profound. Some families refuse to accept that their family member is LGBT. Those that cannot accept the sexual orientation or gender identity of their loved ones can go to extreme measures to try to convince youth they are not lesbian, gay, bisexual, or transgender. Some hope that professional counseling and guidance will help their children realize that they *are* the sexual orientation or gender that their families think they are *supposed to be*. We refer to such measures as extreme corrective behavior modifications or conversion attempts. Families engaging in such measures attempt to change the thoughts and behaviors of LGBT youth or to convert their identities.

Transgender youth may incur corrective behavior modification or conversion attempts through professional counseling or in the home. They may be prohibited from acting, dressing, or thinking about being a different gender than the sex they were born with. Family members may force children to dress in clothing, wear hairstyles, and play with toys that reflect the gender they believe their child to be—not the gender the child feels she, he or ze is. Transgender youth who live in homes where they are unable to express their gender identity encounter similar risks to those experienced by lesbian, gay, and bisexual youth who are rejected. Risks can include depression, suicide, or the abuse of illegal substances.[16]

In extreme attempts at corrective behavior modification or conversion therapy, lesbian, gay, or bisexual youth can be sent to ex-gay camps or programs that claim to make LGB people heterosexual. Ex-gay programs use a myriad of efforts to make people heterosexual, such as electrostatic shocks, intensive therapy, prayer, readings, or extreme physical activity. While ex-gay organizations claim success, they rarely accomplish anything but making LGB people despise themselves more than they already do. In fact, there are websites, books, and blogs designed to help individuals cope with the pain of having participated in an ex-gay organization.[17] Many individuals who have suffered through ex-gay programs offer testimony about the lack of success of those programs. Moreover, through *ex* ex-gay internet sites, young people like Patrick and Seth share narratives of survival. They also offer inspiration to those being pressured by family to become heterosexual. In an op-ed piece, Patrick tells the story of being enticed at the age of 12 by a leader of a popular ex-gay organization that targets youth. The anti-gay propaganda he internalized through that organization plunged him into years of shame and self-hatred.[18] After ten years of painfully trying to be heterosexual, Patrick found a way to accept and love himself as a gay man. A portion of Seth's story is posted on the Beyond Ex-Gay website and reads: "One day my father asked me to go for a ride with him, during which he played a promotional cassette tape filled with what I can only describe as anti-gay propaganda and religious theory describing homosexuality in terms of 'unnatural attractions' and 'sexual brokenness.' The speaker advertised special religious institutions where one could send their 'confused' loved one to get them 'treatment' for unwanted same-sex attractions. My dad perceived that my sexual orientation was a problem and was urging me to submit myself to a religious reorientation and treatment program. I felt completely humiliated and angry."[19] No matter how well intentioned, sending LGBT youth to an anti-gay organization is a form of rejection. Trying to turn a child into a heterosexual can cause deep emotional harm and damage to a parent-child relationship.

Families that do not send their children to counselors, religious organizations, or ex-gay programs for conversion might use other tactics, such as "bargaining."[20] The bargain often involves parental love and support in exchange for LGBT youth denying their same-sex thoughts and feelings. As long as youth act as if they are not LGB or transgender (i.e., lie about who they really are), LGBT youth can live at home and receive support— at least financially. Such bargains invalidate the lived realities of LGBT youth and force them to try to become someone they are not. The message: I don't love you the way you are, so you must change.

Another form of invalidation is telling LGBT youth that they are merely confused or "going through a phase." As we described in Chapter 2, adopting an LGBT identity is a process—sometimes a lengthy, painful, or confusing one. It is not helpful for family members to add to the confusion by suggesting that LGBT youth are somehow confused about their feelings and thoughts. Believing in children *and* believing their stories are essential aspects of familial resilience.[21]

Less overt forms of rejection of a child's sexual orientation or gender identity are just as harmful as more obvious ones. Emotional rejection or psychological harm can come in many forms. LGBT youth who witness family members telling gay jokes, using gay slurs, or discriminating against LGBT people are at risk for emotional scarring. When families engage in such behaviors, they can make the home environment unsafe for LGBT youth. Josie explained the pain she endured while she struggled with her lesbian identity in a household where being a lesbian was not okay. She described how her mother frequently used gay slurs and told offensive "fag" jokes. Since Josie was still figuring out her lesbian identity, she had neither the language nor the courage to challenge her mother. Not only did her mother's verbal barbs offend, but they also made her feel horrible about herself.

While many youth endure environments filled with vocal anti-gay rhetoric, others experience invalidation in the form of silence. Jim came out to his parents when he was in high school. His parents did not respond with violence, but with silence. They told him they did not want to hear about his "lifestyle" or his boyfriends. In short, they did not want to know anything about who he really was. Unfortunately, during his second year of college, Jim took his own life. Downplaying, ignoring, or not talking to LGBT youth about their identities sends a clear message that they are not loved, accepted, or wanted. In fact, some scholars refer to a phenomenon of LGBT youth creating "false selves" as they attempt to hold on to family relationships with loved ones who do not want to know about their sexual orientation.[22] Remaining in the closet or hiding their true identity can have serious mental health consequences for LGBT youth.

While Jim's pain was too much to bear, silence in Alex's family had different consequences. Alex's family members showed their discomfort about LGBT issues by avoiding conversations about sexuality or relationships. But youth like Alex are keenly aware of this avoidance. Alex explained how his parents always asked him about his high-school relationships with girls. They wanted to know who she was, what she was like, and how happy she made him. During those formative years, Alex's family engaged in connected conversations. Once Alex came out, his parents became uncomfortable with relationship conversations and they ceased. While going away to college can reduce the length and frequency of connected parent-child conversations, an absence of such conversations sends a clear message: we really don't want to know about your life. Alex's connection to his parents became distant and strained as a result of their silence about his sexual orientation.

Some primary caregivers fear that others may attribute their child's sexuality or gender identity to poor or inadequate parenting.[23] Poor parenting does not cause a child to be LGBT. Youth who identify as LGBT come from all walks of life and all types of families—none which cause a youth to become lesbian, gay, bisexual, or transgender. Nonetheless, many parents are dismayed or distraught at the thought that they may have done something wrong, something to cause their child to be "abnormal." Sometimes, family members fear what neighbors or relatives might think. Consider the story of Jon, documented by Gerald Mallon and Teresa DeCreecenzo. Jon, a 13 year old biological male, was being raised by his great-grandmother. The following is a summary of a session with a social worker:

> Jon's great-grandmother explained that it was causing her great distress that Jon was insisting that he was a girl. She feared losing her standing in the community because neighbors were beginning to ask her what she had done to make the child "that way." She was embarrassed by Jon's cross-dressing, by his insistence on being called by his preferred name, "Simone," and by other gender-nonconforming mannerisms and behaviors. Jon simply said, "I can't be what I am not, and I am not a boy." Jon's great-grandmother said to the [social worker], "Mister, I have one question for you. Can you change him back?" When [the social worker] replied, "No," she responded, "Then you can keep him."[24]

When family members worry more about what others think than their child's well-being, they are acting in a way that is very parent-centric.

In Jon's case, his caregiver was ready to disown her great-grandchild. In less extreme cases, caregivers focus so much on the stress of what they have done wrong that they ignore the struggles of LGBT youth. They also convey powerful messages. The first message is that other people matter more to me than you. The second: you are not normal and it is my fault. Parents and other family members must be mindful of the messages they send to LGBT youth. Children learn at a very young age that when a parent is upset, it means that something bad has happened. In cases where parents blame themselves, children can learn to see themselves as bad or abnormal. Such messages can inspire shame and self-hatred in LGBT youth. When Solidad came out to her mother, her mother asked, "What did I do wrong?" Solidad assured her that she had done nothing wrong, that her sexual orientation just *was*. Brave words, the right words, but when Solidad hung up, she had a lead weight in her chest the size of shame. Safe spaces for LGBT youth are those where shame has no home.

Action Steps

- Have you exhibited any of these unsafe or unsupportive behaviors toward youth in your life? What can you do to repair those relationships? Consider seeking support of an LGBT-friendly counselor or pro-LGBT community organizations.

- Do you have a distant relative who you suspect is LGBT? Consider how you can best support that youth. How connected are you? Do you have a deep enough relationship where you can assure them that confiding in you is safe? It may not be appropriate to ask "Are you gay?" to a youth with whom you do not have a strong relationship. Reach out more often and begin building a relationship of trust.

- Have you witnessed familial violence against an LGBT youth? Don't ignore it. Report it to police or child services. The violence you witness may be merely the tip of the iceberg for that child.

Beyond Your Family

Youth who live in hostile or unsupportive home environments may seek guidance from other adults in their community. They look to neighbors, teachers, coaches, and other role models for support. Candy struggled with her sexual orientation in middle school, but she dared tell no one. By the time she reached high school, she was ready to burst. She thought her parents might respond negatively to the news that their daughter was bisexual, but she had to tell someone. The person she first came out to was a trusted school guidance counselor. Candy's guidance counselor listened, suggested community resources, and talked with her about how to best approach her family. When Candy's family initially responded with shock and disbelief, the guidance counselor provided a shoulder to cry on. When her family eventually began to adapt to and accept her sexual orientation, she had a mentor to rejoice with.

You do not have to be a guidance counselor to create safe spaces for neighborhood youth. No matter who you are, there are many ways you can support local youth. One of the best ways to support LGBT youth is to create welcoming spaces in your home or neighborhood for those who are struggling with their sexual orientation or gender identity. Consider Brenda's story. Brenda, a mother of three, shared how she and her husband tried to create a safe space for community youth. They always welcomed friends of their children into their home. While Brenda and her husband were careful not to cross boundaries into "parenting" LGBT youth, they did make an effort to let children know that their home was a safe space where they could "be themselves." Brenda explained that "sometimes youth just need to know that a caring adult is interested in and will validate their experiences." Word spread rapidly among the youth in their neighborhood, and on more than one occasion, lesbian and gay youth sought refuge in their home.

Brenda and her husband created a temporary safe space in her home for LGBT youth. Another way to create more a permanent safe space for LGBT youth is to consider being a foster parent. As we described elsewhere, a disproportionate percentage of LGBT youth become homeless. Many end up in the foster system after being rejected or abused by biological families. Those young people need safe environments where they can heal. A supportive foster environment may provide not only physical safety, but also the emotional space where youth can rebuild their self-esteem and resilience. In Chapter 3, we explained how being an ally included acts large and small. Becoming a foster parent would certainly fall into the large category. Are you in a position to offer this kind of safe space to an LGBT youth?

Supporting LGBT youth is the premise of this book. Here, however, we broaden our scope. Sometimes the best way to support youth is to support their families. Young people are not the only ones who need allies. For many families, the journey toward supporting their LGBT youth can feel like a long, lonely road. By supporting entire families, you can help create and maintain safe spaces for LGBT youth. From affirming smiles, to engaging conversations, you can do much to support parents, grandparents, aunts, uncles or other relatives who are trying to support their LGBT youth. Consider the experience of Tom and Jennifer, whose biological son wanted to dress in girls' clothes and wear nail polish. When they allowed their son to express himself in public, Jennifer and Tom needed the support of other community adults. Instead, they received snickers and jeers. Or imagine the story of Karen, a single parent whose daughter had just come out as a lesbian. As Karen struggled to support her child, she wished for other adults with whom she could talk, cry, and explore her options. By lending a listening ear or referring parents like Karen to community organizations like PFLAG, concerned community members help create safe spaces. There are many parents like Tom, Jennifer, and Karen who could use the support of adults like you.

Finally, we would be remiss if we did not mention the need to support youth (heterosexual, cisgender and LGBT) who grow up in same-sex-headed households, many of which include children. Youth with same-sex parents need the support of community adults who validate their family structure. Adult allies can help normalize having two moms or two dads. Such normalization is a first step toward creating safe spaces for youth and their families. Like Brenda, you may have a household where youth feel safe expressing themselves. Some of those young people may have two moms or dads. Supporting youth as they learn to navigate a society in which having same-sex parents is outside the norm is just as important as supporting youth who identify as LGBT.

We hope the stories in this chapter inspire you to create safe spaces for the youth in your family and community. Whether you are part of the immediate or extended family of an LGBT youth or a concerned community member (i.e., neighbor, coach) helping LGBT youth find acceptance and support is paramount to their safety and well-being. Supporting heterosexual youth who live in same-sex families can also be a role you play. Finally, you can support other adults who need assistance as they journey toward supporting their LGBT loved one.

Action Steps

- Consider roles you play in your community. Are you a scout leader, school volunteer, coach, or concerned citizen? How can you make the spaces where you engage with community youth safe for those who may be lesbian, gay, bisexual, or transgender?

- Do you have friends or coworkers whom you suspect of creating unsafe environments for the LGBT youth in their lives? Consider talking to them about alternatives. Guide them to supportive resources listed in the Appendix.

- Your neighbor's child seems to be hanging out at your home more frequently. The youth is so comfortable in your home that she, he or ze comes out to you. Listen. Show that you care. Refer the youth to appropriate and safe resources in your community.

- At a local community event, you notice that the parents of an LGBT youth are being excluded from conversations. Make an effort to get to know them. Include them in conversations.

Chapter 5

Inside the Classroom Walls

Classroom walls create an impression of dichotomy—the academic arena within, the personal arena without. The reality, of course, is much more complicated. The walls are permeable: students (and teachers) bring their personal experiences into the classroom and carry their classroom experiences with them when they leave. Parents, coaches, and religious leaders are present in our classrooms in the knowledge, attitudes, and beliefs that students have learned from them. In turn, classroom experiences spill over into family, extracurricular, and religious life. In this way, classroom walls, though they mark off a space distinctive in purpose and language patterns, are something of a fiction.

Still, classroom spaces leave their mark on all of us. We know what it is like to walk through the door of a classroom and wonder what is in store. Most of us have experienced the relief that comes from slipping into a saved seat (prime real estate for anyone in an unfamiliar setting) and the dread that comes from knowing that no such seat awaits. Students understand that classrooms are not neutral spaces—they are charged with emotion. Far from being beside the point, feelings of relief and dread *are* the point for young people. And we adults need to pay attention because the stakes are high: these moments shape attitudes and ideologies, and these attitudes and ideologies have physical and psychological consequences—particularly for LGBT youth.

Classrooms lay the foundations for an inclusive and safe society: a just community where common interests and individual differences coexist. To the extent that teachers, school administrators, and college professors create an atmosphere in which difference is not only tolerated but expected, explored, and embraced, students will be more likely to develop perspectives that result in respectful behaviors. Without the deliberate creation of an inclusive atmosphere, however, what happens inside classroom walls reproduces the prejudices that exist outside these walls: straightness and gender conformity are assumed; LGBT identity is deviant.

Any adult interested in creating safe spaces for LGBT youth needs to consider the impact of schooling on the social and psychological development of young people. Teachers and peers usher children from the relative protection and insulation of family life into the classroom, where (perhaps for the first time) children encounter cultural and ethnic norms different from those of their family. If our homes are incubators, keeping our children safe as they grow into the patterns of family life, schools are "outcubators"—places that introduce new ways of thinking and behaving. Social and psychological development progresses as young people move through our educational system—kindergarten through college.

In this chapter we discuss ways that educators can validate the experiences of LGBT youth. We also describe how some educators reinforce LGBT exclusionary attitudes and beliefs that find expression in everyday acts of discrimination against LGBT people. Most educators do not set out to marginalize LGBT youth. They simply follow paths of least resistance.[1] They put one foot in front of the other in what seems the natural, even the right, direction without critically examining the journey or the destination. Heterosexism is one of those unexamined avenues of privilege. Assumptions that everyone is (or should be) heterosexual shape most classroom interactions, whether academic or social. Assumptions about gender binaries and appropriate gender roles also pervade our classrooms. Educators, indeed all adults, must forge new paths or widen existing ones to make room for all youth. Challenging assumptions is difficult work, however, and we need tools to do it well, to do it at all.

Tammy Aaberg spoke to this challenge in the aftermath of her 15-year-old son's suicide. Justin, a promising musician, was bullied because of his sexual orientation. He took his life after finishing his freshman year. After Justin's death, his mother campaigned to change district policies that required teachers to remain neutral regarding issues of sexual orientation. Tammy Aaberg named the problem: "Most of the teachers and principals . . . mean well—they want to intervene. But the teachers still don't know what they can and can't do."[2] LGBT students need advocacy and protection, not neutrality. This chapter and the next offer guidance—stories of educators who have made schools safer for all students, including LGBT youth. We've divided these stories into two sections. First are stories of transformative *curricula*. Second are stories of transformative classroom *communication*.

Curriculum and communication—distinct but inter-related aspects of classroom life. Neglect one, and the other is bound to suffer; improve one, and the other will likely benefit.

Curriculum

Curriculum, the word we use to mean a course of study, is derived from the Latin word *currere*, "to run," specifically to run a race. And, of course, when there is a race, there are winners and there are losers. We contend that the winners are those who see themselves in textbooks, art, film, and other educational materials. Youth who see themselves as wise or powerful main characters or heroes worthy of celebration and emulation will feel validated, included, and safe inside their classrooms. LGBT youth rarely have this experience. As youth proceed through the system of American schooling, they might see negative representations of the LGBT community in the health or biology classroom, where they learn about HIV/AIDS as a gay-related disease.[3] Otherwise, the traditional curriculum typically ignores the experiences or contributions of LGBT people. Below are some examples of this erasure in our elementary, secondary, and higher education settings.

Sexual orientation topics are entirely absent from nearly half our elementary teacher education programs in the United States.[4] It is therefore unsurprising that LGBT people are largely absent from elementary curricula or classroom discussions. Take the topic of family, for instance—a unit of study that is part of every (or nearly every) early childhood curriculum. The oft-stated objective is for children to learn that families come in different shapes and sizes, live in different dwellings, observe different traditions, and celebrate different holidays. Teachers around our nation narrate stories about single-parent families, adoptive families, divorced families, and foster families. The idea is that tolerance will grow as students gain appreciation for difference. We can learn from each other and enjoy each other's ways of being family. So far, so good—until the family is two moms and their children or two dads and their adopted daughter. Such families rarely make the curricular cut—they are invisible.

While it might seem to be the safest and least political of all curriculum units, the study of family can either reinforce or interrupt heteronormative beliefs and attitudes. Most teachers are reinforcers. They teach their students the status quo; they shrink from challenging dominant social patterns and expectations, especially in relation to sexual orientation or gender identity. Even teachers who describe themselves as social justice advocates fail to challenge homophobic or transphobic language and images in many early childhood settings.[5] Powerful social messages are responsible (at least in part) for this noncritical allegiance to traditional perspectives. Consider the following story as an example of how the forces beyond the classroom pave paths of heterosexism.

The PBS television series *Postcards from Buster*, partially funded through the federal government's Ready-to-Learn initiative, is a literacy intervention for early elementary English language learners. Each episode features Buster, an 8-year-old animated rabbit who travels throughout North America with his musician father. At each stop, Buster meets children who introduce him to the local culture, and the rabbit captures these encounters on his trusty camcorder. In an episode entitled "Sugartime!" Buster's adventures take him to Vermont, where he meets David, Emma, James, and their two moms, a blended family that teaches Buster the art of maple sugaring. The lesbian moms are featured incidentally, with Emma simply stating that she loves both of them very much. Sexual orientation is never explored; the words "gay" or "lesbian" are never used.

Even so, when the "Sugartime!" installment was brought to the attention of then Secretary of Education Margaret Spellings, she expressed strong opposition. She warned the president of PBS, "Many parents would not want their young children exposed to the life-styles portrayed in this episode."[6] PBS pulled "Sugartime!" from its lineup.[7] Still, the controversy severely damaged the program's funding stream—*Postcards from Buster* lost its 2004 underwriters and other traditional funding sources. As a result, the 2005 season featured only 10 episodes, a drastic reduction from the 40 episodes in 2004. Marc Brown, the creator of *Postcards*, expressed his disappointment: "What we are trying to do in the series is connect kids with other kids by reflecting their lives. In some episodes, as in the Vermont one, we are validating children who are seldom validated."[8] Instead, Ready-to-Learn validated heterosexism. We wonder whether the only relevant question here is a child's readiness to learn. Perhaps adults need a Ready-to-Teach initiative.

The young children prevented from viewing "Sugartime!" grow up. They move on to our secondary schools where the experiences and contributions of LGBT people are once again absent or rendered invisible. Let's start with literature: Whitman's *Leaves of Grass*, a staple in secondary literature anthologies, demands exploration of the poet's not-so-oblique references to romantic relationships between men. Scholars see the work as evidence of the pre-modern attitude toward same-sex orientation—but this central aspect is routinely and carefully avoided as a subject for examination in our secondary classrooms.

It is important to note that we are not arguing for an explicit discussion of sex in our classrooms. But just as recognition of heterosexual romantic themes can help students understand literary passages, so can the recognition of same-sex attraction. Kevin Jennings, founder of the Gay, Lesbian, Straight Educators Network, lamented this widespread treatment of *Leaves of Grass*: "To teach Whitman without acknowledging these pervasive themes in his work is nothing less than dishonest and inaccurate, yet it is the standard way in which he is presented in most classrooms in America."[9] Apparently, educators would rather omit or veil important themes in Whitman's poetry than broach a topic they consider taboo. Such a decision keeps LGBT people outside the walls of our classrooms and, by extension, outside the canons of polite society.

History classrooms are no different, even though the themes of oppression and the struggle for civil rights are routinely examined. In these discussions, students learn of the exacting campaigns for human dignity and constitutional protections waged by African Americans, women, and people with disabilities. These history lessons promote democratic ideals: they celebrate freedom and reinforce our commitment to justice. But they can also mislead. First, such history lessons often relegate the civil rights struggle to the past, as if all underrepresented groups have attained equal rights. As we described in Chapter 1, this is far from true. Second, such history lessons typically overlook one campaign for dignity and constitutional protections: that of the LGBT community. The bus boycott of Montgomery, yes; resistance at Stonewall, no. Once again, LGBT people are erased, even from the struggle to be recognized. In a groundbreaking move to reverse this discriminatory practice, the state of California recently passed the Fair, Accurate, Inclusive, and Respectful (FAIR) Education Act, which requires public school social science curricula to include the contributions of LGBT individuals. To the strident opponents of the new law, Jay Willis responded, "[O]fficially acknowledging the roles of LGBT individuals in the development of this country's history could help significantly undermine the harmful stereotypes that have contributed to recent suicides attributed to antigay bullying."[10] In other words, straight-laced history not only bends the historical record, it also bends attitudes.

The erasure of LGBT people is sometimes ensconced in textbooks or standardized tests; at other times, the erasure is a result of a teacher's assumptions about heterosexuality and gender conformity. These assumptions often blindside us. Maria, a sophomore at a college in the Northeast and an "out" lesbian, liked her Spanish class, liked her Spanish teacher. She considered herself a Spanish student, not a lesbian Spanish student. Nothing in the class had caused her to feel invisible or unsafe. One afternoon, all that changed. She got her test back with a red mark next to her response to this question: "Do you have a sweetheart?" Her answer, "Si, yo tengo una novia" was crossed out. In its place was "novio," the masculine form of the Spanish word for sweetheart. She wondered what she should do. Talk to the teacher and ask that her grade be changed? Forget it? She wondered whether she should have written the expected answer instead of asserting her identity. Did it always have to be a choice of denying herself or explaining herself? Maria was tired and disappointed. And, yes, a little angry because the teacher assumed her sweetheart was a boy. Maria's lived reality as a young lesbian was erased by the teacher's red pen.

Assumptions, if left unchallenged and unexamined, can devolve into active bigotry. Bigotry is a heat-seeking missile—it will find its target. Jess, a transgender student, was one such target. He had chosen to shorten his given name—the abbreviated form was gender-neutral, more reflective of his gender identity. His teacher, however, refused to honor Jess's choice. He continued to call him the name on the official roster.

We contend that such teacher-student interactions compromise the education and safety of our youth . . . *all* youth, not just LGBT youth. Adrienne Rich described erasure this way: "When someone with the authority of a teacher, say, describes the world and you are not in it, there is a moment of psychic disequilibrium, as if you looked into a mirror and saw nothing."[11] Our classrooms need to be "mirrors and windows"[12] for all students— mirrors in which youth see themselves in the curriculum and recognize their place in the group; windows through which youth see beyond themselves to experiences connected with, but not identical to, their own. Creating safe spaces for *all* students means not ignoring or erasing the experiences of LGBT people in K–12 and higher education curricula.

Erasure might be preferred, however, to the anti-LGBT teaching that some states mandate in their health curriculum. Utah, South Carolina, Mississippi, Arizona, and Oklahoma are among those states that explicitly prohibit affirmation of same-sex relationships. Alabama goes even further: It mandates that students be apprised of sodomy laws and told that homosexuality is a deviant lifestyle that poses a public health risk.[13] One LGBT student reported that her college instructor compared homosexuality to bestiality. Although Lai knew that such a comment was "not okay," she also understood that many students silently endure such denigration for fear of reprisal. Such teaching can incite verbal and physical bullying of LGBT youth. When the official curriculum stigmatizes or, worse yet, vilifies LGBT people, bullies can feel like moral champions, like guardians of the American way. More on bullying in the next chapter.

Reflection Point

- What messages did you receive about the LGBT community when you were in school? Which messages were explicit, which were implied?
- Did you ever question these messages? If so, what empowered you to do so? If not, what would have helped you to question them?
- What do you know about the gay civil rights movement? (Stonewall, for example?)
- Do you talk to the youth in your life about what they are learning about the LGBT community in their curriculum? If not, what would help facilitate this conversation?

Thus far we have offered many examples of behaviors and perspectives that are harmful to LGBT youth. Now we turn to examples of how educators can create safe spaces through their curricular decisions. The following vignettes offer portraits of curriculum decisions that both reflect and expand student experiences. The teachers in the following pages use a variety of tactics to create inclusive curricula. Their strategies can reach beyond the walls of our classrooms to create safe spaces for LGBT youth.

Zeke Lerner, a kindergarten teacher, includes a unit on family in his curriculum. In this way he is no different from most kindergarten teachers. Zeke's family unit, however, bears little resemblance to those of his colleagues. When teaching young students about our society's most basic social structure, Zeke implemented two strategies: *integration* and *interpretation*. What follows is a description of these strategies that can guide educators, parents, and other youth workers as they interact with children and teens around issues of difference.

Possibly sensitized to the need to integrate LGBT individuals in his treatment of family by his student Cody, a child with lesbian moms, Zeke chose three books as centerpieces for his family unit: *The Family Book, Who's in a Family*, and *Tango Makes Three*.[14] The first two books present a variety of family structures: Kevin and his brother live with their mother and grandmother; Laura and Kyle live with their two moms. *Tango* is the true story of two male penguins in the Central Park Zoo who hatched an abandoned egg. They raised Tango, the baby chick, feeding her from their beaks and teaching her to swim. These curriculum choices go beyond mere inclusion: they *integrate* the LGBT experience into the mainstream curriculum. The story of Laura and Kyle and their two moms, for example, was not treated separately from the range of conventional families that Zeke discussed in his classroom. The story of *Tango* became as much a story about adoption as it was a story about gay penguins and their chick. Zeke's integration of the LGBT experience is a difficult act to follow. Too often, well-intentioned teachers "tack on" an image or an example of an LGBT individual in the pursuit of an inclusive curriculum. Students see this for what it is: tokenism. Zeke's resources avoided this pitfall.

Zeke's second strategy was *interpretation*. Children hold assumptions not only about what exists, but about what is good and what is safe. Surrounded as they are by heteronormative images and messages, our students need to know that LGBT individuals are not a threat to their well-being. Zeke targeted these value assumptions in his family unit. He *interpreted* Laura and Kyle's family experience: He wanted his students to associate this lesbian family with care, love, and normalcy. As he held up the photo of Laura and Kyle's family, he explained that their moms "take care of them." With this assertion, Zeke implied something good, something desirable, about Laura and Kyle's moms. He described Robin's dads in the same way: they took care of Robin. Thus, positive values of love and caring were associated with same-sex couples and their families.

If applied across all disciplines and grade levels, *integration* and *interpretation* of LGBT experiences and contributions can transform our classrooms into safe spaces. While it is true that teachers sometimes have little control over the official curriculum, they can orchestrate or recognize teachable moments, using them to integrate or interpret the LGBT community for their students. Zeke deliberately chose to incorporate LGBT-inclusive texts in his family unit. He read these texts aloud; everyone experienced these stories as a collective. Curriculum extends beyond these classroom lessons, however. From bookshelves to bulletin boards to films, curriculum involves any written, visual, or auditory resources made available to students in their course of study. When teachers (or parents) assemble a reading list or stock their bookshelves, they have opportunities to include resources that make visible the lives and concerns of groups that have historically been erased, including LGBT people.

LGBT students need to see themselves in the world of ideas and experiences offered up by their teachers if they are to become academically and socially connected in the classroom. Heterosexual students with LGBT family members or friends need to see their loved ones reflected in the images and stories that shape ideologies. Heterosexual students who have no LGBT friends or family also need positive LGBT representations if they are to have a full understanding of the human experience. And yet, when asked if they were taught about LGBT people or history, less than 12 percent of LGBT students replied in the affirmative.[15]

One reason educators take the path of least resistance is their fear of negative repercussions from parents or administrators. Ask Johanna Habeisen, a school librarian who was issued a letter of reprimand by her principal after she introduced *And Tango Makes Three* to second-grade students at her school. Her principal explained her objection this way: "I'd love that [book] to be available to counselors that work with families that maybe have this situation. But in this society here, in this town anyways . . . I don't know if it's our job to expose [children]."[16] To relegate LGBT books to the counseling center, however, marginalizes the LGBT community and identifies homosexuality with illness.

Or ask Kimberly, a reading specialist who decided to expand her classroom library. She ordered a number of books from online booksellers that represented the experiences of LGBT individuals in a healthy and positive light. Tucked inside several books (not all from the same bookseller) were handwritten messages directing her to bible verses, ones that have been interpreted as condemnations of homosexuality. Kimberly was stunned and a bit shaken. She worried that she was wrong to share these LGBT-friendly resources with youth. Aimed at a teacher who wanted LGBT youth to see themselves represented in the literature in her classroom, these anti-gay sentiments packed a powerful punch.

Like Kimberly, Sean wanted his classroom bookshelves to represent a broad range of human experience, including that of the LGBT community. Anticipating administrative and parental complaints, he chose a practical and defensible course of action: he configured his shelves to reflect the demographics of his middle school community. Thus, 12 percent of his classroom library represented the Latino community, 4 percent highlighted African Americans, and 10 percent explored the LGBT experience in the U.S. Sean explained his reasoning: "So if a parent ever complained, I could say, 'Well, it matches our community, and here are the statistics.'"

Sean's approach, although a step in the right direction, has its limitations. Marshaling statistics will not eliminate the political risk that LGBT-inclusive texts pose. And some would say that matching resources with the demographics of the community does not go far enough. Megan Boler, for example, argues that educators committed to a just society should exercise a form of affirmative action in their classrooms. She suggests that to make up for years of invisibility, classrooms should over-represent the experiences of those who have been excluded or erased from history.[17] From this perspective, *more than* 12 percent of Sean's bookshelf should be devoted to Latino experiences, *more than* 4 percent to African American experiences, and *more than* 10 percent to LGBT experiences. Imagine Sean's bookshelves bursting with books that chronicle the range of human experience—both mainstream and marginalized youth would benefit.

Sometimes the journey toward an inclusive curriculum requires adding to our bookshelves or to our units of study; at other times it requires integrating positive LGBT images into existing assignments. John Kellermeier tried this. He framed 1 percent of his word problems for a college statistics class around LGBT themes, referencing LGBT demographics as background information or data. "In teaching a particular statistics concept," Kellermeier explains, "it does not matter whether we use as an example the percentage of red balls in an urn or the percentage of lesbians and gay men in a group of people. By using the latter, we can bring the issue of sexual orientation into the classroom." Most responses to his LGBT statistics were positive; students welcomed the opportunity to connect their academics to current societal concerns. He did receive complaints, however, and some students indicated that his references to the LGBT community were "just too much." Instead of abandoning references, Kellermeier conducted classroom research to see if *increasing* the percentage of LGBT-themed word problems changed student feedback. It did—for the better. He concluded,

> In the end it seems that the best way to deal with students' complaints that [LGBT] materials are just 'too much' is to integrate more of it into our courses. [If LGBT] issues are repeated often enough, they become commonplace. Then, as the issues become commonplace in the classroom, students may be better prepared to accept, support and appreciate gays, lesbians and bisexuals out of the classroom as well.[18]

Marley follows a similar approach in her college course where she trains budding educators to take on teaching roles in K–12 classrooms. She asks collegians how issues of race, class, gender, and social orientation matter in an educational experience. Marley offers examples of how LGBT issues play out in her classroom: She assigns an article that describes the systemic prejudice that renders a teacher unable (or unwilling) to come out as a lesbian. "What do you make of that?" she prods. Then there's the Carlson article. Even the title of the article gets their attention. "Gayness, Multicultural Education, and Community" explicitly takes on heterosexism and its effects, not only on isolated gay students and teachers but also on the living organism of our democratic society. Marley doesn't stop there. She reads *Heather Has Two Mommies* and *King and King*. She asks students to consider their obligation to Heather and students like Heather who come from gay and lesbian families. And when the king and king discreetly kiss behind a red heart that covers their lips, she asked students to weigh in on the lawsuit facing a Massachusetts teacher who read the story to her first-grade class, reminding them that same sex marriage is legal in that state. Unfortunately, some of the college student responses "cut Marley off at the knees." For instance, one student commented,

> I see myself as a relatively open-minded person who is open to diverse viewpoints. I am open to learning about people's cultures, but I am not as open in the idea of educating children about the importance of LGBT. In my opinion, children at any age shouldn't be educated about that [because] I see it as perversion and not as a natural way of loving someone. I believe that when a young child is educated about it, they naturally accept it as a natural way to live.

Is this the same student who expressed outrage at seeing Medgar Evers marshaled off the Ole Miss campus? Apparently, some forms of discrimination and hatred are acceptable to teacher candidates. Very disappointing. Still, Marley sees other students question their heteronormative assumptions and recognize their potentially harmful stances on LGBT issues. Marley tirelessly continues her work to educate future teachers in hopes that they may someday follow her role modeling and create safe spaces in their own classrooms for LGBT students.

John and Marley are not alone in their efforts to integrate LGBT content into higher education curricula. Edmon Tucker and Miriam Potocky-Tripodi[19] cited 17 studies of curricular interventions on the university level that sought to reduce students' anti-LGBT bias in classes ranging from social work and psychology to medicine. The interventions included panel presentations by members of the LGBT community, written and audiovisual content about the experiences of LGBT individuals, and a documentary on the life of an assassinated gay politician. The point is this: instructors committed to inclusion find ways to bring the voices of the LGBT community into their curriculum. Perhaps when a chorus of these voices are heard across our college campuses, anti-LGBT violence will cease. Tucker and Potocky-Tripodi put it this way: "[I]t remains to be seen whether any short-term interventions can create lasting shifts that translate into behavioral changes toward LGB individuals. It seems likely that attitude shift is a cumulative process resulting from repeated exposure to consistent information that is deemed credible."[20]

Educators like Zeke, Johanna, Kimberly, Sean, Marley, and John Kellermeier give their students consistent and credible information that includes the experiences of LGBT people. Mostly, they do this by making sure LGBT youth see themselves and their families represented in literature, history, and mathematics. We contend that including LGBT people and issues in the curriculum is an important first step toward creating safe spaces for LGBT youth. We say first step because, as educators, we know that visibility and normalization alone cannot transform our schools into safe and affirming spaces. Educators also need to teach students to critically examine all texts for bias, whether in the form of LGBT exclusion or negative stereotypes. They can encourage students to "talk back" to the curriculum, to look for assumptions, and to question what is presented to them as knowledge. This work is not reserved for educators. Parents, coaches, club advisors, and religious leaders can teach young people to examine what they see and hear (and what they don't see and don't hear) in the media. Better yet, they can model it. Teaching young people to "read the world"[21] goes a long way toward nurturing sophisticated and democratic thinkers.

Reflection Point

- When you were a student, do you remember any teacher's attempts to integrate the LGBT experience into the curriculum? If so, how were these attempts received by you, your peers, and your parents?

- As a parent, how would you feel if your child were in Zeke or Sean's classroom? How would you respond to a friend who objected to Zeke's lesson? How might you respond to your child's questions that arise in response to *Who's in a Family*?

- Integration and interpretation of the LGBT experience (paired with noting its exclusion) can serve as guiding principles beyond the classroom walls. As a parent, how might you introduce the topic of families headed by lesbians or gay men? How might you "normalize" same-sex romantic relationships in your everyday conversations with the youth in your life?

- As an educator, can you identify opportunities to incorporate LGBT voices into your curriculum? What support would you need to take this step?

- As a principal (or school board member), how would you field objections to Zeke's lessons or Sean's bookshelves? What professional development opportunities might you offer to your faculty around LGBT curriculum development?
- Take a look at a current textbook. Do you see any trace of the LGBT experience? If so, are these experiences integrated or tacked on?

Communication

Language is a tool. As such, we believe that speech is *performative*—it *does* things.[22] Words invite or exclude, recognize or erase, empower or intimidate, examine or assume. Far from what the children's chant would have us believe, words *are* sticks and stones. And those sticks and stones can either build bridges or break bones. Nowhere is this more apparent than in the classroom. In this section on communication, we offer cautionary tales and portraits of inclusion. In the former, we see the words performing exclusion, erasure, intimidation, and assumption. In the latter, we see words perform invitation, recognition, empowerment, and examination. First, the cautionary tales.

Seven-year-old Marcus was sent to the principal's office and assigned in-school suspension for using the word "gay" in school. Marcus was not calling one of his classmates gay. Nor was he using the word to refer to something cheesy. No—Marcus was describing his family. He explained to another child that he had two moms, that his mom was gay, and that "gay is when a girl likes another girl." In her official report of the incident, his teacher wrote, "Marcus decided to explain to another child in his group that his mom is gay ... This kind of discussion is not acceptable in my room. I feel that parents should explain things of this nature to their own children in their own way."[23] The teacher saw this conversation for what it was: a teachable moment. But what did she teach? The message to Marcus and to his classmates was that Marcus's family was shameful, something to be hushed. The teacher's words were indeed performative— they taught Marcus that he should have "cep [his] mouf shut."[24]

Let's imagine a "do-over." In our hypothetical scenario, Marcus's teacher overhears Marcus's explanation and listens for his classmate's response. She is poised to intervene on Marcus's behalf, to confirm that families come in various configurations. Perhaps she makes a mental note to use the term "parents" instead of "mom" or "dad." Marcus goes to recess instead of the principal's office. The classmate's understanding of the human experience expands, and Marcus's feelings about his family are not compromised. In this "do-over," the educator used positive communication to create a safe classroom space for Marcus.

Our second cautionary tale takes place in high school. It is day one of Identity and Ethnic Studies, "getting to know you" day. The teacher has prepared a game she calls "Stand and Declare." The directions are simple: She will read a statement, a declaration. Students who identify with that statement stand silently. She starts off with what might seem like a basic statement: "Stand if you are a girl." For Erica, a freshman looking for an ally in a teacher, the declaration could not have been more unsettling. Ze had been struggling against the universal binary of boy/girl, male/female since elementary school. Erica identified as transgender and felt like *neither* a boy or a girl. Yet this educational activity forced hir to choose. This educator, "an otherwise excellent and caring teacher," unwittingly alienated Erica by forcing hir to participate in a public activity where ze had to stand up in front of hir peers and identify as a girl. Erica's reality as a transgender student was erased by this activity.[25]

Nonverbal communication can also make classrooms unsafe spaces. Angel, who was born a biological male, found joy and peace in dressing in skirts and heels. In that attire, she was able to show the world who she truly was . . . most of the world, anyway. For Angel admitted that she often skipped her business class when she wore women's clothing. The one time she did attend that class in a skirt, her college professor winced and grimaced; he ignored her when she raised her hand to speak. This professor's business lesson was hijacked by transphobia; the students likely learned more from Angel's unspoken contributions than anything that was said that day. Angel and Erica would be unsurprised to learn that nearly 50 percent of transgender youth between the ages of 13 and 20 who participated in a National School Climate Survey reported skipping at least one class and an entire school day within the past month due to physical or emotional duress.[26]

We do not tell Marcus's, Erica's and Angel's stories in order to vilify teachers, for they did not set out to shame or alienate LGBT youth. Nevertheless, students from privileged groups were not challenged to think critically about their perceptions, and students from marginalized groups were, well, marginalized. In these instances, teachers missed opportunities to invite discussion, challenge stereotypes, and raise awareness of privilege and discrimination based on sexual orientation and gender identity.

In the absence of meaningful discussion that combats homophobia and transphobia, students use and hear language that denigrates and abuses their LGBT peers. Anti-LGBT slurs masquerading as playful banter are nothing less than verbal assaults. Thus, teachers, parents, or community leaders committed to creating inclusive environments for LGBT youth must wrestle with an essential question: How do I respond to students' homophobic or transphobic language? (The assumption implicit in that question, of course, is that all adults hear or read such comments. It's not a question of *if*; it's a question of *when*.) Some teachers scold. Some snicker. And, most disturbing, some join in. Imagine a student's despair when the presiding adult proves to be not a protector but an abuser. Rory experienced this betrayal. She was under verbal assault when her teacher intervened, but not on Rory's behalf. With a wink and a nod, the teacher pulled the perpetrator aside and confided that Rory was actually a witch who would cast a spell on him if he didn't stop teasing her.[27] Such blatant disregard for a student's physical and psychological safety is rare. Many, perhaps most, teachers pretend to not hear anti-gay comments. (By the way, youth almost always know when adults adopt this "hear no evil" posture. The message youth receive is not that your hearing is compromised—it is either that you agree with the prejudicial sentiment or lack the courage to address it.) As we described in Chapter 3, silence in the presence of anti-LGBT statements suggests acceptance and approval.

Educators need to be clear about what is objectionable about homophobic and transphobic language. Rules against abusive language are only a beginning. Merely outlawing certain words does little more than create a verbal underground of anti-gay insults. This memorized response suggested by the NEA is a start, but not a complete remedy.

"_____" is a word that insults gay and lesbian people. I want to remind you that there are or there may be gay and lesbian people at this school, and when you use words like that you make them feel unsafe and unwelcome. It is important to me that everyone at this school feel safe and welcome. I do not want you to use that word anymore.[28]

Patrick takes a different path with his fifth graders, one of directness and humor. What follows are two encounters with his student Derek. The first occurred after Derek called a classmate "gay." Patrick immediately intervened. As the students were laughing, he told them to take out their dictionaries and look up the word "gay." He instructed Derek to read the definition to the class. Was that what Derek meant when he called his classmate "gay"? No? Well, then, use another, more accurate, word. This is school, after all. Use language appropriately.

It wasn't long before Derek provided Patrick with another opportunity to interrupt homophobic language. This time, Derek accused another student of being bisexual. Overhearing the exchange, Patrick asked, "Really? What does bisexual mean?" When Derek answered that bisexual means "you like both," Patrick probed: "Both what? Like ketchup and mustard? I use both ketchup and mustard on my hamburgers." Derek squirmed but finally said that it means "you like both girls and boys." Patrick then made his point: "Okay, well, I have friends that are men; I have friends that are women. Your definition (is) still not really making much sense to me. I'm just trying to understand why you use this particular word, because if you're going to use it I feel like we should be able to talk about what it means, especially if you're going to do it in my presence." In describing his approach to such incidents, Patrick simply concluded, "That is what a teacher does."

Patrick does not scold. He does not snicker. And he certainly doesn't pretend that he does not hear. He explores the negative usage of words such as "gay" or "bisexual." He prods and questions, requiring students to define the terms. Patrick's actions promoted discussion and understanding: He asked students to students to think about the power of their harmful language. We believe that Patrick is right: That is what a teacher does. That is what any concerned adult does.

Reflection Point

- Do the teachers in your local school receive training on how to confront homophobic or transphobic comments?
- What do the youth in your community say about the acceptability of anti-LGBT comments in their schools?

Good Intentions Are Not Enough

Teachers cannot legislate friendships or alliances; they cannot single-handedly change minds or hearts. Educators can, however, create inclusive and safe classrooms. In this chapter, we described two ways that educators can create environments that recognize and empower LGBT youth. First, educators must ensure that the *curriculum* includes the perspectives, experiences, and history of LGBT people. Second, educators must ensure that *communication* inside the classroom walls validates the LGBT experience. But you can't validate an experience you never talk about. Thus, educators need to become as comfortable using the words that refer to sexual orientation and gender identity as they are using words that describe other differences in the human experience. When the words "gay," "lesbian," "bisexual," and "transgender" are heard positively in the course of classroom discussion, the stigma associated with them diminishes. All of a sudden, these words describe a community—they are constructive and instructive instead of destructive and provocative. Such comfort on the part of an educator invites youth to consider new ways of thinking and behaving with regard to LGBT people. In turn, LGBT students will see educators as approachable, as allies, as safe adults.

Good intentions are not enough; trying to see all students as the same is not enough. Being a fair-minded individual is not enough. We argue that educators must publicly commit to creating classroom climates of inclusivity and respect with the pledged cooperation of all students. Only then can we begin to create classrooms that are safe for LGBT youth.

We conclude this chapter by acknowledging that the work of creating safe spaces for LGBT youth is ongoing and complex; it is not a "once and done" affair, neither is it continual progress. Expect setbacks. Expect mistakes and admit them. Like paths of resistance, the roads to safe spaces are made by walking.[29] What will be your next step?

Action Steps

- Consider the power of curriculum in your schools. Also, consider how an inclusive curriculum might translate into your everyday life.
- Do the schools in your community include LGBT topics in their curricula? Participate in school committees where you can ensure that LGBT-inclusive curriculum is discussed.
- Do you know of teachers who have been discouraged from or reprimanded for using LGBT-friendly resources? If so, consider writing a letter to the principal or superintendent.
- While this chapter was about classrooms, all adults can learn from the actions of teachers like Zeke, Johanna, Kimberly, Sean, John, and Patrick. Those educators addressed LGBT issues in their classrooms. How might you include LGBT-friendly literature, film, or discussions in your home, religious institution, or community organization?
- Consider the power of communication in your life. The next time you hear someone use a derogatory term, consider the following approaches to dialogue: Ask children what they mean by a particular word. Find out their knowledge and clarify misinformation. Don't merely tell someone to stop using a particular term without explaining why. Talk about the power of

words. Words can hurt or heal; discuss possible alternatives to offensive terms. Providing more inclusive alternatives to inappropriate or derogatory terms is always educational. Be candid. Share how derogatory terms offend you—as a heterosexual or LGBT person. Knowing we have hurt or offended someone we care about can be a positive motivator to change behavior.

Chapter 6

Outside the Classroom Walls

Let's play a word association game. The word is "school." List as many images and feelings that arise from this memory-laden concept. (Really, take a moment and jot down these associations.) Your immediate associations were most likely academic in nature—images of books, calculations, and exams. If your school experiences were anything like ours, however, not far down on your list were associations having to do with social dynamics. For many of us, memories of school-based relationships (e.g., friends, cliques, and alliances) retain their sharp outlines and angles long after memories of academic pursuits get fuzzy around the edges. These associations persist because school experiences shape more than our academic lives—school shapes our lives as social and emotional creatures, both present and future, both individually and together.

Because schooling is a multifaceted and complex phenomenon, a discussion about safe schools cannot be limited to classroom experiences. As vital as a classroom teacher is to the well-being of an LGBT student (see Chapter 5), a vulnerable young person eventually leaves the protection of an adult ally for what too often are the treacherous terrains of unmonitored hallways, stairwells, bathrooms, locker rooms, residence halls, and athletic fields. The unstructured and largely unsupervised snatches of time that most students find liberating pose substantial risk for LGBT students. A few short minutes between periods can seem like an eternity, and the stairwell between one classroom and the next is nothing less than a gauntlet. Nor does the dismissal bell signal the end of harassment for targeted LGBT students—graphic and humiliating messages follow them home or to their residence halls via social networking Internet sites and cell phones.

Nearly 85 percent of 7,000 LGBT high school students who participated in a 2009 nationwide survey reported being the victims of verbal taunts because of their sexual orientation, and 40 percent of the respondents reported physical abuse.[1] One of these students described his experience this way: "[H]arassment in the schools is a norm. Kids would scream the word 'faggot' as they saw me the halls. None of the teachers said a word, and that is what scared me."[2] It should come as no surprise, then, that LGBT high school students are more than three times more likely to miss a class because they feel unsafe than are secondary students in general.[3] Listen to the words of a female student as she reflects on her senior year of high school: "I stayed home because everyone hated me so much that it made me hate myself, and I thought there was something completely wrong with me. I missed almost three weeks in a row to avoid seeing the other students."[4]

Colleges and universities can also be unsafe spaces for LGBT students. In a recent collegiate study of more than 5,000 LGBT students, faculty and staff, almost a quarter reported experiences with harassment.[5] One transgender participant in that study explained, "gender identity and expression is still a source of a lot of pain/harassment/violence" on campus.[6] Another student described the effects of harassment as follows: "Anyone who is gender variant has transferred out [of the college] within their first year."[7]

We can also draw a straight line from bullying to lowered academic achievement—the grade point averages of LGBT students fall as incidents of harassment rise.[8] Jess sat quietly through math and English, never hearing a word. He was too worried about recess, the fourth "R," to pay attention to reading, 'riting, and 'rithmetic. Sitting right in front of his teacher, he missed most of fourth grade. Archer also had a hard time paying attention in his introductory psychology class. Three rows behind him sat members of the university hockey team who regularly told fag jokes and directed gay slurs at him. Because Archer paid more attention to the bullies than he did to class lectures, he did not pass college psychology.

Absenteeism and lowered academic achievement, although serious, are not the worst outcomes of bullying. Words like "faggot" and "girlie" become far more than verbal blows: Such unrelenting gay-related taunts drove 11-year-old Carl Walker Hoover (who did not identify as gay) to suicide.[9] His is not an isolated tragedy. As we write this, the LGBT community and their allies are reeling from a succession of teen deaths and injuries that have been traced to anti-gay violence and bullying. These losses cried out for a response. The vulnerability of LGBT youth was suddenly undeniable. The "It Gets Better" online campaign[10] urged teens to "hang in there," promising them a rich and full life beyond bully-ridden classrooms and schoolyards. A common theme throughout these ads was that a community awaits that will accept you "just the way you are."[11] Although the campaign was compelling and hopeful, the obvious question remains: Why should LGBT youth have to endure such abuse until they attain adulthood? Is bullying an inevitable reality, with perpetrators and targets permanent fixtures in the landscape of childhood and adolescence? In his remarks for the "It Gets Better" campaign, President Obama insisted, "We've got to dispel the myth that bullying is just a normal rite of passage—that it's some inevitable part of growing up. It's not."[12] We agree. We've got to do better than promise LGBT young people that it will get better—we've got to *make it better.*

A fierce debate regarding the school's role in preventing anti-gay violence rages as we write this chapter. While LGBT advocates call for explicit inclusion of sexual orientation in anti-bullying curriculum, others insist that teaching tolerance for LGBT individuals "promote[s] unhealthy and harmful behaviors and practices."[13] Tom Pritchard of the Minnesota Family Council was one such vocal opponent of expressly addressing anti-gay bullying in schools. He represents individuals who regard attention to LGBT concerns as "homosexual indoctrination" and who attribute the rash of suicides to an "unhealthy lifestyle" rather than anti-gay bullying.[14]

It is not our contention that most school officials subscribe to Pritchard's ideology or that most educators intend to jeopardize LGBT youth. The problem, we believe, is more subtle and thus less responsive to cookie-cutter recipes for happily-ever-afters. Administrators, teachers, and community leaders who wish to create safe schools need to recognize the complexities of human interactions. The rub is in the definition of "safe schools." Too often, the term "safety" conjures up visions of vigilant teachers roaming hallways and barging into restrooms or campus safety officers who patrol all corners of campus. While these measures might be necessary, authentically safe spaces require commitment to an expanded vision of safety. We argue that safe schools provide *physical, psychological,* and *social freedom* for all students. Students need more than just physical security—they also need a sense of belonging, a settled confidence that their contributions are valued and that their needs are taken seriously. Anti-bullying policies are a good start, especially those that specifically address sexual orientation. We devote a section of this chapter to the discussion of effective policies. We believe, however, that an inclusive school community must be measured not only by what it prohibits, but also in what it nurtures. An anti-gay slur in a safe school will seem as unnatural as a hailstorm in the Sahara Desert. The climate will not sustain it. But how does a school staff generate the conditions needed for a respectful and safe school climate? Aren't such matters beyond our control? Climate, after all, is a mysterious interplay of infinite factors: it cannot be engineered. Boys will be boys, just as the rain in Spain falls mainly on the plain.

While such rationalizations pass for conventional wisdom, they are simply wrong. Climate change is challenging and complex, but it *is* possible. Each moment, each decision, each individual contributes to the ethos or culture of a school community, but the resulting climate is a complex phenomenon that cannot be reduced to any one of these factors. Thus, we contend that the design of a safe school involves *designed measures* (i.e., planned, deliberate actions) that give rise to *dynamic responses* (i.e., unplanned but deliberate actions). Both are necessary components to the creation of an inclusive learning community—in short, a safe school. Further, these designed measures and dynamic responses need to address the *physical*, *psychological*, and *social* aspects of personal safety. This chapter chronicles the physical, psychological, and social struggles of LGBT students and describes both designed measures and dynamic responses that would effectively alleviate these struggles.

The concept of design presumes intentional and deliberate actions undertaken to achieve a desired effect. Designers seek to create a specific experience for those who view their work or enter their spaces. The designer asks what must be done to achieve a sense of wonder, of serenity, or of adventure. For the designers of safe schools, the desired effect is a sense of belonging. What follows are specific and concrete steps that school administrators can take to set the conditions for a safe educational environment. We've organized the discussion into three sections: *policies*, *professional development*, and *physical plant*.

Policies

The obvious place for schools to begin their journey toward safety and inclusion is with the adoption of an anti-bullying policy. Policies offer a structure within which a human rights violation can be remedied. That said, it is vital to recognize that not all anti-bullying policies are created equal. Forty-seven states have enacted anti-bullying legislation that obligates school boards to formulate policies concerning harassment and bullying.[15] Most states stipulate that schools must define bullying behavior and delineate intervention and reporting procedures. Thus, policies need to describe what constitutes harassment. The Office for Civil Rights, in a letter to school personnel, clarifies:

> Harassing conduct may take many forms, including verbal acts and name-calling; graphic and written statements, which may include use of cell phones or the Internet; or other conduct that many be physically threatening, harmful, or humiliating. Harassment does not have to include intent to harm, be directed at a specific target, or involve repeated incidents. Harassment creates a hostile environment when the conduct is sufficiently severe, pervasive, or persistent so as to interfere with or limit a student's ability to participate in or benefit from the services, activities, or opportunities offered by a school.[16]

The letter goes on to explain that, while all harassment is harmful to the target's physical and psychological health, certain types of harassment constitute a civil rights violation. Such "discriminatory harassment" is subject to federal intervention. So it is that some states, following the language in Title VI of the Civil Rights Act of 1964, specifically prohibit bullying conduct that targets students on the basis of their race, color, national origin, sex, or disability.

Conspicuous by their absence from this list, of course, are sexual orientation and gender identity. Thus, far too few anti-bullying policies specifically protect LGBT individuals. LGBT advocates see this omission as an insidious loophole, one that implies that anti-LGBT bullying will be disciplined with a wink and a nod. Some policies actually call for "neutrality" regarding discussions of sexual orientation, a message that one district supervisor admitted "may have created an impression among some teachers, students, and outsiders that school staff wouldn't intervene aggressively to combat anti-gay bullying."[17] The Safe Schools Improvement Act (SSIA), a bill presently pending in Congress, would change all this. SSIA would require all schools that receive federal funds to adopt anti-bullying policies. More to the point, SSIA would require schools to explicitly prohibit harassment based not only on the traits currently protected under OCR (see above), but also on a student's actual or perceived sexual orientation or gender identity.[18]

The need for anti-bullying policies is also a reality for colleges and universities. While some individual post-secondary institutions have implemented university-specific anti-harassment or zero tolerance policies, statewide efforts to change entire higher education systems have been less successful. Part of the challenge is that public post-secondary institutions have unique reporting relationships to governing/coordinating boards and state legislatures, while private universities have even more complex relationships with those entities. Despite political hurdles, California attempted to pass legislation to protect LGBT college students. AB 620 is a bill that was intended to combat harassment and bullying in California public colleges and universities. A May 2011 amendment removed most of the anti-bullying and harassment language from the bill, including requirements that higher education institutions "train faculty with respect to . . . address[ing] harassment of individuals based on sexual orientation and gender identity, train campus public safety officers about hate crimes and harassment based on sexual orientation and gender identity."[19] With this language removed, anti-bullying legislation in California public higher education has no teeth. LGBT college students in California, and in many other states, continue to have little protection from bullying.

Preston Witt underwent harassment based on his sexual orientation and believes that explicit prohibition of anti-LGBT harassment would have made school more tolerable for him. As early as kindergarten, Preston knew he was different from his classmates. He didn't have the language that named this difference, but he did know that "Smear the Queer," a favorite dodgeball game played in his elementary P.E. class, made him uncomfortable. Preston told the coach he didn't like "Smear the Queer" and asked if they might choose a different game. Not only did the coach refuse, he designated Preston "queer for the day." The message to Preston was clear: behavior policies that instructed students to treat each other with respect did not protect him from taunts and intimidation. Preston imagines that LGBT-inclusive policies might have offered him protection:

> Just putting a sign on the wall including sexual orientation and gender identity makes that difference . . . Once I realized what gay actually meant, if I had seen on there "gay students," I would have reported [the harassment] much more. If it's, "Oh, guess what? You get to be the queer and everyone gets to throw the ball at you," that student is much less likely to report it ever again."[20]

While some, though not all, religious groups voice strident opposition to anti-bullying policies, LGBT students in schools with anti-bullying policies that explicitly mention sexual orientation and gender identity report fewer incidents of harassment than do their counterparts in schools without such policies.[21] Whether SSIA will become law remains to be seen as does the power of AB 620. Meanwhile, school personnel who ignore harassment based on sexual orientation or gender identity can under certain circumstances face legal liability. In the aforementioned letter to school personnel, OCR cautions schools against a narrow application of anti-bullying policies. The letter points out that verbal or physical intimidation of LGBT students can, in fact, be forms of "discriminatory harassment," calling for federal intervention under Title IX of the Education Amendments of 1972. Although most school personnel correctly associate Title IX with sexual harassment or sex discrimination, they might not understand that this federal statute "prohibits harassment of both male and female students regardless of the sex of the harasser—i.e., even if the harasser and target are members of the same sex."[22] Title IX also prohibits harassment based on non-stereotypical expressions of gender identity and extends to *all* students, including those identifying (or perceived) as LGBT.

Transgender students face an additional hurdle unique to them. School-generated forms and university applications often ask students to identify as male or female—a demographic distinction that creates unease for those whose gender expression does not coincide with their anatomy and for those whose gender identity cannot be reduced to a simple binary. Designers of comprehensive nondiscriminatory policies recognize that boxes marked M or F cause undue distress for transgender students. Thus, when sex or gender identification is a necessary and pertinent point of information, inclusive forms simply provide space for a student to respond to these questions.

Students who have lesbian moms or gay dads face a similar dilemma when registration forms or permission slips reflect the assumption that all parents are heterosexual. Better to simply ask for parent or guardian signatures. Chris, a transgender parent, appreciated one preschool that listed "Parent 1" and "Parent 2" and then provided a space for a description of how the child's family structure might be unique. This school was in a town that had antidiscrimination legislation with language that included both sexual orientation and gender identity. Then Chris moved to a city where the protections of the more progressive communities were glaringly absent. All school communications are now addressed to mother and father. A conventional family structure is assumed, and many school events are gendered. Invitations to "Take Your Mom to Lunch," are hardly applicable to Chris. Inclusive alternatives to these gendered events are manifold. All it takes is the political will to invite all parents to participate in the school community.

Let us reiterate—safe schools create community, a sense that, although different in appearance or outlook, everyone belongs. Easy enough to say, a devil to implement. Odd, is it not, given the universal need to belong?[23] If everyone seeks belonging, why are we not more committed to inclusivity? The truth is that the concept of belonging is only one side of an ironic social equation: Our sense of belonging rises in direct proportion to the number and types of people who do not belong. In this twisted view, belonging is diminished if *everyone* belongs.

Heterosexism is nowhere as evident as in the politics surrounding the crowning social event of high school: the senior prom. The social importance of this "coming-of-age" event is hard to overstate: "From movies to television series and video games, these cultural artifacts all present prom as a milestone not to be missed, a day that will be memorialized for the rest of a young girl's life. Many teens accept this message as standard wisdom and believe that prom will be a defining moment in their lives."[24] "Defining" turns out to be the operative word. Amy Best contends that proms often function as a rite of passage into white and, more to the point of our discussion, straight adult life.[25] Constance McMillan discovered this implicit agenda when her plans to attend her senior prom with her girlfriend ran afoul of Itawamba County School District policy that required prom dates to be of the opposite sex.[26] In a meeting with the superintendent, Constance was given other unpleasant news: Only males were allowed to wear tuxedoes. And if her presence made other students uncomfortable, she would be asked to leave. When, on Constance's behalf, the American Civil Liberties Union sought a policy change that would address blatant discrimination against LGBT youth, school officials canceled the prom.

Community proms that openly welcome same-sex couples offer an alternative experience for some LGBT students near large metropolitan areas—a modern manifestation of the "separate but equal" doctrine that we know to be inherently unjust. LGBT youth at safe schools attend their prom with dates of their choice, wearing the clothing of their choice. Although still rare, inclusive proms are becoming more common.[27] The presence of LGBT youth at senior proms might complicate this rite of passage that has been laden with heterosexist assumptions. All the better.

Action Steps

- Ask for a copy of your school's anti-bullying policy. Does it explicitly prohibit harassment based on a student's perceived or actual sexual orientation or gender identity? If not, start a discussion with school administrators and school board members. Contact GLSEN or the ACLU for help. See GLSEN's Public Policy Webpage (www.glsen.org) for more information

- Launch a phone, e-mail, or letter campaign that asks your U.S. senators and representatives to support the passage of SSIA.
- Research policies relative to social events, e.g., proms. Challenge attendance policies or dress codes that discriminate on the basis of sexual orientation or gender identity. See GLSEN (www.glsen.org) for suggestions.

Antidiscrimination policies pave the way for another measure that contributes to safe schools: gay-straight alliances (GSAs). GSAs are student-led organizations that work toward a safe and inclusive school community for all students, regardless of sexual orientation or gender identity. GSAs exist in many colleges and universities, high schools, and even some middle schools.

The beauty of a GSA is codified in its name: alliance. GLBT students work alongside straight and cisgender students to educate, advocate, and celebrate. They might organize events for an LGBT Pride Week or promote GLSEN's Day of Silence, a day in April during which LGBT individuals and their allies remain silent to protest the silencing of the LGBT community. Perhaps they simply organize social events during which students can get to know each other. Each group sets its own agenda, but a common theme is support. Here is safety for LGBT students and their allies who might otherwise feel isolated and afraid. In a review of research on gay-straight alliances, GLSEN reports that GSAs make a significant difference in school climate: LGBT students hear fewer homophobic comments and can identify supportive adults more readily in schools that have GSAs. But perhaps the most persuasive data has to do with school attendance: LGBT students in schools with GSAs are less likely to skip school due to fear of harassment. GLSEN concludes, "As part of a comprehensive safe schools initiative, GSAs can create positive changes in school climate that endure over time, outlasting changes in the student body, faculty or administration."[28]

And yet most LGBT students and their allies lack this support. GSAs can be found in all regions of the country and in growing numbers, but their organizers often meet with resistance. Principals and college administrators sometimes deny LGBT students and their allies permission to organize. Many do so illegally. The Equal Access Act, a federal law enacted in 1984, stipulates that a school that allows even one non-curricular student organization to meet on school grounds during or after school cannot discriminate against student organizations that they or their constituents might consider controversial. Thus, students may form clubs to advance religious, political, and social agendas. Administrator and/or parent objections must be met with clear information and determination. GSAs are not a privilege that have to be earned or granted; they have a right to exist. Easier said than done. Ask Ginger, a high school student who was told that she could not form a GSA in her public high school. When the principal refused to reconsider the decision, Ginger and her friends decided to protest at a school board meeting. Although reluctant, the board overturned the principal's decision. Marisol, a student at a private Catholic college also met with resistance when she tried to start a GSA. Unlike Ginger's protest, Marisol's appeals were denied. She was informed by university administrators that there would never be a GSA at the Catholic institution. Never.

Students like Ginger and Marisol need adult advocates who will help them negotiate the process of establishing GSAs. Often they do not know where to turn, which brings us to our final policy discussion: the hiring, and, more to the point, the firing of LGBT teachers (and allies who openly advocate for the LGBT community). Although most schools do not openly discriminate on the basis of sexual orientation or gender identity, few explicitly protect, and even fewer encourage, the expression of LGBT identity. Schools are by and large heterosexist institutions, i.e., they assume everyone is (or should be) heterosexual. Schools also reinforce gender binaries and normative forms of gender expression. In such environments, many LGBT teachers fear sanction or dismissal and so remain closeted. While straight teachers freely share aspects of their personal life with their students, humanizing themselves and making connections vital to student learning, LGBT teachers often withhold such anecdotes. References to family or social events pose risks to a closeted teacher. LGBT teachers can even be reluctant to intervene on behalf of a harassed student or to integrate LGBT related references in their teaching. So it is that LGBT students who would benefit from having a role model, an advocate, remain isolated and unprotected.

Fear of "coming out" to students and colleagues is not unreasonable. Consider this: A fourth-grade student asked student teacher Seth Stambaugh if he was married. Stambaugh replied that he was not. When asked why, Stambaugh explained that he couldn't get married because he would marry a man. It would be illegal. The student then asked Stambaugh if he "liked to hang out with other guys." Stambaugh said yes. Honest answers to honest questions. A teachable moment that might lead a student to question whether a law that prevented Mr. Stambaugh from getting married could be fair. A parent who overheard the conversation thought otherwise and lodged a complaint. The upshot? District administrators requested that Stambaugh be reassigned.[29] The LGBT students in Stambaugh's school (and, yes, many LGBT individuals recognize their sexual orientation as early as elementary school) and LGBT teachers everywhere were once again put on notice: Be on guard—you are a stranger in a strange land. Your visa is strictly conditional—any explicit expression of your identity is cause for deportation.

Unlike many, Stambaugh's story has a happy ending: The school district, after being charged with discriminating against Stambaugh on the basis of sexual orientation, not only reversed its decision but also agreed to "provide leadership training concerning issues related to sexual orientation, gender identity and gender expression."[30] Stambaugh was not alone in his resistance to this act of heterosexism. Twenty-seven teachers petitioned district officials to reconsider their prejudicial action. Parents and staff spoke out against the decision. In their solidarity, they echoed the experience of Maya Angelou when she said, "The need for change bulldozed a road down the center of my mind."[31]

Parents in Stambaugh's school district worked as allies for change. As we mentioned in Chapter 3, heterosexual and cisgender allies may encounter marginalization or violence for their actions. Christina, a heterosexual college faculty member described herself as someone who "stands up for LGBT students." While it isn't always safe for educators to stand up against heterosexism, she believes it is the right thing to do. Christina argued that "in every possible space [I'm] an advocate and an educator about the issue . . . It's political . . . It's hard. It's painful. You take the knocks for it. And sometimes you choose to take knocks so other people don't have to." Sometimes LGBT educators and their allies take more than a few "knocks" when they stand up for LGBT students. The fear of being fired or not earning tenure is real for many faculty members. And, students can sense fear. When teachers are afraid to be allies, it is obvious to students. Gloria, a student at Christina's university, was keenly aware of the challenges faced by LGBT faculty and allies. As LGBT students on that campus began to organize a new GSA, they found few faculty who were willing to be advisors. Gloria explained, "I get the sense that some of the faculty that want to be a sponsor of [LGBT] groups or want to be involved don't feel safe to do so, especially if they don't have tenure. I wish there was something that I could do as a student about that, but I just get that sense that it's really pretty risky still." Gloria's wish to support her faculty is profound. Should the responsibility to support LGBT teachers fall on the shoulders of students? We think not. All of us have a duty to support both teachers and LGBT youth who wish for more inclusive schools. How can you make sure such educators never feel alone when they "stand up" to support LGBT youth?

Action Steps

- If your high school does not have a GSA, consider organizing one. The GSA network (gsanetwork.org) and *GLSEN's Jump-Start Guide for Gay-Straght Alliances* offer helpful advice to get you started.
- Provide training for GSA leadership. Many opportunities exist. The gay-straight alliance for Safe Schools offers an annual Leadership Training Institute. See http://www.gsaforsafeschools.org/.
- Reach out: Encourage your GSA leadership to offer workshops or educational programs not only in their high school or college, but also to local elementary schools or community organizations.
- Encourage collaboration between local college and high-school GSAs for educational programs and mentoring.

Professional Development

The leadership, faculty, and students of Seth Stambaugh's school district will benefit from the distress he suffered when removed from his initial student teaching placement. The controversy occasioned by his informal reference to marriage (in)equality resulted in opportunities for extensive professional development related to creating safe spaces for LGBT teachers and youth. The need for this intervention became obvious. In the absence of legal or public pressure, however, the need for professional development around issues of sexual orientation, gender identity, and gender expression often remains unaddressed. The needs are profound; the response is profound silence.

We've made the point that LGBT students (as well as those who are perceived to be LGBT) face elevated risks for physical attack (see Chapter 1). This is probably unsurprising to most readers. What might be surprising is that not all high-school teachers feel a responsibility to protect LGBT students. Only 73 percent of high-school teachers who participated in an online, nationwide survey strongly agreed that they "have an obligation to ensure a safe and supportive learning environment for LGBT students."[32] If a full 27 percent of high school teachers believe that the safety of LGBT students falls outside their purview, it is little wonder that perpetrators of anti-LGBT violence often act with impunity.

Teachers sometimes operate under a narrow definition of anti-LGBT violence. Although aware of intimidation and taunts, some teachers, perhaps reluctant to become involved, do not intervene unless and until they witness physical violence. They might act differently if they knew that nonphysical threats can drive LGBT students to self-harm. Jess was one such student. He sat alone in the school cafeteria, visited the nurse to avoid the locker room, and dreaded opening his locker where "Death to fags" messages were likely to greet him. "Faculty did not want to deal with it," Jess recalls. "They said I wasn't getting hurt." The presumption nearly killed Jess. We contend that the victim gets to decide what constitutes "hurt."

For Asher Brown, a straight-A middle-school student of small stature who identified as gay, school was a nightmare that ended only with his suicide. Bullies physically tormented him with simulated sexual acts in the locker room and tripping him in the stairwell. The harassment was brutal and unrelenting, leading Asher's parents to claim that he was "bullied to death."[33] Whether Asher's teachers and administrators intentionally ignored harassing behaviors and their resulting complaints is under debate. Nevertheless, systematic harassment of any student calls all adults to a serious examination of their responsibilities to create and maintain safe school environments. Most educators and administrators want to protect all students, but good intentions are not enough. School personnel need strategies that address the full cycle of harassment: they need to recognize vulnerabilities, interrupt verbal or physical assaults, and restore safety. This work often requires considerable skill. Karen Izzo, a high-school English teacher and GSA advisor, warns teachers and community leaders that anti-LGBT harassment can be subtle. Bullies are often "so skilled that they make it look as though they are not doing anything negative."[34] We cannot assume that all adults possess the competency to recognize and interrupt subtle or overt harassment, but we know that, without such competencies, our LGBT students will continue to suffer. Thus, we believe that mandatory professional development is crucial to a safe school climate.

We contend that our definition of safe schools provides a framework for effective professional development. We call our model Three by Two. The "Three" refers to LGBT students' *physical*, *psychological*, and *social* safety; the "Two" refers to *designed measures* that deliberately create safe spaces and the *dynamic responses* that reinforce those measures. Figure 6.1 offers a visual representation of this comprehensive model. Central to the model is the perforated circle that surrounds interlocking physical, psychological, and social safe spaces. Whether inside or outside classroom walls, safe

FIGURE 6.1   Three by Two Professional Development Model

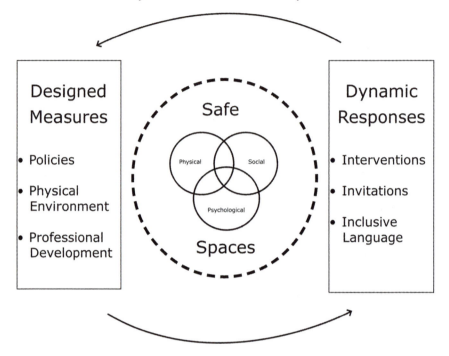

spaces are not closed; they allow designed measures and dynamic responses to shape the environment. The arrows indicate the dynamic nature of community; designed measures can shape dynamic responses and vice versa.

Comprehensive professional development requires commitment. Although some groups will provide diversity training free of charge, workshops always take time: time to organize and time to implement. Climate change does not occur in 90-minute blocks—it takes place over days, weeks, and months. The insights and strategies gained through professional development sessions need to be tested, refined, and shared. All of this takes time. And time, of course, is money. Many union contracts require that educators and other school personnel (inclusive of office and custodial staff) receive compensation for mandatory professional development. Administrators might protest that they lack the resources to devote to such comprehensive professional development. We would encourage such administrators to assess the costs of ignoring this need. LGBT advocates and those who value a diverse society recognize that time and money spent on anti-bullying professional development fosters democratic values in *all* participants—from elementary school students through college administrators. It is money and time well spent.

Reflection Points

- Administrators at unsafe schools often resist or reject professional development offers.[35] What might account for such resistance? How might parents or community leaders encourage schools to commit to comprehensive professional development?

- Consider the relevance of the professional development model for a community organization. What designed measures and dynamic responses could make any community organization a safe space for LGBT people?

- Given the importance of peer allyship, how might the professional development model be helpful for student leader training? How could teaching students to take ownership of designed measures and dynamic responses in their student organizations make those extracurricular spaces safe?

- Some religious communities believe that homosexuality is immoral. Does holding such a belief exempt a teacher from being an advocate for LGBT students? How does the answer to this question affect the broader school community?

Physical Plant—Outside In

Form follows function, so the architects say. School campuses are designed with their constituents in mind: *who* is going to use the space and for what purpose? Thus, spaces are never neutral. By virtue of their design and their decoration, they encourage some activities and discourage others; they accommodate some and stigmatize others. In other words, they reflect the priorities of the designers. Academic spaces can be designed to facilitate cooperation (large, open areas with moveable tables and chairs) or to promote competition (rows of individual desks facing front). The same is true of the larger physical plant. The walkways and hallways, the bathrooms and locker rooms, the residence halls and dining halls of our schools and campuses provide not only the *location* for behavior and emotion, they *shape* behavior and emotion. LGBT students feel the power of physical space keenly. We say that they experience school *outside-in*. Although LGBT students experience all spaces outside-in, we concentrate on the most problematic—bathrooms, locker rooms (and their extension—athletic fields), and residence halls.

The Suicide Prevention Resource Center offers this bit of counsel to school and university administrators who are concerned about the safety of LGBT youth: create unisex bathrooms.[36] The reason is simple: safe bathroom access is a requirement for full participation in school life (to say nothing of health concerns). Fear and anxiety related to bathroom access has caused some LGBT students to miss school or to drop out entirely. Bathrooms are precarious spaces for LGBT students for several reasons. First, because they are usually unmonitored by adults, bathrooms tend to become porcelain empires presided over by bullies whose graffiti intimidates even when they are not physically present. At one university, students complained to the administration that there were LGBT slurs in many of the restrooms. They took the complaint seriously and inspected all 30 bathrooms, finding homophobic and transphobic comments in a good portion of them. When one administrator called maintenance to have the stalls painted to cover the graffiti, they asked, "Do you know how much that will cost?" She replied, "The cost of doing nothing is far greater."

The second reason is related to the first: students whose gender identity does not correspond with their anatomy face physical and emotional risks when forced to use gendered bathrooms. Armando, a cisgender student, admitted that he feared for the safety of his transgender friends. While his campus has a handful of unisex bathrooms on campus, his friends were not always able to get to those bathrooms as they rushed between classes. Armando mused, "Do they go to the guy's room? Do they go to the girl's room? We need more unisex bathrooms!" As an ally, Armando constantly raises the issue of gender-neutral bathrooms, not only for his friends, but for anyone who feels more comfortable in a private bathroom. Every student should have the ability to find a restroom that they can use—safely. Safe schools provide all students the option of accessing a gender-neutral bathroom. Until all bathrooms are harassment-free, schools and colleges can reduce LGBT students' anxiety by publicizing the location of gender-neutral bathrooms.[37]

Locker rooms are as precarious as bathrooms for all the same reasons. They pose additional risk, however, when students are expected to undress in front of their peers. Safe schools allow students to use locker rooms that align with their gender identity and provide private areas for changing. Coaches and athletic directors can extend the dignity afforded LGBT students in the locker room by enforcing and modeling inclusive language and granting LGBT athletes equal opportunity to develop their abilities (i.e., playing time and coaching attention that reflects their ability and dedication). School administrators can make athletic fields safe spaces by enacting and enforcing language policies that prohibit anti-LGBT slurs from players or spectators. See Chapter 7 for more information about safe athletic environments.

While bathrooms and locker rooms pose real threats to the physical, psychological, and social safety of LGBT students, they are not home. Students might comfort themselves with the promise of a safe place when their school day is at an end. University residence halls, on the other hand, *are* home. Consider the following scenarios, both taken from real life: A biologically female student who indicates a male gender identity on an intake form might be assigned to a male residence hall but not "pass" as male. Or a biologically female student identifies as female and is assigned to a women's residence hall, but her gender expression is male. She is consistently "read" as male.[38] These are just two examples of students who would find residential campuses that offer gender-neutral housing more welcoming than those that force them to choose between gender binaries. Gender-neutral housing has its naysayers. Glenn Stanton of Focus on the Family is one. When Ohio University announced its intention to pilot a gender-neutral housing program, Stanton remarked, "The schools have a responsibility to say 'We want to help you and protect you and keep you focused on what you came here to focus on.'"[39] His remarks suggested that inclusive and safe living arrangements would somehow keep students and schools from focusing on education. Yet, that's exactly what gender-neutral housing allows LGBT students to do.

Action Steps

- Conduct several "learning walks" at different times of the day through your school's physical plant. (Going with other allies is even better.) Your goal: Imagine negotiating these spaces as a vulnerable student. Record your impressions (positive and negative) and share them with school administrators.

- Ask your local school or college if they have a list of all the gender-neutral restrooms on campus. Are they in all buildings or just a few? Suggest that the school consider converting more restrooms into gender-neutral spaces.

- Ask whether your school has a policy governing language at athletic events. If it doesn't, draft one and submit it for approval. Find a pledge at http://www.athleteally.com/.

From Beyond the Classroom Walls to Beyond Schools

In this chapter we explained how policies, professional development and physical plant can influence the lives of LGBT youth in K–12 schools, colleges, and universities. Whether you are an educator, administrator, volunteer, coach, school board member, or concerned citizen, we hope this chapter offered you insight into what it takes to create safe educational environments. There is no easy answer or simple solution to making schools safe and welcoming spaces for LGBT youth. We argue, however, that the need for safety stretches far beyond the classroom walls. In order for LGBT youth to feel a sense of physical, psychological, and social safety, inequitable policies, unsafe physical plant, and comprehensive professional development must be addressed. Throughout the chapter, we offered tangible suggestions on how to tackle some of these persistent issues.

This chapter is titled "Outside the Classroom Walls." But, the lessons learned here can transcend even school settings. Imagine safety far beyond the classroom walls. We hope that you will consider using lessons from this chapter in all realms of your life. Whether it be in your workplace or other community organization, issues of exclusionary policies and unsafe physical plant are paramount to LGBT people. LGBT people need physical, psychological, and social safety anywhere they go—not just schools. Armed with tools in this chapter, you can help make many settings safe for LGBT people. For instance, the Three by Two professional development model can be used to teach just about anyone (not just school personnel) to engage in designed measures and dynamic responses to heterosexism, homophobia, and transphobia. How might you use the lessons learned in this chapter to make your schools *and* other settings safe spaces for LGBT people? As you ponder your answer, we encourage you to read Chapter 7, where we describe the need for LGBT safety in a variety of community settings.

Chapter 7

We Are Our Communities

In a groundbreaking work entitled *Bowling Alone*,[1] Robert Putnam documents the decline of civic structures that have historically created a sense of interpersonal connection in local communities. He argues that drastic declines of adult participation in political life and community organizations reflect a disturbing trend that, left unaddressed, could erode the social underpinnings of our democracy. Our commitments to one another matter.

But if Putnam's data on adult isolation chill our souls, certainly the near frenetic pace at which youth participate in community activities should warm us up. Opportunities for youth to participate in community events and activities seem endless: Children and young adults join scout troops, take dance or music lessons, or participate in community events such as trips, art projects, or library read-a-thons. Recreational sports are particularly popular: One study reports that over 80 percent of youth between the ages of 6 and 17 participate in at least one community sport or activity."[2] Youth also spend significant amounts of time in their neighborhoods, community centers, or local religious organizations. These spaces have become essential to the physical, social, and psychological development of our youth. While the developmental benefits of extracurricular involvement abound, but we must listen for a discordant note in the chorus of praise for the opportunities available to our young people. LGBT youth often find these community and neighborhood spaces unwelcoming, even unsafe.

Creating safe communities for LGBT youth is the responsibility of everyone. We are our communities. We cannot rely on police officers or community officials to make our communities safe for LGBT youth. Instead, parents, neighbors, coaches, religious figures, librarians, and other community members must work together to create safe community spaces. Consider a historical example, the neighborhood watch. While neighborhood watch structures vary, they share an underlying tenet that safety and community are collective responsibilities among neighbors. Members agree that it is their responsibility to create a safe community. We argue that our neighborhoods, community centers, youth leagues, and spiritual centers are an extension of our homes and schools. Therefore, it is our responsibility to make them safe for everyone, including LGBT youth. Consider the roles you play in your community. Whether you are a local politician, scout leader, school volunteer, coach, or concerned citizen, you can work to make community activities safe for lesbian, gay, bisexual or transgender youth.

Community Sports

Beginning in early childhood, our nation's youth participate in the wide-ranging world of sports, from t-ball to fencing, gymnastics to hockey. In fact, 30 to 40 million children play organized sports each year.[3] Community programs (i.e., nonschool) account for almost 80 percent of these activities.[4] Many youth enjoy sports as a way to socialize outside the confines of school and home. In one study, more than 65 percent of youth reported that they participated in sports to be with friends.[5] Community, socialization, and just plain fun—all positive aspects of team sports. But sport has an unsavory underbelly: Heterosexism, homophobia, and transphobia pervade many athletic teams. It is not uncommon for teammates, opponents, spectators, or coaches to erupt in anti-gay slurs. These taunts start early in children's lives. Consider the peewee league or t-ball team where boys as young as five or six use the term "sissy" to taunt players on the opposing team. And the abuse persists. Imagine teenage softball players who endure slurs such as "dyke" or "lezzie."

Beyond locker rooms, gymnasiums, and fields, the overall atmosphere of an athletic event can be toxic for LGBT people. Heterosexism often permeates even the spectator stands. Victoria shared her experience at a community basketball game. She was cheering on her team when the boys sitting behind her began their own chants: "Number 33 is a Faggot," "Has Number 24 Ever Seen a Vagina?" and "This is not softball season, stop being pussies!" The fun was over. And when Victoria asked them to stop, she was met with a fresh stream of abuses that ended with a misguided appeal to their First Amendment rights. They shouted, "Shut up! We don't care what you think. It's America, we have freedom of speech here." Sadly, too many fans, players, and coaches believe that hateful speech is free; free of harm, that is. Quite the opposite is true. Derogatory language aimed at LGBT people comes at a high cost, sometimes the ultimate cost. It is no wonder many lesbian, gay, bisexual, and transgender youth choose not to participate in or even attend organized sporting events. And even though Victoria considered herself an ally (see Chapter 3), this encounter made her fearful of speaking out on behalf of her LGBT peers.

Gender-nonconforming students may avoid organized sports for a host of reasons. First, traditional American culture includes pressure for boys to be ultra masculine or for girls to be ultra feminine.[6] These norms follow youth onto fields, courts, and rinks. To avoid being ostracized for gender nonconformity, many youth avoid sports—especially those that are considered most feminine (ice skating, dance) or masculine (wrestling, hockey). Imagine being a biological boy who wants to join the girls dance team or a transgender youth who wants to try out for the football team. Many gender-nonconforming youth *expect* taunts and stares and consequently decide that sport participation isn't worth the abuse. Even the most courageous transgender youth who defy team restrictions and gender norms often face exclusion from coaches, verbal taunting from fans, or violence from teammates.

Transgender athletes also face logistical hurdles. Sex restrictions on "all girls" or "all boys" teams can prohibit transgender students from participating in a team of their choice. Even if a youth is allowed to participate on a team, other technical considerations arise. For instance, locker rooms can be problematic spaces for transgender athletes. Is there a safe locker room they can use at home or at away games? Will that athlete be barred from pregame, halftime, or postgame team meetings held in the team locker room? Questions like these, unthinkable to most youth, plague transgender or gender-nonconforming athletes.

The marginalization of athletes starts as early as a child can toss a ball, shoot hoops, or swing a racket. Heterosexism and the pressures of gender conformity follow children throughout their youth. When children outgrow little leagues, they move on to high-school, college, or adult leagues, but anti-LGBT sentiments follow close on their heels. Justin Bourne, a former professional hockey player, admits that heterosexism and homophobia were everyday occurrences in the locker room. It was not until years after he retired that he realized the harm his taunts and homophobic language may have caused. He explained, "The lack of a homosexual presence in hockey must mean one of two things: either homosexual men don't play the game or they don't feel comfortable admitting it—in which case I, and my brethren, were offending some teammates with our close-mindedness, and furthering what must have been unsettled feelings of fear and general exclusion."[7] Unfortunately, Justin was not talking about an isolated incident or a phenomenon limited to professional hockey. Whether it be tennis, basketball, baseball, softball, field hockey, or any other sport, hostile team interactions and unsafe playing fields incite fear and exclude LGBT athletes, young and old.

The gray haze of anti-LGBT violence and harassment, while pervasive in community sports, has been broken by occasional rays of hope. Kye Allums, a George Washington University (GWU) student, recently became the first openly transgender student to play NCAA basketball. Kye's stardom offers transgender players hope for the future. Kye's team experiences send a positive message to young LGBT athletes: safe and affirming team environments *do exist*. Of GWU teammates, Kye said, "My teammates have embraced me as the big brother of the team. They have been my family, and I love them all."[8]

Making athletics safe for LGBT youth is up to the whole team, but we believe that adults shoulder a large share of the responsibility. Coaches, athletic directors, and other adults who serve as role models for youth must take deliberate steps to create cohesive and loyal team cultures. Unfortunately, many coaches are unaware of the difficulties faced by LGBT youth. Less than 20 percent of the 2 to 4 million adults who coach our youth have received any type of training.[9] Many volunteers who coach community sports are parents. In fact, 85 percent of coaches are fathers coaching their own children.[10] Volunteer coaches receive even less training than those who are paid. We contend that without basic training, coaches are more likely to ignore and perpetuate heterosexism and strict gender roles with their team.

Without access to formal anti-bias training, community coaches may take their cues from professional coaches. Unfortunately, professional coaches often reinforce traditional gender roles and marginalize lesbian, gay, or bisexual players. In one case of negative role modeling, University of Hawaii coach Gregg McMackin used a gay slur to refer to the Notre Dame football team.[11] The upshot of this hurtful comment, however, might have been the emergence of an LGBT ally. In his apology, McMackin expressed remorse, calling the incident a "life lesson" and promising to work alongside the LGBT group on campus. We welcome his advocacy.[12]

McMackin is not alone; other coaches have served as allies to LGBT youth. In Chapter 3 we shared the story of Bill, who taught his son's youth team why using the term "fag" was inappropriate and hurtful. Additionally, Russ Rose, coach of the Penn State Women's volleyball team, has been heralded as a gay-positive leader. He shared the following message with ESPN fans: "I think you can only be your best when you're the most comfortable. If you have to live in a closet, life's really hard. You're alone. Life's tough enough when you have to interact with people. It's really tough if you have to do it alone."[13] LGBT-affirming coaches like Bill and Russ Rose serve as role models to coaches and spectators alike, as they make athletic environments safe for LGBT youth.

Action Steps

- Suggest that all community sport participants (including spectators) sign an anti–hate-language pledge. Be prepared to design the pledge and enlist the help of community members to enforce the pledge on game days. Learn more and find a sample pledge at http://www.athleteally.com/
- Find out if community coaches receive any anti-bias training on LGBT issues or anti-bullying. If not, encourage the community organization to require training for all paid staff and volunteers.
- Direct LGBT youth to blogs like http://bradrobertben.wordpress.com/[14] that highlight the positive experiences of LGBT athletes.
- The Women's Sport Foundation offers a free training video titled *It Takes a Team*.[15] This video describes the experiences of LGBT athletes and how it takes a team to ensure that all athletes are safe and respected. Another valuable resource is Changing the Game: The GLSEN Sports Project (sports .glsen.org). Use these resources during team orientations and/or coach trainings.

Civic Organizations

Every year, scores of youth join community clubs and local organizations such as Scout troops, 4-H, or other groups in search of friendship. Parents often encourage their children to engage in these community organizations so that they can learn leadership skills, enjoy outdoor adventures, and develop meaningful relationships. Many youth organizations, such as those discussed in this section, have mission statements that purport to focus on youth leadership development, character building, and civic engagement. Sounds good. The reality, however, is that although some of these organizations offer safe spaces for LGBT youth, some do not. Imagine Edward, a seven-year-old boy whose gender expression does not fit the norm. Many of the youth in his class are active in a local community youth organization. His peers share stories of adventure and fun. Of course, he wants to join, too. Will Edward find friendship, fun, and role models, or will he experience exclusion?

In this section we describe three nationally recognized youth organizations and show how LGBT youth like Edward can feel either welcome or excluded in those spaces. Although a comprehensive review of civic youth organizations is beyond the scope of this book, we have chosen three of the most well-known youth organizations in the nation as examples. These organizations, however, are among thousands of local, state, and national organizations designed for youth. From these examples, we hope readers will see that *any* youth organization can be a welcoming place to youth. We also argue that the most well-intentioned organizations, even those with impressive mission statements, can be unsafe spaces for LGBT youth.

In their 100-year history, the Boy Scouts has served over 100 million youth through their programming and camping experiences.[16] "The Boy Scouts of America provides a program for young people that builds character, trains them in the responsibilities of participating citizenship and develops personal fitness."[17] Certainly, the Boy Scouts offers young boys an opportunity to develop a host of beneficial skills. Yet the Boy Scouts may not be a safe space for LGBT youth. Just ask former assistant scout master Dale Certiorari, who was removed from his position for being an openly gay man and gay rights activist. In June of 2000, the Boy Scouts convinced the U.S. Supreme Court that it had the right to remove a gay man from his position on the basis of his sexual orientation.[18] His firing and subsequent court ruling sends a symbolic message to all current (or would-be) Boy Scouts. The message: the values we hold and promote are not inclusive of LGBT people.

The Girl Scouts has supported 3.3 million girls in the past 90 years.[19] The organization's website has an entire page dedicated to the safety of young girls that includes statistics about the bullying and harassment faced by young people who identify as lesbian, bisexual, or transgender and describes those statistics as unacceptable.[20] The message: We affirm all girls, no matter their sexual orientation or gender identity. But because the Girls Scouts of America seems to be a welcoming organization for lesbian, bisexual, and transgender youth, they have been attacked by conservatives for this openness. Hans Zeiger, a congressman from Washington State, stated in his blog, "One might wonder why the Girl Scouts have been spared the painful attacks that have been launched upon the Boy Scouts by the Left in recent years. The reasons are simple: the Girl Scouts allow homosexuals and atheists to join their ranks, and they have become a pro-abortion, feminist training corps." Zeiger also said in his post, "If the Girl Scouts of America can't get back to teaching real character, perhaps it will be time to look for our cookies elsewhere."[21] The Girl Scout organization attempts to create safe spaces for youth, and are marginalized by political leaders for doing so. Sadly, this is a common story—organizations that welcome and affirm LGBT youth face political pressure to be less inclusive.

Despite the efforts of the Girl Scouts to document their openness, the reality is that Girl Scout events may not always *feel* welcoming for lesbian, bisexual, or transgender youth. Caring scout leaders, activity coordinators, and community volunteers can serve as allies and role models to LGBT youth. Sadly, they can also contribute to the marginalization of young people. In reflecting on his experiences, Bevin, a transgender male, remembers his Girl Scout experiences. He would have preferred to join the Boy Scouts to go hiking and tie knots. But, as a biological girl, the Girl Scouts was his only option. Instead of tying knots and hiking, he learned to braid hair and knit. Bevin explained that while the Girl Scouts is designed to help girls make friendships and gain confidence, he mostly felt different and excluded. Luckily, Bevin's mother served as the troop leader. She ensured there were activities that met his needs. Unfortunately, when his family moved states, Bevin got a new troop leader who was not so open-minded.

Open to both males and females, 4-H celebrated its 100th anniversary in 2002. More than 6.5 million youth across the U.S. participate in 4-H.[22] Similar to the Scouts, 4-H promotes the healthy development of young people. Their mission statement reads: "4-H empowers youth to reach their full potential, working and learning in partnership with caring adults."[23] In 2009 a young boy experienced bullying at a 4-H summer camp in West Virginia. Once the incident was reported, two of the bullies were sent home—a bold, symbolic move by the 4-H leadership.[24] In this instance, 4-H sent a message to campers, parents, and the community that harassment would not be tolerated. 4-H also takes an inclusive stance it its virtual community. On its website, 4-H states that it reserves the right to remove any discriminatory or derogatory language, including negative comments about sexual orientation.[25]

Unfortunately, these messages of inclusion are not the only ones 4-H sends to young people. Many local 4-H chapters host pageants. Like most pageants, award criteria codify gender norms by rewarding young girls for their appearance, poise, and modeling. Young people whose gender expression pushes the boundaries of normativity would certainly not feel welcome at these contests. Moreover, the mere presence of such events in our communities can send a powerful message to transgender youth: you are not, nor will you ever be a winner.

Action Steps

- Consider the civic organizations in your community. Are they structured in ways that include LGBT youth? Do they send symbolic messages of inclusion or exclusion? Is there local political pressure for those organizations to be exclusionary? Find allies who will join you in making the organization feel safe for LGBT youth.
- Before you allow youth in your life to join a community organization, find out if it is LGBT friendly. If not, fight for change or take your business and children elsewhere.

Religious and Spiritual Communities

Places of faith are community spaces that LGBT youth may seek when grappling with sexual orientation or gender identity issues. The responses that LGBT youth receive from religious and spiritual organizations are as diverse as the organizations themselves. There are hundreds of spiritual and religious options available, far too many to address here. Instead, we offer a snapshot of two organized religions and encourage readers who are interested in the complexity of religion, spirituality, and sexual orientation to seek additional resources. (See our appendix for a list of faith organizations that welcome LGBT people.)

Religious and spiritual communities can offer refuge to LGBT youth. Too often, however, they deliver condemnation instead. Listen to Todd's story: By middle school, Todd suspected he was gay. He could not tell his devout Christian parents, however, because he knew all too well the teaching of their church: LGBT people will spend eternity in hell. Todd had internalized this belief system, so he was determined to fight his same-sex attraction. To no avail, he tried to "pray away the gay." By the time he reached college, Todd knew he could not *keep himself* from being gay. Since his church would not welcome him as a gay man, he decided to abandon his religion. Todd was forced to renegotiate his religious and gay identities, a complex process we describe in Chapter 2.

Too often, LGBT youth are ostracized by religious organizations that portray LGBT people as a danger to the moral fabric of our society. Perhaps Todd did not abandon his faith community after all; perhaps his faith community abandoned him. It is rarely pointed out, however, that some religious communities and many people of faith actively support gay rights. Bill Trench, a New England Methodist minister, is one such ally. In his blog "Thinking Faith," Bill called on the people of Maine to defeat a bill that would overturn marriage equality in their state.[26] In churches such as those led by Bill Trench, LGBT youth can find safe spaces.

In another part of the country, the North Carolina Council of Churches became the first Southern state church council to elect an openly gay man as its president. Stan Kimer is a lay leader in a Metropolitan Community Church (MCC), a denomination founded as a spiritual home for the LGBT community. He now leads this ecumenical council in its pursuit of unity and social justice. The *Charlotte Observer* found Kimer's election newsworthy: "As the newly elected president of the N.C. Council of Churches, Stan Kimer is typical of those who have served before him: a retired business executive, longtime churchgoer and member of several nonprofit organization boards. He is also openly gay. And that sets him apart." [27] We long for a day when the election of an LGBT church leader will not be newsworthy.

LGBT allies can resist discriminatory policies in their churches. The Roman Catholic Church of Minnesota recently encountered such grassroots opposition to its DVD campaign against marriage equality. During the gubernatorial race of 2010, the archdiocese mailed DVDs to more than 400,000 Catholics across the state, urging them to call for an amendment to the state constitution that would "put the one man, one woman definition of marriage beyond the reach of the courts and politicians." The campaign had unintended results. Instead of rallying behind a movement to ban same-sex marriage, many Minnesotans were outraged. These brave allies believed it was their responsibility to make their religious community safe for LGBT people. Indeed, they exemplified the notion that "we are our communities." One local artist created an art piece representing equality from recycled DVDs. Another group of parishioners started Return The DVD.org,[28] a project that sent a message to the Catholic Church that marginalization of LGBT people was unacceptable.[29] Through their artistic and political protests, these parishioners sent a message to their church and LGBT people everywhere: LGBT exclusion is not a religious value.

In Tennessee, Deb Word, Catholic mother and grandmother, single handedly challenged the church for denying Communion to LGBT individuals (and gay rights supporters). Deb created a postcard that she mailed to every Catholic bishop in the United States, urging them to open their hearts and minds and to build a truly inclusive church:

> The postcard reads, "Dear bishop: I house discarded LGBT youth—eight so far this year. I have bandaged a child who has been beaten. I've prayed over the near lifeless body of a child who attempted suicide. I house, feed, counsel and love these children . . . and I remind our clergy not to tell these children they are hell-bound because of their orientation," Word says, "Bishop, you might call me a gay activist, and I am. And I would ask you to join me."[30]

Or consider the story of a lesbian couple in Rhode Island whose experiences highlight the impact of everyday people working with their religious communities to send LGBT-affirming messages to youth. Gwen and Abigail had both been members of religious communities that they had to leave when they became a couple. They were invited to attend a Methodist church, where they forged a tentative place for themselves, hoping for nothing more than tolerance. Instead they were invited to teach the high-school youth group. Would Gwen and Abigail consider it? They hesitated, and then Abigail said, "You probably don't know this, but we are a couple." They were told, "Exactly. We like couples to lead the youth." Community faith organizations send implicit messages to youth about LGBT issues based upon whom they include or exclude. High-school youth in Gwen and Abigail's Sunday school classroom learned more than words from the Bible; they learned that their church valued, respected, and appreciated all people, including those who identified as LGBT.

Just as in Christianity, Jewish perspectives about lesbian, gay, bisexual, and transgender issues vary widely. Recently, Conservative Jews took a step toward LGBT inclusion in the form of an updated mahzor, the prayer book for the High Holy Days (which begin with Rosh Hashanah and end with Yom Kippur).[31] The modernization process took 12 years, and was the first update in the Conservative movement's prayers in almost 40 years. The new prayer book is called Lev Shalem, and, while it remains close to traditional Hebrew texts, it adds commentaries and optional readings to help make the prayer book more modern. The updates include a prayer for a deceased "partner," an attempt to include gay Jews, and a prayer for "a parent who was hurtful." The changes may seem small, but they reflect attempts to be inclusive of LGBT people within the Conservative Jewish movement.[32]

Congregation BeitSimchat Torah (CBST)[33] seeks to be a safe space for LGBT youth. It has a message for people regarding the subject of LGBT bullying and LGBT suicide. It goes something like this: being gay is not an abomination; hate is the abomination. That premise forms the core of Strength Through Community, a new project launched by CBST, alongside organizations Keshet[34] and Nehirim.[35] Building off the success of the It Gets Better project, Strength Through Community reaches out to LGBT youth who are coming to terms with their sexual orientation or gender identity. By sharing stories of Jewish LGBT people, these young people find a wealth of support in the Jewish community.[36]

The importance of supporting LGBT youth extends beyond Christianity and Judaism to all communities of faith. Whether you are part of an organized religion like Islam, Buddhism, Hinduism, Christianity, or Judaism, or of another spiritual group, you can play a role in making your community safe for LGBT youth. The stories in this chapter are few and represent only a small slice of spiritual diversity in the United States and around the world. Our examples were not meant to exclude. Instead, we aimed to show how any religious or spiritual community can become a safe space for LGBT youth.

Action Steps

- Stand up for LGBT youth in your spiritual or religious community. Find ways to make sure your religious leaders know how important it is to support LGBT youth.
- Sponsor a dialogue or book group to examine the basic tenets of your faith. Talk about how these tenets relate to creating safe spaces for LGBT youth.

Public Libraries

Athletics, religion, and civic organizations are not for everyone. Some youth seek the comfort of books for answers to life's dilemmas. Laurie was one of those kids. Laurie struggled with her same-sex feelings but had no one to talk to. In junior high she decided that the librarian seemed like a trustworthy soul. So she asked him if there was a book where she could read about girls who liked girls or boys who liked boys. The librarian helped Laurie find a variety of books, many of which were on reserve or had to be specially requested because they were challenged. She read everything he gave her. Laurie admitted that these LGBT resources "saved my life." Having access to books with LGBT characters and positive LGBT messages was invaluable to Laurie's safety and identity development. The stories helped her learn that she was not alone in her same-sex feelings. In fact, there were many people like her. Laurie read about the lives of gay and lesbian characters long before she had the opportunity to meet another LGBT youth. Through books, she made friends and met adult role models. These fictional characters helped her persist in a home and school environment where she never fit in. In books, however, she always felt affirmed and safe.

Unfortunately, not all libraries are safe spaces for youth. As we described in Chapter 1, books with LGBT characters or content are often banned or challenged. Whether a library bans the book or makes it difficult to access, the effect on LGBT youth is the same. Youth such as Laurie who are desperate to read about characters who are "like them" may be forced to read books that reinforce heterosexism and traditional gender norms. While select local libraries may ban or challenge books, the American Library Association (ALA) values intellectual freedom and has been a longtime supporter of LGBT literature. In 1971 the ALA launched the Stonewall Book Award for adult readers. Since 2008 the ALA has published an annual Rainbow Bibliography of children's and young adult books with LGBT content.[37] The bibliography serves as a guide for librarians, bookstore managers, and readers. It is not a celebratory award, however; it is merely a resource list. Recently, the American Library Association announced the creation of a new award honoring LGBT literature for youth, called the Stonewall Children's and Young Adult Literature Award that honors quality books with LGBT content.[38] The award serves as a symbol of what ALA values—diversity and inclusion.

Beyond books, libraries serve as an important community resource. Since their inception, public libraries have been committed to improving local communities. Moreover, the profession of librarianship itself is dedicated to advancing causes such as literacy, intellectual freedom, equitable access to information, and lifelong learning.[39] Through programs, classes, and other events, public libraries teach young people about topics such as safety, literacy, and career development. Because of their commitment to diversity, some libraries have offered programs about bullying. The It Gets Better video project was created after a rash of LGBT youth suicides so that adults could share their stories about how life changes and gets better in the LGBT community. In Maine, a local reporter noticed the lack of voices coming out of Maine. In response, a dozen community organizations and three local gay-straight alliances hosted an event at the local library where community members could record an "It Gets Better" message. The event also included a screening of the film *Bullied*, which documents Jamie Nabozny's experiences with anti-gay bullies and his federal lawsuit against his school district.[40]

Libraries can also serve as important community spaces where young people can congregate. The American Library Association argues, "The most dangerous time of the day is from 3 PM to 6 PM. Public libraries provide teens with a constructive place to go during these hours, where teens can organize and participate in supervised recreational and educational activities."[41] Whether they come to read, use the Internet, or do their homework, libraries can serve as safe havens for LGBT youth. Frequent LGBT patrons may also have an opportunity to get to know the library staff. Through those connections, youth may find allies and role models in a local librarian.

Action Steps

- Investigate the availability of LGBT literature in your local library. Does your library have quality LGBT-themed literature? Is it accessible to the youth who need it? What library policies exist to prevent the censorship of LGBT literature?
- Suggest that a library display be created around National Coming Out Day or during Gay Pride Month.
- Work with your local library to sponsor a showing of the documentary film *Bullied*. The free *Bullied* kit includes the film and a discussion guide. You can order a free copy from Southern Poverty Law Center.[42]

Neighborhoods and Other Public Spaces

Libraries are not the only community spaces where LGBT youth seek refuge. LGBT youth look for a variety of community spaces where they can freely express their sexual orientation or gender identity—coffee shops, community centers, arcades, and LGBT-friendly businesses. Some youth also spend significant amounts of time playing, socializing, or working in their neighborhoods. Whether they are walking home from school, playing on a jungle gym, headed to work, or just "hanging out," safety is paramount for LGBT youth. Too often, however, LGBT youth are bullied or victimized in our community spaces.

In 1981 John Walsh's son, Adam, was abducted from a shopping mall. This tragic event started a community discussion about how adults deceive children and lure them into dangerous situations. Many of us who were growing up during this time were given "code words." These were prearranged words that an adult would use to indicate they were a safe person in case of emergency. As LGBT youth navigate our communities, they are constantly on the lookout for signals or code words indicating safe spaces. Community spaces, businesses, and organizations can do simple things to help LGBT youth identify as safe. For instance, safe-zone stickers or LGBT flags can serve as codes, or visual symbols, for LGBT youth in need of physical safety.

Frank and Ursula worried about their son, Gage, who was regularly bullied in his middle school. What they feared most was his walk home from school alone. What if bullies followed him? To allay their fears, Frank and Ursula identified a number of safe spaces along Gage's walking route. These spaces included neighbors' homes and a few local businesses. They told Gage that if he ever felt unsafe, he should run to one of those safe spaces and call them immediately.

Gage's story is an all-too-common one—LGBT youth bullied or victimized in public spaces. We argued in the introductory portion of this chapter that we should not have to rely on police to make our communities safe. In Gage's case, it was neighbors and local business owners, not police officers, who kept Gage safe. However, the role of law enforcement in our local neighborhoods cannot be ignored. Law enforcement officials can use the power vested in their positions to send positive messages to LGBT youth: bullying and harassment will not be tolerated. Unfortunately, many youth do not see police or security as symbols of safety. Anna and Stacy were two lesbian college students who lived in an apartment off campus. One day they came home to find one of their cars vandalized. The next week their windshield was smashed. They reported the incidents to the police. What they didn't tell the police was that they occasionally heard people yelling gay slurs outside their apartment. Two weeks after the most recent vandalism, they heard the slurs again. One person yelled, "I wonder if the faggots are home." Terrified, Anna called the police and reported the yelling outside the window. A police car arrived a few minutes later and Anna heaved a sigh of relief. Through the window she heard portions of the three minute talk between the officer and bullies. The officer said: "Keep it down and have a good night." The officer smiled at the bullies and drove away, leaving Anna and Stacy speechless and afraid. Not only did the officer fail to take action, but the police never followed up with Anna or Stacy to see if they were ok. So much for the power of police protection.

In Anna and Stacy's case, police refused to take action against LGBT bullies. In other instances, LGBT youth endure negative treatment from public safety officers. When LGBT youth are bullied and end up in a physical altercation, they can often be labeled as trouble makers. Security and police officers sometimes treat all fight participants equally, giving little attention to how LGBT youth may be defending themselves against bullying. In other cases, young people who "hang out" in public areas can be harassed by police for loitering or trespassing. Imagine being a gay or lesbian youth who is afraid to come out to family. Youth who are fearful of bringing same-sex friends or dates home may find alternative places to hang out. One particular site of contention has been Manhattan's Pier 45, which has become a regular hangout spot for LGBT youth. One transgender youth explained how the Pier was a place of safety and support. She said, "For me, the pier is a place where I can feel affirmed in who I am as a young queer woman of color. It's a place where I know I will find others who look like me. I can relax there. I can breathe knowing that no one will look at me funny—try to stare me down with disapproval, or figure out why I'm a 'girl' wearing 'boy's' clothing."[43] Unfortunately, law enforcement agents regularly expelled youth from the Pier and surrounding public spaces. Youth complained about being harassed for walking down the street, hanging out at a public pier, and even using public restrooms.[44] LGBT youth in the Pier 45 area refused to be victims of societal heterosexism, transphobia, and police harassment. They'd had enough. Enter FIERCE, a nonprofit organization for LGBT youth of color. After years of youth complaints, FIERCE created a "Cop Watch" program. Through that program, FIERCE officials and community youth engaged in regular talks with police about the unacceptable treatment of innocent LGBT youth.

Of course, not all youth are innocent of crimes. However, LGBT youth who commit crimes often experience differential treatment from the criminal justice system. A recent study showed that, for similar misconduct, LGBT adolescents were roughly 1.25 to 3 times more likely to be sanctioned than their straight peers.[45] The researchers also concluded that the sexual-orientation disparity was greatest for girls. Girls who identified themselves as lesbian or bisexual experienced fifty percent more police stops and reported more than twice as many juvenile arrests and convictions as other teen girls in similar trouble.[46] These stories and statistics should cause us to pause and reflect upon how safe our community spaces are.

In the United States, there is a long history of LGBT people and people of color being targeted or profiled by law enforcement.[47] In response to the prevalence of bias in law enforcement, the Anti-Defamation League

(ADL) offers anti-bias workshops for law enforcement agencies. On its website, the ADL explains the need for its services:

> The unique role of law enforcement officials in any community makes cross-cultural understanding imperative. In addition to the need to ensure officer-to-officer sensitivity, to accurately represent its constituents, law enforcement officials need understanding, respect, and a willingness to communicate with all segments of the population. If members of the community feel that their own concerns are not understood, their confidence in law enforcement personnel to meet these needs may be severely diminished.[48]

In the previous paragraphs, we have shared narratives of LGBT youth who had lost confidence in law enforcement.

Reflection Point

- Can LGBT youth in your community turn to the police for help when they are bullied or victimized? Or will they merely be re-victimized by the very officers who should be making our communities safer?
- Does your law enforcement agency engage in diversity training whereby they learn to support LGBT youth? Recommend anti-bias training from the Anti-Defamation League.

Physical and Virtual Community Centers

In response to the lack of safe spaces, many communities have constructed community centers designed to support LGBT youth. One of the most comprehensive lists of LGBT-friendly community spaces is the Centerlink Community Center Directory, which offers maps and contact information for GLBT-friendly centers around the world.[49] Among the centers listed in the directory is District 202, a Minneapolis community center specifically designed for LGBT youth. When it opened its doors in 1991, the center was a safe space where LGBT teens held dances, drank coffee, read books, formed friendships, and met their first boyfriend or girlfriend. At the time of District 202's founding, most schools in the Twin Cities did not have gay-straight alliances or other support networks for gay youth. Internet use was not as widespread as it is today, and many youth had never talked to someone they knew was lesbian, gay, bisexual, or transgender. The LGBT landscape has changed over the past decade and District 202 has adapted to the emergence of younger, more tech-savvy LGBT youth. District 202 no longer has a centralized location. Instead, it sponsors events all over the Twin Cities so that preteens can access the events. District 202 also offers a Queer and Ally Blog and provides links to YouTube videos to spark online discussion.

The use of online resources, blogs, and social media has become an integral part of how many LGBT organizations connect with youth. The social worlds of LGBT youth orbit around cell phones, instant messaging, posting and watching online videos, and social networking.[50] In fact, youth spend more time with media than with any other activity, including sleeping.[51] The internet allows youth to meet other LGBT people who share similar struggles. In communities where LGBT youth feel like they are "the only one," interpersonal connection via technology can be a lifeline.

A model program that utilizes the power of technology to connect LGBT youth to their communities is Youth Guardian Services (YGS).[52] This is an entirely Internet-based organization that facilitates the fostering of relationships between young people. It also connects youth to social service and crisis-response organizations in their local communities. YGS utilizes e-mail as its primary communication tool. E-mail lists provide a forum for LGBT youth to share their stories of activism and organizing. To prevent cyber bullying and the targeting of LGBT youth, YGS has strict guidelines for accessing the lists and protocols for acceptable list submissions.

One group of LGBT youth that is especially dependent on cyber communities is rural LGBT youth. Rural youth often do not have access to LGBT community centers or LGBT events. Plenty of gay and lesbian people live in rural communities yet; the vast majority of programs for LGBT young people are in metropolitan areas. While all LGBT youth face tremendous challenges, rural youth go noticeably underserved. Because of their geographic isolation, rural students can be extremely difficult to reach. The Finance Project offers a useful resource entitled "Finding Resources to Support Rural Out-of-School Time Initiatives."[53] This document shares the unique transportation challenges, limited access to technology, and other barriers to creating effective youth programming in rural America. While the Internet is perhaps the only avenue through which rural young people can access such information, a great digital divide exists between metropolitan and nonmetropolitan Internet access and must be considered when designing rural LGBT spaces. Many rural communities are not reached by high-speed Internet cable, keeping many LGBT youth from home access to the Internet. Additionally, the public facilities that rural students use to access the Internet (schools, libraries, etc.) often have policies in place that censor LGBT-friendly websites.

Action Steps

- If you live in a rural community, volunteer to sponsor events in partnership with urban LGBT centers or provide transportation to metropolitan events.
- Research Internet policies in public-access areas and challenge homophobic filters that deny access to LGBT-friendly websites.
- Identify LGBT-friendly centers in your community and share the information with other adults (i.e., coaches, educators, community leaders) who may need to refer LGBT youth to those centers.

LGBT youth navigate a host of community spaces in search of recreation, learning, friendship, and support. While civic participation for adults is at an all-time low, youth are highly involved in community activities and organizations. In fact, youth spend countless hours in community spaces like libraries, playgrounds, and popular teenage hangout spots. The stories in this chapter confirm that often, community spaces are not safe for LGBT youth.

Narratives in this chapter also show that while some community adults are supportive of LGBT youth, many are not. Young people's stories reveal how coaches, volunteers, and police can be active agents of exclusion and harm. If we are our communities, it is everyone's responsibility to ensure that LGBT youth feel included, affirmed, and safe. You are your community. How will you make it safe for LGBT youth?

Conclusion

We began this book by listing the names of LGBT youth who have committed suicide. Throughout *Safe Spaces*, we described many ways youth can be marginalized in home, school, and community settings. Harsh realities, indeed. We end this book, however, on a very different note. This chapter is about what our home, school, and community spaces *can* and *should* be. Here, we envision not merely safe spaces, but utopia. Utopia is often thought of an ideal or perfect place, and thus, some argue that utopia is unattainable. We disagree. Let us tell you why.

In the following pages, each of the authors describes her utopian visions for the future. Gerri describes family utopia while Megan and Annemarie describe educational utopias. We believe these utopias *are* attainable; we are not skipping down the road with Dorothy on her way to Oz. Instead, utopias reflect spaces that are *more* than safe: they are validating, affirming, and celebratory. Such spaces are not impossible to create. In fact, *Safe Spaces* is filled with stories of LGBT youth and their allies who challenge LGBT marginalization in contemporary society. The courage and success of these activists and allies offer us hope that society *will* change for the better. Utopia is precisely what they are working to achieve.

Readers like you also give us hope. You are reading *Safe Spaces* because you understand how important it is to create welcoming and safe environments for LGBT youth. As we conclude this book, we invite you to create safe spaces for the youth in your life. Once you achieve that goal, we hope that you do not become merely content or satisfied with safety. Ask yourself, is safe really good enough? Do youth deserve more than mere safety? If you believe, as we do, that LGBT youth deserve open, affirming, and validating environments, we invite you to set your sights on utopia. We have.

Gerri's Utopia: It's a Family Affair

As of this writing, Rhode Island's bill for marriage equality has been shelved, at least until the 2012 legislative session. The heteronormative vision of marriage and family has succeeded once again in keeping same-sex relationships on the fringes of social and legal legitimacy. I watched the hearings: Opponents argued that "gay marriage" would shred the moral fabric on which our nation was founded; advocates argued that marriage equality is nothing less than a civil right currently meted out on the basis of sexual orientation. Rubbing shoulders in the crowded courtroom, opponents and advocates were worlds apart. On one point, however, they agreed: the stakes are high . . . so high, in fact, that marriage equality forms the basis of Gerri's utopian vision:

The Defense of Marriage Act has been repealed, replaced with the Marriage Equality Act. Parents imagine a dignified future for their son or daughter who identifies as lesbian, gay, bisexual, or transgender . . . one that includes marriage and family. The extension of this constitutional right has created social structures that afford invitation and possibility, essential ingredients for parental hope. And parents who have hope remain connected, invested. For LGBT youth, home is a safe space.

LGBT individuals participate in all the benefits and responsibilities of family life. Lesbian moms, gay dads, and transgender parents are active in school and civic life. Their children freely share stories about their families. Their friends are frequent guests in their homes. They see their parents in the kaleidoscope of family images they encounter, in the literature they read and the TV shows they watch. For children with LGBT parents, home is a safe space.

Heterosexual youth freely enjoy the company and friendship of their LGBT peers. Their parents and social justice legislation have taught them that family values have nothing to do with the sexual orientation or gender identity of the parents. For heterosexual children, loving homes are safe spaces.

Martin Luther King, Jr. reminded us that "The moral arc of the universe is long, but it bends toward justice." Let it bend.

Megan's Utopia: School Days

I imagine a K–12 school system that warmly welcomes LGBT youth. Teachers and administrators work together to create classrooms, playgrounds, locker rooms, and bathrooms where bullying knows no home . . . hate speech has no voice. Within the school environment, youth feel not only safe, but also validated and affirmed.

They see teachers, administrators, custodians, and volunteers who are openly gay, lesbian, bisexual, or transgender. In this utopian school system, LGBT youth feel strong connections with "out" LGBT role models and strong, vocal heterosexual allies. No matter what their identity, all school personnel use inclusive language, model appreciative behavior, and challenge policies and practices that exclude. In fact, utopian schools have outgrown the need for the professional development model we presented in Chapter 6. No longer must educators be trained on how to design inclusive policies or develop dynamic responses to create physical, psychological, and social safety for LGBT youth. The school environment, policies, and educator interactions with youth are inclusive.

Across the curriculum, children young and old learn about LGBT history and famous lesbian, gay, bisexual, and transgender people. School libraries and classroom bookshelves overflow with quality LGBT memoirs, works of nonfiction, and fictional tales—all invaluable resources for LGBT youth who are navigating identity journeys. In utopia, youth do not "struggle" with their LGBT identity because it is no longer outside societal norms. But, in the rare exceptions when children do struggle, they are surrounded by caring teachers and administrators who are properly trained to support youth on that journey. Moreover, educators support gay-straight alliances and other extracurricular clubs where students can explore their identity. In utopian schools, LGBT groups are as commonplace as student government and the basketball team.

Schools embrace LGBT youth with the same enthusiasm that they embrace other students. Teachers and administrators partner with LGBT families to ensure there is a seamless line of support between home and school. Finally, no parent ever fears that her, his or hir child will be treated in a manner that is anything but nurturing, because the school welcomes and affirms all types of families.

Annemarie's Utopia: Reaching Higher Education

From the initial college application to commencement ceremonies, LGBT college students are valued and appreciated in my utopian vision. Recruitment materials for college campuses include pamphlets and websites filled with diverse, smiling faces. Not uncommon are images of student groups with same-sex couples holding hands next to heterosexual couples doing the same. Messages of inclusion continue seamlessly from recruitment, through admission, to new student orientation. At college orientation, LGBT students meet campus officials, future mentors and role models, many of whom are openly gay, lesbian, bisexual, and transgender.

LGBT students see signs and symbols of LGBT acceptance everywhere. Campus events include famous LGBT speakers, comedians, and musicians. The general education curriculum offers an array of courses about LGBT history, identity, and politics.

In utopia, gay-straight alliances might be a relic of the past. Or, where they do exist, they do not serve the purpose they do today—islands of support at campuses ensconced in heterosexism and transphobia. Instead, LGBT campus groups serve as spaces for collegians to socialize with LGBT peers, not because they need to, but because they want to.

In utopia, LGBT students *feel* at home on campus. Inclusive residence-hall policies thoughtfully pair LGBT roommates so that LGBT students never have to worry about being uncomfortable in their living space. LGBT commuters park their cars with no fear of vandalism. Unsafe bath and locker rooms are a vestige of the past and gender-neutral restrooms are located in every campus building. LGBT students attend sporting events where out LGBT athletes receive as many cheers as their heterosexual teammates. From the dining halls to the laboratories, LGBT students freely express their sexual and gender identities. They openly express affection with their boyfriends, girlfriends, or partners without anyone blinking an eye.

The Road to Utopia

While these utopian views may not come to fruition soon, they offer us something to strive for. Until we reach such utopian realities in our homes, schools, and communities, we must work diligently to create *safe* and *welcoming* spaces for LGBT youth. All LGBT people, including youth, deserve to live, learn, and play in safe and welcoming spaces.

Our road to utopia is not made of yellow bricks, and we cannot reach our destination by simply clicking our heels. Nor will safe spaces happen by merely reading this book. Creating safe spaces requires effort. Throughout this book, we offered readers a plethora of *Action Steps*, tangible activities that can create safe and welcoming spaces for LGBT youth. We hope that you will review those *Action Steps* now. Which actions will you engage in today to bring your home, neighborhood, school, or community one step closer to utopia?

Queerossary of Terms

Why a Queerossary instead of Glossary? To queer something means to do it in a manner that is unconventional or nontraditional. Conventional glossaries offer one definition for each key term. Instead of providing a single definition for each LGBT term, we provide many. Terms used to describe the lesbian, gay, bisexual, and transgender community can vary slightly from source to source. These variations are as insightful as the definitions themselves. The multiplicity of definitions shows that there is fluidity in the ways we make sense of LGBT realities. While the quotation marks have been removed, each definition is *directly quoted* from an original source listed in the endnotes.

ally. (1) Someone who advocates for and supports members of a community other than their own. Reaching across differences to achieve mutual goals.[1] (2) A self-identified heterosexual person who supports and respects sexual diversity, acts accordingly to interrupt and challenge homophobic and heterosexist remarks/behaviors [and] is willing to explore these forms of bias within her/himself.[2] (3) A person who supports and honors sexual and gender diversity, challenges biased remarks and behaviors, and who openly explores one's own biases.[3]

androgynous. (1) [An individual] having high levels of both masculine and feminine characteristics; blended.[4] (2) . . . reflecting an integration of masculine and feminine qualities—androgyny, by definition.[5]

asexual. (1) Having no evident sex or sex organs. In usage, may refer to a person who is not sexually active, or not sexually attracted to other people.[6] (2) Often refers to an enduring lack of sexual desire, but can also refer to a lack of maleness or femaleness.[7]

biphobia. (1) Biphobia can be defined as a fear or dislike of people who do not choose to identify as either heterosexual or gay/lesbian (Hutchins & Kaahumanu, 1991), that is, people who do not identify as at one or the other end of the dichotomy. For gay men and lesbians, this manifests as heterophobia, and for heterosexuals, this manifests as homophobia.[8] (2) The negative attitudes, prejudices and stereotypes that exist about people whose sexual attraction to others cannot be contained fully within the categories gay or lesbian or heterosexual.[9]

bisexual. (1) A person whose emotional, romantic, sexual, spiritual affectional, and/or relational attraction is to men and women or to many genders. Degree of attraction and choice of primary relationship partner varies for each bisexual person.[10] (2) Bisexuality blurs the boundary between heterosexuality and homosexuality in two ways. First, bisexuals themselves are neither clearly homosexual nor clearly heterosexual, thus blurring the conceptual boundary between these two types of sexuality. Second, unless bisexuals confine their romantic involvements to other bisexuals, they probably engage in the most intimate of social relationships with both homosexuals and heterosexuals, again blurring the social and political boundary between these two types of people.[11] (3) A person emotionally, romantically, sexually and relationally attracted to both men and women, though not necessarily simultaneously; a bisexual person may not be equally attracted to both sexes, and the degree of attraction may vary as sexual identity develops over time.[12]

cisgender. (1) People who possess a gender identity or performing in a gender role that society considers appropriate for one's sex.[13] (2) Cisgender refers to a person who is not transgender.[14] (3) A person who is gender-typical or non-transgender.[15]

clocked / being read. When others do *not* see a transperson as the "other" gender.[16]

closeted/in the closet. (1) Used as slang for the state of not publicizing one's sexual identity, keeping it private, living an outwardly heterosexual life while identifying as Lesbian, Gay, Bisexual, or Transgender, or not being forthcoming about one's identity. At times, being in the closet also means not wanting to admit one's sexual identity to oneself.[17] (2) Describes a person who is not open about his or her sexual orientation.[18]

coming out. (1) The process in which a person first acknowledges, accepts and appreciates his or her sexual orientation or gender identity and begins to share that with others.[19] (2) A lifelong process of self-acceptance. People forge a lesbian, gay, bisexual or transgender identity first to themselves and then may reveal it to others. Publicly identifying one's orientation may or may not be part of coming out.[20]

cross-dresser/cross-dressing. (1) The most neutral word to describe a person who dresses, at least partially or part of the time, and for any number of reasons, in clothing associated with another gender within a particular society. Carries no implications of "usual" gender appearance, or sexual orientation. Has replaced "transvestite," which is outdated, problematic, and generally offensive, since it was historically used to diagnose medical/mental health disorders.[21] (2) A person who, regardless of motivation, wears clothes, makeup, etc. that are considered by the culture to be appropriate for another gender but not one's own (preferred term to "transvestite").[22] (3) To occasionally wear clothes traditionally associated with people of the other sex. Cross-dressers are usually comfortable with the sex they were assigned at birth and do not wish to change it. **"Cross-dresser" should NOT be used to describe someone who has transitioned to live full-time as the other sex or who intends to do so in the future**. Cross-dressing is a form of gender expression and is not necessarily tied to erotic activity. Cross-dressing is not indicative of sexual orientation.[23]

dominant. When we say that a system is dominated by a privileged group, it means that positions of power tend to be occupied by members of that group.[24]

dominant culture. The cultural values, beliefs, and practices that are assumed to be the most common and influential within a given society.[25]

drag. Wearing clothes considered appropriate for someone of another gender.[26]

drag king. A FTM crossdresser (typically a lesbian) . . . who employ[s] gender-marked clothing, makeup, and mannerisms for their own and other people's appreciation or for entertainment purposes.[27]

drag queen. (1) A man who dresses as a woman.[28] (2) MTF crossdresser (typically a gay man) . . . who employ[s] gender-marked clothing, makeup, and mannerisms for their own and other people's appreciation or for entertainment purposes.[29]

F2M/FTM. See **transmen**.

gay. (1) A word describing a man or a woman who is emotionally, romantically, sexually, and relationally attracted to members of the same sex.[30] (2) A man who is physically and emotionally attracted to other men. It can also be used to describe men and women who have primarily same-sex desires.[31]

gaydar. (1) The word "gaydar" seems to have emerged as a short form for "gay radar." On a superficial level, "gaydar" supposedly allows lesbians, gays or queers to identify other people whom they believe are lesbian, gay or queer without explicitly being told. This recognition may occur instantaneously or over a period of time.[32] (2) Generally defined, Gaydar is simply the notion that some people, gays and lesbians in particular, have an innate ability to identify other gays and lesbians without having prior knowledge of an individual's sexual preference.[33]

gender. (1) Gender is a complex phenomenon that some believe to be independent of sex and some believe to be interchangeable with sex. Like sex, it is generally assigned at birth based on one's visible genitalia and in the context of cultural norms. Although Western cultures tend to limit gender to two categories (man and woman), some cultures allow for a wider range of possibilities.[34] (2) Gender (though also technically a noun) should be considered a verb, in that it is defined by actions. Specifically, gender describes the ways in which we perform our perceived (or even preferred) sex.[35] (3) The social construction of masculinity and femininity in a specific culture. It involves gender assignment (the gender designation of someone at birth), gender roles (the expectations imposed on someone based on their gender), gender attribution (how others perceive someone's gender), gender expression (how someone presents their gender), and gender identity (how someone defines their gender).[36]

gender expression. (1) How one chooses to express one's gender identity to others through behavior, clothing, hairstyle, voice, body characteristics, etc.[37] (2) How a person behaves, appears or presents him- or herself with regard to societal expectations of gender.[38]

gender identity. (1) The gender role that a person claims for his or her self—which may or may not align with his or her physical gender.[39] (2) Gender identity refers to a person's *inner* experience of gender: what a person *feels* she or he is, regardless of the gender attribution of others. Because gender identity is shaped by many factors (psychological considerations, cultural and social norms and taboos, family expectations, environmental forces, and so on), it can change over time for the individual.[40] (3) An individual's internal sense of being male, female, or something else. Since gender identity is internal, one's gender identity is not necessarily visible to others.[41]

genderqueer. (1) A word people use to describe their own nonstandard gender identity, or by those who do not conform to traditional gender norms.[42] (2) A term used by individuals, mostly transgender youth, who identify as neither female nor male, as both, or as somewhere in between. Genderqueers may transition partly, completely, or not all, and may dress and present exclusively as one gender, vary their presentation, or present androgynously. The one commonality between genderqueers is that they understand themselves in ways that challenge binary constructions of gender.[43] (3) Those who identify their gender outside the gender binary system of male and female, who may be fluid with gender presentation or may not conform to gender norms and may use gender neutral pronouns such as "sie, hir, hir, hirs, hirself" or "zie, zir, zir, zirs, zirself" or choose to use the pronoun closest to the end of the masculine or feminine spectrum they are presenting. Other terms that gender nonconforming people use are boy dyke, dyke boy, boi, femme queens, butch boi, drags, or aggressives (AGs).[44]

gender variant. (1) Alternative terms for transgender, meaning one who varies from traditional "masculine" and "feminine" gender roles.[45] (2) A person whose gender identity and/or gender expression varies from the culturally-expected characteristics of their assigned sex.[46]

heteronormative. (1) Those punitive rules (social, familial, and legal) that force us to conform to hegemonic, heterosexual standards for identity. The term is a short version of "normative heterosexuality."[47] (2) The term heteronormativity has traditionally been used in critical scholarship (esp. queer theory) to refer to (and question) the hegemonic perspective that normalizes heterosexual relationships and lifestyles, thereby excluding alternatives and insisting upon "conventional" binaries of gender and sexuality such as male/female . . . A heteronormative perspective or bias is one that implicitly or explicitly believes that the only "normal" perspective is one which is heterosexual, which understands gender and sexual identity as static concepts, and which inherently desires to be in a monogamous, committed relationship.[48]

heterosexism. (1) The assumption that all people are or should be heterosexual. Heterosexism excludes the needs, concerns, and life experiences of lesbian, gay, bisexual, and other non-monosexual people as well as asexual, transgender, and intersex people, while it gives advantages to heterosexual people. It is often a subtle form of oppression which reinforces realities of silence and invisibility.[49] (2) The belief that heterosexuality represents a standard of some kind, and that all other sexual orientations, if acknowledged at all, are merely a deviation from this. Heterosexist statements are statements that assume all people are straight or that fail to recognise the variety of sexual orientations that exist. For example, referring to husbands and wives rather than partners can be heterosexist, depending on the context of the statement.[50] (3) The assumption that everyone is heterosexual and that heterosexual relationships are natural, normal and worthy of support. These assumptions are systemic and institutionalized.[51]

heterosexual privilege. (1) An advantage given to heterosexual persons simply because they are heterosexual.[52] (2) Benefits derived automatically by being (or being perceived as) heterosexual that are denied to homosexuals, bisexuals, and queers.[53] (3) The benefits and advantages heterosexuals receive in a heterosexual culture. Also, the benefits lesbians, gay men, and bisexual people receive as a result of claiming heterosexual identity or denying gay, lesbian, or bisexual identity.[54]

homophobia. (1) Negative attitudes about homosexuality and/or homosexual people.[55] (2) The fear and hatred of or discomfort with people who love and are sexually attracted to members of the same sex.[56] (3) The negative attitudes, stereotypes and prejudices that still exist in society about individuals who are not heterosexual. It is most often directed at individuals who are gay or lesbian or thought to be gay or lesbian.[57]

internalized homophobia. Self-identification of societal stereotypes by a GLBT person, causing them to dislike and resent their sexual orientation or gender identity.[58]

intersex. (1) Intersex, replacing the term hermaphrodite, refers to people born with sex characteristics (i.e., chromosomes, reproductive organs, and genitalia) that do not "fit" standard definitions of "male" or "female" sex categories.[59] (2) A person who is born with "sex chromosomes," external genitalia, or an internal reproductive system that is not considered "standard" for either male or female (preferred term to "hermaphrodite"). About one in 2,000 children, or five children per day in the United States, are born visibly intersex.[60]

lesbian. (1) A woman who is emotionally, romantically, sexually and relationally attracted to other women.[61] (2) A woman who is physically and emotionally attracted to other women.[62]

M2F/MTF. See **transwomen**.

omnisexual. A person who is physically and emotionally attracted to people of all genders, which could include people that identify as female, male, intersex, genderqueer, transgender, or transsexual.[63]

oppression. (1) A systemic social phenomenon based on the perceived and real difference among social groups that involve ideological domination, institutional control, and the promulgation of the oppressor's ideology, logic system, and culture to the oppressed group. The result is the exploitation of one social group by another for the benefit of the oppressor group.[64] (2) Oppression refers to the vast and deep injustices some groups suffer as a consequence of often unconscious assumptions and reactions by well meaning people in ordinary interactions, media, cultural stereotypes, and structural features of bureaucratic hierarchies, and market mechanisms—in short the normal processes of daily life. Oppressed people suffer some inhibition of their abilities to develop and exercise their capacities and express their needs thoughts and feelings. Oppression's causes are embedded in unquestioned norms, habits, and symbols, in the assumptions underlying institutional rules and collective consequences of following those rules.[65] (3) The experience of oppressed people is that the living of one's life is confined and shaped by forces and barriers which are not accidental or occasional and hence unavoidable, but are systematically related to each other in such a way as to catch on, between, and among them and restrict or penalize motion in any direction. It is the experience of being caged in.[66] (4) Oppression exists when one social group, whether knowingly or unconsciously, exploits another social group for its own benefits. Oppression is distinct from a situation of simple brute force, in that it is an interlocking system that involves ideological control of the social institutions and resources of a society, resulting in a condition of privilege for the agent group relative to the disenfranchisement and exploitation of the target group.[67]

out. (1) "Being out" is a subcultural term with multiple related meanings. As used here, "being out" refers to perceiving oneself as lesbian or bisexual.[68] (2) Refers to varying degrees of being open about one's sexual orientation and/or sex identity or gender identity. [69]

outing. (1) **Outing** is telling other people, to whom a person is not out, that you know that person is LGBT.[70] (2) Exposing someone's sexual orientation or gender identity as being gay, lesbian, bisexual or transgender to others, usually without their permission; in essence "outing" them from the closet.[71] (3) The act of publicly declaring (sometimes based on rumor and/or speculation) or revealing another person's sexual orientation or gender identity without that person's consent. Considered inappropriate by a large portion of the LGBT community.[72]

passing. (1) To appear and be perceived by others as something, such as successfully assuming a gender role different than the one assigned to a person based on biological sex when interacting with society. One can also "pass" as straight in terms of sexual orientation . . . Passing can be intentional or not.[73] (2) Passing is the term used to assert that a transperson is so successful at presenting himself or herself in public as the "other" gender that she or he is perceived by nontranspeople as that gender. Passing is thus a benchmark achievement for most transsexuals and for some cross-dressers.[74]

queer. (1) A term that is inclusive of people who are not heterosexual. For many GLBT people, the word has a negative connotation; however, many younger GLBT people are comfortable using it.[75] (2) A formerly derogative term that has been reclaimed in a positive way to reflect the diversity and breadth of sexual and gender identities. This can include transgender, intersex and questioning people as well as people who consider themselves heterosexual and engage in same-sex sex even though they do not identify as bisexual or gay.[76]

questioning. (1) A person who is questioning their sexual orientation or gender identity.[77] (2) Anyone who is exploring his or her sexuality and/or gender identity and does not fit the label "straight."[78] (3) The process of considering or exploring one's sexual orientation and/or gender identity.[79]

sex. (1) Sex is a noun that describes a genetic body.[80] (2) Sex refers to anatomy and biology. Most societies promote the theory that there are only two "opposite" sexes and give physicians the authority to interpret and assign sex at birth based, by and large, on external genitalia. In reality, however, sex is best understood along a complex continuum that involves five sets of biological factors: genetic material (chromosomes and genes), hormones (testosterone and estrogen), gonads (testes and ovaries), genitals (internal and external), and a variety of secondary sex characteristics (e.g., body hair, fat distribution, breasts, facial features, etc.). Although all of these factors are biological, none of them is entirely free of cultural assumptions and implications. Our ideas about sex (what it means, what is allowed to members of each sex, what is thought to be "natural" to each sex) are shaped by the norms of the society in which we live.[81]

sexual identity. (1) Sexual identity, or orientation, may or may not be biological in nature, but the meaning of sexual identity appears to be socially constructed.[82] (2) Sexual identity denotes self-identification as lesbian/gay, bisexual, or straight.[83]

sexual orientation. (1) Sexual orientation, as commonly defined in the literature (e.g., Kinsey et al., 1948; Meyer-Bahlburg, 1993; Sanders, Reinisch, & McWhirter, 1990), consists of cognitive components (i.e., the individual's erotic attractions, fantasies, and arousal response to erotica which, in combination, we call cognitive sexual orientation for brevity's sake) and sexual partner activity.[84] (2) Sexual orientation involves one's feeling of sexual attraction (revealed through fantasies, erotic and romantic feelings, etc.) and is distinguishable from sexual behavior, which involves sexual acts.[85] (3) An enduring emotional, romantic, sexual and relational attraction to another person; may be same-sex orientation, opposite-sex orientation or bisexual orientation.[86]

transgender. (1) Transgender is an umbrella term that describes many people who transcend "normative" embodiments of masculine and feminine, including trans-sexuals, crossdressers, drag queens and kings, genderqueers, and other gender variant people. Most misuse transgender synonymously with transsexual, which identifies people whose gender identity conflicts with their ascribed gender, and they may take hormones and/or undergo surgery.[87] (2) Transgender is an umbrella term that designates someone who does not fit neatly into the societally accepted boxes called "male/man" and "female/woman," and who intentionally rejects the gender assigned to him or her at birth. Thus, it incorporates all persons who consciously transgress or violate gender norms, whether they intend or attempt to "pass" or not.[88] (3) A term describing a broad range of people who experience and/or express their gender differently from what most people expect. It is an umbrella term that includes people who are transsexual, cross-dressers or otherwise gender non-conforming.[89]

transmen. Transmen are people who were assigned female at birth but identify as male.[90]

transphobia. (1) The fear and hatred of, or discomfort with, people whose gender identity or gender expression do not conform to cultural gender norms.[91] (2) Individual or social ignorance or fear of transgender or transsexual people. Transphobic actions can include prejudice, discrimination, harassment, and act[s] of violence or hatred.[92] (3) Fear or hatred of transgender people; transphobia is manifested in a number of ways, including violence, harassment and discrimination.[93]

transsexual. (1) A person whose gender identity is different from their assigned gender at birth. Transsexuals often undergo hormone treatments and gender reassignment surgeries to align their anatomy with their core identity, but not all desire or are able to do so.[94] (2) Transsexual refers to an individual whose internally felt gender identity does not match the biological body she or he was born with and/or the gender she or he was assigned at birth.[95] (3) . . . transsexual, which identifies people whose gender identity conflicts with their ascribed gender, and they may take hormones and/or undergo surgery.[96] (4) A medical term describing people whose gender and sex do not line up, and who often seek medical treatment to bring their body and gender identity into alignment.[97]

transwomen. Transwomen are people who were assigned male at birth but identify as female.[98]

two spirit. (1) This term describes indigenous people who fulfill one of many mixed gender roles found traditionally among many Native Americans and Canadian First Nations indigenous groups. These roles included wearing the clothing and performing the work that is traditional for both men and women. Dual-gendered, or "two-spirited," people are viewed differently in different Native communities. Sometimes they are seen without stigma and are considered emissaries from the creator, treated with deference and respect, or even considered sacred, but other times this is not the case. "Two-spirit" is the closest thing to an appropriate umbrella term in referring to these gender traditions among Native peoples. However, even "two-spirit" is contested in modern usage.[99] (2) A Native American/First Nation term for people who blend the masculine and the feminine. It is commonly used to describe anatomical woman in the past (preferred term to "berdache"). The term is also often used by contemporary LGBT Native American and First Nation people to describe themselves. [100]

Appendix: LGBT Resource List

Hotline Numbers

Gay & Lesbian National Hotline 1-888-THE-GLNH (1-888-843-4564)

Gay, Lesbian, Bisexual, and Transgender (GLBT) Youth Support Line 1-800-850-8078

National Adolescent Suicide Hotline 1-800-621-4000

National LGBTQ Talk Line/Support Line (Trained Youth Supporter) 1-800-246-PRIDE

Suicide Hotline 1-800-273-8255

The Trevor HelpLine (specializing in LGBT youth suicide prevention) 1-800-850-8078

LGBT Family Resources

Children of Lesbians and Gays Everywhere
www.colage.org
COLAGE is a network and organization for youth who have one or more LGBT parents. This website provides numerous resources for youth seeking mentorship and support.

Family Acceptance Project
www.familyproject.sfsu.edu
This organization focuses on the role of family when addressing LGBT youth wellness issues such as HIV, substance abuse, suicide, and homelessness. The website provides research and resources for families looking to support the LGBT youth in their lives.

Family Equality Council
www.familyequality.org
The Family Equality Council works on legislative actions that support the rights and opportunities of all families. The website offers a variety of ways to be involved at the local and national level. It also has a resource wiki. The Family Equality Council sponsors family events and family camp at locations across the United States.

Parents, Families and Friends of Lesbians and Gays
www.pflag.org
PFLAG is the largest national organization offering support, education, and advocacy for LGBT individuals and their families. The website offers a multitude of resources as well as ways to connect with PFLAG chapters across the United States.

LGBT Educational Resources

Advocates for Youth
www.advocatesforyouth.org
Advocates for Youth focuses on the sexual health of youth. The organization is based on the tenets of rights, respect, and responsibility. Advocates for Youth sponsors two additional websites that focus primarily on the needs of LGBT youth, including one for Spanish-speaking youth.

Campus Pride
www.campuspride.org
Campus Pride is an organization that works with student leaders and campus groups to create safer campus environments for LGBT youth. The website offers resources, programs, and services for LGBT youth and their allies.

Consortium of Higher Education LGBT Resource Professionals
www.lgbtcampus.org
The Consortium of Higher Education LGBT Resource Professionals focuses on the needs of LGBT students, staff, faculty, administrators, and alumni on college campuses in the United States. In addition to curriculum resources, climate improvement projects, and policy initiatives, the Consortium encourages the development of LGBT centers and offices on all college campuses.

Gay, Lesbian and Straight Educators Network
www.glsen.org
GLSEN is an organization for youth, parents, and teachers at all levels of education. GLSEN currently sponsors over 4,000 GSA organizations across the United States. It also coordinates the Day of Silence Project. The website offers numerous resources for educators, administrators, and parents who seek to reduce hate language and bullying in schools.

The Gay-Straight Alliance Network
www.gsanetwork.org
The GSA Network connects GSAs with one another to foster peer support networks, leadership development, and training opportunities. The website offers extensive resources for new GSAs and GSAs looking to expand leadership and advocacy experiences.

GLBT Historical Society
www.glbthistory.org
The Gay, Lesbian, Bisexual, Transgender Historical Society's mission is to preserve and exhibit the rich history of LGBT individuals. The website offers links to an online gallery and museum located in San Francisco, California.

National Youth Advocacy Coalition
www.nyacyouth.com
Focused on ending discrimination of LGBT youth, The National Youth Advocacy Coalition seeks to strengthen the role of youth in the LGBT rights movement. NYAC works nationally to build the capacity of LGBT youth leaders and is committed to sharing the stories of LGBT youth.

The Point Foundation
www.pointfoundation.org
The Point Foundation offers scholarship opportunities for LGBT college and graduate school students. The website highlights some of the current Point Scholars and includes an application for prospective Point Scholars.

Scouting for All
www.scoutingforall.org
Scouting for All promotes diversity and acceptance within the Boy Scouts of America.

Southern Poverty Law Center – Teaching Tolerance
www.tolerance.org
The SPLC and Teaching Tolerance promote the reduction of hate and bigotry for all populations. The Teaching Tolerance website offers curriculum

resources for all age levels on the topics of bullying, hate speech, and historical incidences of intolerance. On a national level, SPLC fights for the civil rights of LGBT individuals and youth.

The Trevor Project
www.thetrevorproject.org
The Trevor Project is dedicated to reducing suicide among LGBT youth. The organization runs a 24/7 crisis hotline, an online chat program, and a youth advisory council. The Trevor Project website also offers resources for those who would like to use the movie *Trevor*, the original inspiration for the Trevor Project.

LGBT Political/Legal Organizations

American Civil Liberties Union
www.aclu.org
The ACLU is a resource for LGBT individuals who feel that their First Amendment rights, rights of due process, right to privacy, or rights to protection are being violated. The website offers an extensive FAQ section and a variety of ways to connect with the ACLU for counsel.

Equity Project
www.equityproject.org
The Equity Project examines the treatment of LGBT youth throughout all stages of the juvenile justice system. The website offers a listserv and numerous resources for individuals involved with LGBT youth and the court system.

First Amendment Center
www.firstamendmentcenter.org
Dedicated to the rights of the First Amendment, the FAC offers lesson plans, resources, and support. The archives section offers cases and strategies for GSAs and other LGBT individuals who feel that their First Amendment rights are being violated.

Freedom to Marry
www.freedomtomarry.org
Freedom to Marry is working to end federal marriage discrimination and bring the rights of same-sex marriage to states across the nation. For states that do not currently recognize same-sex marriage, resource kits are available for individuals seeking to start conversations in their community and with local policymakers.

Gay and Lesbian Advocates & Defenders
www.glad.org
GLAD is an organization that works to end discrimination based on sexual orientation, HIV status, gender, and gender expression. The website has a section on knowing your rights and an info line for those seeking further counsel.

The Gay & Lesbian Alliance Against Defamation
www.glaad.org
GLAAD works to ensure that LGBT voices are heard and fairly represented in news, entertainment, and social media. Every year GLAAD awards the GLAAD media awards, which celebrate the achievements of LGBT individuals and allies working to bring the mission of GLAAD to the large and small screen.

The Human Rights Campaign
www.hrc.org
HRC is the largest national organization working for the rights of LGBT individuals and allies. HRC focuses on educational outreach, media outreach, and the election of individuals who support the HRC mission. The HRC website has an extensive section of resources on topics ranging from aging, to the military, to religion and faith.

Lambda Legal
www.lambdalegal.org
Lambda Legal strives to end discrimination of LGBT individuals through public policy work, impact litigation, and education. The website offers state specific legislation information and a hotline for those in need of legal counsel.

LatinoJustice PRLDEF
www.latinojustice.org
LatinoJustice PRLDEF focuses on the civil rights of Latina/o individuals. The website offers visitors numerous ways to become involved with the mission of the organization. It also provides a web link to contact the organization for legal counsel.

The National Black Justice Coalition
www.nbjcoalition.org
The NBJC focuses on the civil rights of Black LGBT individuals. The NBJC examines the interaction of race and homophobia and provides legal services as well as educational training across the country.

The National Center for Lesbian Rights
www.nclrights.org
NCLR litigates cases that advance the rights and privileges of all LGBT individuals. NCLR has a variety of legal resources on many topics LGBT individuals face in the workplace, home, and school.

The National Center for Transgender Equality
www.transequality.org
NCTE is dedicated to advancing equality for transgender individuals. NCTE strives to ensure the specific rights and needs of transgender individuals are included in the creation of laws and policies.

The National Gay and Lesbian Task Force
thetaskforce.org
The National Gay and Lesbian Task Force is home to Our Policy Institute, a think tank devoted to developing policies and grassroots movements that advance the rights of LGBT individuals. The website offers extensive resources for individuals looking to act locally or nationally.

Sylvia Rivera Law Project
www.srlp.org
SRLP's mission is to end discrimination for gender-nonconforming individuals, especially those who are poor or individuals of color. SRLP offers services and trainings, including a movie *Toilet Training*, as part of their quest to end discrimination.

Transgender Law and Policy Institute
www.transgenderlaw.org
The TLPI provides an extensive set of web links for state and federal laws that impact the lives of transgender individuals. They have information on hate crime laws, laws that impact schools and colleges, medical and health care policies, and employer and union policies.

LGBT Faith Organizations

Affirmation
www.affirmation.org
Affirmation offers support and resources for Mormon LGBT individuals.

Dignity USA
www.dignityusa.org
Dignity USA offers support and resources for Catholic LGBT individuals.

The Evangelical Network
www.t-e-n.org
The Evangelical Network offers support and resources for Evangelical
LGBT individuals.

Evangelicals Concerned
www.ecwr.org
Evangelicals Concerned offers support and resources for Christian LGBT
individuals.

Friends for Lesbian, Gay, Bisexual, Transgender, and Queer Concerns
flgbtqc.quaker.org
Friends for Lesbian, Gay, Bisexual, Transgender and Queer Concerns offers
support and resources for Quaker LGBT individuals.

Gay and Lesbian Vaishnava Association
www.galva108.org
GALVA offers supports and resources for Vaishnava and Hindu LGBT
individuals.

The Gay Christian Network
www.gaychristian.net
The Gay Christian Network offers support and resources for Christian
LGBT individuals.

GayChurch.org
www.gaychurch.org
Gay Church offers support and resources for Christian LGBT individuals.

Gay, Lesbian, and Affirming Disciples Alliance
www.gladalliance.org
The GLAD Alliance offers support and resources for Disciples of Christ
LGBT individuals.

Integrity
www.integrityusa.org
Integrity offers support and resources for Episcopalian LGBT individuals.

Interfaith Alliance
www.interfaithalliance.org
Interfaith Alliance is focused on preventing religious bigotry and celebrating
religious freedom. The website offers numerous resources for individuals
looking to address LGBT issues in their spiritual or religious community.

Kinship
www.sdakinship.org
Kinship offers support and resources for Seventh Day Adventist LGBT individuals.

Lutherans Concerned
www.lcna.org
Lutherans Concerned offers support and resources for Lutheran LGBT individuals.

Metropolitan Community Church
mcchurch.org
MCC offers support and resources for LGBT individuals in the Metropolitan Community Church.

More Light Presbyterians
www.mlp.org
More Light Presbyterians offers support and resources for Presbyterian LGBT individuals.

Reconciling Ministries Network
www.rmnetwork.org
Reconciling Ministries Network offers support and resources for United Methodist LGBT individuals.

Soulforce
www.soulforce.org
Soulforce is an organization that challenges religious and political oppression through nonviolent acts of resistance. The website offers resources and blogs for individuals seeking to learn more about a nonviolent approach to sparking change at local and national levels.

UCC Coalition for LGBT Concerns
www.ucccoalition.org
The Coalition offers support and resources for LGBT individuals in the United Christ Church.

Welcoming & Affirming Baptists
www.wabaptists.org
Welcoming and Affirming Baptists offers support and resources for Baptist LGBT individuals.

World Congress of GLBT Jews: Keshet Ga'avah
www.glbtjews.org

The World Congress offers support and resources for Jewish LGBT individuals.

Other LGBT Resources

BeyondEx-Gays
www.beyondexgay.com
BeyondEx-Gay is an online community for survivors of ex-gay experiences. The website offers narratives, art, and statements from ex-gay participants.

BiNet USA
www.binetusa.org
Focusing on the unique experience of bisexuals and pansexuals, BiNet USA offers resources and educational materials to help promote the visibility of the bisexual and pansexual communities. The website also includes information for a variety of bisexual organizations throughout the United States.

CenterLink: The Community of LGBT Centers
www.lgbtcenters.org
This website contains information for those seeking to find an LGBT center in their area or individuals looking to strengthen the current operations of their local LGBT center. The website offers resources in the areas of social, health, political, and educational development.

Equality Federation
www.equalityfederation.org
The Equality Federation focuses on the connections between statewide initiatives for LGBT equality. Additionally, this organization ensures that every state has the resources needed to address important issues at the state level.

GLBT National Help Center
www.GLBTnationalhelpcenter.org
The GLBT National Help Center offers telephone and internet counseling for LGBT individuals and allies on topics of suicide, substance abuse, and coming out. The website also provides local resources for LGBT individuals in a special section titled *GLBT Near Me*.

International Foundation for Gender Education
www.ifge.org
The International Foundation for Gender Education supports issues of those in the transgender community both nationally and internationally.

National Coalition for LGBT Health
lgbthealth.webolutionary.com
Concerned with health needs of LGBT individuals, the Coalition advocates and conducts research to advance the opportunities for specialized quality care for LGBT individuals. The website offers research and resources for those in the health care professions about best practices for working with LGBT individuals.

Oasis Magazine
www.oasisjournals.com
This is a webspace for LGBT youth seeking to share their writing with other individuals. The website contains stories from youth across the country and provides a safe forum for young people to share their experiences.

SAGE: The LGBT Aging Project
www.lgbtagingproject.org
SAGE is focused on support and services for the aging LGBT population. Care providers, organizations, and older LGBT individuals all have separate sections on this website that explain resources, research, and best practices for elderly LGBT individuals. Additionally, the website can connect visitors with local resources.

TransGenderCare
www.transgendercare.com
TransGenderCare is an extensive archive on the many health needs of the transgender community. The website can be searched by topic and is monitored by current health practitioners to ensure the accuracy and reliability of site information.

Trans-Health
www.trans-health.com
Trans-Health is an online magazine that addresses health and fitness issues for transgender individuals.

Youth Guardian Services
www.youth-guard.org
Youth Guardian Services provides LGBT youth a safe and confidential e-mail/listserv. Individuals are screened before they are accepted to the e-mail/listserv and the lists are monitored by youth trained by Youth Guardian Services.

Notes

Introduction

1. Lauren Smiley, "LGBT Suicides: Aiyisha Hassan, Daughter of Marin Non-Profit Executive Director, Takes Life," *San Francisco Weekly*, October 12, 2010, http://blogs.sfweekly.com/thesnitch/2010/10/lgbt_suicides_aiyisha_hassan_d.php; Patrick Connors, "Gay Teen Suicide an Epidemic: 50 Cent Offers His Novel Take," *San Francisco Weekly*, http://blogs.sfweekly.com/thesnitch/2010/10/gay_suicide .php; Advocate.com Editors, "Gay R.I. Student Commits Suicide," *Advocate.com*, October 1, 2010, http://www.advocate.com/News/Daily_News/2010/10/01/Suicide _Takes_Life_of_Gay_RI_Student/.

2. Lisa and Christina, "About Onely and Heteronormativity," *Onely* (blog), http://onely.org/our-mission.

3. Jocelyn Gregoire and Christin M. Jungers, *The Counselor's Companion: What Every Beginning Counselor Needs to Know* (Mahwah, NJ: Lawrence Erlbaum Associates, Inc, 2007), 61.

4. See Colette Daiute and Cynthia Lightfoot, eds., *Narrative Analysis: Studying the Development of Individuals in Society* (Thousand Oaks, CA: Sage, 2004); and Catherine Kohler Reissman, *Narrative Analysis* (Newbury Park, CA: Sage, 1993).

Chapter 1: The Marginalization of LGBT People

1. Janice Ristock and Norma Timbang, "Relationship Violence in Lesbian/Gay/Bisexual/Transgender/Queer [LGBTQ] Communities," Minnesota Center Against Violence and Abuse, last modified March 25, 2009, http://www.mincava.umn.edu/documents/lgbtqviolence/lgbtqviolence.html.

2. "The State of the Workplace for Gay, Lesbian, Bisexual and Transgender Americans," Human Rights Campaign Foundation, last modified February 12, 2010, http://www.hrc.org/about_us/7061.htm.

3. "Title VII of the Civil Rights Act of 1964," U.S. Equal Employment Opportunity Commission, 2010, http://www.eeoc.gov/laws/statutes/titlevii.cfm.

4. "S. 2238—103rd Congress: Employment Non-Discrimination Act of 1994," GovTrack.us (database of federal legislation), http://www.govtrack.us/congress/bill.xpd?bill=s103-2238. "H.R. 4636—103rd Congress: Employment Non-

Discrimination Act of 1994," GovTrack.us (database of federal legislation), http://www.govtrack.us/congress/bill.xpd?bill=h103-4636.

5. "The State of the Workplace for Gay, Lesbian, Bisexual and Transgender Americans," Human Rights Campaign Foundation, last modified February 12, 2010, http://www.hrc.org/about_us/7061.htm.

6. Sophia Yan, "Virginia Is for Lovers. But How About Gay Ones?" *Time*, last modified March 11, 2010, http://www.time.com/time/nation/article/0,8599,1971393,00.html.

7. Charlie Joughin, "Tennessee Governor Signs Bill Promoting Discrimination into Law," Human Rights Campaign, May 24, 2011, http://www.hrcbackstory.org/2011/05/tennessee-governor-signs-bill-promoting-discrimination-into-law/.

8. Anahad O'Connor, "Crude Videos aboard an Aircraft Carrier," *The Lede* (blog), *New York Times*, January 2, 2011, http://thelede.blogs.nytimes.com/2011/01/02/crude-videos-aboard-an-aircraft-carrier.

9. Department of Veterans Affairs, *The Post-9/11 Veteran's Educational Assistance Act of 2008*, Department of Veteran Affairs, October 2008, http://www.gibill.va.gov/pamphlets/ch33/ch33_pamphlet.pdf.

10. "Transgender-Inclusive Benefits: Colleges and Universities," Human Rights Campaign, 2010, http://www.hrc.org/issues/workplace/benefits/college-university-transgender-benefits.htm.

11. Lee M. V. Badgett, *Unequal Taxes on Equal Benefits: The Taxation of Domestic Partner Benefits*, Center for American Progress and The Williams Institute, December 2007, http://www.americanprogress.org/issues/2007/12/pdf/domestic_partners.pdf.

12. "Marriage and Relationship Recognition," Human Rights Campaign, 2010, http://www.hrc.org/issues/marriage.asp.

13. Office of the General Counsel, *Letter to House of Representatives Committee of the Judiciary, B-275860*, Washington, D.C., 1997.

14. Presidential Memorandum, "Respecting the Rights of Hospital Patients to Receive Visitors and to Designate Surrogate Decision Makers for Medical Emergencies," 75 Fed. Reg. 20511, Apr. 20, 2010.

15. "California Student Safety and Violence Prevention," California Department of Education, 2010, http://www.cde.ca.gov/re/lr/sv/.

16. "American Library Association Banned and Challenged Books," American Library Association, 2010, http://www.ala.org/ala/issuesadvocacy/banned/index.cfm.

17. *David Parker et al. v. William Hurley et al.*, 06-10751 MLW (2006).

18. Lucas L. Johnson, "Tenn. Senate OKs Ban on Teaching of Homosexuality," USA Today, May 21, 2011, http://www.usatoday.com/news/topstories/2011-05-20-4100520317_x.htm.

19. Michael Apple, *Ideology and Culture*, 3rd ed. (New York: Routledge Falmer, 2004).

20. Patricia McDonough, "TV Viewing Among Kids at an Eight-Year High," *Nielsen Wire* (blog), October 26, 2009, http://blog.nielsen.com/nielsenwire/media_entertainment/tv-viewing-among-kids-at-an-eight-year-high/.

21. "*Harsh Realities* Finds Transgender Youth Face Extreme Harassment in School," Gay, Lesbian, Straight Education Network (GLSEN), last modified March 17, 2009, http://www.glsen.org/cgi-bin/iowa/all/news/record/2388.html.

22. GLSEN, *The 2007 National School Climate Survey: Executive Report* (New York: Gay, Lesbian, Straight Education Network, 2007).

23. Sue Rankin, Genevieve Weber, Warren Blumenfeld, and Somjen Frazer, *2010 State of Higher Education for Lesbian, Gay, Bisexual and Transgender People* (Charlotte, NC: Campus Pride, Q Research Institute, 2010).

24. GLSEN, *The 2007 National School Climate Survey: Executive Report* (New York: Gay, Lesbian, Straight Education Network, 2007).

25. "ISU Researchers Publish National Study on Cyberbullying of LGBT and Allied Youths," Iowa State News Service, last modified March 4, 2010, http://www.news.iastate.edu/news/2010/mar/cyberbullying.

26. Mark Hatzenbuehler, "The Social Environment and Suicide Attempts in Lesbian, Gay, and Bisexual Youth," *Pediatrics* 127, no. 5 (2011): 896–903. doi: 10.1542/peds.2010-3020.

27. Caitlin Ryan, David Huebner, Rafael M. Diaz, and Jorge Sanchez, "Family Rejection as a Predictor of Negative Health Outcomes in White and Latino Lesbian, Gay, and Bisexual Young Adults," *Pediatrics* 123, no. 1 (2009): 346–352. doi: 10.1542/peds.2007-3524.

28. Nicholas Ray, *Lesbian, Gay, Bisexual and Transgender Youth: An Epidemic of Homelessness* (New York: National Gay and Lesbian Task Force Policy Institute and the National Coalition for the Homeless, 2006).

29. Colleen Sullivan, Susan Sommer, and Jason Moff, *Youth in the Margins: A Report on the Unmet Needs of Lesbian, Gay, Bisexual and Transgender Youth in the Foster Care System* (New York: Lambda Legal Defense and Education Fund, 2001).

30. Noelle M. Hurd, Marc A. Zimmerman, and Yange Xue, "Negative Adult Influences and the Protective Effects of Role Models: A Study with Urban Adolescents," *Journal of Youth and Adolescence* 38, no. 6 (2009): 777–789. doi: 10.1007/s10964-008-9296-5.

Chapter 2: LGBT Identity

1. Vivienne C. Cass, "Homosexual Identity Formation: A Theoretical Model," *Journal of Homosexuality* 4, no. 3 (1979): 219–23. doi: 10.1300/J082v04n03_01 5; Eli Coleman, "Developmental Stages of the Coming Out Process," *Journal of Homosexuality* 7, no. 2/3 (1982): 31–43. doi:10.1300/J082v07n02_06; Lisa M. Diamond, "Development of Sexual Orientation Among Adolescent and Young Adult

Women," *Developmental Psychology* 34, no. 5 (1998): 1085–1095. doi: 10.1037/0012-1649.34.5.1085; Lisa M. Diamond, "Sexual Identity, Attractions, and Behavior Among Young Sexual-Minority Women Over a 2-Year Period," *Developmental Psychology* 36, no. 2 (2000): 241–250. doi:10.1037/0012-1649.36.2.241; Lisa M. Diamond, "Was It a Phase? Young Women's Relinquishment of Lesbian/Bisexual Identities Over a 5-Year Period," *Journal of Personality and Social Psychology* 84, no. 2 (2003): 352–364. doi: 10.1037/0022-3514.84.2.352; Ruth E. Fassinger and Brett A. Miller, "Validation of an Inclusive Model of Sexual Minority Identity Formation on a Sample of Gay Men," *Journal of Homosexuality* 32, no. 2 (1996): 53–78. doi: 10.1300/J082v32n02_04; Susan R. McCarn and Ruth E. Fassinger, "Revisioning Sexual Minority Identity Formation: A New Model of Lesbian Identity and Its Implications for Counseling and Research," *The Counseling Psychologist* 24, no. 3 (1996): 508–534. doi:10.1177/0011000096243011; Gary J. McDonald, "Individual Differences in the Coming Out Process for Gay Men: Implications for Theoretical Models," *Journal of Homosexuality* 8, no. 1 (1982): 47–60. doi:10.1300/J082v08n01_05; Richard Allen Stevens, Jr., "Understanding Gay Identity Development within the College Environment," *Journal of College Student Development* 45, no. 2 (2004): 185–206, http://muse.jhu.edu/journals/journal_of_college_student_development/v045/45.2stevens.html; Richard R. Troiden, "Becoming Homosexual: A Model of Gay Identity Acquisition," *Psychiatry* 42 (1979): 362–373; and Richard R. Troiden, "The Formation of Homosexual Identities," *Journal of Homosexuality* 17, no. 1/2 (1989): 43–73. doi:10.1300/J082v17n01_02.

2. Anthony R. D'Augelli, "Identity Development and Sexual Orientation: Toward a Model of Lesbian, Gay, and Bisexual Development," in *Human Diversity: Perspectives on People in Context*, eds. Edison J. Trickett, Roderick. J. Watts, and Dina Birman (San Francisco, CA: Jossey-Bass, 1994), 312–333.

3. Ritch C. Savin-Williams, *The New Gay Teenager* (Cambridge, MA: Harvard, 2005), 84.

4. Erik Erikson, *Identity, Youth, and Crisis* (New York, NY: W.W. Norton, 1968).

5. Annemarie Vaccaro, "Intergenerational Perceptions, Similarities, and Differences: A Comparative Analysis of Lesbian, Gay, and Bisexual Millennial Youth with Generation X and Baby Boomers." *Journal of LGBT Youth*, 6, no. 2-3 (2009): 122. doi: 10.1080/19361650902899124.

6. Anthony Greenwald, "A Social-Cognitive Account of the Self's Development," in *Self, Ego, and Identity: Integrative Approaches*, eds. Daniel K. Lapsley and F. Clark Power (New York, NY: Springer-Verlag, 1988), 30–42.

7. Barbara Hansen Lemme, *Development in Adulthood*, 3rd ed. (Needham, MA: Allyn & Bacon, 2002), 419–457.

8. Michael Brinkle, *Return to Michael: A Transgender Story* (Lincoln, NE: iUniverse, 2007); Jennifer Finney Boylan, *She's Not There: A Life in Two Genders*

(New York, NY: Broadway, 2003); Katherine Cummings, *Katherine's Diary: The Story of a Transsexual* (Victoria, Australia: Mandarin, 2007); Lannie Rose, *Lannie: My Journey from Man to Woman* (Pittsburgh, PA: Sterlinghouse, 2007).

9. Kristen A. Renn and Brent Bilodeau, "Queer Student Leaders: An Exploratory Case Study of Identity Development and LGBT Student Involvement at a Midwestern Research University," *Journal of Gay and Lesbian Issues in Education* 2, no. 4 (2005): 49–71. doi:10.1300/J367v02n04_04.

10. Aaron H. Devor, "Witnessing and Mirroring: A Fourteen Stage Model of Transsexual Identity," *Journal of Gay and Lesbian Psychotherapy* 8, no. 1/2 (2004): 41–67. doi:10.1300/J236v08n01_05.

11. Patricia Gagne, Richard Tewksbury, and Deanna McGaughey, "Coming Out and Crossing Over: Identity Formation and Proclamation in a Transgender Community," *Gender and Society* 11, no. 4 (1997): 478–508. doi:10.1177/089124397011004006.

12. Arnold H. Grossman and Anthony R. D'Augelli, "Transgender Youth," *Journal of Homosexuality* 51, no. 1 (2006): 111–128. doi:10.1300/J082v51n01_06.

13. Jan Hoffman, "Boys Will Be Boys? Not in These Families," *New York Times*, June 10, 2011, http://www.nytimes.com/2011/06/12/fashion/new-challenge-for -parents-childrens-gender-roles.html?tntemail1=y&_r=1&emc=tnt&pagewanted =print.

14. Annemarie Vaccaro, "Intergenerational Perceptions, Similarities and Differences: A Comparative Analysis of Lesbian, Gay, and Bisexual Millennial Youth with Generation X and Baby Boomers," *Journal of LGBT Youth: Special Edition on Millennial Teens* 6, no. 2–3 (2009): 113–134. doi:10.1080/19361650902899124.

15. Ritch C. Savin-Williams, *The New Gay Teenager* (Cambridge, MA: Harvard, 2005).

16. Elisa S. Abes and Susan R. Jones, "Meaning-Making Capacity and the Dynamics of Lesbian College Students' Multiple Dimensions of Identity," *Journal of College Student Development* 45, no. 6 (2004): 612–632. doi:10.1353/ csd.2004.0065; Elisa S. Abes, Susan R. Jones, and Marylu K. McEwen, "Reconceptualizing the Model of Multiple Dimensions of Identity: The Role of Meaning-Making Capacity in the Construction of Multiple Identities," *Journal of College Student Development* 48, no. 1 (2007): 1–22. doi:10/1353/csd.2007.0000; Susan R. Jones, "Constructing Identities at the Intersections: An Autoethnographic Exploration of Multiple Dimensions of Identity," *Journal of College Student Development* 50, no. 3 (2009): 287–304. http://muse.jhu.edu/journals/csd/summary/v050/ 50.3.jones.html; Dafina Lazarus Stewart, "Perceptions of Multiple Identities among Black College Students," *Journal of College Student Development* 50, no. 3 (2009): 253–270. http://muse.jhu.edu/journals/csd/summary/v050/50.3. stewart.html.

17. For a description of how Christian scripture is often cited inappropriately as a rationale for homophobia and discrimination, see Reverend Dr. F. Jay Deacon,

"What Does the Bible Say about Homosexuality?" in *Readings for Diversity and Social Justice*, ed. Maurianne Adams, Warren J. Blumenfeld, Carmelita Castaneda, Heather W. Hackman, Madeline L. Peters, and Ximena Zuniga (New York, NY: Routledge, 2000), 290–292.

18. Rosemarie Garland-Thompson, "Integrating Disability, Transforming Feminist Theory," in *The Disability Studies Reader*, ed. Lennard J. Davis (New York: Routledge, 2006), 257–274.

Chapter 3: Sharing the Struggles: The Role of Allies

1. DU Queer and Ally Commission, *Why Is It Important to Be an Ally? Training Materials from the University of Denver* (Denver, CO: University of Denver Queer and Ally Commission, 2007).

2. Peggy McIntosh, "White Privilege and Male Privilege: A Personal Account of Coming to See Correspondences through Work in Women's Studies. Working Paper 189," (Wellesley College Center for Research on Women, Wellesley, MA, 1988), 1–2.

3. McIntosh, "White Privilege and Male Privilege: A Personal Account of Coming to See Correspondences through Work in Women's Studies. Working Paper 189," 16.

4. McIntosh, "White Privilege and Male Privilege: A Personal Account of Coming to See Correspondences through Work in Women's Studies. Working Paper 189," 12.

5. Peter Ji, Steve N. Du Bois, and Patrick Finnessey, "An Academic Course that Teaches Heterosexual Students to be Allies to LGBT Communities: A Qualitative Analysis," *Journal of Gay & Lesbian Social Services* 21, no. 4 (2009): 402–429.

6. Linda Christensen, "Warriors Don't Cry: Acting for Justice," *Rethinking Schools Online* 18, no. 3 (2004): http://www.rethinkingschools.org/brown/acti183.shtml.

7. Peter Ji, Steve N. Du Bois, and Patrick Finnessey, "An Academic Course that Teaches Heterosexual Students to be Allies to LGBT Communities: A Qualitative Analysis," *Journal of Gay & Lesbian Social Services* 21, no. 4 (2009): 402–429.

8. Peter Ji, "Being a Heterosexual Ally to the Lesbian, Gay, Bisexual, and Transgender Community: Reflections and Development," co-published simultaneously in *Journal of Gay & Lesbian Psychotherapy* 11, no. 3/4 (2007): 173–185; and Judith M. Glassgold, and Jack Drescher (eds.), *Activism and LGBT Psychology* (Philadelphia, PA: The Haworth Medical Press, 2007): 173–185.

9. Keith E. Edwards, "Aspiring Social Justice Ally Identity Development: A Conceptual Model," *NASPA Journal* 43, no. 4 (2006): 39–60.

Chapter 4: Family: From Exclusion to Nurturance

1. David H. Olson, Candyce S. Russel, and Douglas H. Sprenkle, "Circumplex Model of Marital and Family Systems: VI. Theoretical Update," *Family Process* 22 (1983): 69–83.

2. Ritch C. Savin-Williams and Eric M. Dubé, "Parental Reactions to Their Child's Disclosure of a Gay/Lesbian Identity," *Family Relations* 47, no. 1 (1998): 7–13.

3. Glenda M. Russel and Jeffrey A. Richards, "Stressor and Resilience Factors for Lesbians, Gay Men and Bisexuals Confronting Anti-GLBT Politics," *American Journal of Community Psychology* 31, no. 3–4 (2003): 313–328. doi:10.1023/A:1023919022811.

4. Laurie Harrington and Justin A. Lavner, "Coming to Terms with Coming Out: Review and Recommendations for Family Systems-Focused Research," *Journal of Family Psychology* 22, no. 3 (2008): 329–343. doi:10.1037/0893-3200.22.3.329.

5. Rosie Ensor and Claire Hughes, "Content or Connectedness? Mother-Child Talk and Early Social Understandings," *Child Development* 79, no. 1 (2008): 201–216. doi:10.1111/j.1467-8624.2007.01120.x.

6. Carly K. Friedman & Elizabeth M. Morgan, "Comparing Sexual-Minority and Heterosexual Young Women's Friends and Parents as Sources of Support for Sexual Issues," *Journal of Youth Adolescence* 38, no. 7 (2008): 920–936. doi:10.1007/s10964-008-9361-0.

7. Ritch C. Savin-Williams, *The New Gay Teenager* (Cambridge, MA: Harvard University Press, 2005), 118.

8. Gilbert H. Herdt and Bruce Koff, *Something to Tell You: The Road Families Travel When a Child Is Gay* (New York: Columbia University Press, 2001).

9. Mark Hatzenbuehler, "The Social Environment and Suicide Attempts in Lesbian, Gay, and Bisexual Youth," *Pediatrics* 127, no. 5 (2011): 896–903. doi:10.1542/peds.2010-3020.

10. Caitlin Ryan, *Helping Families Support Their Lesbian, Gay, Bisexual, and Transgender (LGBT) Children* (Washington, D.C.: National Center for Cultural Competence, Georgetown University Center for Child and Human Development, 2009), http://nccc.georgetown.edu/documents/LGBT_Brief.pdf.

11. Ibid.

12. Nicholas Ray, *Lesbian, Gay, Bisexual and Transgender Youth: An Epidemic of Homelessness* (New York: National Gay and Lesbian Task Force Policy Institute and the National Coalition for the Homeless, 2006), http://www.thetaskforce.org/downloads/HomelessYouth.pdf.

13. Urban Peak, *Annual Report* (Denver, CO: Urban Peak, 2009), http://www.urbanpeak.org/documents/UPannualreport2009-web.pdf.

14. Nicholas Ray, *Lesbian, Gay, Bisexual and Transgender Youth: An Epidemic of Homelessness* (New York: National Gay and Lesbian Task Force Policy Institute and the National Coalition for the Homeless, 2006), 51, http://www.thetaskforce.org/downloads/HomelessYouth.pdf.

15. Linda Dame, "Queer Youth in Care in Manitoba: An Examination of Their Experiences Through Their Voices," *The Canadian Online Journal of Queer*

Studies in Education 1, no.1 (2004), http://jps.library.utoronto.ca/index.php//jqstudies/article/view/3270/1397.

16. Gerald P. Mallon and Teresa DeCrescenzo, "Social Work with Transgender and Gender Variant Children and Youth," in *Social Work Practice with Transgender and Gender Variant Youth*, 2nd ed., ed. Gerald P. Mallon (New York: Routledge, 2009), 65–74.

17. Jallen Rix, *Ex-Gay, No Way: Survival and Recovery From Religious Abuse* (Scotland: Findhorn Press, 2010); "An On-Line Community for Those Who Have Survived Ex-Gay Experiences," Beyond Ex-Gay, http://www.beyondexgay.com/; Scott Moore, "Ex-Ex-Gay. Peterson Toscano: A Survivor of the Ex-Gay Movement," *The Portland Mercury* (Portland, OR), January 25, 2007, http://www.portlandmercury.com/portland/Content?oid=110772&category=34029; Patrick McAlvey, "Ex-Gay Survivor to Exodus: 'Leave Kids Alone,' " *Truth Wins Out* (blog), November 24, 2010, http://www.truthwinsout.org/blog/2010/11/13042/.

18. McAlvey, "Ex-Gay Survivor to Exodus: 'Leave Kids Alone,'" *Truth Wins Out* (blog).

19. "The 'Ex-Gay' Movement and the Negative Impact It Has Had on My Life," Seth Guyette, *Beyond Ex-Gay*, http://www.beyondexgay.com/narratives/seth.

20. Ritch C. Savin-Williams and Eric M. Dubé, "Parental Reactions to their Child's Disclosure of a Gay/Lesbian Identity," *Family Relations* 47, no. 1 (1998): 7–13, http://www.jstor.org/stable/584845.

21. Bonnie Benard, "Using Strengths-Based Practice to Tap the Resilience of Families," in *Strengths Perspectives in Social Work*, 4th ed., ed. David Saleebey (Boston: Allyn & Bacon, 2006), 197–220.

22. Herdt and Koff, *Something to Tell You: The Road Families Travel When a Child Is Gay*, 87.

23. Robert A. Bernstein, *Straight Parents' Gay Children: Keeping Families Together* (New York: Thunder Mouth Press, 1995).

24. Mallon and DeCrescenzo, "Social Work with Transgender and Gender Variant Children and Youth," in *Social Work Practice with Transgender and Gender Variant Youth*, 2nd ed., 74.

Chapter 5: Inside the Classroom Walls

1. Allan Johnson, *Privilege, Power and Difference* (Mountain View, CA: Mayfield Publishing, 2001). The image of "paths of least resistance" is adapted from Johnson's work.

2. David Crary, "After Suicides, Schools Rethink Efforts," *Providence Sunday Journal*, October 10, 2010.

3. Vicky L. Snyder and Francis S. Broadway, "Queering High School Biology Textbooks," *Journal of Research in Science Teaching* 41, no. 6 (2004): 617–636. doi:10.1002/tea.20014.

4. Todd Jennings and Gary Sherwin, "Sexual Orientation Topics in Elementary Teacher Education Programs in the USA," *Teaching Education* 19, no. 4 (2008): 261–278. doi:10.1080/10476210802436328.

5. Kerry Robinson, "Making the Invisible Visible: Gay and Lesbian Issues in Early Childhood Education," *Contemporary Issues in Early Childhood* 3, no. 3 (2002): 415–434. doi: 10.2304/ciec.2002.3.3.8.

6. Dennis Gaffney, "Censured PBS Bunny Returns, Briefly," *The New York Times*, December 18, 2006.

7. Several member stations aired the episode, including flagship stations WGBH in Boston, WNET in New York, and KCET in Los Angeles.

8. Julie Salamon, "Culture Wars Pull Buster into the Fray," *The New York Times*, January 27, 2005.

9. Kevin Jennings, "Out in the Classroom: Addressing Lesbian, Gay, Bisexual, and Transgender (LGBT) Issues in the Social Studies Curriculum," in *The Social Studies Curriculum: Purposes, Problems, and Possibilities*, 3rd ed., ed. E. Wayne Ross (Albany NY: State University of New York Press, 2006), 255–264.

10. Jay Willis, "The FAIR Education Act: Intertwining History and Tolerance in California Public Schools," *Harvard Law and Policy Review*, April 19, 2011, http://hlpronline.com/2011/04/fair-education-act/

11. Adrienne Rich, *Invisibility in Academe*, cited in Renate Rosaldo, *Culture and Truth* (Boston: Beacon Press, 1989), ix.

12. Emily Style, "Curriculum as Window and Mirror," in *Listening for All Voices: Gender Balancing the School Curriculum*, proceedings of a conference held at Oak Knoll School, Summit, NJ, 1988, 6–12.

13. Michelle Parsons, "States Continue to Mandate Anti-LGBT Curriculum in the Classroom," *Edge* (Boston, MA), May 28, 2010, http://www.edgeboston.com/index.php?ch=news&sc&sc2=news&sc3&id=106221.

14. Robert Skutch, *Who's in a Family?* (Berkeley, CA: Tricycle Press, 1995); Todd Parr, *The Family Book* (Boston, MA: Little, Brown Books for Young Readers, 2003); Justin Richardson and Peter Parnell, *And Tango Makes Three* (London: Simon & Schuster, 2007).

15. GLSEN, *The 2009 National School Climate Survey Executive Summary: Key Findings of the Experiences of Lesbian, Gay, Bisexual, and Transgender Youth in our Nation's Schools* (New York: Gay, Lesbian, Straight Education Network, 2009).

16. " 'And Tango Makes Three' Prompts Serious Challenge in Massachusetts School," *School Library Journal*, last modified May 8, 2007, http://www.school libraryjournal.com/slj/articlescensorship/863185-341/quotand_tango_makes_three quot_prompts.html.csp.

17. Megan Boler, "All Speech Is Not Free: The Ethics of 'Affirmative Action Pedagogy,' " in *Democratic Dialogue in Education (Counterpoints: Studies in the Postmodern Theory of Education: 240)*, ed. Megan Boler (New York: Peter Lang, 2006), 3–13.

18. John Kellermeier, "Queer Statistics: Using Lesbigay Word Problem Content in Teaching Statistics," *NWSA Journal* 7, no. 1 (1995): 98–108.

19. Edmon W. Tucker and Miriam Potocky-Tripodi, "Changing Heterosexuals' Attitudes Toward Homosexuals: A Systematic Review of the Empirical Literature," *Research on Social Work Practice* 16, no. 2, (2006), 176–190.

20. Ibid.

21. Paulo Freire, *Pedagogy of the Oppressed, 20th Anniversary Edition* (New York: Continuum, 1993).

22. J. L. Austin, *How to Do Things with Words* (Oxford: Clarendon Press, 1962).

23. "School Says Gay Mom Misunderstood Son's Punishment," ABC News, last modified December 4, 2003, http://abcnews.go.com/WNT/story?id=131672&page=1.

24. "Student Behavior Contract: Marcus McLaurin, Lafayette, LA," American Civil Liberties Union, last modified December 1, 2003, http://www.aclu.org/lgbt-rights_hiv-aids/student-behavior-contract-marcus-mclaurin-lafayette-la.

25. Ericka Sokolower-Shain, "When the Gender Boxes Don't Fit," *Rethinking Schools* 24, no.1 (2009).

26. GLSEN, *Harsh Realities: The Experiences of Transgender Youth in Our Nation's Schools* (New York: Gay, Lesbian, Straight Education Network, 2009).

27. "Lesbian Gay Bisexual Transgender Queer Youth Anti-Bullying Forum" (panel discussion, Rhode Island Department of Education, Providence, RI, November 8, 2010).

28. National Education Association, *Strengthening the Learning Environment: A School Employee's Guide to Gay, Lesbian, Bisexual, and Transgendered Issues*, 2nd ed. (Washington, D.C.: National Education Association of the United States, 2006).

29. Myles Horton and Paulo Freire, *We Make the Road by Walking: Conversations on Education and Social Change*, ed. Brenda Bell, John Gaventa, and John Peters (Philadelphia: Temple University Press, 1990). This image is borrowed from Horton and Freire's work.

Chapter 6: Outside the Classroom Walls

1. Joseph G. Kossiw, Emily A. Greytak, Elizabeth M. Diaz, and Mark J. Bartkiewicz, *The 2009 National School Climate Survey: The Experiences of Lesbian, Gay, Bisexual and Transgender Youth in Our Nation's Schools* (New York: GLSEN, 2010), http://www.glsen.org/binary-data/GLSEN_ATTACHMENTS/file/000/001/1675-2.pdf.

2. Shawn Harrison, "Ministering to Gay Teens: A Student's Environment," *Six:11 Ministries* (blog), January 3, 2011, http://six11.wordpress.com/youth-workers/issues-of-sexuality/glbt/ministering-to-teens/.

3. Joseph G. Kossiw, Emily A. Greytak, Elizabeth M. Diaz, and Mark J. Bartkiewicz, *The 2009 National School Climate Survey: The Experiences of Lesbian, Gay, Bisexual*

and Transgender Youth in Our Nation's Schools (New York: GLSEN, 2010), http://www.glsen.org/binary-data/GLSEN_ATTACHMENTS/file/000/001/1675-2.pdf.

4. Shawn Harrison, "Ministering to Gay Teens: A Student's Environment," *Six:11 Ministries* (blog), January 3, 2011, http://six11.wordpress.com/youth-workers/issues-of-sexuality/glbt/ministering-to-teens/.

5. Sue Rankin, Genevieve Weber, Warren Blumenfeld, and Somjen Frazer, *2010 State of Higher Education for Lesbian, Gay, Bisexual and Transgender People* (Charlotte, North Carolina: Campus Pride, Q Research Institute, 2010).

6. Ibid.

7. Ibid.

8. Joseph G. Kossiw, Emily A. Greytak, Elizabeth M. Diaz, and Mark J. Bartkiewicz, *The 2009 National School Climate Survey: The Experiences of Lesbian, Gay, Bisexual and Transgender Youth in Our Nation's Schools* (New York: GLSEN, 2010), http://www.glsen.org/binary-data/GLSEN_ATTACHMENTS/file/000/001/1675-2.pdf.

9. Michelle Garcia, "One Year Later: Carl Walker-Hoover," *The Advocate*, April 6, 2010, http://www.advocate.com/News/Daily_News/2010/04/06/One_Year_After_the_Death_of_Carl_Walker_Hoover/.

10. Dan Savage, *It Gets Better Project*, 2010, http://www.itgetsbetter.org/.

11. Laura Meckler, "Obama Joins 'It Gets Better' Campaign; Dan Savage Says: Make It Better," *Washington Wire* (blog), *The Wall Street Journal*, October 22, 2010, http://blogs.wsj.com/washwire/2010/10/22/obama-joins-it-gets-better-campaign-dan-savage-says-make-it-better/.

12. "It Gets Better video transcript: Remarks of President Barack Obama, Video for the 'It Gets Better Project,' Washington, D.C.," The White House (n.d.), accessed on July 25, 2011, http://www.whitehouse.gov/it-gets-better-transcript/.

13. Andy Birkey, "Minnesota Family Council pushes back in Anoka-Hennepin anti-bullying controversy," *The Minnesota Independent*, October 4, 2010, http://minnesotaindependent.com/71696/minnesota-family-council-pushes-back-in-anoka-hennepin-anti-gay-bullying-controversy/.

14. Ibid.

15. Joey DiGuglielmo, "Va. Lawmakers Introduce Anti-Bullying Bills," *Washington Blade*, January 5, 2011, http://www.washingtonblade.com/2011/01/05/va-lawmakers-introduce-anti-bullying-bills/.

16. Ali Russlyn, *Dear Colleague Letter: Harassment and Bullying*, letter from Assistant Secretary of Secretary of Civil Rights, United States Department of Education, October 26, 2010, http://www2.ed.gov/about/offices/list/ocr/letters/colleague-201010.pdf.

17. Associated Press, "Suicide Surge: Schools Confront Anti-Gay Bullying," *Minnesota Public Radio*, October 9, 2010, http://minnesota.publicradio.org/display/web/2010/10/09/anti-gay-bullying/.

18. Safe Schools Improvement Act, S. Con. Res. 3739, 111th Cong. (2010), accessed January 6, 2011, http://www.gpo.gov/fdsys/pkg/BILLS-111s3739is/pdf/BILLS-111s3739is.pdf.

19. Bill Documents. "Documents Associated with AB 620 in Session," May 27, 2011, http://www.leginfo.ca.gov/cgibin/postquery?bill_number=ab_620&sess=CUR&house=B&author=block.

20. Lauren Cox, " 'Smear the Queer': Gay Students Tell Their Stories," ABC News/Health, last modified April 17, 2009, http://abcnews.go.com/Health/Mind MoodNews/story?id=7352070&page=1.

21. Harris Interactive, Inc., & Gay, Lesbian, Straight Education Network, *From Teasing to Torment: School Climate in America, a Survey of Students and Teachers* (New York: GLSEN, 2005), http://www.glsen.org/binary-data/GLSEN_ATTACHMENTS/file/499-1.pdf.

22. Andy Birkey, "Minnesota Family Council pushes back in Anoka-Hennepin anti-bullying controversy," *The Minnesota Independent*, October 4, 2010, http://minnesotaindependent.com/71696/minnesota-family-council-pushes-back-in-anoka-hennepin-anti-gay-bullying-controversy/.

23. William Glasser, *Choice Theory: A New Psychology of Personal Freedom* (New York: Harper Collins, 1998).

24. Lynn Peril, "Prom," in *Girl Culture: An Encyclopedia*, eds. Claudia A. Mitchell and Jacqueline Reed-Walsh (Westport, CT: Greenwood Press, 2008).

25. Amy Best, *Prom Night: Youth, Schools, and Popular Culture* (New York: Routledge, 2000).

26. "Mississippi School Sued for Canceling Prom Over Lesbian Student," CNN Living, last modified March 11, 2010, http://articles.cnn.com/2010-03-11/living/mississippi.prom.suit_1_prom-students-aclu?_s=PM:LIVING.

27. "Creating an Inclusive School Prom," GLSEN, last modified May 15, 2002, http://www.glsen.org/cgi-bin/iowa/all/news/record/547.html.

28. "Gay-Straight Alliances: Creating Safer Schools for LGBT Students and their Allies," GLSEN Research Brief (New York: Gay, Lesbian and Straight Education Network, 2007).

29. Wendy Owen, "Student Teacher Says Beaverton School District Discriminated against Him," *OregonLive.com*, October 1, 2010, http://www.oregonlive.com/beaverton/index.ssf/2010/10/student_teacher_says_beaverton_school_district_discriminated_against_him.html.

30. Dominique Fong, "Beaverton School District will Pay $75,000 to Settle Discrimination Claim by Gay Student Teacher," *OregonLive.com*, February 11, 2011, http://www.oregonlive.com/beaverton/index.ssf/2011/02/beaverton_school_district_will_pay_75000_to_settle_discrimination_claim_by_gay_student_teacher.html.

31. Maya Angelou, *I Know Why the Caged Bird Sings* (New York: Random House), 259.

32. Harris Interactive, Inc., & Gay, Lesbian, Straight Education Network, *From Teasing to Torment: School Climate in America, a Survey of Students and Teachers* (New York: GLSEN, 2005), http://www.glsen.org/binary-data/GLSEN _ATTACHMENTS/file/499-1.pdf.

33. Peggy O'Hare, "Parents Say Bullies Drove Their Son to Take His Life: They Claim School District Took No Action," *Houston Chronicle*, September 29, 2010, http://www.chron.com/disp/story.mpl/metropolitan/7220896.html.

34. Karen Izzo, "Lesbian Gay Bisexual Transgender Queer Youth Anti-Bullying Forum" (panel discussion, Rhode Island Department of Education, Providence, RI, November 8, 2010).

35. James Robinson, "Lesbian Gay Bisexual Transgender Queer Youth Anti-Bullying Forum" (panel discussion, Rhode Island Department of Education, Providence, RI, November 8, 2010).

36. Suicide Prevention Resource Center (SPRC), "Preventing Suicidal Behavior among Lesbian, Gay, Bisexual, and Transgender Youth: Developing LGBT Cultural Competence" (SPRC, 2010), http://www.sprc.org/library/PreventingSuicidal BehaviorLGBTYouth.pdf.

37. Brett Beemyn, Andrea Domingue, Jessica Pettitt, and Todd Smith, "Suggested Steps to Make Campuses More Trans-Inclusive," *Journal of Gay and Lesbian Issues in Education* 3, no. 1 (2005): 89–94. doi: 10.1300/J367v03n01_09.

38. Jeanette Bradeen, Emily Sandoval, and Nancy Tubbs, "Gender-Neutral Housing and Stonewall Hall: Innovative Living Options for the TransGeneration" (presentation, University of California, Riverside), http://architect.lgbtcampus.org/ housing/gender-neutral-housing-and-stonewall-hall-pre/download.

39. Stephanie Samuel, "Ohio U to Offer Gender-Neutral Dorms," *The Christian Post*, January 14, 2011, http://www.christianpost.com/news/ohio-u-to-offer -gender-neutral-dorms-48489/.

Chapter 7: We Are Our Communities

1. Robert D. Putnam, *Bowling Alone: The Collapse and Revival of American Community* (New York, NY: Simon & Schuster, 2000).

2. Kristin Moore and Jennifer Ehrle, "Snapshots of America's Families: Children's Environment and Behavior: Participation in Extracurricular Activities" (Washington, D.C.: Urban Institute, National Survey of America's Families, 1997), C5, http://www.urban.org/UploadedPDF/900869_1997Snapshots.pdf.

3. Regis Tremblay, "Troubling Signs from Youth Sports," *The Center for Kids FIRST in Sports* (2003), http://www.thecenterforkidsfirst.org/pdf/Statistics.pdf.

4. Fred Engh, *Why Johnny Hates Sports* (New York, NY: Avery, 1999), 73.

5. Regis Tremblay, "Troubling Signs from Youth Sports," *The Center for Kids FIRST in Sports* (2003), http://www.thecenterforkidsfirst.org/pdf/Statistics.pdf.

6. Pat Griffin et al., *It Takes a Team! Making Sports Safe for Lesbian, Gay, Bisexual, and Transgender Athletes and Coaches*, eds. Donna Lopiano, Marjorie Snyder, and Lisa D. Thompson (Women's Sports Foundation, 2002).

7. Justin Bourne, "It's Time to End the Use of Gay Slurs in Hockey," *USA Today*, November 3, 2009, http://www.usatoday.com/sports/hockey/columnist/bourne/2009-11-02-hockey-culture_N.htm.

8. CNN Wire Staff, "First Transgender Athlete to Play in NCAA Basketball," CNN U.S., November 3, 2010, http://articles.cnn.com/2010-11-03/us/transgender.basketball.player_1_transgender-athletics-staff-basketball-team?_s=PM:US.

9. John Gerdy, ed., *Sports in School: The Future of an Institution* (New York, NY: Teacher's College Press, Columbia University, 2000), 55.

10. Fred Engh, *Why Johnny Hates Sports* (New York, NY: Avery, 1999), 73.

11. Associated Press, "Hawaii Coach Apologizes for Gay Slur," *ESPN News*, July 30, 2009, http://sports.espn.go.com/ncf/news/story?id=4366952.

12. "UH Football Coach Greg McMackin Apologizes For Gay Slur," YouTube video, 3:14, posted by "Xlnt1080," August 1, 2009, http://www.youtube.com/watch?v=W9mG0tX08Ag.

13. Cyd Ziegler Jr., "Penn State Volleyball Coach is Gay-Positive," last modified December 21, 2010, http://outsports.com/jocktalkblog/2010/12/21/penn-state-volleyball-coach-is-gay-positive.

14. Brad Usselman, Robert, and Ben Newcomer, *Walk the Road: One Common Goal* (blog), http://bradrobertben.wordpress.com.

15. "About It Takes a Team!," Women's Sports Foundation, http://www.womenssportsfoundation.org/home/advocate/know-your-rights/coach-and-athletic-director-resources/about-itat.

16. "100 Years in Review, 1910–2010," Boy Scouts of America, 2010, http://www.scouting.org/About/FactSheets/100_years.aspx.

17. "Scouting," Boy Scouts of America, http://www.scouting.org/.

18. Boy Scouts of America v. Dale, No. 99-699 (June 28, 2000), http://law.onecle.com/ussc/530/530us640.html.

19. "Who We Are: Facts," Girl Scouts of the United States of America, http://www.girlscouts.org/who_we_are/facts/.

20. "Facts and Findings: Safety," Girl Scouts of the United States of America, http://www.girlscouts.org/research/facts_findings/safety.asp.

21. Michael Jones, "GOP Politician: Girl Scouts are Indoctrinating Girls with Lesbianism and Atheism," *Change.org*, September 16, 2010, http://gayrights.change.org/blog/view/gop_politician_girl_scouts_are_indoctrinating_girls_with_lesbianism_and_atheism.

22. "FAQ," 4-H, http://www.4-h.org/about/4-h-history/faq/.

23. "About 4-H," 4-H, http://www.4-h.org/about/.

24. Amanda Barren, "Mother: Gay Son Suffered Brutal Harassment at Camp," WSAZ News Channel 3, July 17, 2009, http://www.wsaz.com/news/headlines/ 51064322.html.

25. "Social Media," 4-H, http://www.4-h.org/get-involved/social-media.

26. Bill Trench, "The Mercies of God," *Thinking Faith*, July 10, 2009, http:// thinkfaithfully.blogspot.com/2009/07/mercies-of-god.html.

27. Yonat Shimron, "Gay Man Leads N.C. Church Association," *Charlotte Observer* (Charlotte, NC), December 27, 2010, http://www.charlotteobserver.com/ 2010/12/27/1936344/gay-man-leads-nc-church-association.html.

28. *ReturnTheDVD.org*, http://returnthedvd.org.

29. Michael Jones, "Catholics Tell Minnesota Archbishop: Jesus Wouldn't Fight Civil Rights for Gay Couples," *Change.org*, December 10, 2010, http://gayrights .change.org/blog/view/catholics_tell_minnesota_archbishop_jesus_wouldnt_fight _civil_rights_for_gay_couples.

30. Michael Jones, "The Catholic Grandmother with a Powerful Message for Her Church on Gay Rights," *Change.org*, November 30, 2010, http://news.change .org/stories/the-catholic-grandmother-with-a-powerful-message-for-her-church -on-gay-rights.

31. Advocate.com Editors, "Gays in Updated Jewish Prayer Book," *Advocate.com*, September 17, 2010, http://www.advocate.com/News/Daily_News/ 2010/09/17/Gays_in_Updated_Jewish_Prayer_Book.

32. Jordan Rubenstein, "Jewish Prayers Now Include LGBT People," *Change.org*, September 21, 2010, http://news.change.org/stories/jewish-prayers -now-include-lgbt-people.

33. "The LGBT Synagogue – CBST," Congregation Beit Simchat Torah, http:// www.cbst.org.

34. "Welcome to Keshet," Keshet, http://keshetonline.org.

35. "Nehirim: GLBT Jewish Culture and Spirituality: Creating Transformative Programs and Community for Gay, Lesbian, Bisexual, Queer, and Transgendered Jews," Nehirim GLBT Jewish Culture and Spirituality, http://www.nehirim.org.

36. Michael Jones, "A Jewish Response to Hate, Bullying, and Suicide," *Change.org*, November 16, 2010, http://news.change.org/stories/a-jewish -response-to-hate-bullying-and-suicide.

37. "Rainbow Books," Gay, Lesbian, Bisexual, and Transgendered Round Table and the Social Responsibilities Round Table of the American Library Association, http://glbtrt.ala.org/rainbowbooks/.

38. Dana Rudolph, "New Award Honors LGBT Children's and Youth Litera- ture," *Change.org*, November 2, 2010, http://news.change.org/stories/new-award -honors-lgbt-childrens-and-youth-literature.

39. "ALA | Key Action Areas," American Library Association, http://www .ala.org/ala/aboutala/missionhistory/keyactionareas/index.cfm.

40. Brandon Miller, "Maine Residents Join Together to Fight Anti-Gay Bullying," *Change.org*, December 19, 2010, http://news.change.org/stories/maine-residents-join-together-to-fight-anti-gay-bullying.

41. "ALA | Teens: Annotated Public Library Talking Points," American Library Association, http://www.ala.org/ala/issuesadvocacy/advocacy/advocacyuniversity/additup/13to18/anntk_public.cfm.

42. "Southern Poverty Law Center," SPLC: Southern Poverty Law Center, http://www.splcenter.org.

43. Emerson Brisbon, "Taking Back the Piers. Op-Ed: LGBTQ Youth Fight Gentrification Along Manhattan's Historic Piers," Fierce NYC, May 3, 2009, http://www.fiercenyc.org/index.php?s=100&n=55.

44. "FIERCE – Cop Watch," Fierce NYC, http://www.fiercenyc.org/index.php?s=117.

45. Kathryn E. W. Himmelstein and Hannah Brückner, "Criminal-Justice and School Sanctions Against Nonheterosexual Youth: A National Longitudinal Study," *Pediatrics* 127, no. 1 (2011): 49–57. doi:10.1542/peds.2009-2306.

46. Donna St. George, "Gay and Lesbian Teens are Punished More at School, by Police, Study Says," *Washington Post*, December 6, 2010, http://www.washington-post.com/wp-dyn/content/article/2010/12/06/AR2010120600035.html.

47. Jabari Asim, *Not Guilty: Twelve Black Men Speak Out on Law, Justice, and Life* (New York, NY: Harper Collins, 2001).

48. "ADL/LEARN: Law Enforcement Anti-Bias Training," Anti-Defamation League, http://www.adl.org/learn/learn_main_training/anti_bias_training.asp?LEARN_Cat=Training&LEARN_SubCat=Anti_Bias_Training.

49. "Gay Lesbian Bisexual & Transgender LGBT Community Centers," Center-Link, The Community of LGBT Centers, http://resources.lgbtcenters.org/Directory/Find-A-Center.aspx.

50. Victoria J. Rideout, Ulla G. Foehr, and Donald F. Roberts, "Generation M2: Media in the Lives of 8- to 18-Year-Olds: A Kaiser Family Foundation Study," January 2010, http://www.kff.org/entmedia/upload/8010.pdf.

51. Donald F. Roberts and Ulla G. Foehr, "Trends in Media Use," *The Future of Children* 18, no. 1 (2008), http://futureofchildren.org/futureofchildren/publications/docs/18_01_02.pdf.

52. "Youth Guardian Services," *Youth Guardian Services*, http://www.youth-guard.org/.

53. Elisabeth Wright, "Finding Resources to Support Rural Out-of-School Time Initiatives," *The Finance Project* 4, no. 1 (2003), http://76.12.61.196/publications/ruralost.pdf.

Queerossary of Terms

1. "LGBT Resources – Definition of Terms," University of California, Berkeley Gender Equity Resource Center, accessed on February 9, 2011, http://geneq.berkeley.edu/lgbt_resources_definiton_of_terms.

2. "GLBT Online Resource: Terms, Culture, Definitions," Appalachian State University, accessed on February 9, 2011, http://glbt.appstate.edu/index.php?module =pagesmith&id=4.

3. "LGBT Resources – Definitions," Southern Illinois University, Edwardsville, accessed on February 9, 2011, http://www.siue.edu/lgbt/definitions.shtml.

4. "LGBT – University at Albany – SUNY: Definitions," University at Albany, accessed on February 9, 2011, http://www.albany.edu/lgbt/definitions.shtml.

5. Robert L. Quackenbush, "Sex Roles and Social-Sexual Effectiveness," *Social Behavior & Personality* 18, no. 1 (1990): 35–39.

6. "LGBT Resources – Definition of Terms," University of California, Berkeley Gender Equity Resource Center, accessed on February 9, 2011, http://geneq .berkeley.edu/lgbt_resources_definiton_of_terms.

7. "LGBT – University at Albany – SUNY: Definitions," University at Albany, accessed on February 9, 2011, http://www.albany.edu/lgbt/definitions.shtml.

8. Sari H. Dworkin, "Treating the Bisexual Client," *Journal of Clinical Psychology* 57 (2001): 671–680, doi:10.1002/jclp.1036.

9. Janice Ristock and Norma Timbang, "Relationship Violence in Lesbian/Gay/ Bisexual/Transgender/Queer [LGBTQ] Communities." Minnesota Center Against Lesbian/Gay/Bisexual/Transgender/Queer [LGBTQ] Communities," Minnesota Center Against Violence and Abuse, last modified March 25, 2009, http:// www.mincava.umn.edu/documents/lgbtqviolence/lgbtqviolence.html.

10. DU Queer and Ally Commission, *Terms Commonly Associated with the Lesbian, Gay, Bisexual, Transgender, Intersex, Queer and Questioning Communities* (Denver, CO: University of Denver Queer and Ally Commission, 2007).

11. Paula C. Rust, "The Politics of Sexual Identity: Sexual Attraction and Behavior Among Lesbian and Bisexual Women," *Social Problems* 39, no. 4 (1992): 382–383. http://www.jstor.org/stable/3097016.

12. "HRC | Glossary of Terms," Human Rights Campaign, accessed on November 16, 2010, http://www.hrc.org/issues/3336.htm.

13. Jocelyn Gregoire and Christin M. Jungers, *The Counselor's Companion: What Every Beginning Counselor Needs to Know* (Mahwah, NJ: Lawrence Erlbaum Associates, Inc, 2007), 61.

14. Tre Wentling, Elroi Windsor, Kristen Schilt, and Betsy Lucal, "Teaching Transgender," *Teaching Sociology* 36 (2008): 50. doi:10.1177/0092055X0803 600107.

15. Genny Beemyn, *Transgender Packet: Transgender Terminology* (Amherst, MA: The Stonewall Center, University of Massachusetts, Amherst, 2008).

16. Michael D. Shankle, ed., *The Handbook of Lesbian, Gay, Bisexual, and Transgender Public Health: A Practitioner's Guide to Service* (New York: Harrington Park Press, 2006), 152.

17. "Glossary of Important LGBT Terms," New York University, accessed on November 16, 2010, http://www.nyu.edu/life/student-life/diversity-at-nyu/

lesbian-gay-bisexual-transgender-and-queer-student-center/glossary-of-important
-lgbt-terms.html.

18. GLAAD, *Media Reference Guide*, 8th ed. (New York: GLAAD, 2010): 6–9.
http://www.glaad.org/document.doc?id=99.

19. "HRC | Glossary of Terms," Human Rights Campaign, accessed on November 16, 2010, http://www.hrc.org/issues/3336.htm.

20. GLAAD, *Media Reference Guide*, 8th ed. (New York: GLAAD, 2010): 6–9.
http://www.glaad.org/document.doc?id=99.

21. "LGBTQIA Glossary – UC Davis LGBT Resource Center," University of California, Davis, accessed on November 16, 2010, http://lgbcenter.ucdavis.edu/
lgbt-education/lgbtqia-glossary.

22. Genny Beemyn, *Transgender Packet: Transgender Terminology* (Amherst, MA: The Stonewall Center, University of Massachusetts, Amherst, 2008).

23. GLAAD, *Media Reference Guide*, 8th ed. (New York: GLAAD, 2010): 6–9.
http://www.glaad.org/document.doc?id=99.

24. Allan G. Johnson, *Privilege, Power, and Difference* (Boston, MA: McGraw-Hill, 2001), 97.

25. "LGBT Resources – Definition of Terms," University of California, Berkeley Gender Equity Resource Center, accessed on February 9, 2011, http://geneq
.berkeley.edu/lgbt_resources_definiton_of_terms.

26. Genny Beemyn, *Transgender Packet: Transgender Terminology* (Amherst, MA: The Stonewall Center, University of Massachusetts, Amherst, 2008).

27. Ibid.

28. Jocelyn Gregoire and Christin M. Jungers, *The Counselor's Companion: What Every Beginning Counselor Needs to Know* (Mahwah, NJ: Lawrence Erlbaum Associates, Inc, 2007), 61.

29. Genny Beemyn, *Transgender Packet: Transgender Terminology* (Amherst, MA: The Stonewall Center, University of Massachusetts, Amherst, 2008).

30. "HRC | Glossary of Terms," Human Rights Campaign, accessed on November 16, 2010, http://www.hrc.org/issues/3336.htm.

31. Janice Ristock and Norma Timbang, "Relationship Violence in Lesbian/
Gay/Bisexual/Transgender/Queer [LGBTQ] Communities," Minnesota Center Against Violence and Abuse, last modified March 25, 2009, http://www
.mincava.umn.edu/documents/lgbtqviolence/lgbtqviolence.html.

32. Andrea Noack, "Building Identities, Building Communities: Lesbian Women and Gaydar" (master's thesis, York University, 1998), 1. http://www
.collectionscanada.gc.ca/obj/s4/f2/dsk2/ftp01/MQ39217.pdf.

33. Cecil F. Abrams, Jr., "Perception of Sexual Orientation as a Function of Amount and Type of Stereotype" (master's thesis, San Jose State University, 2008), 1. http://scholarworks.sjsu.edu/etd_theses/3496/.

34. Michael D. Shankle, ed., *The Handbook of Lesbian, Gay, Bisexual, and Transgender Public Health: A Practitioner's Guide to Service* (New York: Harrington Park Press, 2006), 150.

35. Emily Lenning, "Moving Beyond the Binary: Exploring Dimensions of Gender Presentation and Orientation," *International Journal of Social Inquiry* 2, no. 2 (2009): 40.

36. Genny Beemyn, *Transgender Packet: Transgender Terminology* (Amherst, MA: The Stonewall Center, University of Massachusetts, Amherst, 2008).

37. Ibid.

38. GLAAD, *Media Reference Guide*, 8th ed. (New York: GLAAD, 2010): 6–9. http://www.glaad.org/document.doc?id=99.

39. Ibid.

40. Michael D. Shankle, ed., *The Handbook of Lesbian, Gay, Bisexual, and Transgender Public Health: A Practitioner's Guide to Service* (New York: Harrington Park Press, 2006), 150.

41. Genny Beemyn, *Transgender Packet: Transgender Terminology* (Amherst, MA: The Stonewall Center, University of Massachusetts, Amherst, 2008).

42. "HRC | Glossary of Terms," Human Rights Campaign, accessed on November 16, 2010, http://www.hrc.org/issues/3336.htm.

43. Genny Beemyn, *Transgender Packet: Transgender Terminology* (Amherst, MA: The Stonewall Center, University of Massachusetts, Amherst, 2008).

44. Janice Ristock and Norma Timbang, "Relationship Violence in Lesbian/ Gay/Bisexual/Transgender/Queer [LGBTQ] Communities," Minnesota Center Against Violence and Abuse, last modified March 25, 2009, http://www.mincava .umn.edu/documents/lgbtqviolence/lgbtqviolence.html.

45. Genny Beemyn, *Transgender Packet: Transgender Terminology* (Amherst, MA: The Stonewall Center, University of Massachusetts, Amherst, 2008).

46. "LGBTQIA Glossary – UC Davis LGBT Resource Center," University of California, Davis, accessed on November 16, 2010, http://lgbcenter.ucdavis.edu/ lgbt-education/lgbtqia-glossary.

47. "Definition: Heteronormativity," Purdue University, accessed on February 9, 2011, http://www.cla.purdue.edu/english/theory/genderandsex/terms/ heteronormativity.html.

48. Lisa and Christina, "About Onely and Heteronormativity," *Onely* (blog), http://onely.org/our-mission.

49. "LGBTQIA Glossary – UC Davis LGBT Resource Center," University of California, Davis, accessed on November 16, 2010, http://lgbcenter.ucdavis.edu/ lgbt-education/lgbtqia-glossary.

50. "Glossary," LGBT Community, accessed on November 16, 2010, http:// www.lgbtcommunity.org.uk/glossary.html.

51. Janice Ristock and Norma Timbang, "Relationship Violence in Lesbian/ Gay/Bisexual/Transgender/Queer [LGBTQ] Communities," Minnesota Center

Against Violence and Abuse, last modified March 25, 2009, http://www.mincava
.umn.edu/documents/lgbtqviolence/lgbtqviolence.html.

52. Brandy Smith, "GLBT-Definitions," NACADA Clearinghouse of Academic Advising Resources, accessed on March 29, 2011, http://www.nacada.ksu.edu/clearinghouse/Advisingissues/GLBT-Definitions.htm.

53. "LGBT Resources – Definition of Terms," University of California, Berkeley Gender Equity Resource Center, accessed on February 9, 2011, http://geneq.berkeley.edu/lgbt_resources_definiton_of_terms.

54. DU Queer and Ally Commission, *Terms Commonly Associated with the Lesbian, Gay, Bisexual, Transgender, Intersex, Queer and Questioning Communities* (Denver, CO: University of Denver Queer and Ally Commission, 2007).

55. Michele J. Eliason, "The Prevalence and Nature of Biphobia in Heterosexual Undergraduate Students," *Archives of Sexual Behavior* 26, no. 3 (1997): 317. doi:10.1023/A:1024527032040.

56. "HRC | Glossary of Terms," Human Rights Campaign, accessed on November 16, 2010, http://www.hrc.org/issues/3336.htm.

57. Janice Ristock and Norma Timbang, "Relationship Violence in Lesbian/Gay/Bisexual/Transgender/Queer [LGBTQ] Communities," Minnesota Center Against Violence and Abuse, last modified March 25, 2009, http://www.mincava.umn.edu/documents/lgbtqviolence/lgbtqviolence.html.

58. "HRC | Glossary of Terms," Human Rights Campaign, accessed on November 16, 2010, http://www.hrc.org/issues/3336.htm.

59. Tre Wentling, Elroi Windsor, Kristen Schilt, and Betsy Lucal, "Teaching Transgender," *Teaching Sociology* 36 (2008): 50. doi:10.1177/0092055X0803600107.

60. Genny Beemyn, *Transgender Packet: Transgender Terminology* (Amherst, MA: The Stonewall Center, University of Massachusetts, Amherst, 2008).

61. "HRC | Glossary of Terms," Human Rights Campaign, accessed on November 16, 2010, http://www.hrc.org/issues/3336.htm.

62. Janice Ristock and Norma Timbang, "Relationship Violence in Lesbian/Gay/Bisexual/Transgender/Queer [LGBTQ] Communities," Minnesota Center Against Violence and Abuse, last modified March 25, 2009, http://www.mincava.umn.edu/documents/lgbtqviolence/lgbtqviolence.html.

63. Ibid.

64. "Privilege, Allyship & Safe Space," Multicultural Resource Center, Oberlin College, http://new.oberlin.edu/dotAsset/2012201.pdf.

65. Iris Marion Young, "Five Faces of Oppression," in *Readings for Diversity and Social Justice*, ed. Maurianne Adams, Warren J. Blumenfeld, Rosie Castaneda, Heather W. Hackman, Madeline L. Peters, and Ximena Zuniga (New York: Routledge, 2000), 36.

66. Marilyn Frye, *The Politics of Reality: Essays in Feminist Theory* (Freedom, CA: The Crossing Press, 1983), 4.

67. Maurianne Adams, Lee Anne Bell, and Pat Griffin, *Teaching for Diversity and Social Justice: A Sourcebook*, 2nd ed. (New York, NY: Routledge, 1997, 2007), 17.

68. Rust, *The Politics of Sexual Identity: Sexual Attraction and Behavior among Lesbian and Bisexual Women*, 371.

69. "LGBT Resources – Definition of Terms," University of California, Berkeley Gender Equity Resource Center, accessed on February 9, 2011, http://geneq.berkeley.edu/lgbt_resources_definiton_of_terms.

70. "Glossary," Equality Network, accessed on August 8, 2011, http://www.equality-network.org/Equality/website.nsf/webpages/E275794AB1A4E5F980256FB80049F872?OpenDocument.

71. "HRC | Glossary of Terms," Human Rights Campaign, accessed on November 16, 2010, http://www.hrc.org/issues/3336.htm.

72. GLAAD, *Media Reference Guide*, 8th ed. (New York: GLAAD, 2010): 6–9. http://www.glaad.org/document.doc?id=99.

73. "Terms to Know," SUNY College at Oneonta, accessed on November 16, 2010, http://www.oneonta.edu/development/gsrc/terms.html.

74. Michael D. Shankle, ed., *The Handbook of Lesbian, Gay, Bisexual, and Transgender Public Health: A Practitioner's Guide to Service* (New York: Harrington Park Press, 2006), 152.

75. "HRC | Glossary of Terms," Human Rights Campaign, accessed on November 16, 2010, http://www.hrc.org/issues/3336.htm.

76. Janice Ristock and Norma Timbang, "Relationship Violence in Lesbian/Gay/Bisexual/Transgender/Queer [LGBTQ] Communities," Minnesota Center Against Violence and Abuse, last modified March 25, 2009, http://www.mincava.umn.edu/documents/lgbtqviolence/lgbtqviolence.html.

77. DU Queer and Ally Commission, *Terms Commonly Associated with the Lesbian, Gay, Bisexual, Transgender, Intersex, Queer and Questioning Communities* (Denver, CO: University of Denver Queer and Ally Commission, 2007).

78. Megan Coffey, "A Gay Rights Alphabet Soup Glossary," Examiner.com, last modified August 9, 2009, http://www.examiner.com/sonoma-county-civil-rights-in-san-francisco/a-gay-rights-alphabet-soup-glossary.

79. "Privilege, Allyship & Safe Space," Multicultural Resource Center, Oberlin College, http://new.oberlin.edu/dotAsset/2012201.pdf.

80. Emily Lenning, "Moving Beyond the Binary: Exploring Dimensions of Gender Presentation and Orientation," *International Journal of Social Inquiry* 2, no. 2 (2009): 40.

81. Michael D. Shankle, ed., *The Handbook of Lesbian, Gay, Bisexual, and Transgender Public Health: A Practitioner's Guide to Service* (New York: Harrington Park Press, 2006), 149.

82. Jennifer H. Dworkin, "MOREboys: Generating and Expending Social Capital," Social Science. Paper 4 (2005): 674.

83. Margaret Rosario, Heino F. L. Meyer-Bahlburg, Joyce Hunter, Theresa M. Exner, Marya Gwadz, and Arden M. Keller, "The Psychosexual Development of Urban Lesbian, Gay, and Bisexual Youths," *The Journal of Sex Research* 33, no. 2 (1996): 113.

84. Rosario et al., "The Psychosexual Development of Urban Lesbian, Gay, and Bisexual Youths," 113.

85. Michael D. Shankle, ed., *The Handbook of Lesbian, Gay, Bisexual, and Transgender Public Health: A Practitioner's Guide to Service* (New York: Harrington Park Press, 2006), 150.

86. "HRC | Glossary of Terms," Human Rights Campaign, accessed on November 16, 2010, http://www.hrc.org/issues/3336.htm.

87. Tre Wentling, Elroi Windsor, Kristen Schilt, and Betsy Lucal, "Teaching Transgender," *Teaching Sociology* 36 (2008): 49. doi:10.1177/0092055X0803 600107.

88. Michael D. Shankle, ed., *The Handbook of Lesbian, Gay, Bisexual, and Transgender Public Health: A Practitioner's Guide to Service* (New York: Harrington Park Press, 2006), 150–151.

89. "HRC | Glossary of Terms," Human Rights Campaign, accessed on November 16, 2010, http://www.hrc.org/issues/3336.htm.

90. Tre Wentling, Elroi Windsor, Kristen Schilt, and Betsy Lucal, "Teaching Transgender," *Teaching Sociology* 36 (2008): 51. doi:10.1177/0092055X08 03600107.

91. "HRC | Glossary of Terms," Human Rights Campaign, accessed on November 16, 2010, http://www.hrc.org/issues/3336.htm.

92. "Homosexual Definitions," Gay Family Support, accessed on February 9, 2011, http://www.gayfamilysupport.com/homosexual-definitions.html.

93. "LGBT Resources – Definition of Terms," University of California, Berkeley Gender Equity Resource Center, accessed on February 9, 2011, http://geneq .berkeley.edu/lgbt_resources_definiton_of_terms.

94. Genny Beemyn, *Transgender Packet: Transgender Terminology* (Amherst, MA: The Stonewall Center, University of Massachusetts, Amherst, 2008).

95. Michael D. Shankle, ed., *The Handbook of Lesbian, Gay, Bisexual, and Transgender Public Health: A Practitioner's Guide to Service* (New York: Harrington Park Press, 2006), 152.

96. Tre Wentling, Elroi Windsor, Kristen Schilt, and Betsy Lucal, "Teaching Transgender," *Teaching Sociology* 36 (2008): 49. doi:10.1177/0092055X08036 00107.

97. "HRC | Glossary of Terms," Human Rights Campaign, accessed on November 16, 2010, http://www.hrc.org/issues/3336.htm.

98. Tre Wentling, Elroi Windsor, Kristen Schilt, and Betsy Lucal, "Teaching Transgender," *Teaching Sociology* 36 (2008): 51. doi:10.1177/0092055X0803 600107.

99. "LGBTQIA Glossary – UC Davis LGBT Resource Center," University of California, Davis, accessed on November 16, 2010, http://lgbcenter.ucdavis.edu/lgbt-education/lgbtqia-glossary.

100. Genny Beemyn, *Transgender Packet: Transgender Terminology* (Amherst, MA: The Stonewall Center, University of Massachusetts, Amherst, 2008).

Index

Page numbers followed by f indicate figure.

Aaberg, Tammy, 84–85
AB 620 bill, 106
Abandonment, LGBT youth and, 56, 73
Absenteeism, bullying and, 102
Abusive language, 97
Academic achievement, bullying and low, 102
Academic spaces, 115
Activities, community, 6, 18, 120; gender-segregated, 38; LGBT youth and, 18, 22–23
Adaptability, family and, 66, 67–68
ADL. See Anti-Defamation League (ADL)
Adolescence/adolescents: feelings during, 4; identity and, 4; identity integration in, 34; LGBT, sanctioning of, 133
Adult advocates, 110
Adults: checking feelings and identity, 69; creating safe spaces for youth, 42, 45; distracted, 69, 70; gender expression and, 3; on heterosexism, 1; homophobia, transphobia, and, 67; marginalization of youth, 23–24; supportive, importance of, 32, 34, 41, 55; transgender youth and, 18; workplace discrimination and, 17; worry about children, 72; youth and, 23–24
Advocates for Youth, 152
Affirmation, 88, 156
ALA. See American Library Association (ALA)
Allums, Kye, 122
Ally(ies): benefits and challenges of, 62–63; defined, 47–49, 141; effective, 6; family members as, 68; identity, building, 49–50; personal dimension of, 49–52; public dimension of, 52–56; teaching about LGBT discrimination, 63. See also Ally development indicators; Allyship

Ally development indicators: anti-ally behaviors, 56–57; being safe person/confidant, 57–58; challenging oppression systems, 61–62; confronting oppression, 58–59; educating oneself and others, 59–61. See also Ally(ies)
Allyship: as equal-opportunity adventure, 52–54; identity development as facet of, 53, 54; key indicators of, 56–63
American Civil Liberties Union, 108, 154
American Library Association (ALA), 130, 131
And Tango Makes Three, 19
Androgynous, 141, 144
Angelou, Maya, 111
Anti-ally behaviors, 56–57
Anti-bias training, on LGBT issues, 123
Anti-bullying legislation, 104
Anti-bullying policies, 103–12
Anti-Defamation League (ADL), 133–34
Antidiscrimination legislation, 107
Anti-gay discrimination, 52
Anti-gay language, 1
Anti-gay slurs, 120
Anti-gay violence, 102
Anti–hate language pledge, 123
Anti-LGB environments, 32
Anti-LGBT behavior, 21
Anti-LGBT bullying, 105–12
Anti-LGBT slurs, 97
Anti-LGBT teaching, 88–89
Arizona, affirmation of same-sex relationship and, 88
Asexual, 2, 36, 42, 141, 145
Athleteally.com, 117
Athletic events, LGBT people and, 120

"Bargaining," as alternative tactic, 76
Bathrooms, 116, 117
Behavior(s): anti-ally, 56–57; anti-LGBT, 21; modifications, transgender and, 74–75
Best, Amy, 108
Beyond Ex-Gay, 75, 159
Bible verses, homosexuality and, 91
BiNet USA, 159
Biphobia, 48, 141–42
Bisexual, 54; defined, 142; exploring, 32; identity, Chinese family and, 41–42; meaning of, 98; support of, 78–79
Blog: of Bill Trench, 127; District 2002, 134–35; on effects of heteronormativity, 2; on experiences of LGBT athletes, 123; of Hans Zeiger, 124
Books: challenged, 19; lack of LGBT characters, 19; learning about LGBT through, 19; for LGBT community, 91–92
Bourne, Justin, 121
Bowling Alone, 119
Boy Scouts, 124
Brown, Asher, 113
Brown, Marc, 85
Bullied (film), 131
Bullying: absenteeism and, 102; anti-LGBT, 105–12; bill for fighting, 106; confronting, 52; low academic achievement and, 102; from peers, 23; policies concerning, 104–5; suicide and, 102

California AB 620 bill, 106
California Student Safety and Violence Prevention Act (AB 537), 17
Campus Pride, 152
CBST. *See* Congregation BeitSimchat Torah (CBST)
Celebrities, youth and, 21
Centerlink Community Center Directory, 134
CenterLink: The Community of LGBT Centers, 159
Certiorari, Dale, 124
Challenges: of being an ally, 62–63; of faculty and allies, 111; of finding trustworthy adults, 42; of integrating into gay-straight alliance, 42
Charlotte Observer, 127
Children: as allies for parents, 54–55; believing in, 76; connected conversations with, 70;

early in life, 4; intersexed, 36; positive family talk and, 68–69, 72
Children of Lesbians and Gays Everywhere, 151
Chinese family, bisexual identity and, 41–42
Christensen, Linda, 51–52
Cisgender, 20, 142
Cisgender privilege, 50–51
Citizenship, allyship as aspect of, 62
Civic organizations, 123–26
Civil Rights Act of 1964 (Title VI), 105
Classroom(s): affirmative action in, 92; from beyond schools to beyond, 117–18; curriculum, 85–95; family description in, 95–96; impact on youth development, 83–84; LGBT issues in, 92–93; nonverbal communication in, 96; outside, 101–18. *See also* School(s)
Climate change, 104, 114
Clocked/being read, 142
Cohesion, family and, 66, 68
College courses, LGBT issues and integrating of, 92–93
"Coming-of-age" event, 108
Coming out: deciding against, 68; defined, 142; to family, 70; fear of, 110–11; LGB people and, 33; transgender individuals and, 37
Commitment: of allies, 54; to diversity, libraries and, 130; intellectual and ethical, 49–50; professional development and, 114; space spaces and, 103
Communication, power of, 95–98
Community(ies): activities, 6, 18, 120; rural, 135–36; safe, creating, 120–21; talking to, 22. *See also* Physical and virtual community centers
Community leaders, impact on youth, 21–22
Community organizations, LGBT youth and, 20
Community proms, 108
Community sports, 120–23
Companion, 57
Comprehensive professional development, 114
Confrontation, allies and, 53
Confusion: identity beginnings and, 29, 31, 34; LGB youth and, 28; Congregation BeitSimchat Torah (CBST), 128–29; Connected conversations, 69; Consortium of Higher Education LGBT Resource Professionals, 152
Context and identity, 26–27

Conversion attempts, 74–75

"Cop Watch" program, 133

Corrective behavior modifications, transgender and, 74–75

Cross-dresser/cross-dressing, 2, 142–43

Cuccinelli, Ken, 11

Cultural background: identity processes and, 42; learning about, 43; Cultural heritage, 43

Curriculum, 85–95; erasure of LGBT people in, 87–88; health, 88; hidden, 20–21; history lessons, 87; inclusive, 92; interventions on university level, 93; LGBT exclusion from, 20; traditional, 85; unit on family in kindergarten, 89

Cyberbullying, 23

Day of Silence, 59, 109

Defense of Marriage Act, 138

Depression, 23, 73, 75

Derogatory language, 23, 29, 68, 120, 125

Developmental milestones, identity and, 24

Dignity USA, 156

Disabilities, LGBT identity and, 39, 42

Discrimination: anti-gay, 52; against LGBT people, 10, 15, 22; policies on, 11. See also Employment discrimination; Nondiscrimination policies

"Discriminatory harassment," 105, 107

District 202, 134–35

Dominant, 143

Dominant culture, 143

"Don't Ask, Don't Tell" (DADT) policy, 13

Drag, 143

Drag king, 3, 143

Drag queen, 36, 143

Dynamics, of family, 66, 67

Education: about LGBT issues, 72; role of ally and, 61

Education Amendments of 1972, Title IX, 107

Educational entities: employment discrimination and, 11–12; LGBT people and, 11

Educational environment, LGBT identity development and, 45

Educational resources, LGBT families and, 71

Education programs, sexual orientation in, 85

Educators: on abusive language, 97; on creating safe classrooms, 98–99; standing up for heterosexism, 111

Elementary curricula, sexual orientation in, 85

Elementary schools, family description in classrooms of, 95–96

Emotional rejection, 76

Emotional response, 66–67

Emotional violence, 22

Emotions, talking about, 69

Employees firing, LGBT people and, 10

Employment benefits, LGBT people and, 13–14

Employment discrimination, LGBT youth and, 12

Employment Non-Discrimination Act (ENDA), 11

ENDA. See Employment Non-Discrimination Act (ENDA)

Environment(s): anti-LGB, 32; LGBT development and, 26–27, 28f, 45; positive, 31–32; supportive foster, 79; unsupportive home, 78–79; vocal anti-gay rhetoric, 76

The Equal Access Act, 1984, 109–10

Equality: inspiring people to work for LGBT, 49, 51; LGBT and state of, 10–17; racial, 71; road to, 64

Equality Federation, 159

Equality road to LGBT, 63–64

Equity Project, 154

Erikson, Erik, 27

Ethnicity, identity and, 41

Evangelical Concerned, 157

The Evangelical Network, 157

Evers, Medgar, 93

Ex ex-gay organizations, 75

Ex-gay programs, 75

"Fag" jokes, 76, 102

Fair, Accurate, Inclusive, and Respectful (FAIR Education Act), 87

"False selves" phenomenon, 76

Family(ies): beyond, 78–81; gender attraction and, 4; in kindergarten curriculum, 89; negative reactions about sexual orientation, 23; shapes and sizes of, 65; study of, 85; toward safe family spaces, 66–73; unsafe familial spaces, 73–78

Family Acceptance Project, 151–52

The Family Book, 89

Family communication, 68

Family Equality Council, 152

Feelings: during adolescence, 4; of children, adults and, 69

FIERCE, 133

Finance Project, 135

Finding Resources to Support Rural Out-of-School Time Initiatives, 135

Firing employees, LGBT people and, 10

First Amendment Center, 154

Focus on the Family, 117

Foster-care system, 23, 79

Foster parent, 79

Foster system, 73–74

4-H, 125–26

Freedom to Marry, 154

Friendly organizations, 33

Friends for Lesbian, Gay Bisexual, Transgender, and Queer Concerns, 157

Gay, defined, 143

Gay and Lesbian Advocates & Defenders, 155

The Gay & Lesbian Alliance Against Defamation, 155

Gay and Lesbian Vaishnava Association, 157

The Gay Christian Network, 157

Gay jokes, 76

Gay, Lesbian, and Affirming Disciples Alliance, 157

Gay, Lesbian, and Straight Education Network (GLSEN), 109

Gay, Lesbian and Straight Educators Network, 33, 87, 153

Gay Pride Month, 131

Gay-related taunts, 102

Gay Rights Movement of the 1970, 19

Gay slurs, 22, 76, 102, 132

The Gay Straight Alliance Network, 153

Gay-straight alliances (GSAs), 20, 35, 109–10, 112

GayChurch.org, 157

Gaydar, 143

"Gayness, Multicultural Education, and Community," 93

Gender: defined, 143–44; transgender individuals and, 36–37. *See also* Gender identity

Gender conformity, children and, 121

Gender expression, 144

Gender identity, 144; rejection of, 76; social class identity and, 42–43; in state of Virginia, 11–12; transgender youth and, 75

Gender-neutral bathroom, 116

Gender-neutral pronouns, 55

Gender nonconforming, 2, 121

Gender-segregated activities, 38

Gender variant, 36, 144

Genderqueer, 2, 36, 144

Girl Scouts, 124–25

GLBT Historical Society, 153

GLBT National Help Center, 159

GLSEN. *See* Gay, Lesbian, and Straight Education Network (GLSEN)

GSAs. *See* Gay-straight alliances (GSAs)

Guidance counselor, 78–79

Habeisen, Johanna, 92

Harassment: of adults to transgender youth, 18; bill for fighting, 106; forms of, 105; in jobs, 11; of LGBT students at universities, 102; from peers, 23; policies concerning, 104–5; verbal, 22, 55

Healthcare: coverage of health plans, 14; LGBT people and, 14–15

Healthcare professionals, transgender patients and, 14

Health problems, LGBT youth and, 73

Heather Has Two Mommies, 93

Heteronormative, 144–45

Heterosexism: children and, 121; defined, 9, 145; educators standing up for, 111; LGBT youth in Pier 45 area and, 133

Heterosexist language, 12

Heterosexual privilege, 48, 50, 145

Heterosexuals: allies as, 55; community organizations encouragement of, 20; employment benefits and, 13–14; pretending to be, 31; teachers and, 91; U.S. policies to, 15

High school, family description in, 96

Higher education curricula, integrating LGBT issues in, 93–94

History classrooms, 87

Home environment, LGBT identity development and, 45

Homeless youth, 73, 74

Homophobia, 67, 145

Homophobic language, 97, 98, 121

Homosexuality, 29–30, 75, 88, 91

Hoover, Carl Walker, 102

Hospital visitation, LGBT people and, 14, 15

Hotline numbers, 151

HRC, 33

Hughes, Langston, 20
The Human Rights Campaign, 14, 155

Identity(ies): beginnings of, 27–31; complexity
    of, 43–45; context and, 26–27; definition and
    background, 25–26; explorations, 31–34;
    hiding, 77; integrations, 34–35; queer,
    claiming, 38–43; religious, 39, 40–41;
    transgender, 36–38
Identity development, allyship and, 52
Identity intersections, 39
Identity models, 26, 29, 34, 36
Illegal drugs, 73
Inclusive terms, use of, 57
Inspiration, allies and, 63
Integration: families of LGBT and, 71;
    kindergarten curriculum and, 89–90; of
    LGBT images to curriculum, 92; of LGBT
    individuals or experience, 89–90
Integrity, 157
Interactions: identities and, 27; with peers, 41;
    teacher-student, 88
Interfaith Alliance, 157
Internalized homophobia, 145
International Foundation for Gender
    Education, 159
Internet, people in unsafe environment and, 33
Interpersonal relationships, allies and, 62–63
Interpersonal violence, 22
Interpretation strategy, in kindergarten
    curriculum, 89–90
Intersex, 3, 36, 145
Intersexed children, 36
Invalidation, 76
Itawamba County School District policy, 108
"It Gets Better" campaign, 55, 102–3, 129, 130
It Takes a Team, 123
Izzo, Karen, 113

Jennings, Kenneth, 87
Jews, conservative, LGBT and, 128
Ji, Peter, 52, 53

Kimer, Stan, 127
Kindergarten curriculum, family in, 89
King and King, 93
Kinship, 158

Lambda Legal, 23, 155
Language: abusive, 97; anti-bullying and

harassment, 106; anti-gay, 1; derogatory, 68,
    120, 125; hate, 39; hurtful/harmful, 56, 98;
    offensive, 58
Latino culture, 41
LatinoJustice PRLDEF, 155
Law enforcement officials: LGBT people and,
    133–34; role of, 134; use of power, 132
Leadership, training for GSA, 112
Leaves of Grass, 86, 87
Legislation: anti-bullying, 104;
    antidiscrimination, 107; firing LGBT
    and, 10
Lerner, Zeke, 89
Lesbian: defined, 145; at very young age, 30–31
LGB adults, normal, 32
LGB-affirming environments, 29
LGB people, as allies to transgender
    individuals, 55
LGB youth realities, 28
LGBT affirmative messages, 58
LGBT and Straight Alliance, 55
LGBT educational resources, 152–54
LGBT Faith Organizations, 156–59
LGBT family resources, 151–52
LGBT-friendly books, 19
LGBT-friendly educational resources, removal
    of, 19–20, 21
LGBT identity development, people, places, and
    social identities influencing, 44, 44f
LGBT people: of color, 41; development and, 44,
    44f; development and influence of, 28f; safe
    spaces and, 9–10; state of equality of, 10–17
LGBT Political/Legal Organizations, 154
LGBT Pride Week, 109
LGBT resource list, 151–60
LGBT students, teachers and, 90–91
Lifestyle, gender identity and, 37
Literature, LGBT people in, 18–19
Local public figures, youth and impact of, 21
Locker rooms, 116–17
Lutherans Concerned, 158
Luv Ya Bunches, 19

Main squeeze, 57
Marginalization of LGBT people: impact of,
    9–10; LGBT youth, 17–24; state of equality
    for LGBT people, 10–17
Marriage-related benefits, LGBT people
    and, 14, 15
Massachusetts, teachers in, 19

McIntosh, Peggy, 48, 49
McMackin, Gregg, 122
McMillan, Constance, 108
Media images, LGBT youth and, 21, 22
Mental problems, LGBT youth and, 73, 77
Metropolitan Community Church
    (MCC), 127, 158
Military, LGBT people and, 13
Minneapolis community center, 134
Minnesota Family Council, 103
Mississippi, affirmation of same-sex relationship
    and, 88
Models of family systems, 66
More Light Presbyterians, 158
Movies, LGBT youth and, 20
Multiple identities, 39, 43, 44

Nabozny, Jamie, 131
The National Black Justice Coalition, 155
The National Center for Lesbian Rights, 156
The National Center for Transgender
    Equality, 156
National Coalition for LGBT Health, 160
National Coming Out Day, 59, 131
The National Gay and Lesbian Task Force, 156
National Youth Advocacy Coalition, 153
Negative emotions, 49
Negative talk, on LGBT issues, 73
Negative terms, adults and, 70
Negative thoughts: LGB-affirming environments
    and, 29; LGB identity and, 28
Neighborhood: LGBT identity development and,
    45; seeking refuge in, 131–34
The New Gay Teenager, 39
Non-birth parents, LGBT people and, 15–16
Nondiscrimination policies, 11, 12
Nondiscrimination statements, LGBT youth
    and, 17
Nonverbal communication,
    in classrooms, 96
Normal LGB adults, 32
North Carolina Council of Churches, 127
Notre Dame football team, 122

Oasis Magazine, 160
Obama, Barack, 103
Observations, identities and, 27
OCR. See Office for Civil Rights (OCR)
Offensive language, 58
Office for Civil Rights (OCR), 105, 107

Oklahoma, affirmation of same-sex relationship
    and, 88
Omnisexual, 146
Online resources, 135
Oppression: allies and confronting, 53, 56–57,
    58–59; challenging systems of, 61–62;
    defined, 146; engaging in active or passive, 56
Out, 146
"Outcubators," 84
Outing, 146

Parents: anti-gay language and, 1; messages to
    LGBT youth and, 78; response, 66; role in
    helping children, 69; support of children, 66;
    teachings about family, 95–96; transgender,
    LGBT people and, 16
Parents, Families and Friends of Lesbians and
    Gays, 152
Partner, 57
Passing, 146–47
Peers: anti-gay language and, 1; gender
    attraction and, 4; harassment and bullying
    from, 23; harassment of transgender youth,
    18; interactions with, 41; pretending to be
    heterosexuals to, 31; shaping identity
    and, 27, 29
People of color, law enforcement and, 133–34
The Perks of Being a Wallflower, 19
Personal dimension, allies and, 49–52
PFLAG, 33, 80
Physical abuse, from family members, 23, 74
Physical and virtual community centers, 134–36
Physical plant, outside in, 115–17
Physical violence, 22
Places, LGBT development and, 44, 44f
The Point Foundation, 153
Policy(ies): anti-bullying, 1, 103–12;
    discriminatory or non-inclusive, 22;
    exclusionary, 16, 17, 20, 56; legally
    married, U.S. and, 15
Politicians: LGBT-friendly resources and, 21;
    role of, 120
Positive family talk, children and, 68–69, 72
Postcards from Buster, 86
Post-9/11 GI Bill, 13
Potocky-Tripodi, Miriam, 93–94
Preferred Gender Pronoun (PGP), 55
Prejudice: LGB, 28; against LGBT people, 10
Pride, identity integration and, 34
Pritchard, Tom, 103

Privilege, 48
Professional counseling, 74
Professional development, 112–15
Promotions, LGBT people and, 11
Psychological harm, 76
Public acts, personal dimension of, 51
Public dimension, allies and, 52–56
Public libraries, 129–31
Public spaces, seeking refuge in, 131–34
Putnam, Robert, 119

Queer, 2, 39, 147
Queer and Ally Blog, 135
Queer identity, claiming, 38–39
Queerossary of terms, 141–49
Questioning, 147

Race privilege, 48
Rainbow Bibliography, 130
Ready-to-Learn initiative, 86
Reconciling Ministries Network, 158
Reflections, identities and, 27
Rejection, emotional, 76
Rejection, LGBT youth and, 73, 76, 78
Relationships: of adults with LGBT people, 70; allyship and, 60, 62–63; family, transgender individuals and, 68
Religious and spiritual communities, 126–29
Religious community, 115, 127, 129
Religious figures, youth and impact of, 21
Religious identities, 39, 40–41
Residential campuses, 117
Rhode Island's bill for marriage equality, 138
Role models, interactions with, 41
Rose, Russ, 122–23

Safe family spaces, 66–73
Safe person/confidant, 57–58
Safe School Improvement Act (SSIA), 105, 106
Safe schools, 103–4, 113
Safe spaces: family members and, 65–81; LGBT youth and access to, 18; permanent, 79
Safety, sharing concerns about, 72, 73
Safe-zone sign, 58
SAGE: The LGBT Aging Project, 160
Same-sex feelings, 29–30, 129–30
Same-sex–headed households, support of youth growing up in, 80
School dances, LGBT youth and, 20
School officials, impact on youth, 21

School registration forms, 107
School(s): from beyond classrooms to beyond, 117–18; exploring students identities in, 34; LGBT people marginalization in, 18–19; on LGBT topics in curricula, 98; messages about LGBT community, 83, 85, 87. See also Classroom(s); Curriculum
School skipping, LGBT youth and, 22
Scouting for All, 153
Secret identity, 32
Self-education allies, 54
Self-esteem, 23, 30, 31, 79
Self-examination, allies and, 50
Self-hatred, identity beginnings and, 29
Self-image, transition of, 32
Self-love, identity integration and, 34
Self-tolerance, identity beginnings and, 29
Self-worth, searching for, 31
Semi-private places, violence against LGBT youth in, 18
Sense of belonging, 103, 108
Sense of identity, checking children's, 69
Sense of self, positive, 31, 32
"Separate but equal" doctrine, 108
Sex, 147
Sexual identity, 70, 147
Sexual orientation: defined, 147; in elementary curricula, 85; exploring, 33; feeling good about, 35; negative reactions from families about, 23; rejection of, 76; self and, 34; in state of Virginia, 11–12; struggles with, 78–79
Shelters, 73
Significant other, 57
Silence, 50, 56, 76, 77
"Smear the Queer" game, 106
Social class, gender identity and, 42–43
Social class identities, 42–43
Social identities, LGBT identity development and, 39, 40f, 44, 44f
Social support, people's movement and, 35
Social workers, role of, 74
Soulforce, 158
South Carolina, affirmation of same-sex relationship and, 88
Southern Poverty Law Center, 131, 153–54
Spellings, Margaret, 86
SSIA. See Safe School Improvement Act (SSIA)
Stage theories, 26
Stambaugh, Seth, 110

"Standing by," allies and, 52–53

Stanton, Glenn, 117

Stonewall Book Award, 130

Stonewall Children's and Young Adult
Literature Award, 130

Straight Alliance, 55

Stressor, 66

Substance abuse, 73

"Sugartime!," 86

Suicide: of Asher Brown, 113; bullying and, 102;
negative reactions from families and, 23;
parents' silence and, 76; unsupportive family
environment and, 73

Suicide Prevention Resource Center, 115–16

Support: of families, 79–80; of LGBT youth, 78,
79; of peers, 55; of youth growing up in
same-sex–headed households, 80

Sylvia Rivera Law Project, 156

Tango Makes Three, 89, 91

Teachers: addressing LGBT issues, anti-gay
language and, 1; K-8, Tennessee state and,
20; LGBT books and, 19; LGBT students and,
90–91; in Massachusetts, 19; responsibility
of, high-school, 112; role of, 85–86. See also
Educators

Teacher-student interactions, 88

Technology, youth and use of, 70

Tennessee, state of: bill restricting LGBT issues
in classroom, 20; LGBT people and, 12

Tensions, 66

"Thinking Faith" (Bill Trench blog), 127

Three by Two model, 113–14, 114f, 118

Title IX of the Education Amendments
of 1972, 107

Title VI of the Civil Rights Act of 1964, 105

Title VII of the Civil Rights Act of 1964, 11

Training: anti-bias, LGBT issues and, 123; for
GSA leadership, 112

Transformation, personal, 52, 53

Transgender, 24; defined, 148; harassment of
adults to, 18; on identifying gender, 107;
identities of, 36–38; individuals in umbrella
of, 2, 36, 38; LGB persons as allies to, 55;
marginalized, 18; PGP and, 55; professional
counseling and, 74–75

Transgender athletes, 121

Transgender Law and Policy Institute, 156

Transgender parents, LGBT people and, 16

Transgender people, marginalization of, 9

TransGenderCare, 160

Trans-Health, 160

Transmen, 148

Transphobia: adults and, 67–68; an ally and, 48,
49; athletic teams and, 120; defined, 148;
LGBT youth in Pier 45 area and, 133

Transphobic comments, 98, 116

Transphobic language, 86, 97

Transsexual, 2, 36, 148

Transwomen, 148

Trench, Bill, 127

The Trevor Project, 154

Tucker, Edmon, 93–94

Two spirit, 148–49

UCC Coalition for LGBT Concerns, 158

Unitary transgender identity theory, 36

United States: sexual orientation in curricula, 85;
state of equality for LGBT people in, 10–17

Universities: anti-bullying policies in, 105–6;
LGBT or queer studies at, 20; as unsafe
spaces, 102. See also Academic spaces

University applications, gender identification
and, 107

Unsafe familial spaces, 73–78

Utah, affirmation of same-sex
relationship and, 88

Verbal abuse, from family members,
23, 74

Victimization, 73

Violence, 78; anti-gay, 102; emotional, 22;
interpersonal, 22; physical, 22

Violence against LGBT people, 67, 72, 122

Virginia attorney general, 11

Vocal anti-gay rhetoric environment, 76

Walsh, John, 131

Welcoming & Affirming Baptists, 158–59

Whitman, Walt, 20

Who's in a Family, 89

Willis, Jay, 87

Witt, Preston, 106

Women's Sport Foundation, 123

Word, Deb, 127

Workplace discrimination, 10, 11, 12, 17

Youth Guardian Services (YGS), 135, 160

Zeiger, Hans, 124–25

About the Authors

ANNEMARIE VACCARO, PhD, is a faculty member in the Department of Human Development and Family Studies at the University of Rhode Island. Her research on diversity and social justice in higher education has been published in journals such as *The Journal of GLBT Family Studies, The Journal of LGBT Youth,* and *Equity and Excellence in Education.*

GERRI AUGUST, PhD, is a member of the Foundations faculty in the Department of Educational Studies at Rhode Island College. Her research focus is transformative pedagogy. During the 2010–11 academic year, she was honored as an Education Alliance Fellow at Brown University.

MEGAN S. KENNEDY, PhD, is a faculty member in the Department of Education at Westfield State University in Massachusetts. She has written and presented on the topic of queer theory in teacher preparation and the use of LGBT-themed literature in the classroom at both regional and national conferences.